The Faith Moves South

A History of the Church in Africa

Steven Paas

With contributions by

Klaus Fiedler

Kachere Books no. 27

Kachere Series
Zomba 2006

Copyright© 2006 Steven Paas

All rights reserved. No part of this publication may be reproduced, stored in a retrieval system, or transmitted in any form nor by any means, electronic, mechanical, photocopying, recording or otherwise, without prior permission from the author.

ISBN: 99908-76-65-7   ISBN-13: 978-99908-76-65-9

Kachere Books no. 27

The Kachere Series is represented outside Africa by:
African Books Collective Oxford (orders@africanbookscollective.com)
Michigan State University Press East Lansing (msupress@msu.edu)

Layout and Cover Design: Willem Hendrik Paas

Cover illustration: Nkhudzi Bay prayer house of the Church of Central Africa Presbyterian (CCAP), located at Kalinjeka, between Mangochi and Monkey Bay, on the coast of Lake Malawi (photography: Rita Paas).

Printed by Lightning Source

Kachere Series,
P.O. Box 1037, Zomba, Malawi
email: kachere@globemw.net
web: www.sdnp.org.mw/Kachereseries

This book is part of the **Kachere Series**, the publications arm of the **Department of Theology and Religious Studies of the University of Malawi**.

Other Mvunguti/ Kachere Books by Steven Paas:
Digging Out the Ancestral Church: Researching and Communicating Church History
Chikonzedwe cha Mpingo: Zosintha Zazikulu za Uzimu 1500-1650
Mpingo Wakale: Mbiri ya m'zaka za 1-500
English – Chichewa/ Chinyanja Dictionary
Chichewa/ Chinyanja – English Dictionary
A Conflict on Authority in the Early African Church: Augustine of Hippo and the Donatists
From Galilee to the Atlantic: A History of the Church in the West
Kaphunziridwe ka Baibulo - A Guide for Bible Study Groups
English Lessons from the Bible – Maphunziro a chiNgerezi m'Baibulo
A Conflict on the Church and the Sacraments: The Religious Disputation at Regensburg in 1541

Other Mvunguti/ Kachere Books by Klaus Fiedler:
Christianity and African Culture: German Protestant Missionaries in Tanzania
Teaching Church History in Malawi
With Paul Gundani, Hilary Mijoga (eds), *Theology Cooked in an African Pot Joseph Booth in Melbourne*
With Janet Y Kholowa, *In the Beginning God Created them Equal*
With Janet Y Kholowa, *Mtumwi Paulo ndi Udindo wa Amayi Mumpingo*
With Janet Y Kholowa, *Pachiyambi Anawalenga Chimodzimodzi*

For titles of other publications in the Kachere Series and of the Mvunguti Books, see the last pages of this book

Table of Contents

Preface 11
Part One   Africa in General 17
Chapter 1 19
Africa on the Eve of Change 19
  1. Earliest Centres of Christianity in Africa 19
    a. Egypt 19
    b. North Africa 20
  2. A New Era of Contact 21
  3. The Situation of Traditional Religions 22
  4. The Situation of Islam 24
    a. Two Gateways 24
    b. The Islamisation of Egypt 25
    c. The Islamisation of North Africa 26
  5. The Fullness of Time 28
  6. The Situation in Sub-Saharan Africa 29
    a. West Africa 29
    b. East Africa 32
    c. South-Central Africa 33
    d. South Africa 34
Chapter 2 36
Nubian and Ethiopian Christianity 36
  1. Nubia excavated 36
    a. Archeological Findings 36
    b. Monophysitism 37
    c. Royal Power 37
    d. Decline 39
  2. Ethiopia 40
    a. Ethiopia until 1100 40
    b. The Zagwe Kings 42
    c. Decline and Survival 44
    d. Jesuit Attempt Fails 45
    e. Conflicts and Disintegration 46
    f. The First Protestant Missionaries in Ethiopia 47
    g. Another Roman Catholic Attempt Fails 48
    h. New Protestant Missions 49
    i. Ethiopia Maintains itself 49
Chapter 3 52
Africa and Early Portuguese Missions 52
  1. Henry the Navigator 52
  2. Islands and the West Coast 53
  3. Congo 55
  4. Angola 57
  5. Southern and Eastern Africa 57

Chapter 4 61
Africa and the Dutch until 1800 61
   1. Gold Coast, Congo, Angola 61
   2. Boers and Khoikhoi 64
   3. Nguni and Tswana 64
   4. Planting of the Dutch Reformed Church 66
   5. Early Mission Work 66

Chapter 5 69
Africa and the British until 1885 69
   1. The Empire extends to Africa 69
      a. Competition 69
      b. Triangular Trade 70
      c. Southern Africa 70
   2. Effects of the Great Awakening 71
      a. Rediscovery of the Centrality of Christ 71
      b. Missionary Movement 72
      c. Anti-Slavery Movement 73
      d. The Classical Missions 74

Chapter 6 75
Western Africa 1800-1900 75
   1. Sierra Leone 75
   2. The Niger Mission 77
   3. Liberia 80
   4. Ghana, Cameroon, Senegal, Gabon, Zaire 80
      a. Ghana and Cameroon 80
      b. Senegal, Gabon and Zaire 81
   5. Angola 82
      a. Comparative Roman Catholic Weakness 82
      b. Opportunities for Protestant Mission 83

Chapter 7 86
Southern Africa 1800-1900 86
   1. The Dutch Speaking Settlers 86
   2. The English Speaking Missions 88
   3. Andrew Murray 91
      a. Scottish-Dutch descent 91
      b. Missionary Strategist 92
      c. Writings 94
      d. Theological Significance 94
   4. Johannes van der Kemp 95
      a. With the London Missionary Society 95
      b. Work among Khoikhoi, San and Xhosa 96

Chapter 8 98
Eastern Africa 1800-1900 98
   1. Mozambique 98
   2. Kenya 99

    3. Tanzania..100
    4. Uganda 101
    5. Madagascar 102
        a. First Roman Catholic Attempts 102
        b. Early work by the London Missionary Society 103
        c. Persecution 103
        d. Freedom Restored 105
        e. French Colony 105
        f. Independence 106

Chapter 9 107
Africa's Old Colonisers after 1885 107
    1. The Scramble..107
    2. The British..109
        a. Egypt and the Sudan...109
        b. South Africa 110
        c. Sierra Leone...110
        d. Ghana 111
        e. Nigeria 111
        f. Kenya 111
        g. Uganda 112
        h. Zanzibar and Tanganyika...112
    3. The Portuguese...113
        a. Extension 113
        b. Lusitanianism 113
        c. Between Concordat and World Council of Churches 114
        d. Wars and Independence..114

Chapter 10 117
Africa's New Colonisers after 1885 117
    1. The Belgians...117
        a. Congo Free State 117
        b. Congo Colony...119
        c. Independence 120
    2. The French...120
        a. Before Berlin 1885...120
        b. From Berlin 1885 121
        c. Decolonisation 122
    3. The Germans 122
        a. The German Scramble 122
        b. The Cameroons and Togo...123
        c. German East Africa..124
        d. South-West Africa 124
        e. Defeat..125

Chapter 11 126
Missions and Colonialism 1885-1960 126
    1. Protestant and Roman Catholic Missions....................................126
    2. Competing Missionary Movements...129

  3. Accusations..131
  4. Neither Soulmates nor Antagonists..132
  5. The 'Hey Day of Missions', 1885-1918 134
   a. Growth 134
   b. Cooperation 135
   c. Aggressiveness..136
  6. Strained Partnership, 1918-1945...137
  7. Final Period, 1945-1960 138

Chapter 12 140
African Instituted Churches..140
  1. Two Traditions 140
  2. Early African Initiatives 141
  3. The Rise of Ethiopianism, 1890-1910.......................................142
  4. The Rise of Prophet-Healing Churches.....................................145
  5. The East Africa Revival...149
  6. The Golden Age of Independency...151
  7. Continuing Independency, after 1960.......................................152

Chapter 13 154
Church and Mission in Independent Africa...............................154
  1. The Joy and the Pain of Change 154
  2. Churches Responding to Independence....................................155
  3. Theology Responding to Independence....................................157
   a. African Theology 158
   b. Liberation Theology...159
   c. Evangelical and Reformed Theology.................................159
   d. Other Theologies 162
  4. Africa and Mainstream Theologies...162

Chapter 14 164
Faith Missions 164
  1. Pre-Classical Missions...164
  2. Classical Missions...164
  3. Revival Ferment...165
   a. Brethren Movement...165
   b. Prophetic Movement 165
   c. Holiness Movement..166
  4. Faith Missions 166
  5. Special Characteristics of Faith Missions.................................168
  6. Faith Missions in Africa..171
   a. Livingstone Inland Mission 171
   b. Africa Inland Mission..171
   c. Sudan Missions 172

Chapter 15 175
Unity and Cooperation...175
  1. What is Unity?...175
   a. Diversity and Truth 175

    b. Analogy Qualified by Scripture 176
    c. Restoration through Salvation by Christ 177
  2. Syncretism.. 177
  3. Examples in Malawi 179
  4. Ecumenism and Christian Cooperation....................................... 180
  5. The Situation in Africa 182
  Part Two   Focus on South-Central Africa 186

Chapter 16 ....**188**

The Church in Malawi...188
  1. David Livingstone 188
  2. Classical Missions.. 189
    a. Universities' Mission to Central Africa 189
    b. Livingstonia Mission... 190
    Work at Cape Maclear 191
    Work at Bandawe 192
    Mission to the Ngoni... 193
    Khondowe 194
    c. Blantyre Mission... 194
    d. Dutch Reformed Church Mission.. 196
    e. Church of Central Africa Presbyterian...................................... 198
    f. The Roman Catholic Mission 199
    Portuguese claims 199
    The White Fathers and the Montfort Fathers 199
    Conflict with the Nyau Societies 201
  3. Post-Classical Missions 201
    a. Joseph Booth and the Industrial Missions 201
    b. Africa Evangelical Church of Malawi 203
    c. Providence Industrial Mission... 204
  4. From Mission to Church... 205
    a. Forms of Cooperation.. 205
    b. Machona Churches... 206
  5. Independent Malawi 207
    a. Church and State 207
    b. New Missions after the 'End of Missions'................................ 209
    c. Revival.. 210
    d. Women's Organisations 210

Chapter 17 ....**212**

The Church in Zambia..212
  1. East Zambia.. 212
  2. South Zambia 212
  3. The Copperbelt... 213
  4. Unity and Dissent... 214
  5. Reformed and Presbyterian Churches.. 216
  6. Independent Zambia... 217

Chapter 18 ....**219**

The Church in Zimbabwe...219

    1. Jesuit and Dominican Attempts..219
    2. Mission before 1890 220
    3. The Era of Colonialism...221
    4. The Reformed Church of Zimbabwe 222
    5. The C.C.A.P. in Zimbabwe 223
    6. Independence..224

Chapter 19 ....**225**
  Pentecostals and Charismatics..**225**
    1. Five Streams 225
    2. Beginnings of Pentecostalism..225
    3. Pentecostal Churches in Malawi 228
    4. Features of Charismatism..229
    5. Charismatic Movement in Malawi 232
    6. Politics 233

Chapter 20 ....**235**
  The Position of Africa's Women..**235**
    1. Biblical Pattern..235
      a. Together with Man...235
      b. Equal to Man..236
      c. Different from Man 236
    2. Cultural Patterns..237
      a. Philosophy..237
      b. Western Culture...237
      c. African and Islamic Cultures 240
      d. Christ is more than Culture..241
    3. Christian Women Today 242
      a. Situation before Independence..242
      b. Present situation...243
    4. The Way Forward 246

Chapter 21 ....**248**
  Conversion..**248**
    1. Conversion in Context...248
    2. God and the African Past...249
    3. New Perspectives on an Encounter...250
      a. Adaptation..251
      b. Functions in Society 252
      c. Mediators of Modernity 252
      d. Position towards the State..252
      e. Agents of Cultural and Social Change? 252
    4. African Conversion...253
    5. The Character of the 'Continuum' 254
    6. Lessons from History...256
  Bibliography..**257**
  Index...**269**

Preface

The idea of writing this book was born when I was teaching African Church History at Zomba Theological College, an institute for the training of ministers of the Word of God in South-Central Africa, mainly in Malawi. I tried to arrange the contents of the book in such a way that it may be used as a Text Book for beginning students at tertiary institutions of theological education. Although, particularly the prescribed curricula of Colleges in Central Africa were taken into account, I trust that the book could also serve students in a wider region within or outside Africa. It is meant as a tool for (future) pastors who are to proclaim the wonderful acts of God, who in Jesus Christ, through the Word and the Holy Spirit, planted his Church, and continues to look after it. Moreover, it is hoped that any individual having an interest in the Church, will find the book useful.

In terms of *Historiography* I have consciously tried to quench bias and to honour *African Church History* in its own rights. I am inclined to follow Verstraelen who uses the term *Southern Christianity* for a great variety of churches and Christian cultures that came into being East and South of the *Roman Empire*. In the book's title, *The Faith Moves South*, I have expressed this sentiment. Verstraelen stresses that 'Christianity was not an exclusive phenomenon in the *Roman Empire* in the North, but struck roots in different socio-cultural contexts in the Southern Hemisphere'. He pleads for 'new modes of rethinking and rewriting Christian History' by telling the full story of this non-Roman and non-Greek Christianity, 'and making it part of Christian history as a whole'.[1] Stretching this thought, other historians derive from the flourishing Christianity of today's Africa the idea that the epicentre of Christianity has critically 'shifted from the North to the South'.[2]

---

[1] F.J. Verstraelen, 'Southern Perspectives on Christian History', in: *Neue Zeitschrift fur Missionswissenschaft*, 53-1997/2, pp. 100, 101; F.J. Verstraelen, 'The Teaching of Christian History and Ministerial Formation Today', in: *Association of Theological Institutions in Southern and Central Africa* (ATISCA), Bulletin 2, 1993, pp. 3-25.
Verstraelen developed ideas of his deceased wife, published in: Gerdien Verstraelen-Gilhuis, *From Dutch Mission Church to Reformed Church in Zambia: The Scope for African Leadership and Initiative in the History of a Zambian Mission Church*, Franeker: Wever, 1982, pp. 13-21 ('Recovering the African Perspective of Mission History', and 'Written and Oral Sources'); Gerdien Verstraelen-Gilhuis, *A New Look at Christianity in Africa*, Gweru: Mambo Press, 1992, pp. 77-98 ('Rewriting the History of Christianity in Africa').

[2] Chukwudi A. Njoku, 'The Missionary Factor in African Christianity 1884-1914', in: Kalu (ed.), *African Christianity: An African Story*, p.220. He refers to David B. Barrett, 'AD 2000: 350 million Christians in Africa', in: *International Review of Mission*, 59 (1970), pp. 39-54, and to: Kwame Bediako, *Jesus in Africa: The Christian Gospel in African History and Experience*, Akropong-Akuapem: Regnum Africa, 2000, pp. 3, 4.

An important consequence of this thought is that African Christianity of course should not be considered as an appendix or an extension of Western Christianity. It is rightfully stressed that 'Christianity was a non-Western religion in the first place'. However, some historians have developed their thought into the the direction of the opposite extreme, suggesting that the beginnings of Christianity are in Africa, geographically and religiously. They have come to adhere to a completely 'new historiography' in which African Christianity is presented as 'an extension of African primal religion'. This approach is not helpful, because, as Kalu admits, it is 'based on many unarticulated assumptions'.[3] It distorts the picture of the course in history that Christianity took. But there is nothing wrong in emphasising that the Gospel of the joyful events of salvation went from Jerusalem either directly to the North and the North East of Africa, or much later, indirectly to Sub-Saharan Africa through the churches in the West. After all, Christians, anywhere in the world, have received the Gospel from the 'outside'. The Church roots in a message that is from the outside (*forensic*), spiritually, and for most of the Church geographically as well. The Christian Church did not start in Africa or the West, but in Jerusalem, and its foundation is located even outside history, it is not possessed by any world view, however primal it may be. Through Christ God has shown his love for the world, so that people of all nations, world views and religions may realise the superiority and the uniqueness of the Gospel of salvation, join together in His Church, and be saved, now in principle, and presently, after the *Parousia*, in perfection. This - in my view - is the perspective for the Historiography of Church History.

I need not apologise that this book is shaped in a European mind that is groomed by classical biblical beliefs as re-iterated in the 16th century *Reformation* and in the ensuing reformed and evangelical awakenings in the 18th and 19th centuries. Starting point is that Church History is not only part of Secular History, but that it is also an aspect of Theology, and that in both cases, in the perspective of divine Revelation in the Holy Scriptures, it shows the deployment of the Church as herald of the ever approaching Kingdom of God. Elsewhere I have explained this view in more detail.[4]

Like any Text Book this book on *African Church History* often refers to other publications on the same topic, either by quoting from them, or by encouraging the students to read them. The older works by Latourette.[5] and Groves,[6] written in the

---

[3] Ogbu U. Kalu, 'Ethiopianism in African Christianity', in: Kalu (ed.), *African Christianity*, p. 259.

[4] Steven Paas, *Digging out the Ancestral Church – Researching and Communicating Church History*, Zomba: Kachere, 2006³, pp. 11-22; Steven Paas, *From Galilee to the Atlantic: A History of the Church in the West*, Zomba: Kachere, 2004, pp. 21-31.

[5] Kenneth Scott Latourette, *A History of the Expansion of Christianity*, 7 volumes, Exeter: Paternoster/

period 1935-1960, are still valuable descriptions, but as pre-independence literature they are limited in that they perceive *African Church History* largely from a European or American angle. They were important sources for Hildebrandt who first published his concise survey of the history of the Church in Africa in 1981.[7] Hildebrandt tries not to neglect the African contribution to Mission. He is apparently sympathetic to the object of his survey, the Church. His main focus is the loyalty of the Church to Jesus Christ as reflected by classical Christian teaching. Didactically this book remains a helpful tool for beginning students, because of its brevity, its clarity and its well defined Biblical position.

Recent Textbooks have increasingly tried to consider *African Church History* in its own rights. Six volumes have drawn special attention, Kalu (2005), Sundkler and Steed (2000), Shaw (1996), Isichei (1995), Baur (1994), and Hastings (1994). Some of them, Sundkler and Hastings followed at some distance by Baur, are fat handbooks constituting rich sources for finding details on practically all missions and churches. They try to be scholarly 'neutral', although they cannot always hide their respective Protestant (Sundkler) and Roman Catholic preferences. Shaw and Isichei are not lacking interesting details, but they are smaller and concentrate more on mainlines. Shaw looks from an Evangelical angle and operates from the interesting idea that *African Church History* can be grasped by kingdom concepts. Kalu's book takes a special position. He serves as the Editor. Except for his own contributions the book contains valuable studies by 18 other writers, almost all of them Africans.[8]

Kalu explicitly defends a way of writing Church History that excludes histories written from an institutional or denominational angle, or written by 'missionaries and their protégés'. Probably that is why he only mentions Shaw's book once, in a rather depreciatory manner, and even does not include the title in his bibliography

---

Grand Rapids: Zondervan, New York: Harper and Row, 1971 [first 1935-1946; on Africa parts of all volumes, except 4]; K.S. Latourette, *Christianity in a Revolutionary Age*, 5 volumes, Exeter: Paternoster/ Grand Rapids: Zondervan/ New York: Harper and Row, 1970 [first 1955-1965; on Africa: parts of volumes 3 and 5].

[6] Charles P. Groves, *The Planting of Christianity in Africa*, 4 volumes, London: Lutterworth, 1948-1964 (vol. I before 1840, vol.II 1840-1878, vol III 1878-1914, vol. IV 1914-1954]

[7] J.Hildebrandt, *History of the Church in Africa, A Survey*, Achimota (Ghana): African Christian Press, 1990 (first edition: 1981].

[8] Ogbu U. Kalu (ed.), *African Christianity: An African Story*, Pretoria: University of Pretoria, 2005; Bengt G.M. Sundkler and C. Steed, *A History of the Church in Africa*, Cambridge: Cambridge University Press, 2000; Mark R.Shaw, *The Kingdom of God in Africa: A Short History of African Christianity*, Grand Rapids: Baker Books,1996; E. Isichei, *A History of Christianity in Africa: From Antiquity to the Present*, London: SPCK, 1995; J. Baur, *2000 Years of Christianity in Africa: An African History 62 – 1992*, Nairobi: Paulines, 1994; A. Hastings, *The Church in Africa: 1450- 1950*, Oxford: Clarendon, 1994.

of 32 pages.⁹ Hildebrandt's book is perhaps even at a lower place in Kalu's hierarchy, because it is not mentioned at all! Kalu thinks it is possible for a church historian to eliminate in his mind the 'images of the church' going 'beyond the biblical images' in the 'myriad denominations' and the 'unique claims of Christianity'. He also claims that this position gives him the possibility to write a Church History that is genuinely 'ecumenical', showing the 'unique Christian perception of reality'. In Kalu's idea of ecumenicity not only individual church traditions are excluded. He also seems to exclude the unique forensic character of the Christian faith, by suggesting that there is 'continuity' between the traditional non-Christian religions of Africa ('primal religions') and African Christianity. According to him, this idea of continuity, is not in danger of opening the door to *syncretism*. Yet, it is not clear how Kalu can evade this danger when he wants Christians to 'engage the interior of the non-Christian worldview and reclaim it from [*from*: sic S.P.] Christ', which to him 'is not merely breaking with the past'.[10]

Kalu says that he is 'ideologically-driven' to 'tell the story as an African story'. Of course we are dealing with an African history. But accepting and honouring this reality does not need the help of an ideology. The conclusion to the character of African Church History is the result of scholarly deliberation, either by Africans or by non-Africans. One who forgets this, does not heed Ki-Zerbo's warning that historians should go for historical truth in a scholarly way in order 'to be sure of not exchanging one myth for another'.[11] Kalu seems to take a new position on the line of 'Africo-liberal ecumenism' (cf Chapter 13.3a), which finds it difficult to admit to its own disposition to bias. While appreciating the important issue Kalu is tabling, I do not think that Scripture demands from church historians to erase denominations and to accept that 'African Christianity is essentially rooted in primal religion'. It certainly would run against the ideas of Byang Kato, the 'founding father of African Evangelical Theology'. Kato is convinced that African Christian self-identity rooted to any extent in pre-Christian or non-Christian religious tradition, will not be able to maintain itself because it compromises the Gospel.[12] I am of the opinion that the History of the Church of Christ can be accounted for in a genuinely catholic spirit that does not first denounce the histories of denominations

---

[9] Ogbu U. Kalu, *African Christianity*, Preface, p.xi, 'Shaw's [book] is rather marred by the extreme application of the kingdom motif, but the maps are very helpful'.
[10] Ogbu U. Kalu, 'The Shape and Flow of African Church Historiography', in: (ed.), *African Christianity*, 2005, pp.2-23.
[11] J.Ki-Zerbo (ed.), *General History of Africa*, p. 3 [through: Verstraelen Gilhuis, *A New Look at Christianity in Africa* pp. 4, 84].
[12] Byang Kato, *Theological Pitfalls in Africa*, Kisumu: Evangelical Publishing House, 1975. See also Keith Ferdinando's DACB article on Kato: http://www.dacb/org/stories/Nigeria/kato.html

and institutions, but describes and evaluates them in the light of the Gospel, just like the writing of Church History involves and evaluates the meeting of the Church with traditional non-Christian worldviews and religions. This may be in disagreement to Kalu's view. Yet, I have gratefully used information in the volume by Kalu and his co-writers, in order to balance possible overrepresentation of the Western element in my account and in the descriptions by other authors which I used.

Writing African Church History not only depends on written sources. There is a growing consciousness of the necessity of collecting the information that has not yet been reduced to writing. Many accounts of African and other agents of African Church History are in the process of being recorded. A commendable work is being done by the organisers and writers of the *Dictionary of African Christian Biography* (D.A.C.B.). Their accounts of recorded oral history, some of which I gratefully used, are not published in books, but digitally on the D.A.C.B.- Website.[13]

D.A.C.B. is not the only source facilitated by the Internet. Fortunately the number of useful Websites is growing. This is important viz a viz the factors that limit the possibilities for studying African Church History: time, money and distance. These factors especially limit the availability of books, libraries and archives. That is why students in an African context increasingly resort to Websites on the Internet.[14]

Particular gratitude I owe to Dr. Klaus Fiedler, who is an Associate Professor in the Department of Theology and Religious Study of the *University of Malawi*, and an experienced teacher of Church History and Missiology, specialised on Africa. He helped me by giving advice, by proof reading and making corrections and improvements throughout the book. He shows his hand especially in sections of chapters 11, 14, 16, and 19.

The illustrations I mainly collected from various free sites of the Internet. Specific sources were only mentioned when apart from the website address, more

---

[13] http://www.dacb.org

[14] The number of helpful Websites is growing rapidly. Here are some examples:
www.chi.gospelcom.net/glimpses/glmps.151.shtml
www.en.wikipedia.org/africanchurchhistory
www.dmoz.org/society/religion_and_spirituality/church_history/afric/
www.fortunecity.com/meltingpot/cecilian/777/edumain.htm
www.bethel.edu/-letnie/Sub-SaharaHomepage.html
www.sul.stanford.edu/depts./ssrg/Africa/history/religion.html
www.fordham.edu/halsall/africa/africasbook.html
www.exploringafrica.matrix.msu.edu.html

details were given and when copy rights regulations were referred to. If unintentionally some pictures are not duly accounted for, please accept my apologies.

I extend my sincere thanks to the students of *Zomba Theological College* who through their questions and comments, made me more conscious of the need to correct mistakes, to improve gaps in my historical knowledge and to strengthen my didactical approach.

Some persons helped in a more than an ordinary way. Mr. Arie van der Poel, Coordinator for Southern Africa of the *Gereformeerde Zendings Bond* (Reformed Mission League) in The Netherlands regularly encouraged me to continue preparations for this book, and he also made some valuable corrections and recommendations. Mr. Willem Hendrik Paas made the lay out of the book and assisted in finding useful illustrations and inserting them properly into the text. I am grateful to them.

Publication and distribution was made possible due to generous financial support by three Dutch institutions, the *Gereformeerde Zendings Bond*, the *Stichting Mitswah*, and the *Christelijke Gereformeerde Pniel Church* in Veenendaal.

My wife Rita played an important role. In many aspects she has facilitated my functioning. I owe her much for her love, loyalty and practical wisdom.

We praise God who in Christ, through the Word and the Spirit, is known to us as our dear heavenly Father. His Name be glorified in the lives of the readers of this book.

Zomba 2006

Steven Paas

Part One

Africa in General

Chapter 1

Africa on the Eve of Change

1. Earliest Centres of Christianity in Africa[1]

Christianity first expanded in the regions around the *Mediterranean Sea*. The earliest centres in Africa were Egypt and North Africa. In Egypt the Greek and the Coptic cultures were dominant, and in North Africa the Latin and the Berber cultures dominated.

a. Egypt

In Egypt Christianity developed first in the context of the Greek culture that was dominant in the eastern part of the Roman Empire, beginning among the many Hellenised Jews living there. Soon the church spread among the other Greek speaking people in the urban areas. Alexandria became an influential centre of Christianity, often in opposition to the Antiochene School of thinking. Clement of Alexandria († 215), Origen († 254), and Athanasius († 373) were among the early church fathers who laid the foundation of Christian theology in the Hellenist world.

A Coptic Church in Aswan, Egypt

At an early stage many non-Hellenised people in the Egyptian countryside also turned to Christianity. They were called *Copts*, and the Bible was translated into the Coptic language. The Copts, after the *Council of Chalcedon* in 451, stuck to the *Monophysite* position in Christology. They were separated from and replaced the official Greek (Melkite) church, using their own Coptic language. The Coptic Church survived first persecutions by pagan Roman emperors, then conflicts with the Catholic Church, and finally oppression under Islamic rule.[2]

---

[1] For a fuller account of North Africa's Christian Era, see: P. Brown, *Augustine of Hippo – A Biography*, London: Faber and Faber, 1967; P. Brown, *Religion and Society in the Age of Augustine*, London, 1972; See also: Steven Paas, *From Galilee to the Atlantic: A History of the Church in the West*, Zomba: Kachere, 2004, pp. 96-112; Steven Paas, *Mpingo Wakale: Mbiri ya m'zaka za 1-500*, Zomba: Kachere, 2004, pp. 90-108; Steven Paas, *A Conflict on Authority in the Early African Church: Augustine and the Donatists*, Zomba: Kachere, 2005[2].

[2] For an effective overview of early Egyptian Christianity see: Kenneth Sawyer and Youhana Youssef, 'Early Christianity in North Africa', in: Kalu (ed.), *African Christianity*, pp. 45-66.

The Faith Moves South

b. North Africa

Church Father Aurelius Augustinus († 430) of Hippo, North Africa.

Another region of early Christian history is North Africa, like Egypt then a province of the Roman Empire. The name *'Africa'* referred to the coastal area with the city of Carthage as the centre, and also to the highlands of Numidia and the more remote Mauritania. The Roman province of North Africa covered more or less the territories of present day Tunisia, Algeria, and Morocco. Unlike Egypt, North Africa was influenced by the western part of the Roman Empire, where Latin gradually became the most important vehicle of culture. Latin Roman names and Latinised African names appear in reports of persecution and condemnation of Christians of the period before 313. The theological school of Carthage became influential. Tertullian († c. 225) and Cyprian († 258) were at the cradle of the development of theology in the Latin language. Much more important, however, was Augustine († 430), whom Baur even calls 'the culminating point of the whole Western theology'.[3]

It is true that the Western church owes much to Africa. That is why the ancient

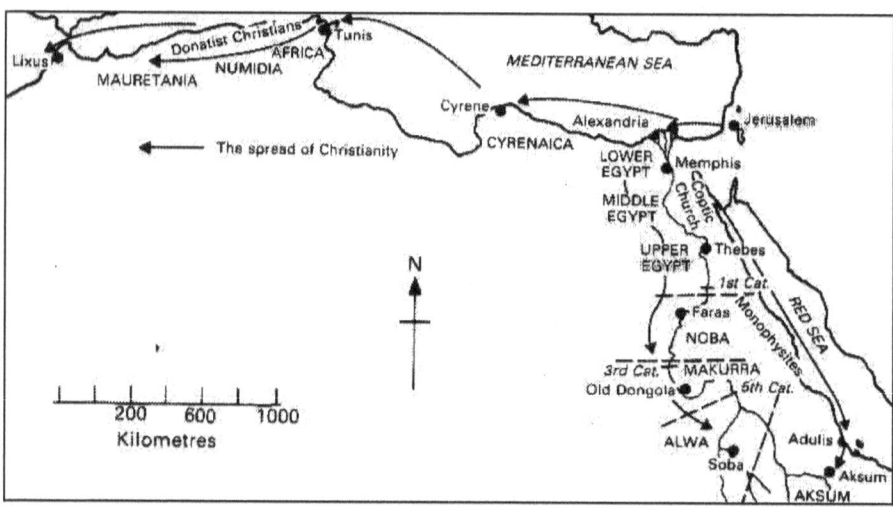

Map of the Spread of Christianity in North Africa from the 1st to the 6th century (from: Shillington, History of Africa, p.67)

---

[3] John Baur, *2000 Years of Christianity in Africa – An African History 62-1992*, Nairobi: Paulines,

church of North Africa still captures the imagination of many modern people. We wonder about its rapid original growth, we also wonder about the internal quarrels and schisms that contributed to its complete eradication. The liberation of Christianity in 313 was followed by a hundred years of internal quarrels that damaged the church of North Africa. These *Donatist* upheavals[4] were followed, just after Augustine's death, by a hundred years of occupation by the Germanic Vandals, who persecuted the African Christians forcing them to accept the heresy of *Arianism*.[5] In the meantime, in the West the Roman Empire had collapsed (476). This historic event had significant consequences for the relationship between Africa and Europe. After the invasion by Arab Muslims in the 7th century North African Christianity faded out.[6] Baur refers to Arab writers who 'mention a few Christian villages still existing in 1400 and a solitary Christian community in Tunis, the New Carthage, in 1500'.[7] Sawyer and Youssef are inclined to be more optimistic. They combine details from Stark and Jenkins[8] and think that the number of North African Christians decreased from 8 million by 500 to 5 million by the year 1000, to 2.5 million by the year 1200, to 1.5 million by the year 1500. They say that the decline accelerated during and after the Crusades.[9]

2. A New Era of Contact

During the European Middle Ages Christianity did not penetrate further into the African continent than North Africa, Egypt, Nubia and Ethiopia. In the 7th century both Egypt and North Africa were conquered by the Arab armies and were included in the Islamic Empire. Both Egyptian and North African Christianity had to compete with Islam, the one survived and the other vanished. The same is true for Christianity in Nubia and Ethiopia (see chapter 2), the former vanished and the latter continued to be a factor of significance. Islam remained the great competitor in the history of the church in much of the rest of Africa. Together with the *Saharan Desert*, Islam had created a barrier between Europe and the large Sub-Saharan part of the African continent. Africans and Europeans did not know much about

---

1994², p. 28.
[4] Cf. Steven Paas, *A Conflict on Authority in the Early African Church: Augustine and the Donatists*, Zomba: Kachere, 2005².
[5] Arianism: The principle heresy which denied the true Divinity of Christ, so called after its author Arius († c.336), maintaining that the Son of God was not eternal but was created.
[6] W.C.H. Frend, *The Donatist Church – A Movement of Protest in Roman Northern Africa*, Oxford University Press, 1985²; P. Hincliff, *Cyprian of Carthage*, London: Chapman, 1974; N.B. McLynn, *Ambrose of Milan – Church and Court in a Christian Capital*, Berkeley/Los Angeles, 1994; Paas, *From Galilee to the Atlantic*, chapters 6, 9, 10.
[7] Baur, *2000 Years*, p.29.
[8] Rodney Stark, *The Rise of Christianity*, Princeton University Press, 1996; Philip Jenkins, *The Next Christendom*, Oxford University Press, 2000.
[9] Sawyer and Youssef, 'Early Christianity in North Africa', in: Kalu (ed.), *African Christianity*, pp. 72, 73.

one another. Especially to Sub-Saharan Africa no early conceptions about Europe were known. Europe's interest in Africa did not go beyond vague imagination, that linked India to Africa, and in which the mysterious Christian king, *Prester John*, played a role.[10]

The European church was at first preoccupied with the evangelisation of pagan European peoples, and then with its own inward affairs. Francis of Assisi belonged to the very few early medieval Christians who were conscious of the church's missionary task for the peoples beyond Europe; he tried to make peace between Muslims and Crusaders.[11] Raymond Lull († c. 1315), a follower of Franscis rather unsuccessfully sought support for his plans to evangelise Muslims and Jews.[12]

Raymond Lull (from: Jorn Barger, 2002)

In the 15th and 16th centuries there was an important change of focus. Attention to the outside world was born out of the movements of the *Renaissance* and the *Reformation*. Profound changes in religion, learning, economy and social life meant the beginning of a *New Era*. Africa and Europe would discover each other!

3. The Situation of Traditional Religions

What was the religious situation in Africa when the *New Era* witnessed the encounter between Europeans and Africans? Although *Christianity* had maintained itself in Egypt and Ethiopia, *Islam* was advancing in North, West and East Africa, and *Traditional Religions* were the major force in most of the continent.[13]

Unlike Northern Africa where Islam barred any Christianisation attempt, Sub-Saharan Africa opened up to Christianity quickly, especially in the 19th century. Sundkler says that four categories of people were the gates through which the Christian faith entered Africa: (1) *kings*, (2) *young men*, (3) *freed slaves and refugees*, and (4) *women*.

First, the *king* was the door through which missionaries had to pass. Using any other way often led to suffering and failure. The centrality of kings was also true

---

[10] Baur, 2000 Years, 42, 43,ff.
[11] *Franciscan Mission among the Muslims: Occasion of the 8th Centenary of Francis' Birth*, A Friar Paper, Assissi, Italy, 1982.
[12] Raymond Lull, or Raimundus Lull(i)us was a Franciscan. He promoted the teaching of Arab and information on Islam to future missionaries, and he was martyred in Ceuta in North Africa in 1315 where he worked as a missionary among Muslims. Cf. J. van Amersfoort and W.J. van Asselt, *Liever Turks dan Paaps?*, Zoetermeer: Boekencentrum, p. 115. For the Portuguese attempts to evangelise Africa (on the way to India) see especially chapter 3.
[13] For this chapter, studt also: Shaw, The *Kingdom of God in Africa*, pp.75-90; Hastings, *The Church in Africa*, pp. 46-53, 188-193, 306-337; K. Shillington, *History of Africa*, London: Macmillan, 1995², pp. 62-225; Sundkler and Steed, *A History of the Church in Africa*, pp. 81-96.

for the lower chiefs who ruled villages and regions with no large scale political structures. Many Africans lived in such units. It was much more true for the kings or chiefs of the bigger African kingdoms with their capital cities that already existed in the Middle Ages. Similar to the Nubian kings and the Egyptian pharaohs, these African traditional rulers were more than secular functionaries, they were sacred kings. Sometimes they even were looked upon as *divine*. They then functioned as *mediator* between heaven and earth, bridging the gap with the ancestors and providing the necessities of life, like rain or victory in war.

The *kingship* in African traditional religion is closely related to *kinship*. Together *kingship* and *kinship* are at the foundation of traditional religion. This kinship means that the individual is part of the whole, s/he cannot exist alone, only corporately. One's identity is found in community. This corporateness includes the *ancestors*. God is seen as the *Great Ancestor*, though conceptions and names of God vary. Kinship ties are hierarchical and generational. Therefore dead ancestors, believed to have continuing impact from the spirit world, are venerated as leaders. This means that the living need contact with the world of the spirits of the ancestors. This explains the necessity of *mediators* who bridge the gap, medicine men and women, diviners, and especially the *sacred kings*. In their priestly function kings were a link between human rule and spiritual government; only they could be heard by the *ancestral spirits*. As such they were 'guardians of the land' or guardians of 'rainmaking' shrines. Like in pharaonic Egypt, some kings were regarded as *semi-divine beings*, superhuman figures. They were the hope of the people, the guarantee of peace and prosperity, the power that can destroy the evils of enemy attacks, diseases, drought and famine.

In certain *cults* there was a kind of competition between the king and the priestly figure at the shrines. The territorial cults of *Mwari* and *Mhondoro* in Zimbabwe were related to what was seen as God, and also to the veneration of human beings that were thought to be divine.[14] The *Mbona* cult in Malawi centres on a prophet-rainmaker who was innocently killed by a king and who revealed himself supernaturally.[15] These cults and those who administered the rites checked the power of the kings.[16]

Secondly, the African Church was primarily a movement of the *youth*. This is because of the many missionaries, who spent their youth, and often their old age as well, in Africa. They preached the Gospel to the heathen, but the African masses were reached largely by the work of young African converts themselves. These young *catechists* and *evangelists* were especially able to preach to Africans of their own age.

---

[14] J.M. Schoffeleers, *Guardians of the Land*, Gweru: Mambo Press/ Kachere Text, 1999², pp.235-310

[15] J.M. Schoffeleers, *River of Blood: The Genesis of a Martyr Cult in Southern Malawi, c. A.D. 1600*, Madison: University of Wisconsin Press, 1992; Schoffeleers, *Guardians*, 131-234;

[16] J.M. Schoffeleers, *Religion and the Dramatisation of Life*, Blantyre: Claim\ Kachere/ Bonn: Culture and Science Publ, 1996, pp.34-65

Thirdly, *uprooted people* were the first to accept the Christian message. *Freed slaves* who were on the run from their masters, and other categories of *refugees* found certainty and comfort in the Gospel of Jesus Christ.

Fourthly, *women* were perhaps the most marginalised category in African society. The Church gave them a position that they had never had before, religiously, in the family, and even in society.

These factors prepared and facilitated the spread of Christianity. However, *African Traditional Religions* harboured strong powers that were ready to counteract the Gospel and the kingdom of God. Deeply rooted conceptions of a distant and unapproachable *Supreme Being* and of the nearly divine role of ancestral spirits as *living dead* had no room for God's immanence in Jesus Christ. In addition to that, all over the continent the powers of *witchcraft* and *magic* had deeply invaded the inner being of society and of individuals. Having victory over these powers would take more than the initial meeting with Christianity.

4. The Situation of Islam

a. Two Gateways

Mark Shaw has characterised Africa as a 'continent with a triple heritage', referring to the long histories of Traditional Religions, Christianity and Islam.[17] Islam reached Africa through two gateways, from the east and from the north.[18] From both directions the carriers of Islam navigated across vast empty spaces, the waters of the Indian Ocean and the sands of the Sahara desert.The *Sahara Desert* and the *Red Sea* and *Indian Ocean* were not great barriers to the spread of Islam. Arabs had lived, travelled and traded in desert conditions for centuries before the founding of Islam. Moreover, since the Arabian Peninsula is bordered on three sides by water, Arabs were experienced sea traders. The regions where Islam first successfully spread are Egypt, North Africa, and North-East Africa, in later stages they were followed by Sub-Saharan Africa in the West, in the East, and in some Southern and Central parts.[19]

---

[17] Shaw, *The Kingdom of God in Africa*, p. 75.

[18] A condensed survey of early expansion of Islam in Sub-Saharan Africa is offered by: Ioan M. Lewis, [Islamic Frontiers in] 'Africa South of the Sahara', in: Joseph Schacht with C.E. Bosworth (eds), *The Legacy of Islam*, Oxford: Clarendon, 1974^2, pp. 105-115.

[19] Cf. Akitunde E. Akinade, 'Islamic Challenges in African Christianity', in: Ogbu U. Kalu (ed.), *African Christianity: An African Story*, Universtity of Pretoria, 2005, pp. 117-138; A.Rahman I. Doi, *The Planting and Diffusion of Islam in Africa, South of the Sahara*, 1971:
http://exploringafrica.matrix.msu.edu/curriculum/lm14/stu_actthree14.html

b. The Islamisation of Egypt

Egypt was the first African country to come under the influence of Islam. At the time of the arrival of the first Muslim traders Egypt was predominantly Christian. Indeed, Christianity had become the main religion in Egypt, hundreds of years earlier, soon after the formation of Christianity.

Saladin (1137/ 1138 - 1193), a Kurdish Muslim general who founded the Ayyubid dynasty in Egypt and Syria. This picture with the words "Saladin, king of Egypt" is from a 15th century manuscript, the globus in his left hand is a European symbol of kingly power

After the collapse of the Roman Empire in the West, Egypt became part of the Eastern Roman Empire, ruled from Constantinople. The Coptic population found Byzantine rule to be corrupt and oppressive. Therefore they did not resist occupation by the Muslim Arabs in the 640s. The Arabs moved the capital from Alexandria in the north to Cairo in the centre of the country, where they were relatively close to the Coptic peasant population. There was a process of Islamisation, generally not through violence, but through indirect means, such as extra taxation of Christians, education in Arabic, and immigration of Arab peasants. By the end of the 10th century Arab rule was pushed aside by an essentially North African Berber movement, the *Fatimids*, who were a kind of *Shi'ites*, claiming descent from Mohammed's daughter Fatima. The greatest Fatimid Caliph was Saladin. He warded off a Christian Crusade army in the 1160s, and recaptured Jerusalem for Islam in 1187, which provoked European leaders to organise the third Crusade. The Fatimids were succeeded by the *Ayyubid* dynasty who returned the Egyptians to the *Sunni* main branch of Islam. In the meantime the process of Arabisation of Egypt continued, especially in the period 950-1350, when large numbers of Arab Bedouin peacefully invaded the country.

Fatimids and Ayyubids both imported Turkish slaves to serve in their armies. These Turks were called *Mamluks*. Gradually they developed into a new military and landed aristocracy that eventually, in 1250, took over the rule of the country. The *Mamluk* military dictatorship extended Egyptian rule to Western Asia, including Medina and Mecca, and defeated the fourth Crusade. Harsh taxation of the Egyptian peasants, among them many Christians, finally weakened the Mamluk regime.

In 1517 the *Ottoman Turks* conquered Egypt. In 1453 the Ottomans had taken Constantinople, ending the Eastern Roman Empire. Egypt was added to their vast Ottoman empire. Now it was ruled from Istanbul, the new name of Constantinople. The Ottomans extended the Egyptian boundary southwards into Nubia in the 1550s, and even Massawa on the Red Sea was occupied. This barred the Portu-

The Faith Moves South

guese soldiers, traders and missionaries from entering the Red Sea and Ethiopia. Egypt became an important gateway through which Islam spread to other parts of Africa.

c. *The Islamisation of North Africa*

From Egypt the Arab armies conquered the regions West to them, calling this vast North African territory *al-Maghrib* (the West). In the 690s, Carthage and the former Roman territories in Africa were conquered, they were called *Ifriqiya* by the Arabs. In the beginning the Berber population of the inlands resisted, but gradually the Muslims pushed on. In 711 they reached the Atlantic coast of Morocco. Berber society soon abandoned Christianity, and many of them formed part of the Islamic army. Arab and Berber intermarriages contributed to the formation of the North African Muslim peoples.

After the 7th century Islam became divided into conflicting movements. The main division was between the *Sunnite* majority and the *Shi'ite* minority. Power over the Sunnite majority was soon seized by the *Ummayad* dynasty, who moved the Muslim capital from Madinah to Damascus. The *Abbasid* dynasty took over and they made Baghdad to be the capital.[20] North African Muslims asserted independence from the Ummayad and Abbasid *caliphs*. They formed the *Kharijite Movement*, which was related to the Shi'ites, and according to Shillington reminiscent of the Berber *Donatists* of the Christian era.[21] The Kharijites were considered heretical by the Sunnite majority of Islam. Kharijite independency preceded the *Fatimid dynasty*, mentioned in the previous section, which took control over most of the Maghrib. They tried to take over power from the Abbasids in the whole Muslim world. In 969 they conquered Egypt.

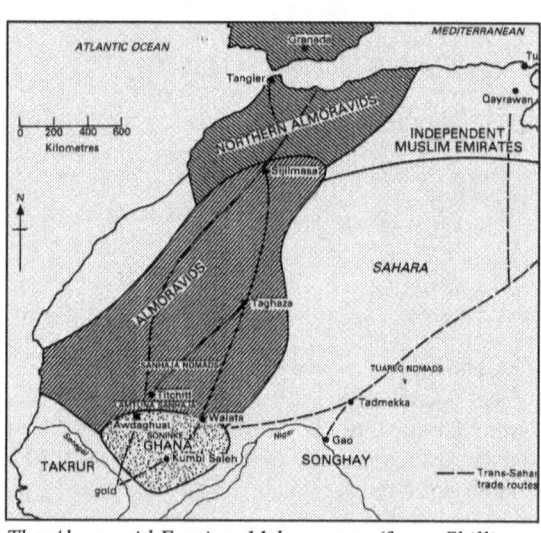

The Almoravid Empire, 11th century (from: Shillington, History of Africa, p.91)

---

[20] Karen Armstrong, *Islam: A Short History*, London: Weidenfield & Nicholson, chapter 2.
[21] Shillington, *History of Africa*, p.77

In the 10th century a revival among Sanhanja Berber converts beyond the Sahara on the Atlantic side led to the emergence of a strict Islamic movement, the Almoravids. Parts of Western Sub-Sahara, Mauritania and Morocco belonged to the *Almoravid Empire*. By the middle of the 11th century the empire split into a southern part that conquered or deeply influenced the Ghana kingdom of the Soninke people, and a northern part that invaded Spain. In 1040 the northern Almoravids were overthrown by more strict Muslim Berbers from the south, who founded the Almohad Empire. In the 12th century the whole of the Maghrib was united in this state, which was, together with Muslim Spain, successful in spreading and strengthening the intellectual achievements of Islam, like in the fields of mathematics, science, physics, astronomy, chemistry.[22] The Almohad unity in the Maghrib collapsed in the 13th century. At the same time the Spanish and Portuguese started to throw the Muslims out of the Iberian Peninsula. In 1492 the Muslims lost Granada, their last foothold in Spain.

The Almoravid and Almohad states contributed much to contacts between peoples in North Africa and south of the Sahara. Especially they played a role in the trade of gold from Sub-Saharan to North Africa and to Europe.

In the meantime the process of Arabisation of the Maghrib intensified. Many Arab Bedouin moved from Arabia into North Africa, spreading Arabic language, culture and their specific type of Islam. Large numbers of Berbers were absorbed by the Arabs, although the Berber language survived in the inlands.

In the 16th century the Ottoman Turkish Empire on the one side, and the Spanish and Portuguese on the other struggled for control of the Maghrib, mainly of the sea ports. The Turks lost dominance of the Mediterranean, when they were defeated at Malta in 1565 and at Lepanto in 1571. But Tripoli, Tunis and Algiers became Turkish ports and the inland became the territory of the Turkish Empire. The Turks supported trans-Saharan contacts.

Morocco was not absorbed by the Turks, neither was it conquered by the Iberians. Under king Ahmad al-Mansur (†1603) a Portuguese invasion was warded off (1578 at the battle of al-Ksar Kebir), and Morocco extended its territory beyond the Sahara in the Western Sudan[23] by occupying Songhay country, thus acquiring control of the trade in gold and slaves.

---

[22] Christian Western Europe learned many skills from the Arabs and Berbers in Spain and North Africa, like paper making, Hebrew grammar, the decimal system, modern medicine, and above all Aristotle's philosophy, which Thomas Aquinas made the foundation of his *Thomistic Theology*, which still is officially recognised in the Roman Catholic Church. Cf. Joseph Schacht with C.E. Bosworth (eds.), *The Legacy of Islam*, Oxford: Clarendon, 1974^2, pp.244-505, offering contributions on the influence of Islam culture on the West for: Art and Architecture (Oleg Grabar and Richard Ettinghausen), Literature (Franz Rosenthal), Philosophy, Theology and Mysticism (George C. Anawati), Science (Martin Plessner and Juan Vernet), Music (O. Wright).

[23] The name *Sudan* in a wider sense applies to a territory South of the Sahara desert, stretching from West to East. It is derived from the Arab name for the whole continent of Africa, *Bilad al-Sudan*, which means *land of the black people* (cf. Akitune E. Akinade, 'Islamic challenges', in: Kalu (ed.), *African Christianity*, p. 118) In a narrower sense *Sudan* is the name of a national state in the East of Africa.

5. The Fullness of Time

God is the ruler of history. His hand has prepared the world for receiving the Gospel of Jesus Christ. This has been so in a special way since the beginning of the history of the Christian Church. The 'fullness of time' had come.[24] Missionaries who went out after the outpouring of the Holy Spirit at Pentecost, penetrated into societies that were disappointed or bored by their pasts, which made them ready for change. God had worked in the hearts and in the circumstances of many people to make them open for receiving the message of salvation through Jesus Christ. For Sub-Saharan Africa, the 'fullness of time' became visible many centuries later. In the New Era, after 1500, changes became increasingly apparent, socially, economically and politically. In the next sections we will see emerging and collapsing kingdoms, movements of migrating peoples, wars feeding disruption and slavery, and the opening of trading routes. *Kings, youth, slaves, refugees* and *women* were the categories that were most affected by these changes. They were the ones through whom, according to Sundkler, the Christian faith would invade Sub-Saharan Africa. The modern missionary enterprise in Africa started in the 19th century. However, Mission and Church had to compete, not only with *African Traditional Religions*, but also with *Islam*.

The occupation by Islam of Egypt, North Africa and Nubia was followed by the Islamic conquest of the Sahara. Then the Eastern and Western coastal areas of Sub-Saharan Africa were penetrated, Niger, East Sudan, West Sudan. This happened hundreds of years before the arrival of the missioinaries. The Hausa belonged to the first Sub-Saharan peoples that were converted to Islam. From about 1750 the Fullani people, voluntarily joined by the Hausa, in a violent way founded a large and powerful Islamic state.[25] Gradually during the 18th and 19th centuries Islam spread southwards, sometimes using violent, sometimes, peaceful methods.[26] In West Africa this expansion could not continue to the South of the continent. But, in the coastal areas of East Africa the influence of Arabic Islam reached the very South, leading to the foundation of Muslim island and city states. Swahili Arabs and allied tribes were active as hunters and traders of slaves. In the East and the South of Africa Islam not only spread from Arabia, but also by means of the migration of workers from India to Africa.

---

[24] *Galatians* 4: 4, 'When the time had fully come, God sent forth his Son'. Cf. Paas, *From Galilee to the Atlantic*, pp. 37-57.
[25] K. Shillington, *History of Africa*, London: Macmillan, 1995, discusses on pp. 90-106 the early spread of Islam in the Sudanic states of West Africa.
[26] Cf. J. S. Trimingham, *Islam in West Africa*, London, 1959; *Islam in the Sudan*, London 1949², repr. 1965, *Islam in East Africa*, London: Oxford University Press, 1964; *The Influence of Islam on Africa* (1968); J. and L. Kritzeck, ed., *Islam in Africa* (1969), E.C. Mwandivenga, *Islam in Zimbabwe*, Gweru: Mambo Press, 1983; D.S. Bone (ed.), *Malawi's Muslims – Historical Perspectives*, Blantyre: Claim, 2000, with annotated bibliography

Christian Mission did not enter a religious vacuum. The older Missions before 1800 and the modern missions of the 19th century had to struggle with the continuing impact of *African Traditional Religions*. Missions and Churches also met with the increasingly powerful presence of Islam in many places.[27] Now, in this chapter let us look separately at each of the Sub-Saharan regions.

6. The Situation in Sub-Saharan Africa

a. West Africa

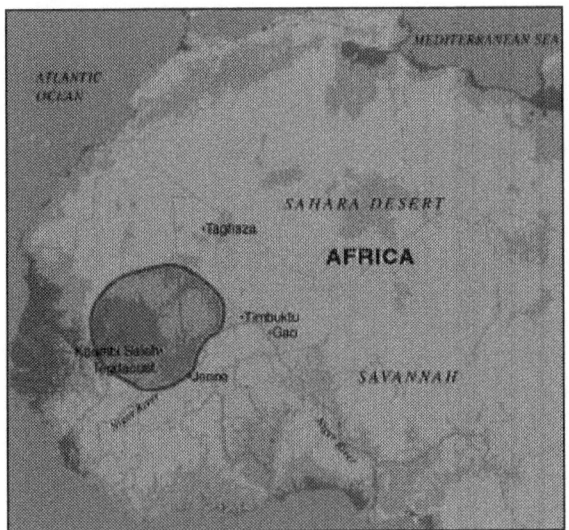

The Soninke kingdom of Ghana, located in what now is south-eastern Mauretania, and part of Mali, in its largest extent, about mid 11th century.

Generally it took many years for West African leaders to be fully convinced of the virtues of Islam and to convert. It was not until the leaders of a kingdom or state had converted that an effort was made, usually with the full support of the leader, to convert ordinary citizens. It often took several generations before the majority of the people in a particular kingdom or societies were practicing Muslim. This gradual process resulted in a situation where people would adopt some Islamic practices and beliefs while maintaining some of their indigenous beliefs and practices. Gradually, Islamic practice became more predominant, but often elements of indigenous belief and practice would continue.

Many Sub-Saharan societies remained loosely organised in villages, joined together in chiefdoms. However, in many other cases, cities played an important role in African society. In the West Sudan they were called *kafu* and were often walled. These cities were the beginning of early kingdoms, with a much more tightly knit organisation. Here are some examples.

---

[27] For a case study of the the life of Mission and Church within a powerful Islamic context, see: Martha Frederiks, *We have toiled all Night: Christianity in The Gambia 1456-2000*, Zoetermeer: Boekencentrum, 2005.

The Faith Moves South

The *Soninke kingdom of Ghana* (900-1100). It was actually situated hundreds of kilometres northwest of modern Ghana. Its inhabitants were mainly the Soninke people. The Soninke state was renowned for its gold trade. It was situated halfway between the Sahara and the gold fields in Senegal. The Soninke traders sold Saharan salt from the north in exchange for gold from the south. Through Berber contacts, especially the Almoravids, either peacefully or violently, the Soninke became Muslims by the middle of the 11th century. One of their kings was Tenkaminen who held court in his capital city of Kumbi. The king controlled both political and religious life.

The *kingdom of Mali* (1200-1400). It was begun by a Soninke chief of Sosso who conquered most of the Ghana kingdom, and also the homeland of the Malinke to the south. The Sosso state was built on violence. This provoked resistance from the Malinke, who under king Sundiata took control of the whole Soninke and Malinke territory. He extended his empire southwards to Bure on the Niger where gold was found. Traditionally the Malinke people believed that contact with the ancestor spirits secured peace and prosperity. The chiefs, or *mansa*, were considered mediators with the ancestors. All political and religious power was in their hands. King Sundiata took over all *mansa*-

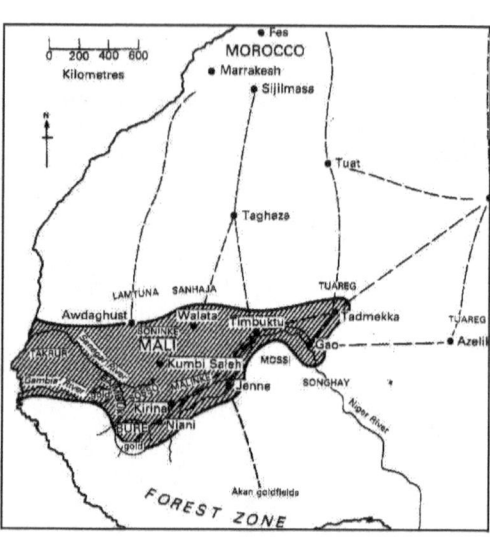

The Mali Empire in the 14th century (from: Shillington, History of Africa, p.95).

titles of lower chiefs; consequently he was treated with extreme respect. Most kings after Sundiata were Muslims, but they never completely rejected traditional religion. Under kings Musa and Sulayman in the 14th century the Mali Empire reached the summit of its glory and wealth. King Musa's free spending of gold in Cairo, where he was on his way to Mecca, even unsettled prices at the Egyptian gold market. Major Mali cities Timbuktu and Jenne were filled with libraries, and schools of law and theology. In the 15th century the empire declined, because outer provinces grasped independence; the most important of them was Songhay.

The *kingdom of Songhay* (1400-1600) consisted of the area around the middle Niger. The first capital was at Kukiya and then Gao. By the beginning of the 11th century the rulers had become Muslims. Under King Sonni Ali (†1492) the Songhay absorbed the kingdom of Mali. Ali was succeeded by a general, Muhammad Ture (†1528), founder of the Askiya dynasty, who became known as the *caliph of the Sudan*. Timbuktu again was a centre of Islamic learning. A Moroccan visitor,

Africa on the Eve of Change

Leo Africanus, visited the town, and observed 'many doctors, judges, priests and other learned men, who are well maintained at the King's cost'. He also saw 'various manuscripts and written books ... sold for more money than other merchandise'.[28] The Songhay kingdom broke down in 1591, when a Moroccan army took the rulers by surprise. Until 1660 the Moroccan sultan was formally in authority in this Sub-Saharan territory on the river Niger.

A 16th century Mosque in Agadez, Niger (from: website, explorin-gafrica)

Some other West-African states were: the *Takrur* in the Senegal valley, who adopted Islam already in the 11th century, and were allies of the Almoravids, and the kingdom of *Kanem-Borno* in the central Sudan, shaped by King Idris Alooma in the 16th century as a federation of three Hausa kingdoms, whose capital was Kano.

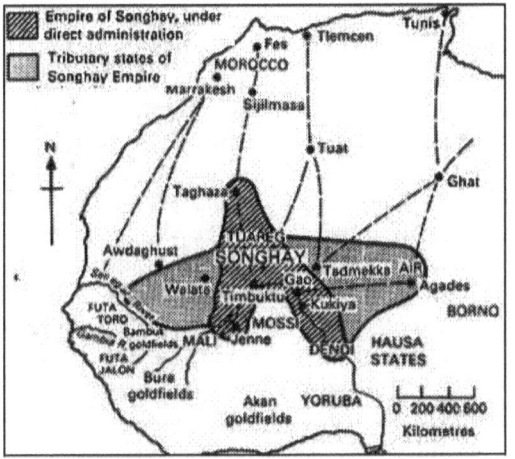

The Songhay Empire in the early 16th century (from: Shillington, History of Africa, p. 102)

The Yoruba speaking people also formed states of their own. Most important were the kingdoms of *Ife, Benin, Oyo,* and *Dahomey.* All these states at times cooperated with the slave trade and profited from it, although the Dahomeian king Agaja (†1740) tried to stop the transport of African slaves across the ocean and have Europeans to establish plantations in Africa where slaves could be put to work.[29]

Let me conclude this survey with a few words on the Akan states, of which the Ashanti kingdom was the most important. The traditional trade route for Akan gold was through the Sahara desert. Slaves were working in the gold mines. But in the 1480s the Akan started trading their gold and their surplus of slaves to the Portuguese. The Akan formed a number of states that in the 1670s joined together to the Ashanti state under king Osei Tutu. Under his successor Opuku Ware (†1750) the Ashanti kingdom covered most of present day Ghana. The gold trade amassed an enormous wealth for the Ashanti kings.

---

[28] Shillington, *History of Africa*, p. 105.
[29] Shillington, *History of Africa*, p. 193

In the 1470s, Portuguese ships for the first time touched the West-African coast, which signalled the beginning of a new era for life in villages, chiefdoms, kingdoms and empires.

b. East Africa

Apart from Ethiopia and Swahili-Arab settlements in the coastal regions, there is very little written evidence of East Africa's history before 1500. Yet, much historical information can be derived from oral sources, archaeological findings and the study of languages. Historians agree that Bantu speaking peoples entered the East African interior south of Ethiopia in the early centuries AD. They increasingly relied on cattle. In the period 1400-1700 Nilotic speaking people from the North also invaded East Africa, also keeping cattle. There was much blending of these two main groups. Political and religious developments in the interior were heavily influenced by what happened at the coast. Greek and Roman traders used to refer to the East-African coast as *Anzania*. The Anzanean people were probably Bantu-speaking fishermen and farmers, at least in the 5th century.

In Arab literature the East African coast and its off-shore islands are called the *land of Zanji (Zenji)*. There was an increasing Arab presence in this region, caused by the spread of Islam in the 7th and 8th centuries. The Arabs, who often intermarried with Africans, were conscious of their mission, but they were also sailors and traders. Gold, slaves, leopard skins, and ivory were traded. Their ships connected the African coast and the Islamic world of West-Asia and India. They established market-towns along the coast, often on the off-shore islands, like Mogadishu, Pate, Mombasa, Malindi, the Lamu Islands, Pemba, Zanzibar, Mafia, Kilwa, the Comoro Islands, Mozambique Island, Sofala, all together some forty towns. In these cities and coastal regions developed the *Swahili culture*. Ki-swahili means 'language of the people of the coast'. It is a Bantu language with Arab additions. The Swahili-Arabs were Islamic in religion and African in language. These merchant city-states were ruled by a council of *wazee* (Swahili: elders) and a kind of king, a *sheikh*. An example is Zanzibar, in the 16th century ruled by a *Mwinyi Mkuu* (Great Master), who was surrounded by the sanctity of a divine chief. Swahili traders depended on inland African tribes for the delivery of goods. Until the arrival of the Portuguese in 1498 there was relative peace in the Swahili *land of Zenj*

In the interlake regions of present day Kenya, Uganda, Rwanda, Burundi and Tanzania also a number of states emerged. The most important one is *Buganda*.. It rose in the 17th century after having asserted itself against the Bunyoro cattle raiders, who in their turn had taken over from the Chwezi state in the 16th century. The Buganda kings were called *kabaka*. In the 18th century kabaka Mawanda founded a strong centralised kingship. To the south, in Rwanda and Burundi, gradually two states shaped in which the Tutsi people dominated. East of Lake Victoria the Maasai entered, being of Cushite stock, probably related to the Oromo of Ethiopia. They settled under various names (e.g. Karamojong, Teso, Turkana, Samburu) in present day Uganda, Kenya and Tanzania. They traded and partially mixed with Bantu peoples they met, for example with the Kikuyu of central Kenya, and the Chagga of the Tanzanian plateau.

c. South-Central Africa

In the South-East of present day Congo chiefs of the Luba people joined together in a kingdom under the Ncongolo dynasty. The Luba kings were given great *mystical and religious authority*. In the 1450s the royal house split, and a rival kingdom was founded, the Lunda. Ideas of centralised religion facilitated later territorial expansion. In the 17th and 18th centuries the Lunda grew to great power. They even founded a new state to the South East in the copper area of present day Zambia, founded by the *Kazembe dynasty*. The Kazembe kingdom traded with ports on

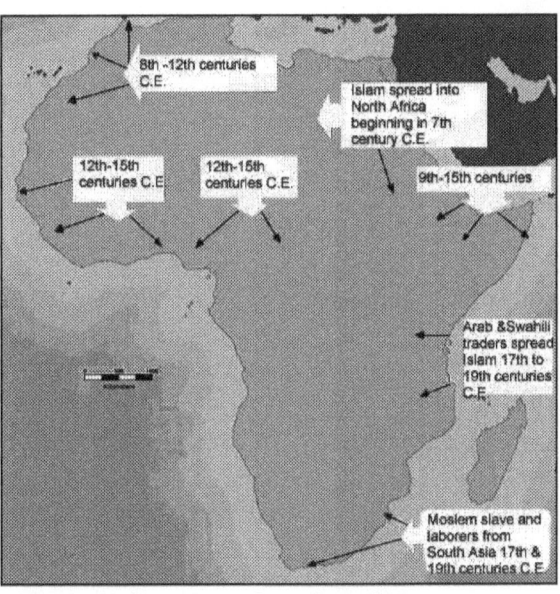

The spread of Islam in Africa through the centuries.

both the Atlantic and the Indian Ocean. Another break-away from the Lunda were the *Kinguri kings*, who founded a raiding state in central Angola, and later were called the Imba-ngala people. In Angola by 1500 the Ndongo people joined together under Ngola, the main guardian of the rainmaking shrine.

In the South West of today's Congo the chiefs of the BaCongo people were united in a single kingdom by 1400. The kings of this *Congo Kingdom* were called ManiCongo. Their authority rested much on the guardians of the rainmaking shrines.

The *Maravi Kingdoms* of central and southern Malawi originated from a wider tradition, the Luangwa, that stretched to half way through Zambia, including Chewa, Bisa and Bemba peoples. The Maravi people consisted of the Nyanja just south of Lake Malawi, the Mang'anja further south in the Shire Valley, and the Chewa to the

A 14th century lithograph of Mansa Musa, celebrating his power on his Hajj to Mecca.

West. They were ruled by respectively the Kalonga dynasty, which was started about the year 1400 by a joining together of the Banda and Phiri clans, and its offshoots, the Lundu, and Undi dynasties. The religious rituals for rain and soil fertility connected to the position of the king, may have come from the Luba tradition. The Maravi peoples traded in ivory and iron. In the 16th century they resisted Portuguese imperialism. Kalonga Masula (†1650) welded the Maravi peoples together to one empire that stretched from the Zambezi to Mozambique Island. He even invaded the Mutapa Empire in Zimbabwe. Due to lack of administration and leadership the Maravi Empire declined. The Yao people took over the Maravi trading routes to the Swahili ports.

South of the Zambezi there were the *Toutswe* communities of eastern Botswana. In western Zimbabwe there were the communities of the *Leopard Kopje culture*, especially the Mapungubwe people. They were cattle breeders and traders. This community of Shona people was the beginning of the rise of the state of *Great Zimbabwe*. They built and extended big stone enclosures (*zimbabwe* comes from *dzimba dzamambwe* = stone buildings) for cattle, for they were able masons. From Great Zimbabwe the Swahili coast, especially Kilwa, was supplied with gold and ivory. But in about 1450 the site was abandoned, leaving the mysteries of the history of Great Zimbabwe unsolved. It was followed by the foundation of the *Torwa State*, that continued the tradition of building stone enclosures. By the end of the 17th century the Torwa rulers were defeated by cattle pirates called *Rozvi* (meaning: *destroyers*), led by one Dombo, who listened to the title *changamire*. Dombo even expelled the Portuguese from the collapsing Mutapa territory, thus forming his own *Rozvi Empire*.

The *Mutapa Empire* started in about 1420 when one Mutota segregated himself from the Great Zimbabwe state. Together with his son, Matope, he formed an alternative state in the Northern Shona region at Dande. They and their successors adopted the title of *Mwene Mutapa* (= conqueror). In the 16th century the Mutapa empire succesfully resisted Portuguese attempts to check it, thus keeping control of trade to the Swahili coast. In the 17th century, however, the Portuguese military influence increased, making the Mutapa Empire crumble, only to be saved by invading Rozvi pirates, who expelled the Portuguese.

d. South Africa

The Khoikhoi and the San are the oldest peoples of South Africa. By 1600 Khoikhoi and San clans lived in southern Namibia and the south-west Cape. The Bantu also claim old rights. Sotho-Tswana presence south of the Limpopo and Vaal Rivers can be traced back to before 1400. South East of Drakensberg another Bantu sub-group, the Nguni-speaking peoples, had settled, the southernmost of them being the Xhosa.

By the 19th century they had developed *Zulu kingdoms* under kings such as Shaka, Dingane, and Mpande. Their wars created a *mfecane*, that is a diaspora of numerous movements of refugees, which as Sundkler stresses,[30] would indirectly contribute greatly to the acceptance and the spread of Christianity. But first, in the 17th century all these peoples were to meet Dutch (see chapter 4) and somewhat later English settlers (see chapter 5).

Islam came to South Africa quite recently. The demand for cheap labor was responsible for the introduction of Islam into this region. Muslims mainly came to South Africa in two waves.

The first group was brought in by, Dutch colonial settlers who in 1652 had arrived at what today Cape Town. The Dutch settler-farmers needed cheap labor to work on their farms. In response to this demand, the Dutch began to import slaves from Dutch colonies in South East Asia (Malaysia and Indonesia). Most of these slaves were Muslim. Throughout the years of slavery and after emancipation in the early 19th century, the descendents of these slaves maintained their strong religious affiliation with Islam. Today, a strong minority of Muslims are living in the area around Cape Town.

The second group of Muslims came to South Africa in the 19th century. At this time, British settler-farmers had developed huge sugar plantations in the province of Natal. Slavery had been abolished, but these farmers were able to recruit inexpensive labour from India. Today, there are more than one million people of Indian heritage living in South Africa. Many of them belong to the Islamic faith.[31]

---

[30] Sundkler and Steed, *A History of the Church in Africa*, pp.82,83.
[31] Akinade, 'Islamic Challenges', in: Kalu (ed.), *African Christianity*, p. 135, quotes the 1993 census which says that half a million South Africans are Muslims, almost half of them Indians, also almost half are Coloureds, the others are a few Blacks and Whites.

Chapter 2

Nubian and Ethiopian Christianity

1. Nubia excavated[1]

a. Archeological Findings

The history of Christian Nubia was hidden and almost forgotten for a very long time. This changed in the period 1959 – 1969 when a series of 59 archeological expeditions, coordinated by UNESCO, uncovered important testimonies of early Christian presence in the region. Here are some of the findings. The reference in *Acts* 8: 26-39 to Candace the Queen of the Ethiopians, whose treasurer was baptised by Philip, does not actually point to present day Ethiopia but to *Kush*,[2] later Meroe, in present day Northern Sudan, where Queens with the title Candace ruled. In the third century the kingdom of Meroe was overrun, probably by Ethiopian warriors. Later, from the ruins of Meroe, the three kingdoms of Nubia were shaped, Nobatia in the North with its capital Faras, Makuria in the Centre with its capital Dongola and Alodia in the South with its capital Soba.[3]

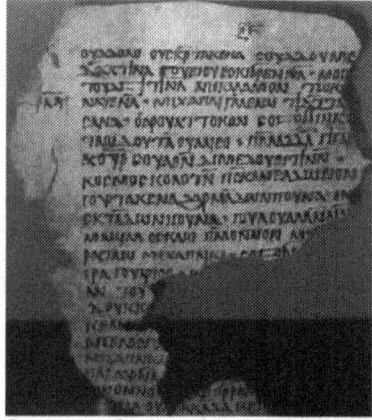

Remnant of a page from a 9th or 10th century translation in Old Nubian of a book on the Archangel Michael, found at Qasr Ibrim (British Museum).

---

[1] For a more extensive survey of the history of the Nubian Church see: R. Werner, W. B. Anderson, and A. Wheeler, *Day of Devastation, Day of Contentment: The History of the Sudanese Church Across 2000 Years*, Nairobi: Paulines Publ., 2000, William B. Anderson and Ogbu U. Kalu (ed.), 'Christianity in Sudan and Ethiopia', in: Kalu (ed.) *African Christianity*, pp. 75-104; M. R. Shaw, *The Kingdom of God in Africa – A Short History of African Christianity*, Baker Books, 1996, pp. 65-72, 92-98; J. Baur, *2000 Years of Christianity in Africa – An African History 62-1992*, Paulines Publ., 1994, pp. 31-34; B.Sundkler and C.Steed, *A History of the Church in Africa*, Cambridge University Press, 2001[2], pp.30-34; K. Shillington, *History of Africa*, London: Macmillan, pp.68, 73, 163, 164.
[2] The Hebrew word *Kush* appears in Scripture, e.g. as the name of one of Noah's sons. Later *Kush* became the name for *Ethiopia* of which it is the Greek translation. Literally the word means 'black man'. (Cf. Anderson and Kalu, 'Christianity in Sudan and Ethiopia', in: Kalu et.al. (eds), *African Christianity*, pp. 75, 76).
[3] Nobatia, Makuria and Alodia are Greek names. Anderson and Kalu, *African Christianity*, p.77, use the Arab names: Nuba, Maqurra and Alwa.

Excavations have uncovered the city of Faras which revealed remnants of Christian churches dating from the early fifth century. These findings agree with reports in Rufinus' *Church History* (appr. 400) who said that Coptic monks from Egypt, travelling Southwards on the river Nile, had penetrated Nubia by that time.

b. Monophysitism

Empress Theodora (c.500-548) of the Byzantine or Eastern Roman Empire, wife of Emperor Justian I, depicted on a mosaic. She sent the Monophysite missionary Julian to Nubia.

In surveys of the history of Nubian Christianity we are reminded of intensive missionary activity supported by Byzantine emperors in the 6th century. Perhaps the year 543 can be looked upon as the official beginning of Nubian Church History. In that year the Coptic priest Julian reached Nubia. He was sent by the Byzantine Empress Theodora. Julian baptised a Nobatian king and his nobles, nominated a bishop, and he converted a pagan temple into a church. At the same time he tried to propagate the ideas of Empress Theodora on the two natures of Christ. She advocated the *Monophysite* view of a union of Christ's divine nature and His human nature, as if the divine nature had absorbed the human nature at the incarnation. This thought deviated from the official stance of the Church as formulated at the *Council of Chalcedon*, in which not only the bond between the two natures was stressed, but also their being distinct. So Nubia became another battleground in the conflict between *Monophysitism* and *Chalcedonian* conceptions of Christology. Julian was followed by another Monophysite missionary, Longinus. He established the Monophysite form of Christianity also in most southern Nubian kingdom, Alwa. The kingdom of Makuria, however, received Orthodox (Melkite) missionaries and accepted Christianity in its Chalcedonian version. Orthodox ideas seem to have gradually triumphed in the whole of Nubia.

c. Royal Power

After the Arab conquest of Egypt in the 640s the Muslim armies pushed southwards. The extension of Arab rule and of Islam isolated Nubia from the Christian culture around the Mediterranean Sea. Yet, for a long time Nubia maintained itself. In 642 a large Nubian army halted the Arabs at Dongola, the capital of Makuria, and confined them north of the cataracts of the Nile. About 700 a peace treaty, the Baqt, secured the Nubians' independence, provided they delivered slaves and goods to the Arab regime in Egypt, respected the presence of a mosque in their capital.

Soon after the *Baqt* treaty the three kingdoms united with Dongola as capital. United Nubia maintained itself for some centuries as a counterbalance to Muslim power. Nubia had influence in Egypt and defended the interests of Egyptian Christians. King Georgios II received official recognition from the Caliph in Baghdad. The Fatimid rulers who seized power in Egypt in 969 were tolerant towards the Christians and friendly with Nubia.

Like in Byzantium (and in Ethiopia) the Nubian Church was headed by the king. Under the king state and church were bound together in a kind of theocracy. Kings even played the role of priests. Impressive church buildings and other Christian monuments were there, but this may not have made Nubian Christianity to become much more than a court religion, only superficially understood by the masses. The largest church building unearthed, is a cathedral in the Nobatian capital Faras, built by king Merkurios (697-707) and bishop Paulos. Paintings and writings on the walls show names and faces of bishops, at least some of whom were blacks. Faras cathedral was hit by a fire in 926, partly destroyed in 1170, and after that it was gradually covered by the sand of the desert.

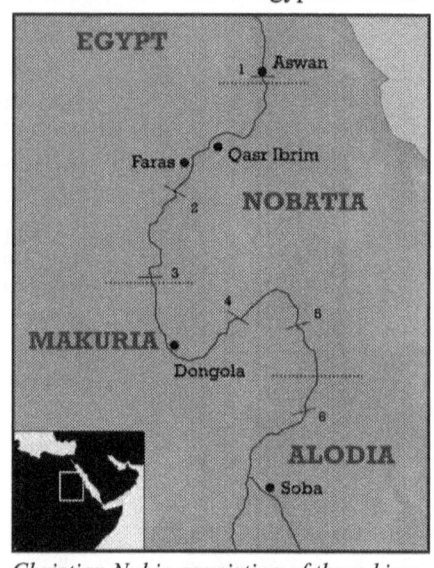

Christian Nubia consisting of three kingdoms, Nobatia, Makuria and Alodia.

The Church in this Northern kingdom of Nobatia, especially in the period of kings Georgios I († 920) and Georgios II, seems to have played a role in supporting and defending the Coptic patriarch of Alexandria and in sending clergy to the ailing Church in Ethiopia. This was not the first missionary challenge. In the beginning of Nubian Christianity Nobatia had been asked by the Southern kingdom of Alodia to send missionaries. In the Christianising of Southern Nubia also traders from Axum (Ethiopia) were active. At Soba the remnants of a cathedral were dug out, which indicates a strong presence of Christianity. Even much farther to the West, at Darfur, halfway from Nile to Niger, Christian symbols originating from Nubia were uncovered.

The Church in Nubia grew from the 6th through the 8th centuries, and it flourished in the period from the 8th through the 11th centuries.

d. Decline

From the 12th century onwards, by Muslim influence and pressure, the Nubian Church went down to almost extinction. In Egypt the Ayyubids ended Fatimid rule and thereafter in 1260 the Turkish *Mamluks* took over. The *Crusades* had made them extra hostile towards Christians. In 1276 a Nubian claimant to the throne, Shekanda, had himself crowned king under Mamluk protection. Under Muslim pressure Shekanda allowed Arab Bedouin to enter the country. This was the beginning of the end. In 1315 Nubia got a Muslim king, Abdallah Marshambo. In 1317 the main church of Dongola was converted into a Mosque. For some centuries a Nubian kingdom continued to exist in further southward in Alwa, but by the beginning of the 16th century it could not resist anymore the invading Arab nomads, and the territory was militarily conquered by Islam from the south, by the Islamised Funji people.

Shaw and Sundkler mention the following reasons for Christianity's demise in Nubia: (a) lack of evangelism, (b) isolation from the rest of Christianity, especially because of the surrounding Islamic forces, (c) influences from and intermarriages with Muslim nomads who had been allowed to enter, (d) lack of locally trained leaders, (e) clericalism, the church did not function without bishops or priests, (f) the church was bound and used by the state, especially by the king, (f) Christianity was mainly court religion, which points to a shallowness of faith, (g) the Nubians got socially uprooted when they changed from agricultural life to a nomadic mode of existence. Anderson and Kalu are of the opinion that the Nubian Church was strong, but that it could not adjust to radical change, like the interference by Muslim Egypt becoming more tense by the *Crusades*, and the imposition of religious taxation (*jizya*) on the Christians after the conquest by Egypt.

Old Nubia comprised the North-East of present day Sudan, the largest country in Africa. Sudan gained its independence from Britain in 1956. The Sudan was declared an Islamic Republic in 1983. Muslims are 70 percent with Sunni Islam in dominance. Almost the entire indigenous northern population is Muslim. There are several powerful Sufi orders, the largest is the Ansar, followers of the Mahdi. Christians comprise 19 percent, most of whom live in the South, in the Nubian mountains, and in Khartoum's Southern section. Traditional religions comprise 9.9 percent of the population.[4]

---

[4] George W. Braswell, Jr., *Islam Its Prophet, Peoples, Politics and Power*, pp. 192-193.

2. Ethiopia[5]

a. Ethiopia until 1100

Ethiopia is said to have become *'the oldest continuing Christian country not only in Africa but in the world'*. Some information is given of the history of Ethiopian Christianity.

The beginning of Christianity in Ethiopia is recorded by Rufinus (c.345-410). Whereas Christianity came to Nubia through the river Nile, it came to Ethiopia through the Red Sea. It began in the northern kingdom of Axum (or Aksum) in the 4th century. The first seeds were sown by two young men from Tyre (present day Lebanon), Frumentius and Aedesius. On their way to India, their ship was intercepted and captured on the Axumite coast, present day Eritrea. The ship's crew was killed, but their lives were spared. They were taken to king Ella-Amida of Axum, who gave them the important positions of steward and cup-bearer. On the king's death Frumentius was even made administrator for successor Ezana who was still under age. Frumentius and Aedesius used their influential positions for allowing Christian traders who arrived through the Red Sea, to spread the Gospel. They also encouraged the establishment of churches. When given leave to return home, Frumentius went to Alexandria to meet patriarch Athanasius. Frumentius was ordained bishop and in 334 he was sent back to Ethiopia in the official capacity of a missionary and Abba Selama, that is Archbishop of Ethiopia.[6] This was the direct preparation for the formation of the Ethiopian Church, and also of its subordination to Alexandria for 1600 years. After Frumentius' return, King Ezana, who in the meantime had enlarged his kingdom, became a Christian. He and his successors created a close connection between the Christian Church and the Ethiopian royal court.

Until the 5th century Christianity was largely confined to the royal court. Missionary work among the ordinary people began to develop by the activities of a group of Syrian monks, the *Nine Saints*. They translated Scripture into the Ge'ez language. They also made a compilation in Ge'ez of Patristic texts, entitled *Qerilos*, which would become fundamental to Ethiopian theological thought. The *Nine Saints* gave Ethiopian Christianity its specific monastic character (*Abba Aregawi*). They built churches and monasteries on almost inaccessible mountain tops. The

---

[5] For a fuller account of Ethiopian Church History, see: Sundkler and Steed, *A History of the Church in Africa*, pp. 35-41, 73-80, 150-168, 694-699, 927-930; Foster, *First Advance*, pp. 110-112; Shaw, *Kingdom*, pp. 62-65, 71-72, 118-119, 183-187, 273-275; Baur, *2000 years*, pp. 34-39, 43-44, 50-54, 153-170, 399-402; Hastings, The *Church in Africa,* pp. 3-45, 130-172, 194-196, 222-241, 611-613; A. Hastings, *A History of African Christianity 1950-1975*, Cambridge, 1979, pp. 35-38, 219-221; K. Ward, 'Africa', in: A. Hastings (ed), *A World History of Christianity*, London, 1999, pp. 197-200; Shillington, *History of Africa*, pp.68-71, 107-115, 164-167, 284-288, 364-366.

[6] Cf. Anderson and Kalu, 'Christianity in Sudan and Ethiopia', in: Kalu et.al. (eds), *African Christianity*, p.106.

Coptic icon of Church Father Athanasius (289-373), Archbishop of Alexandria.

oldest existing monastery is *Debres Damo*. They took the Christian message to the illiterate masses. But their missionary methods were superficial. There was not much teaching and not many preachers were trained. This led to *syncretism*, and real Christian commitment was rarely to be found. The Nine Saints were *Monophysites* (of *Unionite* persuasion); as such they were deviating from Christianity as defined by the great Church councils. Yet, the Christian Church was established among the nobles and the peasants of Ethiopia. Its leading bishop was the *abun*, nominated by the patriarch of Alexandria. But the most central position was that of the king. Christian political responsibility was shown by King Kaleb (†558) who invaded Zafar and Najram in South Arabia to revenge for the massacre of Christians in that region. He established Ethiopian churches there. Perhaps the legend of Ethiopia's link with Old Testament Israel and the house of King Solomon –told in the ancient document *Kebra Nagast*- was born in this time.[7]

In the early Middle Ages there were important changes, the emergence of Islam and the removal of the centre of the Ethiopian Church southwards. The first change was that Christianity had to compete with Islam, the new world religion that emerged in Arabia and rapidly spread from mid 7th century. Shaw opposes the 'popular belief that Christianity in Africa was extinguished by the rise and spread of Islam'.[8] Ethiopian Christianity survived, although not much is known about the 7th through the 9th centuries, Shaw assumes that Ethiopian Christianity in that period developed quite peacefully; its Islamic neighbours to the north did not cut off communications with the patriarchate in Egypt, and pilgrimages to Jerusalem went on. One can wonder about Shaw's picture of a peaceful relationship between Islam and the Church in early Ethiopia when taking into account that the power of Islam has been undermining Ethiopian Christianity in a very apparent way. Sundkler stresses that by 1300 half of Ethiopia was under Islam. In the beginning of the 16th century Muslim military violence nearly swept away the whole of Ethiopian Christianity. The second change in the position of medieval Ethiopian Christianity was that in the 8th century the Ethiopian Church's centre moved from Axum to the central highlands of Ethiopia, taking with it the Ge'ez language, its liturgy and its

---

[7] The story says that Ethiopian queen Medaka visited King Solomon and that out of this a son was born, Ebria Hakim, who as King Menelik I established a Judaistic religion in Ethiopia.

[8] Shaw, *Kingdom*, p. 75f.

Unionite views. This defensive move contributed to its isolation from the outside world.

In the 10th century Ethiopia was threatened from the south by the pagan Agau people who caused a serious decline of Christian rule. The Ethiopian kingdom had become very weak. The Church blamed this decline on unfaithfulness to Ethiopia's calling as the newly chosen people of Israel. The Church also reproached the kings for having severed the ties with the patriarch of Alexandria, so that for a long time no *abun* had been sent.

b. The Zagwe Kings

A new dynasty of kings, the Zagwe, tried to meet with this criticism. Like the kings in Axum line they claimed to be descendants of Solomon. Whereas the Queen of Sheba was said to have given birth to Menelik I, who became the first Axumite king, the king of the Zagwe dynasty said that they were descendants of Solomon and the Queen of Sheba's handmaid.

They swept aside the old house of the Axum kings, killing all its members, except for one as the story goes. The Zagwe moved the capital from Axum in Tigray (or: Tigre) southwards to Wollo. They expanded Ethiopian territory, and revived Christian literature and art.

The most important Zagwe king is Lalibela (1190-1225), also known by his throne name Gare Maskal (*Servant of the Cross*). There are many legends on him. During a near to death experience in his youth, he was said to be carried by an angel to heaven. Returned once more to earth he withdrew into the wilderness then took a wife upon God's command with the name of Maskal Kebra (*Exalted Cross*) and flew with an angel to Jerusalem. As a mystic he lived in Jerusalem for a long time. He viewed himself as king and

St. George's Church, one of the rock cut churches of King Lalibela, built mid 12th century. This cruciform-shaped Church is the most magnificent of the 11 churches.

priest, and as such he reported that a revelation had come to him to build the *New Jerusalem*. There was a theological and a political side to this thought. The *New Jerusalem* is a New Testament image, its foundation had to express honour to Jesus Christ. With this idea Lalibela stressed that he was different from the old Axum kings who derived their symbols of power mainly from the Old Testament. He also broke the Axum tradition of building churches on mountain tops. Lalibela commissioned churches to be carved out of the rock, based on the vision he had.[9] These churches of his *New Jerusalem* were situated near holy and healing waters, accessible to the people. There are twelve churches and chapels, including various shrines. Four churches are monolithic in the strict sense, the others are excavated churches in different degrees of separation from the rock. The walls of the trenches and courtyards contain cavities and chambers sometimes filled with the mummies of pious monks and pilgrims. Legend says that the churches were built with the help of angels within 24 years. One of the churches is called *Bet Abba Libanos*. According to legend, Lalibela's wife, Maskal Kebra, with the help of angels, created this church in one night. It is dedicated to one of the most famous monastic saints of the Ethiopian Church, Abba Libanos.

Despite their achievements the Zagwe kings were not popular. They did not fit into the idea of the sacred calling of Ethiopia as the continuation of Old Testament Israel. The above mentioned national myth of the Queen of Sheba (1 *Kings* 10: 1-13) is related in the *Kebre-Nagast* document. Her son Menelik I, as the first king in the *Solomonide dynasty*, is said to have brought the *Ark of the Covenant* with him from Jerusalem where he visited his father. The document is not friendly to the Zagwe kings. It suggests that they are usurpers. Had they not moved the capital and destroyed the real Solomonic line? Yet, they did not succeed in rooting out completely the supposedly Ethiopian branch of the house of Solomon. The only survivor was hiding in the *Debre Libanos* monastery. In 1270 the leader of this monastery, Tekle Haymanot, helped to restore the ancient line of Axum kings handing over power to the hidden survivor, Yekunno-Amlak, who agreed to the claim that he was a descendant of King Solomon. Yekunno-Amlak contributed much to the creation of a problem that in later ages would harm the Ethiopian Church tremendously. Out of gratefulness he gave the Church one third of Ethiopia's land, making it a big landlord. Later, as a consequence of this the Church would be classified with the exploiters of the landless and the poor. Yekunno-Amlak and his successors expanded the kingdom, at the cost of the Muslims. Under King (by now also called Emperor) Amde-Zion (†1344) there were massive conversions to Christianity.

The Solomonide kings also facilitated a religious revival. The central figure in it was Tekle Haymanot. He had grown up in the southern region of Shoa where Christians suffered from pagan attacks. After a period of personal spiritual crisis and experiences in a monastic community in Tigray in the north, he started a new monastic order (*Dabra Asbo*) that worked successfully among the pagans of Shoa. After Tekle Haymanot's death the revivalist and missionary activities were strengthened by the new *Abun* Yaqob and by new military conquests. A conflict between church and state, mainly of *Abbot* Fillippos and *Abun* Yaqob versus *Emperor* Amde-Zion gave the church more influence in society. *Monasticism* united

---

[9] Anderson and Kalu, 'Christianity in Sudan and Ethiopia', in: Kalu et.al. (eds), *African Christianity*, p.109, 110.

The Faith Moves South

the country, but at times it was also a dividing power, for instance when, in opposition to Tekle Haymanot's community, the order of *Ewostatewos* arose. A bone of contention was the question of whether Saturday or Sunday should be kept as the *Sabbath* for Christians.

The conflict was resolved at a church council convened by Emperor Zar'a-Ya'qob[10] (†1468). The new emperor tried to reform and reunite the Church. He wanted to make new contacts with Rome and the West. Under his rule, although it was harsh and ruthless at times, the Ethiopian church flourished. Around 1430 opposition against Zar'a-Ya'qob's theocratic rule came from the newly founded monastic order of the *Estifanites*. They aimed at a spiritual kingdom of the heart and rejected the emperor's cult of the cross and of Mary.

c. Decline and Survival

After King Zar'a-Ya'qob's death in 1468, Ethiopia came under rapidly increasing pressure of Islam. In the beginning of the 16th century Muslims occupied more Ethiopian territory than Christians, although many Muslim settlements were not connected, and were ruled by Christian overlords. Yet, through slave trade and pilgrimages Ethiopian Muslims communicated with the Arab and Turkish branches of the *ummah*. Anti-Christian sentiments led to a widespread Muslim rising, led by a liberated slave, Imam Ahmad (†1543). People saw him as the Imam of Judgment Day who had returned to lead Islam to final victory. The Turks provided him with modern weapons. In 1529 at Shimbra-Kure the Ethiopian army was crushed by the forces of Imam Ahmad. Much Christian culture was destroyed during the 12 years of his campaigns, including many churches and monasteries. The situation was aggravated by a revolutionary movement of the pagan Oromo in the South, directed against both Christianity and Islam.

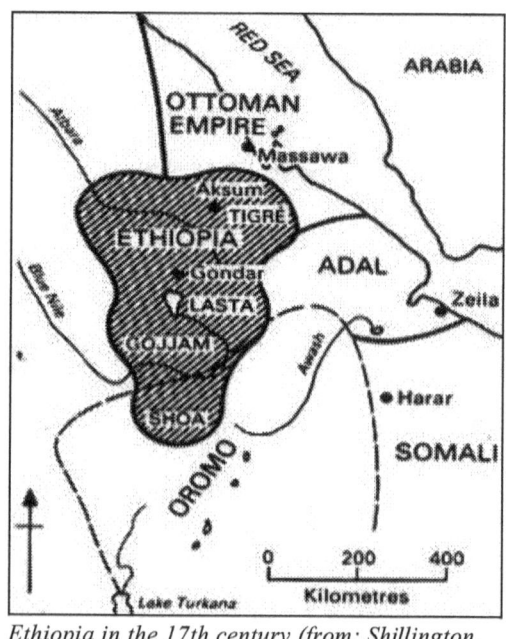

Ethiopia in the 17th century (from: Shillington, History of Africa, p. 166)

---

[10] Seed of Jacob; cf. Anderson and Kalu, 'Christianity in Sudan and Ethiopia', in: Kalu et.al. (eds), *African Christianity*, p.110.

In the meantime, resulting from the Portuguese campaigns of discovery, conquest and mission, a Portuguese embassy had opened in Ethiopia (the *Alvarez Embassy*, 1520-1526). In despair Zar'a-Ya'qob's great-grandson, King Lebna Dengel (†1540) appealed to the Portuguese for assistance. The Portuguese sent a fleet to Massawa with Vasco da Gama's son Christoph as the admiral. Under King Galawdewos (†1559), the Ethiopians and the Portuguese defeated and killed Imam Ahmad in 1543. Christian rule was reinstalled. But church and state had become weaker and more vulnerable. The great vision of the New Israel and the New Solomon was darkened. Many had lapsed to Islam. A book of penitence, *Mesihafe Qedir*, was to teach the way back to the church.

d. Jesuit Attempt Fails

By appealing to the Portuguese a new competitor had been given entrance to the country, the Roman Catholic Church with its universal claims of authority. Some of Christoph da Gama's soldiers remained in the country, and soon they had a bishop of their own, Andrew de Oviedo. Portuguese Roman Catholic activity in Ethiopia was coloured by the European situation where the Roman Catholic *Counter Reformation* tried to root out heretics, including followers of the Protestant Reformation. In the eyes of Rome the Ethiopian Orthodox Church was heretical, and had to be brought under the wings of the Pope. In 1557 Jesuits came to Ethiopia, with the intention to change the Ethiopian church and to unite it with Rome. Of course this challenged the independence of the Ethiopian Church and also the position of the patriarch of Alexandria who nominated the *abun*. King Galawdewos resisted the attempts of the Jesuits to introduce Latin rites and Roman Christology.

In the 17th century the independence of Ethiopian Christianity was again felt to be threatened by Western Jesuits. Pedro Paez, a Spanish Jesuit, entered the country in 1603. He was meant to become the patriarch of a transformed Ethiopian Church under Rome. Paez succeeded in winning the hearts of Kings Za-Dingil and Susenyos. He even convinced them of the christological error of Unionism. In 1622 King Susenyos decided to become a Roman Catholic. In 1626 the union of the Ethiopian church and the Roman Church was officially proclaimed. But in the meantime Paez had died. He was succeeded by Alfonso Mendez, an authoritarian Spanish prelate, who demanded re-baptism of all and re-ordination of the clergy. Mendez also demanded the abolition of Ethiopian rites and customs. This led to a rebellion and much bloodshed, so that King Susenyos in 1632 stopped the campaign of Romanisation by a public proclamation that restored the *Ethiopian Coptic Church*. Subsequently Susenyos abdicated. His son Fasilidas (†1667) withdrew to Gondar where a new capital was established. He chased away the Jesuit missionaries, and cut off relations with the Portuguese. As a reaction to this disappointment with foreigners a period of isolation followed. For two centuries the Ethiopian Church would mainly pay attention to internal affairs.

e. Conflicts and Disintegration

In this period of isolation the church tried to remedy some of its weaknesses. In the South Christianity was definitely weaker than in the North. The Church in the South lacked leadership and communication. They were surrounded by the pagan Oromo people. Two migratory movements supported the Church. Migrants from the North settled in the South and helped the Church in its missionary activity. Many Oromo people migrating to the North were influenced by the Church and became Christians.

Unfortunately this positive development did not stop processes of decline and division in church and state. In Gondar, people quarreled about issues like the right day for the Sabbath, leadership in the Church, and the role of Alexandria. More serious were the controversies on the two natures of Christ. They had split the church into at least four sections, the *Unionites*, the *Unctionists*, the *Unionists*, and the Sost Ledat, that is the *Three Births party*. The Unionites (*tewahido*) were classical *Monophysites*. They claimed that the uniting force of Incarnation had brought about one unique divine-human nature. In practice, however, they only stressed Christ's divine nature. According to the Unctionists the Holy Spirit through His unction (*qibat*) has united Christ's divine and human natures. Thus they were open to the heresy of *Subordinatianism*, putting the Son under the Spirit. The Son-of-Grace-party (*ye-siga-liij*) were kind of *Adoptianists*. They distinguished Christ's eternal sonship by the Father, his temporal sonship by Mary, and his redemptive sonship by the Holy Spirit. By union of his temporal and his redemptive sonship He is adopted as the eternal Son of God. By the end of the 18th century a variant of the Son-of-Grace-party would emerge, the Sost Ledat party, claiming that as a consequence Christ was born three times.

The parties in the controversies on Christology were regionally divided and weakened church and state. Royal policies aggravated the situation. In 1654 King Fasilidas supported the Unctionists, only to provoke rebellion among the Unionists. Also Yohannes I (†1682) favoured the Unctionists. His son Isayu I (†1706), however, forced the Unctionists to accept the Unionist position.

These quarrels divided society very deeply along the lines of the Alexandian patriarchate, the monastic movement of Tekle Haymanot, and the monastic movement of Ewostatewos. The *abun* represented the Alexandrian party which made him unacceptable to others. The *echege* who was sent to Gondar was just a representative of the Tekle Haymanot party. Even Echege Filpos appeared to be powerless. Ethiopian Christianity seemed to be at the verge of total collapse.

In the 18th century the quarrels led to political chaos. The central power of the kings at Gondar ceased to be effective. The power vacuum was filled by local rulers, called *ras*, who were ruling their own mini-states. Attempts by regional chiefs to grasp royal power, failed. One of them, Wibe of Simien, was beaten by Muslim Oromo at Debre Tabor in 1842. A Christian group among the Oromo, the Yeju, managed to take control of the royal house at Gondar, but they could not make their power effective in other parts of the country. In the midst of this the theological disputes went on. Islam was greatly helped by this chaos. Many people were confused and became Muslims. This period of great instability and disorder is called the *Era of the Princes*, or the *Era of the Judges* (Zamena mesa fint). It would last until 1855 when one of the local chiefs fought his way to the top, and became 'king of kings'. His name was Tewodros II (1818-1868).[11] The new king, or emperor, ended the chaos and proclaimed a new era of justice, peace and order. His qualities are summed up by Anderson and Kalu: He told the clergy to forget about disputes on Christology, and just stick to the classical *Monophysite* faith of Alexandria. He attempted to unify the nation, to reform the church, to introduce social programmes for the masses, to redistribute the land, to have the Bible translated in the Amharic language.[12] Besides, Tewodros adopted the claims of his Solomonic predecessors by calling himself 'Son of David'. He behaved independently towards the Patriarch of Alexandria by not accepting him to act as an envoy of Egyptian Muslim rulers. Only when the patriarch sent Selama (†1867) as the new *abun*, the emperor started to show his favour. Selama was educated at a school of the *Church Missionary Society* (C.M.S.) in Cairo. There he was trained in a Protestant Evangelical way, which made him favour Protestantism. Selama was liked by the emperor, which enhanced his influence. Unfortunately later they clashed. Selama was sent to prison where he died. Tewodros remained interested in the Protestants.

f. The First Protestant Missionaries in Ethiopia

Protestant missionaries had already arrived in Ethiopia before the reign of Tewodros started. In the previous section we noticed that Ethiopian Christianity seemed to be collapsing because of divisions and controversies. In this critical period, for the first time Protestant missionaries came to the country. They were Samuel Gobat, Johann Ludwig Krapf, Martin Flad, H.A. Stern and others (1830). They all belonged to the *Church Missionary Society* (C.M.S.), an organisation born out of the Evangelical revival in the Anglican Church. The C.M.S. did not intend to establish new churches. They wanted to purify and strengthen the Ethiopian church and use it as a bridge for evangelisation of eastern and central Africa. The French and German names of these missionaries demonstrate the inability of the C.M.S. to recruit Englishmen for their first enterprises. It also shows the international character of the 19th century missionary movement. Gobat started with the distribution of Bibles and tracts. His influence grew rapidly, e.g. with *Echege* Filpos, and he was even invited to become *abun*. Later he became Anglican bishop of Jerusalem, and kept contact with Ethiopia through visiting pilgrims. Krapf was especially interested in converting the pagan Oromo or Galla in the South. In his view converted

---

[11] Tewodros = Gift of God.
[12] Anderson and Kalu, 'Christianity in Sudan and Ethiopia', in: Kalu et.als (eds), *African Christianity*, pp. 113, 114.

Oromo would be missionaries the central regions of Africa. He made a grammar of the Galla language and translated the Gospels into it. Flad and Stern worked among the Falashas, 'the black Jews of Ethiopia', and led a number of them to the Ethiopian Church.

However, the Ethiopians soon noticed that the C.M.S. missionaries opposed *monasticism*, the prayers to Mary, and the veneration of images. Moreover they felt that their presence might prelude British colonialist attempts. Krapf favoured a British presence in Ethiopia to ward off Roman Catholic missionary attempts. These factors made the Ethiopian *ras* suspicious. That is why these first Protestant missionaries were expelled in 1842 and 1843.

Protestant missionaries showed a keen interest in the work of Bible translation. By mid 19th century the Scriptures had been translated into the Amharic language. When Protestants began working on this, there were already other translations. There was an old translation of the Gospels, made by Peter Heyling in the 17th century. In the 18th century an Ethiopian monk, helped by a French diplomat in Cairo, made a completely new translation of the whole Bible, which was ready in 1840.

Krapf started to improve this translation of the Bible. He continued this work even after his banishment and published his translation in 1870. Orthodox clergy, especially in Tseazega, put this Bible in place of the ancient Ge'ez version and used it for Bible study. In the meantime Krapf had gone to Zanzibar, and Mombasa in Kenya; from there he again tried to approach the Oromo people.

g. Another Roman Catholic Attempt Fails

The period just before the rise of emperor Tewodros also witnessed the arrival of Roman Catholic missionaries. This was the first time since the failure of Jesuit attempts in the 16th and 17th centuries. The coming of Justin de Jacobis to Ethiopia (1839) signaled new Roman Catholic attempts to bring Ethiopian Christianity under Rome. The climate seemed favourable. Many Ethiopians were tired of the chaos and disorder that was brought about in the Era of the Princes. They longed for the order and authority that Rome could give. Moreover, it was thought Rome could end the disputes on Christology, as at least two of the parties, the Unctionists and the Unionists, seemed to be close to Roman Catholic theology.

De Jacobis was an Italian Lazarist. He cooperated with bishop Massaja, a Capuchin, who consecrated him to be bishop. They kept this consecration secret, so as not to arouse suspicions from the Ethiopian clergy, who certainly would disagree with their vision of having Ethiopia united with Rome. They started seminaries, converted people, and managed to win the favour of the *echege* and of Wibe, the local *ras* of Tigray. The latter entrusted De Jacobis with headship of a group that was to ask the patriarch of Alexandria for a new *abun*. Ironically this journey led to the nomination of abun Selama, who was a friend of Protestantism. In 1841 Selama became the new abun of Ethiopia, thus restoring the contacts with the Coptic patriarchate of Alexandria after a long time. He disliked Roman Catholicism, and especially after 1855 when his protector Tewodros became emperor, he opposed the work of Roman Catholic missionaries.

De Jacobis tried to establish an indigenised Roman Catholic Church in the North. Massaja started in 1846. He first worked together with De Jacobis, then he went to the pagan Oromo in the South. And finally until 1879, he worked for the establishment of a Roman Catholic Church in the central Shewa province. In all three places he was expelled, and in the last one even banished from the country.

h. New Protestant Missions

Emperor Tewodros was interested in the technological products of Western Protestant culture, so he re-opened the doors for Protestants. Through the help of Gobat and Krapf able artisans were recruited from Chrischona, a Pietist Lutheran centre near Basle in Switzerland. The first group arrived in 1856. Some of them married Ethiopian wives and never returned to Europe. The country was opened for Protestant missionaries again. After the restoration of Ethiopian unity by Emperor Tewodros, Selama emphatically turned against Roman Catholics, forcing De Jacobis into hiding and expelling Massaja from the South.

Eventually Selama got into conflict with the capricious emperor, and he ended his life in prison in 1867. The emperor too ended his life tragically. Because of the levying of land taxations and the confiscations of church land, he estranged himself from the Church. His desire to be accepted on equal terms by Western powers was not fulfilled. Soon the emperor collided with the British government who did not comply with his wishes for military support against rival leaders. He put all English missionaries in prison. However, instead of giving in, the English sent an expedition navy force. In 1868 his army was crushed by the English, and he committed suicide.

i. Ethiopia Maintains itself

Tewodros was succeeded by Yohannes IV (†1889). The new emperor strengthened the unity of state and church. He also ended the public controversies as to Christology, by calling all parties to the *Council of Boru Meda* in 1878, and forcing them to conform to the classical *Monophysite* position of the *Unionites*. Not only Christians, but also pagans and Muslims were forced to concede to the decision of the Council. In this way the emperor started a successful campaign of forcing non-Christians into Christianity. He also extended Ethiopian territory by building garrison towns (*katema*) at the frontiers of his empire. In these cities the army and the church were actively represented. Many Muslims were brought under Christian rule, and eventually became Christians, especially among the southern Oromo.

Yohannes IV tried to resist the powers of imperialism that threatened Ethiopian independence. He defeated the Egyptians in 1875 and 1876, but he could not pre-

The Faith Moves South

vent the Italians from occupying the coastal town of Massawa. He attacked a new messianic Muslim movement under *mahdi* Muhammad Ahmed, but in the battle of Qallabat in 1880 he was mortally wounded.

During the reign of his successor, Menelik II (†1913), Ethiopia was threatened by Italy which in 1885 occupied Eritrea, seeking to establish a colonial empire in Africa. However, the Ethiopians defeated the Italian army in the *Battle of Adowa* in 1896. This feat contributed much to the movement of *'Ethiopianism'* that soon would spread among the Christians of colonial Africa, and inspire black imagination all over the world.

Menelik II built a new capital, Addis Ababa, welcomed Western artisans and missionaries, and had his cousin's son Ras Tafari Makonnen, later Emperor Haile Selassie I, educated in Europe. In line with his predecessor he tried to turn as many pagans as possible to the Orthodox Church, to be baptised after an absolute minimum of instruction.

Menelek II (1844-1913), Emperor of Ethiopia, whose army under general Ras Makonnen beat the Italians in the Battle of Adowa in 1896.

In the meantime the Evangelical movement continued to spread. Contacts between Evangelical missionaries from Sweden, and Orthodox clergy in Hamasen encouraged the study of the Bible in Amharic. This encounter with Scripture led many to the discovery that there is no salvation but through faith in Christ. Persecution by local rulers made a group of Hamasen Christians flee to Egypt and later to Eritrea, at that time occupied by the Italians. Later they returned to form an indigenous Protestant church in the Hamasen highlands. Among the Oromo an Evangelical church took shape, aided by a new Bible translation in the Oromo language by a liberated slave Onesimus and Aster Ganno, which was completed in 1899.

In 1916 Ras Tafari Makonnen became regent over Ethiopia, and in 1930 he became Emperor Haile Selassie. In 1936 Ethiopia was conquered by Italy. The Pope congratulated the Italian army, and Roman Catholic missionaries began to pour into the country, whereas many Protestant missionaries were expelled.[13] Emperor Haile Selassie started a guerilla war from neighbouring countries, in which many Ethiopians had taken refuge. Many refugees in Kenya met with Anton Jonsson, a Swedish teacher and preacher, and came into contact with Evangelical faith. The Italian occupation lasted until 1941. The Ethiopian Church was forced by the Italians to break ties with the Coptic Church in Egypt. After the occupation the Ethiopian Church became completely independent, not by force but voluntarily. A series of conferences with the patriarchate of Alexandria led to an agreement in 1959.

---

[13] Cf. Hildebrandt, *History of the Church in Africa*, p.235.

In 1944 the government declared a large part of the country a 'no-go-area' for foreign missionaries, who did not cooperate with the Ethiopian Church. This confirmed the policy of some Protestant organisations who cooperated with the Ethiopian Church. Other foreign missions were only allowed to work in pagan Oromoland in the South. Yet, a number of independent Evangelical denominations arose, like the *Word of Life Evangelical Church* (Sudan Interior Mission – S.I.M.) and the *Ethiopian Evangelical Church Mekane Yesus*.[14] The *Mekane Yesus Church* (the name means: the place where Jesus lives) was founded in 1959 with about 20,000 members, as a result of various Lutheran Missions, e.g. the *Bauern Mission* from Hermannsburg. According to the Mission's website the church has more than 3 million members now.

After the end of the Italian occupation, the Roman Catholic Church at first experienced a backlash of Ethiopian revenge, but it soon regained and strengthened its position.

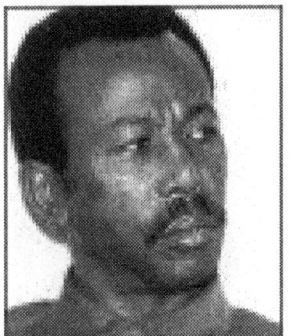

Menghistu Haile Mariam, leader of the Marxist-Leninist revolution in Ethiopia in 1977, who persecuted the Church.

In 1974 Emperor Haile Selassie was overthrown by an army council, the Derg. In 1977 a Communist revolution led by Colonel Menghistu Haile Mariam brought Ethiopia under *Marxist-Leninist* rule, which lasted for a decade. Christianity was suppressed, and the population suffered immensely from the cruelties of this regime. The suffering was intensified by the Ethiopian-Eritrean war. Mengistu especially persecuted the Protestant churches. Buildings were confiscated, organisations were infiltrated by communist agents, many leaders were imprisoned and some murdered. Later the Orthodox Church was hit by waves of persecution. After the end of Menghistu's regime it became clear the churches had survived, either publicly or underground. The Evangelical churches that had suffered most, had seen a tremendous growth of membership. In the Orthodox Church the leadership by non-clergy had grown stronger, and so had the interest in personal and communal Bible study.

---

[14] E.E.C.M.Y., for further information consult their website: http://www.eecmy.org/CO/index.shtml

Chapter 3

Africa and Early Portuguese Missions

1. Henry the Navigator

The defeat of Islam and the establishment of Christian rule was the dream of Prince Henry of Portugal († 1460), which he not only sought to realise in his own country, but also in other parts of the world, not least in Africa. He is known as Henry the *Navigator*, because of his nautical plans and activities. Henry aimed at the discovery of territories beyond the seas, that thus far had been largely unknown to the Europeans. Early world maps show that before 1500 Europeans were greatly ignorant about the geography of Sub-Saharan Africa.[1]

Infante Dom Henrique, Prince of Portugal, known in English as Henry the Navigator (1394-1460), contributed much to the development of Portugal as a seafaring nation and to plans for Portuguese expansion

From Henry the Navigator onwards this situation of ignorance was going to change. Bypassing the Arabs and getting direct access to the gold fields of West Africa was an important motive of the Portuguese seafarers. The ultimate goal was reaching India with its opportunities for the very rewarding trade in spices. Henry's plan to enter Africa to defeat Islam and establish Christianity met with approval by Popes Martin V (1418) and Nicolas V (1452). Henry even got papal blessing for trading in African slaves (1441). The exploration and the conquest (*conquista*) of foreign lands was to be aimed at evangelising the pagans. Therefore Henry's explorations were not only the work of sailors and soldiers, but also of missionary priests. In a special arrangement the pope allowed these priests to work in the system of *padroado* which made them directly responsible to the Portuguese government.

In 1441 Portuguese ships landed in Mauritania. In the 1470s the Fante coast, connected to the Akan gold fields, was reached. Soon the trade routes of gold, that used to run through Songhay and the Sahara desert, were diverted to the Portu-

---

[1] Peter Whitfield, *The Image of the World: Twenty Centuries of World Maps*, San Francisco: Pomegranate Artbooks, 1994, pp.20-26.

guese and other European trading forts on the Atlantic coast. Contacts between Portuguese and the kingdom of Benin (from 1472) provided the Portuguese with Benin slaves whom they used as commodities in exchange for Akan gold. In 1485 Congo was reached, and in 1486 the Cape of Good Hope, by Bartholomew Diaz. In 1494 in the *Treaty of Tordesillas*, Spain and Portugal divided the newly discovered world on either side of the Atlantic Ocean, thus granting Portugal the right to colonise Africa. This move was sanctioned by Pope Julius II in 1506.

In 1498 Vasco da Gama rounded the Cape and discovered the Zambezi, Mozambique Island, and other Swahili city states. The Portuguese discoveries and conquests were immediately followed by missionary efforts. Here is a general survey of early Portuguese missionary work. [2]

Martin V, originally Oddone Colonna (1368-1431) one of the Popes who approved of Portuguese plans to beat Islam and extend Christianity

2. Islands and the West Coast

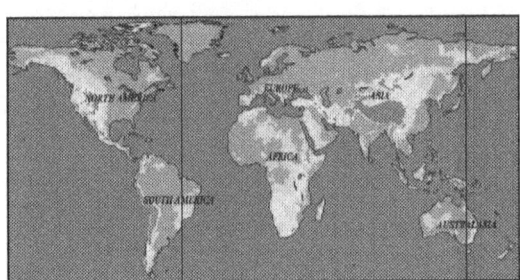

The Treaty of Tordesillas of 1494 divided the world outside of Europe between Portugal and Spain along a north-south meridian west of the Cape Verde Islands (46° 37' W). The lands to the east would belong to Portugal and the lands to the west to Spain.

Franciscan monks had worked on the *Canary Islands* since the beginning of the 15th century alongside commercial activities. By 1500 the bishop of Madeira was overseeing the mission work in Cape Verde, Sao Tomé and the Azores. In the meantime, in 1462, Alfonso de Balano, also a Franciscan, was appointed to oversee the missionary work at the *Guinea Coast*.

Cape Verde. This archipelago off the North Western coast of Africa became a base for slaves. It also became a base for the recruitment of African priests who were to be sent to Lisbon for training before they would enter the African continent as missionaries.

---

[2] On the early Portuguese involvement in Africa, see: Shaw, *Kingdom*, pp. 107-119; Baur, *2000 Years*, pp. 43-99; Foster, *Setback and Recovery*, pp. 180-183; Thomson, *New Movements*, pp. 80-81; Hastings, *African Church*, pp. 71-129; Ward, 'Africa', in: Hastings (ed), *World History*, pp. 200-203; Shillington, *History of Africa*, pp. 170-173, 198-201

The Faith Moves South

Sao Tomé and Principe Islands. On these uninhabited islands Portuguese settlers developed sugar plantations. Slave labour was used, first from southern Russia,[3] and then from the African mainland. Here is the beginning of the slave trade that for centuries would dominate the relations between Europe and Africa, and which was extended to a 'triangular trade' that included America. *Sao Tomé* became the main transit point for slaves being transported by the Portuguese to Brazil. A church was established among settlers, so African slaves were touched by Christianity.

View of Fort Elmina, St. George's castle was built in 1482-6 by the Portuguese, who were the first European builders in West Africa. It is the largest of the fortified buildings on the coast. In 1637 the Dutch took Fort Elmina from the Portuguese (from: Friere, 1546.

Mali and *Ghana*. Diogo Gomez converted a vassal king of Mali in 1457. In 1482 Diogo da Azambuja unsuccessfully tried to convert a local king in Ghana, and the church he founded became a symbol of hostile foreign presence. In 1503 another local king embraced Christianity, but later lapsed. Initial successes by Augustinians, Capuchins and Dominicans all ended in failure. Ghana or Gold Coast was reached in 1482. The Portuguese sailors landed in Elmina, where a Fort was established. Missionary attempts by Jesuits, Dominicans, Franciscans, Augustinians and Capuchins achieved some initial success, until the Fort of Elmina was conquered by the Dutch in 1637.

Benin. During the decades around 1500, the Portuguese received war captives from the Benin kings. These captives they sold as slaves to Akan in exchange for gold. Spanish Jesuits who in 1655 baptised the Benin king, were ordered by Portuguese soldiers to leave.

Early Roman Catholic Mission in West Africa had 'considerably limited success'. Kpobi says that by the end of the 17th century, the mission was, for all practical puposes, over'. Except for some relics, mission had practically died, because it was dominated by trade, and effectively resisted by African culture and religion, whereas the mass baptisms by Roman Catholic missionaries made 'converts' easily lapse into their former religion. Perhaps the greatest drawback to mission was the slave trade. Roman Catholic Portuguese got involved in the purchase and shipment of African slaves. For almost four centuries the Atlantic slave trade affected Africa, not only the West Coast, but also the territories south to it, Congo and Angola. Christian mission 'in such circumstances was most difficult, if not impossible'.[4]

---

[3] Shillington, *History of Africa*, p.171.

[4] N.A. Kpobi, 'African Chaplains in Seventeenth Century West Africa', in Ogbu U. Kalu (ed.), *African*

3. Congo

In 1491 the first group of Portuguese missionaries arrived at Mbanza Congo. In 1493 many Africans were baptised, among them Prince Mvemba Nzinga; he changed his name to Alfonso I (†1543). After ascending the throne in 1506, pushing aside his brother who was the rightful heir, he destroyed the pagan temple and capital, and built a new capital, São Salvador, with a cathedral. He invited many Portuguese missionaries, and sent his sons and grandsons to Lisbon for theological training. In 1531 his son Henrique was ordained bishop.[5] The church was planted throughout the kingdom. However, many Portuguese missionaries were sexually immoral, and also joined the *slave trade*. In 1516 the Benin kings stopped selling slaves. Then the trade shifted southwards to the Congo kingdom. King Alfonso had become very dependent on the Portuguese. His wars of conquest produced many captives whom the Portuguese could use as a trade commodity, and in their plantations on *São Tomé*.

An invasion by the Jaga people in 1568/1569 would have ended the authority of the Congo kings, if the Portuguese army had not saved and re-installed them. In the 17th century the kingdom disintegrated, and its regional factions increasingly built their economies on the trade in slaves.

In the meantime, at the request of King Alfonso's successors, at last more zealous Christian missionaries were sent. In 1625 the Jesuits' presence was strengthened, they constructed a college, headed by Fr. Cardoso, who also translated a catechism into KiKongo. In 1645 the Capuchins[6] arrived. This religious order would remain in Congo for 190 years. They baptised many people and started numerous schools in the Congo capital São Salvador, and also in Mbanza in the coastal province of Soyo. They successfully resisted Protestant missionary attempts in the period 1641-1648 when the Dutch ruled Congo. However, missionary methods of the Capuchins excluded a real understanding of traditional African beliefs, and sometimes raised hostility. Moreover Rome forced them to superficial methods, allowing baptism of those who were 'in the faith of the church' (*in fides ecclesiae*), although they did not understand the Christian faith as such. This opened the door to *syncretism*. Gradually Christianity mixed with *fetishism* and *superstitions*.

When King Antonio I went to war against the Poruguese the Congo Kingdom developed a very serious crisis. In the battle of Ambuila (1665) a Portuguese army from Angola almost ended its existence. The provinces, among them Soyo, made themselves independent. São Salvador became deserted and many missionaries withdrew to Angola. In the chaotic situation the church in Congo/ São Salvador

---

Christianity: An African Story, University of Pretoria, 2005, pp. 144-148.
[5] H. Gundani, 'Iberians and African Clergy in Southern Africa', in Ogbu U. Kalu (ed.), *African Christianity: An African Story*, University of Pretoria, 2005, pp. 176-178.
[6] The *Order of Friars Minor Capuchin* (OFM Cap) is an order of friars in the Roman Catholic Church, the chief and only permanent offshoot from the Franciscans.

almost vanished. According to Baur 'only in the province of Soyo remained a truly flourishing church'.[7] Gray thinks that Soyo Christianity at least for some decades was a 'vigorous and expanding' power.[8]

These positive qualifications of Soyo Christianity cannot deny that the number of missionaries further decreased when in 1759 the anticlerical Portuguese government (Pombal) prohibited missionary work by the Jesuits and in 1834 forbid mission by all religious orders. That is why also the last Capuchins had to leave, in 1835.

The phasing out of missionaries contributed to the 'dying out of Christianity'[9] in the Congo Kingdom, and also to a revival of *African Traditional Religion*. The Christian faith had never been able to take the place of traditional beliefs and customs, such as veneration of ancestors and spirits. This once again opened the door to *syncretism*. Gradually Christianity mixed with *fetishism* and *superstitions*.

This is the context of the movement of prophetesses Maffuta and her successor Donna Beatrice or Kimpa Vita. Influenced by Roman Catholic Mariology, Maffuta had visions of Mary informing the leaders of church and state of Christ's dissatisfaction with them, especially because they had removed the centre from São Salvador to Kibangu. Donna Beatrice also criticised this change of capital. She foretold a glorious future for São Salvador in terms of the New Jerusalem. She was together with a consort, Barro, who was called St. John. Donna Beatrice herself used the name of St. Anthony, the Capuchins' patron saint. She ordered the people to burn their fetishes and even crucifixes. All this challenged the king, his council and the Capuchins.

Prophetess Kimpa Vita, or Dona Beatrice (1684-1706) in Congo.

They agreed to consider her as a rebel. That is why she was condemned and, together with Barro, eventually burnt as a witch in 1706.

In the province of Soyo Christianity mixed with traditional rites to the fertility snake Mumba. Traditional offerings to the fertility spirit for healing, rain and blessing had been replaced in Mpinda by offerings to a wooden statue of Mary, the Mama Nzambi i.e. Mother God, Christianity decayed and finally almost vanished. Baur indicates that, when the *Holy Ghost Fathers* arrived in Congo in 1865, they found *relics* of the church, and also a Christian community still in existence.[10]

---

[7] Baur, *2000 Years*, p. 65.
[8] Richard Gray, *Black Christians and White Missionaries*, New Haven CO: Yale University Press, 1990.
[9] Baur, *2000 Years*, p.70.
[10] Baur, *2000 Years*, pp. 70-73.

4. Angola

Since 1519 the Portuguese have been active in Angola, in 1526 the king of the Ngola (King or Queen) of the Ndongo people was converted, and by 1570 they began to conquer the land. In 1575 the Portuguese settled a colony in Luanda, the capital of the kingdom of Ndongo. The Jesuits also settled there. From the king, the Ngola, the Portuguese bought slaves to be transported to *Sao Tomé* and from there to Brazil. As a result the Ngola kingdom grew militarily and economically at the expense of its enemies in the interior. Mid 18th century Luanda alone exported more than ten thousand captives a year.[11] The Imbangala in the interior cooperated with the Ngola kingdom in the slave trade, and later took over direct contacts with the Portuguese.

Ngola Ann Nzinga Mbande (c.1583-1663) was one of the most famous monarchs in pre-colonial Angola. She ruled over the Ndongo and the Matamba people, and successfully resisted Portuguese colonial expansion during the time of her life.

The Jesuits in Luanda founded a church among settlers and slaves, and they tried to establish African Christian communities, using the village model. They were not very successful. The invasion by the Dutch (1641-1647) stopped their work all together. Later some Africans from Angola were trained for the priesthood on *Sao Tomé*. One of them, called Francisco Necessitades, belonged to the few African priests who continued the work after 1840, when all white missionaries left Angola. The invasion by the Dutch (1641-1647) stopped this work.[12] David Livingstone, when he visited Angola in 1854, found little evidence of Christianity.

5. Southern and Eastern Africa

The first Portuguese naval captain to touch Southern Africa was Bartholomew Diaz. He rounded the Cape in 1488 and he erected a cross at False Island (Kwaaihoek), west of the Bushmans River mouth.[13] After him in 1498 Vasco da Gama sailed past the Cape of Good Hope on his way to discover a sea route to India. He saw a beautiful strip of the coast that he called Terra de Natal. The Portuguese established bases along the Pacific Ocean coast. They succeeded in capturing most of the Muslim-Swahili city-states, especially Sofala, Mozambique Island, Kilwa, Zanzibar, Mombasa, Malindi, Lamu. The first missionary to work in the region of

---

[11] Shillington, *History of Africa*, p.201.
[12] Gundani, 'Iberians and African Clergy in Southern Africa', in: Kalu (ed.), *African Christianity*, pp. 185, 186.
[13] Cf. Paillay and Hofmeyr, *Perspectives on Church History*, p.233.

The Faith Moves South

Fort Jesus, a Portuguese stronghold, built in 1593, on Mombasa Island, Kenya.

Sofala was Gonzalo da Silveira, a Jesuit. Victory over Muslim resistance and domination of the Indian Ocean was achieved by a naval victory in 1509. The Portuguese gradually put stone fortresses in these coastal cities. Fort Jesus in Mombasa (completed 1599) for a long time was the centre of Portuguese power in eastern Africa. In this way the Portuguese began to control the trade by these city-states with the African interior. Missionary work followed, in and around the fortified settlements, and also in the interior.

Like in other African territories, the Portuguese in Mozambique 'made minimal contact with the interior', until the end of the 19th century. Colonial administrators, missionaries, and militaries rarely crossed the line from Sofala to Quelimane. The Dominicans established a station on the Island of Mozambique in 1577. In 1559 the Jesuits arrived, they opened stations along the Zambezi River. But their work was not permanent. The Dominicans trained a few African priests, among them Luiz de Esprito Santo, who mixed his missionary work with political and military involvement in Portuguese actions against Kaparidze, the emperor of the Mutapa Empire and was killed by the latter in 1631.[14]

Vasco da Gama, Portuguese seafarer, who was the first to go beyond the Cape of Good Hope, and along the east coast of Africa to Mombasa in 1497-1498.

Sometimes the Portuguese pressed on for the interior of East Africa, searching for the Empire of Prester John. At one time they thought to have found it in Christian Ethiopia (see chapter 2). At another time they imagined it might exist along the Zambezi River. An army was sent to establish contacts and also to seize control of it and of the trade between Sofala and the Zambezi interior. Instead of finding this great Christian ruler, in 1560 missionary Gonzalo da Silveira, met with Emperor Mwene Mutapa (or Munhumutapa) who resided in Zimbabwe. The Jesuit succeeded in baptising the emperor. His Zimbabwean empire seemed to be open for Christianity. However, Muslim traders convinced the Mwene Mutapa that Silveira was a sorcerer and a spy. This changed the emperor's ideas, and he had the missionary executed. Portuguese attempts at military conquest of the Mutapa state in 1571 and 1574 were not successful.

---

[14] Gundani, 'Iberians and African Clergy in Southern Africa', in: Kalu (ed.), *African Christianity*, pp. 182-185.

Still, a kind of Portuguese overrule was established. Up to the 18th century the Mwene Mutapa had Portuguese names and considered themselves Christians, though there was not much of a church in Zimbabwe. Some Shona were trained as Dominican friars in Goa, but they did not return to Africa.[15] There was more of Christianity in the Zambezi Valley with Tete as its centre, but when the *Enlightenment* began in Europe, and the Portuguese government became hostile to the Roman Catholic Church, no more missionaries could come, and the Zambezi and Zimbabwe missions became extinct. When the *Enlightenment* came to an end, there were only few Roman Catholic priests in the whole of Africa, most of them serving the white settlers on the off shore islands and in a few coastal settlements like Lorenço Marques and Luanda.[16] Gundani says that the shortage of missionary priests, beside the 'vitality of traditional culture', was a main reason for the 'limited impact' of Christianity in the early stages of Roman Catholic mission in the Portuguese territories of Southern and Eastern Africa. He refers to some factors that were behind this. The concept of *padroado* was beyond the capacity of Portugal's resources, entering the unsafe and disease-ridden interior of

Swahili city states on Africa's east coast in the 15th and 16th centuries (from: Shillington, History of Africa, p. 133).

Africa deterred the clergy, the Portuguese State and Rome were at logger heads concerning the recruitment of missionaries.[17] Hildebrandt mentions more reasons why the Portuguese failed to establish a lasting Church, the desire for trade and

---

[15] Gundani, op. cit. pp. 179-182.

[16] Cf. Hildebrandt, *History of the Church in Africa*, pp. 64,65, who says that 'by the end of the 18th century the Portuguese church seems to have completely died out in the interior', and that 'by the beginning of the 19th century there were no Roman Catholics left along the coast, except for some foreign traders'.

[17] Gundani, op. cit. pp. 173, 174.

wealth including the slave trade, lack of understanding for the African culture, and superficial methods of missionaries like the practice of mass baptisms.[18]

Although the Portuguese presence was impressively demonstrated by military constructions like Fort Jesus in Mombasa, the missionary efforts in the city-states along the East coast eventually were not successful. There was a hopeful change when the Augustinian Hermits came to Mombasa. They baptised many people, sometimes providing rice to the new Christians as a reward, in a vast region stretching from the Lamu archipelago to Zanzibar. Missionary success seemed assured when in 1625 the sultan of Mombasa, Yusuf bin Hasan, was converted. But after a conflict with the Portuguese military, the sultan turned against Christianity and started to persecute the Christians, having 300 of them killed. The Portuguese restored their power, but further attempts of Christianisation failed.

Also in Ethiopia, Portuguese and Roman Catholic missionary attempts failed. In chapter 2 we referred to the *Alvarez Embassy* (1520-1526), to Portuguese assistance to ward off Muslim invasions, to the Jesuit mission in Ethiopia, to the official reunion of the Coptic and the Roman churches (1622), the failure to implement this reunion, and in 1632 the cutting off by Ethiopia of ties with Rome and Portugal.

---

[18] Hildebrandt, *History of the Church in Africa*, p.68.

Chapter 4
Africa and the Dutch until 1800

1. Gold Coast, Congo, Angola[1]

The Dutch presence in Southern Africa has become known very much. Yet it should be noted that they touched and influenced other regions in Africa as well. The motive was predominantly commercial, yet there were also some missionary attempts. Portuguese sea power was increasingly challenged by the Dutch. Born out of the Reformation and out of a successful war of independence against Spain, *The Republic of the Seven United Netherlands* developed as a mighty naval force, mainly directed at trade. This force was not under the direct responsibility of the Republic's government, but under the rule of a number of private trading companies.

Gold Coast (Ghana) By 1593 a Dutch trader, Barent Ericzoon and his company were among the first to settle on the Guinea coast. At Moree they built Fort Nassau, near the Portuguese Fort at Elmina, which they captured from the Portuguese in 1637. For many years the Dutch remained the most powerful nation on the African West Coast.

The Dutch, and also Danish, Swedish and Prussian traders continued to compete with the Portuguese military presence and with Portuguese attempts to spread Roman Catholicism. In this way the *Dutch West Indies Company* helped in neutralising Portuguese influence in West Africa. People in Ghana were exposed by the Protestant Dutch to Calvinist teachings. This continued until the 18th century when the Dutch influence began to dwindle.[2] In 1871 Dutch Gold Coast settlements were sold to Britain and incorporated into Gold Coast.

Of some impact was the training and ordination of 'sick-comforters' and ministers who served on the ships and also in the permanent settlements on the African Coast. They contributed in a very modest way to missionary work. Among these pastors were some African converts. For example, Jacobus Capitein, a Fante tribesman, was taken to Holland as a boy. He entered Leyden University in 1737. Five years later, he wrote his *Doctoral Dissertation* in which he put forward the Biblical defence of slavery.[3] He was ordained in Amsterdam and returned to minis-

---

[1] On the early Dutch involvement in Africa, in the framework of local developments, see: Shaw, *Kingdom*, pp. 119-124; Hastings, *Church in Africa*, pp. 197-198; Shillington, *History of Africa*, pp. 212-225, 258-266; G.J. Pillay and J.W. Hofmeyr (eds), *Perspectives on Church History – An Introduction for South African Readers*, Pretoria: De Jager-HAUM, pp.232-247;
[2] Du Plessis. *Evangelization*. pp. 109, 110.
[3] Jacobus Elisa Joannes Capitein, *Dissertatio Politica-Theologica de Servitude, Libertate Christianae non contrario* (Politico-Theological Dissertation on Slavery as not being Contrary to Christian Liberty).

ter in Africa. He established a school, and he did much in promoting the writing of the Fante language, e.g. by translating the *Lord's Prayer*, the *Twelve Articles of Faith* and the *Ten Commandments*, which were published in a booklet that was printed in Holland. Capitein also met with many difficulties that frustrated his work. He died at Fort Elmina in 1747 at the age of 30.[4]

Another African who worked as a minister in Dutch missionary work was Christian Jacob Protten (1715-1769). He was a mulatto, son of a Danish merchant, based at Christiansborg, and an African mother. Together with another mulatto boy, Frederik Pederson Svane, he was taken to Copenhagen. There they studied Theology. After his study Protten went to the Moravian headquarter at Herrnhut. As a missionary of the *Moravian Movement* he went back to Africa. First he was based in the Dutch Fort Elmina, and then in the Danish Fort Christiansborg. Protten worked on reducing the Ga language into writing, and produced translations of Biblical material. He is also reported to have written a Fante grammar book. Frederik Pederson Svane during his study joined the Pietists. He married a Danish wife. As a missionnary he worked at Christiansborg, and returned to Denmark in 1746.[5]

These West Africans reflected the Protestant taste of putting the Scriptures into the language of the local people. This should be positively appreciated as a practical consequence from the Protestant Reformed theology of 'sola scriptura'. The Roman Catholic writer Adrian Hastings is less positive about this. He describes the African chaplain-missionaries as failures. He blames them for not fully maintaining their African identity by marrying white wives, or in the case of Jacobus Capitein no marrying at all, as his intention to wed an African woman was rejected in Holland as 'dangerous'. Often these African evangelists lived in tiny slaving communities, consisting mainly of whites, close to the Fort, working only among the coloured minority of mulattos.[6]

Jacobus Eliza Capitein (1717-1747), was taken to The Netherlands, graduated at the University of Leiden, and became a minister in the Gold Coast.

Congo. The early Dutch contact with the African coast was at Soyo. Trade with the Dutch was considered of such importance that Soyo ruler Garcia III made a successful revolt against

---

The Latin text was translated into Dutch in the same year and saw at least four prints: Jacobus Elisa Joannes Capitein, *Staatkundig – Godgeleerd Onderzoekschrift over de Slavernij, als niet Strijdig tegen de Christelyke Vryheid*, Leyden: Philippus Bonk/ Amsterdam: Gerrit de Groot, 1742.

[4] For a condensed survey of Capitein's life and significance, see: Kpobi, 'African Chaplains', in: *African Christianity*, pp. 156-159; A. Eekhof, *De Negerpredikant Jacobus Elisa Joannes Capitein*, Leiden: Bredee, 1917.

[5] Kpobi, 'African Chaplains', in: Kalu (ed.), *African Christianity*, 163-166.

[6] Hastings, *Church in Africa*, pp. 178, 179.

the Portuguese and the Congo monarchy. The coming, in 1641, of the Dutch in the northern coastal kingdom of Congo boosted Soyo's fortunes. The Dutch traded in guns and ammunition in exchange for copper and slaves. With the Dutch firepower, Soyo's army successfully defeated the Portuguese at Kitombo in 1670. There were earlier victories against the Congolese monarch in 1665 and 1669.

Between 1641 and 1648 the Dutch were powerful in Congo. Some attempts were made to spread Protestantism among the people of Congo. Despite the cordial relationship existing between the Dutch and the Congolese, the former were unable to make tangible inroads with their Calvinistic theology among the Soyo population. The Roman Catholics, through members of the Capuchin order, were much more successful. This is because King Garcia II favoured the Dutch in commerce, but in religion he favoured Roman Catholicism, thus diminishing Dutch Protestant influence. King Garcia II wanted to make clear that they did not really depend on the Dutch, and that their agreement with them was only concerning trade. This thwarted the Dutch hopes of propagating Calvinistic teachings while the Capuchins gained much ground.

No wonder then that after the Portuguese had retained their position in Congo in 1648, Protestant literature spread by the Dutch, was collected and made into a bonfire.[7] Hence the Dutch were unable to make any missionary gains in Congo.

Angola. By 1640 the Dutch had started to conquer some coastal regions of Angola. In 1641 a fleet of 20 ships and 3000 sailors belonging to the Dutch *West Indies Company* (W.I.C.) attacked Luanda and drove the Portuguese out of their trading posts in Angola.[8] Just as the Portuguese Roman Catholics had been barring missionary attempts by people of other faiths, the Dutch were equally anxious to check Portuguese and Roman Catholic progress in Angola.

By 1780 African Protestant Christianity in Angola and other coastal regions was a reality. Yet progress was slow. As we have seen above, the Dutch, English and Danish forts along the slave coasts had had chaplains since the late 17th century. But due to high white mortality rates and other frustrations their work did not develop much. The activities of these chaplains mainly consisted of baptism, worship services on Sundays, and small scale educational work. Dutch and English chaplains did their missionary work under the gloomy cloud of slavery. In some way they were involved in the purchase of fellow human beings and forcibly detaining them before shipping them in overcrowded ships across the oceans to America where their compatriots had opened up new found land, farms and mines in need of intensive cheap labour.[9]

---

[7] Richard Gray, *Black Christians and White Missionaries*, London: Yale University Press 1990, pp. 37, 38, 41; J. Du Plessis, *The Evangelisation of Pagan Africa*, Cape Town: Juta, 1929, p. 26.

[8] cf. S. Paas, *Het Protestantisme in Angola – Tussen Wereldraad en Concordaat*, ICCC, 1973, p.6.

[9] Hastings. *Church in Africa*, pp. 95, 197.

2. Boers and Khoikhoi

The Dutch also competed with the Portuguese in East Asia. The *United East Indies Company* (Verenigde Oostindische Compagnie - V.O.C.) was the main trading organisation. This powerful organisation developed an interest in the southern tip of Africa. For their ships, heading for the East Indies, they needed a refreshment station, for replenishment with fresh food. Therefore, in 1652, Jan van Riebeeck and other V.O.C. employees established a lasting and growing settlement at the Cape. They grew fruits and vegetables for their ships and built a hospital for sick sailors. The Dutch bought fresh meat from the local population, the Khoikhoi and the San.

A Ship of the Dutch East Indies Company anchoring at the Cape of Good Hope.

Jan van Riebeeck (1618/1619-1677), Governor of the Cape 1652-1662 for the Dutch East Indies Company.

However, the gardens and the Khoikhoi cattle were not sufficient to supply the V.O.C. settlement and the passing ships. That is why more people were brought in, who settled as farmers. In Dutch the word farmer means *boer*, hence the indication of South African Dutch as *Boers*. Slaves from Madagascar, Mozambique and Indonesia were imported to work on these farms. The spread of these Boer settlements conflicted with the Khoikhoi and San peoples, who saw their grazing grounds diminished. When the Boers started penetrating deeper into the territory, this led to a series of Khoikhoi-Boer wars. After a period of military resistance most of the Khoikhoi either escaped Boer influence by withdrawing into the interior, or they were forced to work for the Boers. Gradually they adopted much of Dutch culture, including the Dutch language.

3. Nguni and Tswana

In the 18th century Boer penetration into the Eastern interior led to contacts with the Xhosa people. They were the southern fringe of Nguni speaking peoples. At first the contacts were rather peaceful, but in the second half of the century serious conflicts arose between Boers and Xhosa cattle keepers over the use of grazing grounds. During a war in 1799 the Boers were defeated, which temporarily slowed down the white 'trek' northward. In the West there were other peoples who gradually came into contact with the expanding Boer population. The Herero and

Ovambo had moved in from the North, into Namibia. East of the Kalahari the Sotho-Tswana had established their kingdoms (*morafe*), in a political structure that included religious functions for their kings (*kgosi*). There was much blending between Nguni-Xhosa and Soto-Tswana and Khoisan.

Shaka, or Chaka (ca. 1781-1828), Ruler of the Zulu.

In the end of the 18th century the Nguni peoples in the North developed three distinct kingdoms. One of them, the Mthedwa kingdom, included the Zulu people. In the beginning of the 19th century, the Zulu leader Shaka seized power. His regiments soon subdued the armies of fellow Nguni kings. He established a large empire that would clash with the Boers, especially after Shaka's death in 1828. External and internal Nguni conflicts, including the wars of the Shaka Empire, brought about much disruption and chaos. Many peoples were uprooted and scattered. That is why the Soto-Tswana called this period the *Difaqane*, 'the scattering'. The Nguni word for it shows a different angle, *Mfecane*, which means 'the crushing'. Out of the movements of refugees from the Shaka terror new states arose, for example the Sotho State established by Moshoeshoe, and the Ndebele state led by Mzilikazi. In 1835 Nguni groups under Zwangendaba, fleeing from Shaka's successor Dingane, crossed the Zambezi River. After Zwangendaba's death in 1848 they broke apart in various groups that settled in Malawi, Zambia, Mozambique, and Tanzania. [10]

King Moshoeshoe (1786-1870)

In the meantime at the Cape the British had taken over control from the Boers. They complicated the relationship between whites and blacks by mixing the interests of the British Empire into the pattern of Xhosa, Zulu, and Boer aspirations. All these moving and migrating parties were challenged by fundamental changes that created fear and uncertainty concerning the basics of life. That is why the Gospel of peace and new life was found to give hope by many, first among the new arrivals from Europe and then also among the Africans.

---

[10] See: D.D. Phiri, *From Nguni to Ngoni: A History of the Ngoni Exodus from Zululand and Swaziland to Malawi, Tanzania and Zambia*, Limbe: Popular Publ., 1982.

4. Planting of the Dutch Reformed Church

The Dutch settlers at the Cape imported their religion into Africa. They established *Dutch Reformed* church life. Jan Van Riebeeck's group did not include ordained ministers. Pastoral work was mainly done by 'sick-comforters'. Willem Wylant was the first one. Sacraments were administered by visiting ministers. The *Dutch Reformed Church* founded its first congregation there in 1665, at the arrival of Johan van Arckel (†1666), the first minister to settle in South Africa. It was decided that baptised slaves were to have the same rights as any other Christians. Initially mixed marriages of whites and baptised blacks and coloureds were not prohibited. At the Lord's Table all believers joined together.

The second congregation was established at Stellenbosch in 1687, after groups of 'free burghers' had settled there. First sick-comforter Sybrand Mankadan had served them, and then after the institution of the congregation, the ordained ministers Overney and Van Andel came to work there. Soon there was a network of churches. From 1688 the Dutch were joined by *Huguenot* refugees who fled from France when, in 1685, King Louis XIV revoked the *Edict of Nantes*, thus taking away their religious freedom.[11] The Huguenots brought a minister with them to the Cape, Pierre Simond (†1713). Later also Lutherans (from Germany) blended into the Dutch South Africans, or 'Boers', and their Reformed Church. Besides, after much struggle and tension, in 1778 the V.O.C. councillors also allowed Lutheran immigrants to have their own Lutheran Church, the first Lutheran minister being Andreas Kolver (†1799).

5. Early Mission Work

Among the early Dutch settlers there was some recognition of the task of spreading the Gospel to the local population. Perhaps the first convert was the Khoikhoi woman Krotoa, named Eva by the Dutch. She was the niece of a Khoikhoi chief and proved to be such an excellent learner of languages that she soon could serve the Van Riebeeck family and others as translator from the Khoikhoi language into Dutch and Portuguese and the other way around. In 1662 she was baptised into the Dutch Reformed Church and she married a junior Dutch surgeon, Pieter van Meerhof.[12]

Sick-comforter Willem Wylant was the first to do regular evangelism work among the Khoikhoi people. After him a minister, Petrus Kalden (†1739), took up the work. In 1689 Huguenot minister Simond tried to pave the way for a separate

---

[11] Steven Paas, *From Galilee to the Atlantic: A History of the Church in the West*, Zomba: Kachere, 2004, pp. 244,245; Steven Paas, *Chikonzedwe cha Mpingo: Zosintha Zazikulu za Uzimu 1500-1650*, Blantyre: Claim, 2002, pp. 75, 76.

[12] Harriet Deacon, *The Island: A History of Robben Island 1488-1990*. Unfortunately Krotoa's husband was soon killed, she allegedly fell into the habit of beer drinking and irregular behaviour, and she died as a prisoner on Robben Island, in 1674.

mission to the Khoikhoi.[13] There were also some attempts by German and Danish missionaries. In a way these attempts challenged the Dutch Reformed home church in Amsterdam. As the church leadership did not react, some members addressed Count von Zinzendorf and the congregation of *Moravian Brethren* at Herrnhut.[14] The Herrnhutters responded by offering to the Council of the Lords Seventeen to send the Moravian refugee George Schmidt (†1785). In 1737 Schmidt arrived at the Cape. The following year he moved on and settled among the Khoikhoi people at a place that later became known as Genadendal (Valley of Grace). Schmidt gathered a flock of followers. He helped the Khoikhoi with their farming, planting vegetables and fruit trees. He baptised a few people, although he was not ordained. This caused confusion with the Dutch clergy. Soon the Dutch Reformed Church began to mistrust him, also because of some of the teachings of Moravian leader Von Zinzendorf who had criticised Reformed doctrine on predestination. In the meantime Von Zinzendorf had ordained Schmidt, but the Dutch found it impossible to accept his ordination. Neither did they recognise baptisms done by Schmidt.

Though he was not expelled, the nagging treatment by his fellow whites in and around Genadendal (later called Baviaan Kloof) caused him to retreat back to Europe in 1744 only two years after his arrival to South Africa. Officially he left for The Netherlands in order to sort out problems in Amsterdam. But he never came back.[15]

Mission work at the Cape was not started again until the arrival in 1786 of Helperus Ritzema van Lier, a Dutch Reformed minister who became an instigator of the *South African Missionary Society*, founded in 1799. In 1792 he and others welcomed Moravian missionaries Maarsveld, Schwinn and Kuhnel, who re-opened the mission station at Genadendal (Baviaans Kloof). They met an 80 years old Christian, Lena, who had been baptised by Schmidt fifty years earlier. She had been his cook and she showed how she valued contacts with Schmidt by displaying a much treasured New Testament wrapped in a sheepskin that Schmidt himself had given her. The three baptised many people, among them were the descendants of men

Title page of a book on the Khokhoi woman Krotoa, who probably was the first convert of early Dutch Reformed Mission at the Cape (Trudie Bloem, Krotoa-Eva: The Woman from Robben Island, Stormberg, 1999).

---

[13] Hildebrandt, *History of the Church in Africa*, p.70, says 'that the early efforts by pastors of the Dutch Reformed Church to win these people [Khoikhoi] to Christ, did not succeed'. In its absoluteness this statement cannot be true, as there were at least some early Khokhoi conversions.
[14] On the Moravians see: Paas, *From Galilee to the Atlantic*, pp. 313, 314.
[15] Pillay and Hofmeyr, *Perspectives on Church History*, pp. 242,243; Hastings, *The Church in Africa*, p. 197.

and women who had been baptised by George Schmidt half a century earlier.

The Moravian spirit was different from that of the Dutch Reformed Church which at the Cape functioned as a state church. Although in 1792 this Moravian group was warmly welcomed, it was also opposed by some white farmers who saw the Moravians as a threat to their labour and social structure.

By 1798 through marriage and immigration the white community of Moravians had grown considerably. They were devout and practical people helping and teaching their black brethren. The white wives taught the Khoikhoi and coloured wives, women and girls many skills. Together with the black people they numbered 1200 persons. The place was renamed Genadendal like in George Schmidt's times. Prayer, worship and manual labour were the main activities. Soon the local people saw Genadendal as a haven from the oppressive white masters where they could find 'dignity, stability, a modest degree of prosperity and the opportunity to learn'. The Moravians, being somewhat Lutheran in outlook, did not bother to fight against the injustices being perpetrated on the Khoikhoi and coloured people by the white masters, but they assumed a quietist attitude. Their main emphasis was on conversion, rather than on addressing the social evils.[16] In 1808 this thriving Khoikhoi and Moravian Christian community was extended to a new settlement in Mamre (Groene Kloof).

Finally, in 1806, the rule of the Cape by the *Council of the Lords Seventeen* and the the *Batavian Republic*[17] ended. The British occupied the Cape.

---

[16] Adrian Hastings. *Church in Africa*, pp. 198, 201, 216, 218; cf. M. Malikebu, 'Dutch Missionaries in Africa in the Period 1650-1950', an unpublished composition for Zomba Theological College, 2004.

[17] As a result of the *French Revolution* and the subsequent French occupation of large parts of Europe, The Netherlands had temporarily become a French puppet state which had adopted the name *Batavian Republic*.

Chapter 5

Africa and the British until 1885

1. The Empire extends to Africa

a. Competition

Originally commercial interests, rather than territorial ambition, dictated the growth of the early British Empire. England in the 16th century was a poor country, lacking the wealth of Portugal and Spain. Unlike the Spaniards and Portuguese, the English originally were less motivated by mission or colonisation. In the 17th century the English began to realise the huge commercial potential of overseas acquisitions, starting with the lucrative exploitation of sugar and other produce from the West Indies. The union of England with Scotland as Great Britain, in 1707, added to the power for expansion overseas.

The British successfully competed with other seafaring nations that had started to expand overseas trade and territorial acquisitions earlier. The Portuguese were first. They had deployed mainly to the South and the East of the globe. In the West they had to share with the Spaniards. These Iberian nations had been attacked in their overseas trading posts and incipient colonies by the Dutch. Also the French had begun to establish their stations overseas. Now it was time for all to experience the expansion of British sea power. Beside Africa, almost the whole world including South and North America, India, Ceylon, Indonesia and Australia were the places where the struggle of beginning colonial expansion and competition took place. Here we only look at the aspects that directly concern Africa.

William Hawkins of Plymouth probably was the first English trader who settled on the West Coast. Soon other English traders joined him. In 1618 they formed a trading company, and in the meatime they had built forts in the Gold Coast and in the Gambia. Like the Scandinavians and the Dutch, the English made use of chaplains for pastoral work in and around their forts. One of them was Thomas Thompson, a missionary of the *Society for the Propagation of the Gospel* (S.P.G.). He first worked among the Indians in North America. In 1750 he was sent to the West African Cape Coast or Gold Coast. He did not only work among the whites in the forts, but also among the local Africans. Thompson helped in sending Africans for study to England. One of them was Philip Quaicoo (1741-1816). After completion of his studies Quaicoo was the first African to become a priest in the Anglican

Church. He married an English woman, and in 1766 he returned to the Gold Coast as a missionary, where he worked for fifty years.[1]

b. Triangular Trade

In North America, the Thirteen Colonies along the Atlantic seaboard between French Canada and Spanish Florida were firmly established by 1733. The English colonists had begun to plant cotton in the 17th century, and this plantation crop was grown on a very large scale by the late 18th century. This combined with a scattering of forts and trading settlements in West Africa and the trade from the West Indies created the *Triangular Trade*: (a) British ships took manufactured goods and spirits to West Africa. (b) They exchanged them for slaves whom they landed in the West Indies and the southernmost of the Thirteen Colonies. (c) The ships then returned to Britain with cargoes of cotton, rum, sugar, and tobacco, produced mainly by the labour of the slaves. Britain's prosperity was bound up with the slave trade, until it became illegal in 1807, by which time the Empire had ceased to be dependent upon the slave trade as other forms of commerce had become more profitable and Britain was starting to emerge as the leading industrial nation, inevitably reducing the economic demand for slave labour.

c. Southern Africa

After the slave trade was ended by Britain in 1807, the British continued to show interest in Africa. Already before the scramble for territory of the 1880s, various forts, controlling ports, were kept in West Africa, where gold and ivory kept their importance.

An early example was the colony of Sierra Leone founded in 1788 with the taking of a strip of land to provide a home for liberated slaves; a protectorate was established over the hinterland in 1896.

Another early example was South Africa. The Cape of Good Hope was occupied by two English captains 1620, but initially neither the government nor the British *East India Company* was interested in developing this early settlement into a colony. The Dutch occupied it in 1650, and Cape Town remained a port of call for their *United East Indies Company* until 1795, when, French revolutionary armies having occupied the Dutch Republic, the British seized it to keep it from the French. Under the *Treaty of Paris* in 1814, the United Kingdom bought Cape Town from the new kingdom of The Netherlands for $6 million. British settlement began in 1824 on the coast of Natal, proclaimed a British colony in 1843.[2]

---

[1] Kpobi, 'African Chaplains', in: Kalu (ed.), *African Christianity*, pp.160-163; Hildebrandt, *History of the Church in Africa*, pp. 71-74. In his account Quaicoo is called Quaque.

[2] Cf. Hutchinson, *New Century Encyclopedia*; Shillington, *History of Africa*

Africa and the British until 1885

In the previous chapter we noticed that British colonisation of the Cape was emphatically rejected by the Dutch settlers. The need to find new farmland and establish independence from British rule led a body of Boers (Dutch: *farmers*) from the Cape to make the *Great Trek* northeast in 1836, to found Transvaal and Orange Free State. The conflict between the British government and the Boers eventually led to war, as we will see in chapter 9 section 2b.

2. Effects of the Great Awakening

a. Rediscovery of the Centrality of Christ

George Whitefield (1714-1770), Reformed revivalist preacher in England and America, who contributed to the Great Awakening, that paved the way to Mission.

British colonialism aimed at the extension of economical and political power. Slave trade soon became its main pillar. In their colonies in South, Central, and North America the Europeans were lacking labour, therefore slaves were imported from Africa. The Portuguese began this trade in the 16th century, the Dutch played an important part, but in the 18th century Britain dominated the slave trade. It had become the backbone of the economy in these countries.

The selfishness and cruelty of colonialism began to be ameliorated by important developments in the field of religion. Though legal and widely accepted, slavery and slave trade began to be resisted. In Britain and North America the faith rediscovered in the Reformation, but grown cold and weak by the effects of *Enlightenment* and *Orthodoxism*, revived and awakened in the 1730s and 1740s. In England, Scotland and Wales, the preaching of George Whitefield and John and Charles Wesley brought about a profound evangelical revival inside and outside the Anglican Church. It comprised 'Evangelicals within the Church of England, Methodism, Calvinistic Methodism, and Dissenters or Nonconformists'.

Especially influential was the so called *Clapham Sect*, a group of high-ranking Evangelical lay people. The revival led by George Whitefield, Jonathan Edwards, the brothers Gilbert, John and Willam Tennent, and others did the same in North America.[3] Collectively these revivals on both side of the Atlantic Ocean are called *The Great Awakening*.[4] It was characterised by 'three powerful convictions':

---

[3] On this revival and awakening, read: E.E.Cairns, *Christianity through the Centuries – A History of the Christian Church*, Zondervan, 1996³, pp. 383-416, 428-434; T. Dowley (ed.), *The History of Christian-*

(a) the centrality of the death of Christ for salvation, (b) the necessity of the new birth and (c) the certainty of the Second Coming of Christ and his kingdom of righteousness.[5]

b. Missionary Movement

The revivals not only prepared the ground for the rejection and *abolition* of slavery, they also were a strong incentive for a declaration of war against the evil of injustice in society, and for the birth of the modern missionary movement. William Carey (1761-1834) belonged to the foremost who opened the eyes of many for the responsibility of mission. Walls mentions some factors that helped for the emergence of movements for mission and social justice: (a) the realisation that there is a 'human solidarity in depravity ... a spiritual parity of the unregenerate of Christendom and the heathen abroad', (b) a logistic network, creating the interregional, interdenominational and international contacts that formed the backbone of missionary societies, and (c) the staffing of missionary organisations by evangelicals.[6]

William Carey (1761-1834), founding father of the Missionary Movement, inspired to the foundation of the Baptist Missionary Society in 1792.

Walls says that evangelicalism not only addressed the unbelieving world, it was also a 'religious protest against a Christian society that is not Christian enough'. Evangelicalism accepted the idea of a Christian nation with *national righteousness* (therefore no slave trade) and *social righteousness* (therefore a no to children's labour). In the first place, however, there is the necessity of *personal holiness*, that is of personal knowledge of the radical nature of sin, personal trust in Christ's finished work, and a godly personal life. According to Walls the evangelical revivals were 'perhaps the most successful of all reformulations of Christianity in the context of changing Western culture'. They 'contextualised the Gospel for the Northern Protestant world'. They also tried to translate the Gospel overseas. More than elsewhere this enterprise was successful in Africa. The effects of evangelicalism in its anti-slavery movement and in its missionary movement were felt very much in Africa.

---

ity, Lion Publ., 1990[7], pp. 436-457, 518-540.

[4] Cf. Jehu Hanciles, 'Back to Africa: White Abolitionists and Black Missionaries', in: Ogbu U. Kalu (ed.), *African Christianity: An African Story*, University of Pretoria, 2005, p. 194.

[5] Shaw, *Kingdom*, pp. 129-132, where he explains these three convictions.

[6] A.F.Walls, *The Missionary Movement in Christian History – Studies in the Transmission of Faith*, New York/ Edinburgh, 1996, pp. 79-85.

c. Anti-Slavery Movement

The anti-slavery movement or abolition movement started with the activities of Granville Sharp and Lord Mansfield who campaigned for making slavery illegal in Britain. In 1787 three important events enlarged the scope of the movement:

> (a) the establishing of a *colony of freed slaves in Sierra Leone*, (b) the founding of the *Society for the Abolition of the Slave Trade*, with Sharp as chairman and Wilberforce as one of the members, (c) the publication of a *book by the Ghanese ex-slave Ottobah Cuguano*[7] about his life as a slave, which made great impact on the general public.

Members of the *Clapham Sect* continually tried to destroy the legal position of slavery. Gradually public opinion began to favour abolitionism. Helpful was the autobiography of an ex-slave from Nigeria, Olaudah Equiano, who showed that abolition would promote legitimate commerce.[8] The work of William Wilberforce in particular was instrumental in making Parliament accept a bill prohibiting the slave trade in 1807 and finally the *Abolition of Slavery Bill* in 1833.

The year 1871 marked the beginning of Britain's campaign to end the slave trade in East Africa itself and Christianise the people. In 1871 Dr. Livingstone was found in Africa by journalist Henry Morton Stanley. Stanley travelled along with

William Wilberforce (1759-1833) contributed much to the Abolition of Slavery.

Olaudah Equiano, an ex-slave from Nigeria who in 1789 published an influential book against the slave trade.

Henry Morton Stanley (1841-1904), American journalist and explorer who contributed to preparations for the work by missionary organisations.

---

[7] Ottobah, Cuguano, *Narrative of the Enslavement of a Native of Africa*, 1787.
[8] Olaudah Equiano, *The Interesting Narrative of Olaudah Equiano, or Gustavus Vassa, the African*, New York: Dove Publications, 1999 [original edition 1789].

Livingstone, who had been living in Africa for almost 30 years, and began writing stories about Livingstone's life and aspirations to end slavery and spread Christianity. When Stanley published his stories about Livingstone, it aroused a great deal of support among the British people, and it strengthened Britain's movement to abolish the slave trade *de facto*. In 1875 with the strong urging of the British Government, Zanzibar ended their Slave Trading Empire.

d. The Classical Missions

In the meantime evangelicalism had continued to give shape to the beginning of a missionary movement. A number of missionary organisations had been formed, first the *Baptist Missionary Society* (1792), then the *London Missionary Society* (1795), and the *Church Missionary Society*. (1799). This movement would lead to rapid spread of missions in 19th century Africa, and to the real emergence of Christianity in Sub-Saharan Africa. The most important theological innovation for foreign mission work was the idea of the *Mission Society*, which would work with and for the Church, but keep its independence in terms of rules and regulations, leadership personel (and the necessary training), and finances. Such *Mission Societies* could work beyond the natural boundaries of their churches, and it was the *Mission Societies*, not the churches that effectively evangelised Africa. [9]

The success of the anti-slavery movement and the missionary movement was not only fed by a revival of evangelical-biblical faith, but sometimes also by a great optimism with regard to the good potential of Western civilisation, imperialism, and capitalism. Perhaps Shaw is right when he says that in this optimistic activism 18th and 19th century Western evangelicalism 'became an unconscious ally'[10] of the movement it wanted to resist most, the *Enlightenment* with its expectations from man's autonomous rational power.[11]

---

[9] Cf. Klaus Fiedler, *The Story of Faith Missions: From Hudson Taylor to Present Day Africa*, Oxford: Regnum Books, 1994, pp.20-23;

[10] Shaw, *Kingdom*, pp. 132, 138, 140.

[11] Apart from this section, study also: Shaw, *Kingdom*, pp. 127-138; Baur, *2000 Years*, pp. 105-106, 109; Walls, *Missionary Movement*, pp. 79-84; Hastings, *Church in Africa*, pp. 173-188.

Chapter 6

Western Africa 1800-1900

1. Sierra Leone

Kpobi distinguishes three periods in the era of Mission and Church planting in Sub-Saharan Africa. *First* there was the period of the European 'discovery' of the western coast of Africa, starting from about the middle of the 15th century. Kpobi says that during this period 'the church was no more than an appendage to the commercial enterprise and therefore had very little attraction for the African population'. The *second period* of mission in Africa started from

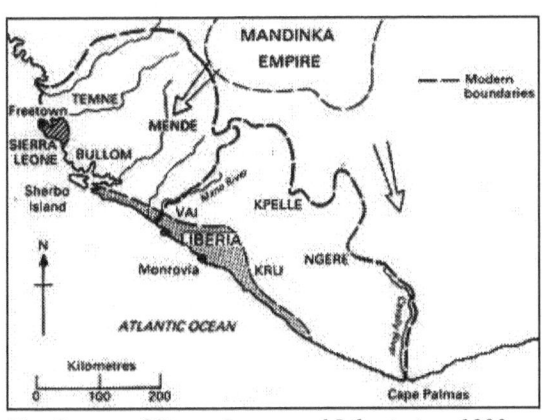

The Coasts of Sierra Leone and Liberia in c.1880 (from: Shillington: History of Africa, p. 240).

the middle of the 18th century 'when attempts were made at evangelisation alongside the slave trade'. Again this was a comparatively 'unfruitful period', as Kpobi maintains. Yet it contributed to the preparation of the ground.[1]

That became apparent in the late 18th century or in the beginning of the 19th century, when the *third period* of mission began, which was its real beginning of the Christianisation of Sub-Saharan Africa. One may wonder why Protestantism waited so long before really starting mission in other continents. At first Protestantism was a weak and persecuted minority. When it had become numerous, free and well established, it had a tremendous task of evangelising the European and American masses who, like Hildebrandt stresses, 'had never heard of salvation through the atoning blood of Jesus Christ'.[2] The major thrust of missionary activity came through the *Great Evangelical Awakenings* in the Protestant churches of Europe and North America in the 18th and 19th centuries.

Yet, modern African Christianity is not in the first place the result of missionary activity from the North. Walls stresses that African Christianity 'has been prin-

---

[1] Kpobi, 'African Chaplains', in: Kalu (ed.), *African Christianity*, pp.140, 141.
[2] Hildebrandt, *History of the Church in Africa*, pp.67, 68.

cipally sustained by Africans, and is to a surprising extent the result of African initiatives'.[3]

Much of modern mission started in West Africa.[4] The first attempt in West Africa was a joint enterprise by whites and blacks, the settlement of a Christian community in Sierra Leone. Under protection of the British government, Sharp and the *Clapham Sect* in 1787 had settled 411 freed slaves of the 'Black Poor', yet including 70 white prostitutes,[5] from London in Sierra Leone on the West African coast. This settlement, enthusiastically called *Province of Freedom*, soon appeared to be a failure. Many settlers died, others became slaves again. Then a *Sierra Leone Company* was formed, which facilitated in 1792 the coming of almost 1200 black British ex-soldiers from Nova Scotia in Canada to Sierra Leone. Many of these black settlers were Baptists. They built a city, Freetown, and organised Christian life according to Puritan principles. Leaders like David George and Thomas Peters established Baptist churches. Methodism was represented by Moses Wilkinson, and there was also the work of Anglican chaplains. Soon missionary initiatives were taken. Hanciles stresses that modern Church and Mission 'began not with white missionary agency, but as the initiative of ex-African slaves'.[6] In 1800 more than five hundred ex-slaves from Jamaica, *Maroons* as they were called, were added to the community. In 1808 Sierra Leone became an official British colony. Agriculture and especially trade began to flourish. Schools were founded, among them in 1827 by the Anglican C.M.S. *Fourah Bay College*, for the training of ministers, teachers, catechists, and missionaries.

After the banning of the slave trade by Britain in 1807, the British navy, intercepting slave ships, brought in thousands of 'recaptives'. These freed slaves were Muslims or African traditionalists. Most of the latter category became Christians, but many Muslims resisted conversion to the Christian faith. The Sierra Leonean immigrants built their own culture (Creole), a mixture of African and Western traditions, and they shaped their own language (*Krio*) with English vocabulary and African syntax.

This new Christian community developed missionary activities far beyond Sierra Leone, supplying 'African missionaries for the rest of West Africa' and elsewhere, even in Kenya.[7] They were helped by Western missionaries. The Methodists sent out pioneers such as Brown, Warren, and Davies. The Quaker missionary Hannah Kilham did language work and started a school for girls. The first C.M.S. missionaries partly failed, but from 1806 with men such as Prasse, Butscher, and

---

[3] Walls, *Missionary Movement*, p. 86.
[4] Besides this chapter, study: Shaw, *Kingdom*, pp. 139-158; Baur, *2000 Years*, pp. 103-152; Hastings, *Church in Africa*, pp. 177-188, 338-358; Ward, 'Africa', in: Hastings (ed), *World History*, pp. 203-209.
[5] Hastings, *Church in Africa*, pp, 179,180.
[6] Jehu Hanciles, 'Back to Africa: White Abolitionists and Black Missionaries', in: Kalu (ed.), *African Christianity*, p. 204.
[7] Walls, *Missionary Movement*, pp. 86, 67.

Nylander the work progressed. However, in the beginning of the 19th century Western missionary activity was not yet the numerous and powerful movement that it would be by the end of the century. The actual outreach in missionary work was done by Africans, in the case of Sierra Leone, by the Creoles.

The most famous indigenous missionary was Samuel Ajayi Crowther († 1891), a Yoruba domestic slave from the Nigerian village of Abeokuta, who was sold to a slaver bound for Brazil, but was freed by the British navy and taken to Freetown ln 1822. He was the first students of *Fourah Bay College*. After his training he served a period as teacher and partaker of an expedition in the Niger area, then he went to London, where he was ordained priest in 1843. In 1864 he became the first African bishop of the Anglican Church.

2. The Niger Mission

Inspired by the success of Freetown, ex-slaves established other Christian communities along the West African coast. Started by two Hausa ex-slaves from Trinidad a settlement was made at Badagry in Nigeria. The Methodist Thomas Birch Freeman, himself an ex-slave, helped to organise a church among the recaptives and to start Christianisation of nearby areas. The chief of Abeokuta allowed ex-slaves to return to his region. 'By 1851 there were alredy some 3000 returned emigrants in Abeokuta alone'. Among the returned exiles was Samuel Crowther, who was reunited with his mother and sisters, who were subsequently baptised. Initial persecutions hindered the Christians at Abeokuta, but after the conversion of some leading diviners (*babalawo*), Christianity was widely accepted.

In the same period Christianity spread to Calabar, Bonny, Lagos and many places along the Niger. The African initiative continued to play an important role. At the same time there was an increase of expatriate missionary efforts. The *Baptist Missionary Society* (B.M.S.), the *London Missionary Society* (L.M.S.), and the *Church Missionary Society* (C.M.S.), were followed by the *American Board for Foreign Missions* (1810), the *Wesleyan Methodists' Mission* (1813), the *Basel Mission Society* (1814), and soon many others sent out their missionaries. These first missionaries in West Africa worked independently from government control, often had little formal education, and were rarely ordained. Many of them worked in the area of language and translation, C.M.S. missionary S.W. Koelle and his *Polyglotta Africana* being a notable example.

Samuel Crowther and other homecoming Sierra Leoneans were ready to contribute to the conversion of the inland of Africa. Many of them belonged to the Yoruba people and had not forgotten their language and culture. Crowther and other Yoruba were trained at *Fourah Bay College* in Freetown, and in 1843 he was the first to be ordained as an Anglican minister. The missionary work in the Sierra Leone, and later also in the Badagry and Abeokuta areas, mainly developed under the responsibility of Anglican Evangelicals of the *Church Missionary Society* (C.M.S.). Soon Crowther was given an important role to play in the activities of the

The Faith Moves South

C.S.M. in West African Inland, along the Niger River, at least in the plans of Henry Venn († 1873), who from 1841 was Secretary of the C.M.S. Venn propagated the 'three selves', the necessity of a self-supporting, self-propagating, and self-governing African church. Also he worked out the idea of cooperation between Christianity and commerce, implying that African economical independence was an important instrument for the shaping of an African church. He developed the idea that the indigenisation of native churches ought to become a national institution that would supersede denominational distinctions.

Samuel Ajayi Crowther (c.1807-1891), the first African who became an Anglican Bishop, leader of the Niger Mission.

Venn was instrumental in making Crowther a bishop of the Anglican Church. Then he placed Crowther at the head of an organisation that was to evangelise a vast area along the Niger. Hanciles calls this 'a bold experiment in African leadership and initiative'.[8] Unfortunately Crowther as a Yoruba was a relative stranger to the Niger area, where many other peoples lived, e.g. Igbo, Nupe and Hausa. He had to cope with a variety of languages and cultures, enormous distances between a series of stations along the River Niger, stiff resistance by Islamicised tribes. The C.M.S. gave him a steamer, which made communications easier, but made him also dependent on traders whose goods he transported for money that he needed for the mission. This dependence was undermining the integrity of the mission, as missionaries were sometimes identified with the ruthless capitalist practices and the immorality of many traders. Besides, some members of Crowther's own group were guilty of misbehaviour, like manslaughter and misappropriation of funds [9] These were considerable hindrances to the work. Yet, the Niger mission did not become a failure. Crowther's qualities as a scholar, pastor and faitful missionary contributed to its relative success. In Onitsha a missionary centre was established, and among the Brass people of the Niger Delta Christianity found acceptance, at least temporarily.[10]

By the end of the century the character of mission changed. There was an increase of missionaries from Europe. Colonial powers had started their 'scramble for Africa'. This decreased the room for Venn's Africanisation programme. In 1890 a C.M.S. committee, consisting of young newly arrived missionaries decided to discharge almost the entire staff of Crowther. Crowther was humiliated and after his death he was replaced by a white missionary. Hastings underlines that this

---

[8] Hanciles, 'Back to Africa: White Abolitionists and Black Missionaries', in: Kalu (ed.), *African Christianity*, p. 206.
[9] Shaw, *Kingdom*, pp. 155, 156.
[10] Hastings, *Church in Africa*, pp. 339-349.

event 'damaged black-white Church relations for many years.[11] These days Crowther's significance is widely recognised. Hildebrandt says: 'There is little doubt that he was one of the greatest African church leaders of the nineteenth century'.[12]

Although the C.M.S. now had less room for the thought of an independent native pastorate, the ideal of Africanisation was kept alive. It was defended by the Afro-American missionary and Liberian statesman Edward W. Blyden (1832-1912). It was also propagated by the Sierra Leonean pastor James Johnson (c.1836-1917), because of his exemplary lifestyle often called 'Holy Johnson. Johnson was born in Sierra Leone to Yoruba parents who were freed slaves. After his study at *Fourah Bay College* he was ordained and became a missionary worker for the C.M.S. In 1874 the C.M.S. sent him to the Lagos area in Nigeria. Although Johnson promoted a Church under African leadership, he never abandoned the Anglican Church. Yet, members of his C.M.S. founded church separated and formed an independent 'Ethiopian' church. This led to a break between Johnson and his former associate Garrick Braide (see chapter 12, section 4). In 1900, ten years after Crowther had left, Johnson became assistant bishop of the Niger Mission.[13]

In south-eastern Nigeria a notable work of the Scottish Presbyterians started in the Calabar area in 1847. A Bible translation in the Efik language was completed in 1868. Four years later Esien Ukpabio, the first baptised convert, was ordained as a minister of the Nigerian Presbyterian Church.[14] From 1888 to her death in 1915 a single missionary lady was working in the area, Mary M. Slessor. She also opened mission stations further to the North in Iboland.[15]

Sierra Leone and the Niger area also witnessed the return of Roman Catholic Mission to Africa. The *Holy Ghost Fathers* or *Spiritans*, led from Algiers by François Libermann, were the first. They also spread to other countries in West Africa and in East Africa (see chapter 11, section 1).

Mary Slessor (1848-1915) was a Scottish missionary for the United Presbyterian Church to Calabar, south-eastern Nigeria She was commonly called 'Ma' Slessor.

---

[11] Hastings, *Church in Africa*, pp. 392.
[12] Hildebrandt, *History of the Church in Africa*, p. 103. Cf. Gerdien Verstraelen-Gilhuis, "Bishop Crowther and the 'Young Purifiers': A Search into the Background of the Conflict of the Niger Mission via an Analysis of the Action of the 'Sudan Party'", Amsterdam: Free University, 1969 [unpublished MTh Thesis in Dutch].
[13] Cf. Norbert C. Brockman's DACB article, on website: http://www.dacb.org/stories/sierraleone/johnson.html
[14] Hildebrandt, *History of the Church in Africa*, p. 105.
[15] Hildebrandt, *History of the Church in Africa*, p. 158, 159.

3. Liberia

Following the example of Britain in Sierra Leone, the United States of America shaped a place for freed slaves on the African West Coast. In 1816 the *American Colonization Society* was formed. This was followed by the founding of Liberia as a home for free blacks in 1821. The first leaders of Liberia, and its main settlement Monrovia, were Jehudi Ashmun and Lott Carey. The latter served the colony as missionary, doctor, governor and soldier. By 1866 the colony had about 18000 inhabitants. In the late 1870s black emigration to Liberia grew substantially. In the Liberian Constitution (1847) more rights were given to the 'homecoming' emigrants than to the indigenous people, which was the cause of increasing tensions.

Edward Wilmot Blyden (1832-1912), Liberian educator and statesman.

Successively missionary work among indigenous Africans was started by black Methodists, Baptists, Roman Catholics, Episcopalians and Presbyterians. Before 1880 almost all black missionaries were sent and financed by white churches and mission boards. To them belonged Joseph and Mary Gomer, Alexander Crummel, and Edward W. Blyden. Other black missionaries were sent by black denominations. Generally they did not work among the indigenous people, but among the settlers who had come from America, and together with them they had 'extremely negative views of African cultures'. In time, however, the interest in *Africanness* was strengthened. Blyden contributed much to the Africanisation of politics and mission. He was a significant missionary and statesman. His book *Christianity, Islam and the Negro Race* (1880) encouraged respect for African languages, cultures and customs. As such he was a father of African *nationalism* and of the movement of *Ethiopianism*.[16]

4. Ghana, Cameroon, Senegal, Gabon, Zaire

a. Ghana and Cameroon

In the Gold Coast, present day Ghana started to work the German and Swiss missionaries of the *Bremen Mission*, and *Basel Evangelical Missionary Society*. Missionaries such as Zimmerman and Christaller did much work in the Twi language. The *Basel Mission* began their own in 1828, after first having sent missionaries through other organisations, like the C.M.S. They faced a lot of hardship and almost all died. An interesting example of early African missionary initiative con-

---

[16] Hanciles, 'Back to Africa: White Abolitionists and Black Missionaries', in: Kalu (ed.), *African Christianity*, pp. 211-214.

cerns two Africans, Joseph Smyth and William de Graft. The former was leader of a British school for colonial administration and the latter a student in that school. They were sincere Christians who organised the spreading of Bibles and Bible study. Later their work was absorbed by the Wesleyan Methodist Mission that came to Cape Coast in 1834.[17] The Methodists had great impact, especially through the work of the West-Indian Thomas Birch Freeman, who arrived in Ghana in 1838 and worked there for fifty years. He contributed much to the Christian awakening in West Africa. In *Cameroon* missionary work started around 1850 among freed slaves on the island of Fernando Po. The mission was started by the *Baptist Missionary Society* worked with Jamaican missionaries Alfred Saker and others, many of them liberated slaves who were very motivated to bring the Gospel back to Africa.

b. *Senegal, Gabon and Zaire*

Original Protestant mission in Gabon, started by Americans of the *Board of Commissioners for Foreign Mission*, was resisted by the French colonial authorities and was handed over to missionaries of the American Presbyterian Church who began work in Gabon in 1861. Roman Catholic attempts in Gabon and Senegal were eventually successful, mainly through the work of the *Holy Ghost Fathers*, founded

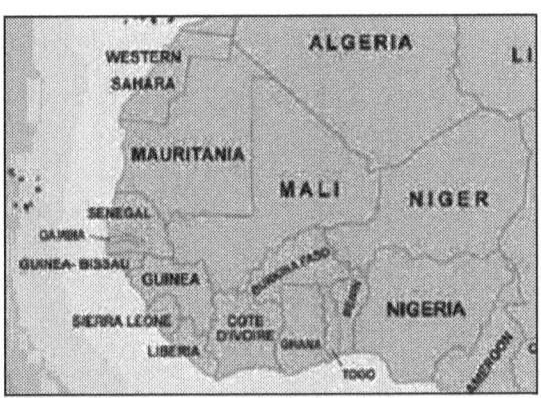

The West Coast of Africa.

by the French (ex-) Jew François Libermann in 1841. Among the workers were Edward Barron, John Kelly, and Jean Bessieux, who founded St. Mary of Gabon, the first modern Roman Catholic mission station in Africa. Through the *Paris Mission Society*, the famous German physician Albert Schweitzer worked in Gabon, at Lambarene, for fifty years. He did a commendable medical work, although his liberal teachings on Scripture weakened his missionary contribution.[18]

In the 1890s missionaries of the *Sacred Heart of Jesus* and *Jesuits* entered the Congo River area where Roman Catholic Christianity had completely collapsed after the death of Congo King Garcia V in 1830, and after the departure of the last Capuchins who were under pressure from an anti-clerical government in Portugal. They were soon followed by missionaries of many other Roman Catholic orders.

---

[17] Hildebrandt, *History of the Church in Africa*, pp. 92, 93.
[18] Cf. Hildebrandt, *History of the Church in Africa*, p.165.

The Faith Moves South

In 1878 Protestant missionaries were welcomed. Thomas Comber and George Grenfell of the interdenominational *Livingstone Inland Mission* began work there.[19] They were actually members of the *Baptist Missionary Society* from Britain. The *Livingstone Inland Mission*, originally led by Fanny Guinness, was the first Faith Mission to start work in Africa. They wanted to establish a chain of mission stations from the coast to the interior. In 1983 they had 10 stations the first and the klast 800 kilometres apart. In 1884 the work was handed over to American Baptists, but the Swedish L.I.M. members continued their work as a Faith Mission, also entering Congo-Brazzavile.[20] In 1910 another Faith Mission entered the Congo in 1912, the *Africa Inland Mission* (A.I.M.), by now led by C.E. Hurlbert, joining together in 1913 with the *Heart of Africa Mission* and its missionary C.T. Studd (See chapter 14, section 6b).

5. Angola

a. Comparative Roman Catholic Weakness

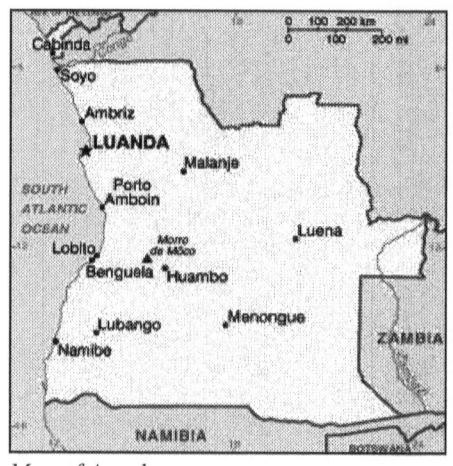

Map of Angola.

Roman Catholic Mission had been favoured by the Portuguese colonial authorities since their arrival in the 15th century. However, by the beginning of the 18th century a serious recession of Roman Catholic mission work began. This period of missionary weakness would last till the beginning of the 20th century. It gave an opportunity to mission by Protestant Churches and organisations. Here are some of the reasons why Roman Catholic Mission grew weak and Protestant mission could penetrate the country: (a) Until the end of the 19th century Portuguese colonial rule was limited mainly to the coastal regions, leaving the interior to other influences. (b) There was a rather strong tradition of anti-clericalism among the Portuguese which also affected the overseas territories. (c) Internal disputes between Portuguese and Spanish Church leaders and the Vatican. (d) Colonial rulers realised that the Portuguese colonial empire needed good relationships with Great

---

[19] Hastings, *The Church in Africa*, pp. 257, 318, 319, 385, 435; Cf. Fiedler, *The Story of Faith Missions*, pp. 169-183.
[20] Fiedler, *Story of Faith Missions*, pp. 37 – 39.

Britain. (e) The *Berlin Conference* of 1884/ 1885, which allowed European states to colonialise Africa, demanded freedom of religion.

By 1850 in almost all parts of the country, except for the South, Roman Catholic mission activity had ended.[21] The *Capuchins* had been active in the South since the 1830s when they were authorised by the Pope to work in this area, but the work went down gradually. [22] In 1866 the French *Holy Ghost Fathers* entered the region. Their main problem was that they were hindered by the Portuguese authorities because of their nationality. That is why their leader Charles Du Pirquet started a seminary for the training of Portuguese members. Later they were re-inforced by clergy from the Portuguese enclave Goa in India. In the eyes of the authorities the presence of Portuguese clergy safeguarded Portuguese culture and theology. In a decade the *Holy Ghost Fathers* took full control of the coastal region of Southern Angola. Many of their missionaries died then. [23]

b. *Opportunities for Protestant Mission*

The comparative weakness of Roman Catholic Mission and Portuguese colonial rule in the interior of Angola provided opportunities for Protestant Mission. Let us look at some of the Churches and organisations which started work in Angola.

(a) *Baptist Missionary Society*. The arrival of English Baptist missionaries in 1878 made them the first Protestants in Angola. From their headquarters in Sao Salvador they opened many stations in the Northern part of Angola.[24]

(b) *Methodists*. They came from America and their leader was William Taylor, who was consecrated 'bishop of Africa' in 1884. Taylor arrived in Angola in 1885. He was a famous preacher and also a missionary strategist. He had made a plan of establishing a chain of mission stations from the Atlantic Ocean to the Indian Ocean. Taylor defended the idea self supportive missions, which in his view was what the Apostle Paul had meant. Between 1885 and 1896 not less than 186 missionaries were sent out. By the 19th Century the mission had done opening the stations at Luanda, Quingwa Pingo –Sundango, Quessna and Malanje.

(c) *Canadian Congregationalists*. They arrived in Angola in 1880 and settled in the Ovimbundu highlands near Lobito. To their leaders belonged W.T. Currie, Gladwyn M. Childs, and John T.Tucker. They established good contacts with the traditional African kings. [25] They built their headquarters and schools at Dondi.[26] In 1911 followed the establishment of a school for the training of native evangel-

---

[21] Hildebrandt, *History of the Church in Africa*, p. 135.
[22] K.S.Latourette, *A History of the Expansion of Christianity* vol. 5, p 398.
[23] Hildebrandt, *History of the Church in Africa*, pp 170,399
[24] Latourette, *Expansion* (vol.5), p. 399; Hildbrandt, *History of the Church in Africa*, p. 170
[25] Baur, *2000 Years*, pp. 99,. 221
[26] Cf. Lawrence W. Henderson, *A Igreja Em Angola: Um Rio Com Várias Correntes*, Lisboa: Al

ists and teachers. [27] Besides, an extensive network of primary schools was organised with thousands of pupils and native teachers. Although the Portuguese didn't want things be done in the native language, the Canadians tried hard to make sure that the vernacular language was used. Soon many portions of the Bible were translated into the vernacular. [28]

(d) *American Board of Commissioners for Foreign Mission.* Du Plessis describes their early attempts, problems and growth. The first party of this mission included American blacks such as Samuel T. Miller, who was educated at Hampton Institute, W.W. Bagster and W.H. Sanders. They landed at Benguela in 1880. In 1882 the group was attacked by fever, and in 1884 the unfriendly Chief Ekwikwi chased away the missionaries. But with the support from the governor, they were allowed back for their work. Yet two stations were formed in the inland. [29] But in the same year they were betrayed by hostile traders. Because of the problems the mission had to withdraw to Benguela on the coast. All this slowed down the progress. In 1889 the mission re-established itself, and especially in the inland. Rapid growth of the church returned after 1914.

(e) *Angola Evangelical Mission.* This non-denominational mission was founded by M.Z. Stober and was mainly supported from people in Britain. It started work in Northern Angola among Congo speaking people in 1898. Its headquarters was in Kabinda.

(f) *Plymouth Brethren* (Garanganze Mission – Christian Mission in Many Lands). They arrived in 1889 and worked in partnership with the Canadian Congregationalists. Their leader was F.S. Arnot, who in his youth was inspired by Livingstone.[30] In 1884 he arrived at Benguela. Here he met Msidi (or Kathanga) who was the chief of the Luba speaking Garanganze, who asked him to settle at his capital Bukenya, in 1886. In 1891 Belgium occupied Katanga. They wanted Msidi's submission but he refused and was shot dead. Arnot was replaced by Swam Faulkner. He wrote a book called *Garanganze* on his 'seven years of pioneer missionary work in Central Africa'. Later he returned to Angola and made great contributions in language work. Finally, because Msidi's Empire had collapsed, the Garanganze Mission dispersed. Arnot died in Johannesburg in 1914.

(g) *Andrew Murray Memorial Mission.* This mission worked in the South-East of Angola. It started under the leadership of A.W. Baily in 1889, [31] and was named after Andrew Murray, the famous South-African instigator of Mission. After some decades of successful work, especially leading to Christian education, the mission clashed with the Portuguese authorities. In 1922 all schools were to be closed. Local Christians were not allowed to preach unless accompanied by the white

---

[27] Hildebrandt, *History*, pp. 215, 243.
[28] Du Plessis, *Evangelisation* (Central Africa), pp. 230-237
[29] Du Plessis, Evangelisation (Central Africa), pp. 234-6
[30] Du Plessis, *Evangelisation* (Central Africa), p. 235
[31] Du Plessis, *Evangelisation* (Central Africa), pp. 239-400

missionary. Faithful Christians were imprisoned. [32] In practice Christians were barred from worhipping God.

(h) *Philafrican Mission.* This mission was a by-product of Bishop Taylor's mission. His missionary approach aroused an interest among a number of Swiss people, some of them Swiss immigrants in America.[33] In 1887 the mission became independent.

Although there was a hardening of resistance against Protestant mission, in 1924 the number of missions in Angola was extended by the arrival of the *South Africa General Mission* and the *Mission of the Seventh Day Adventists*.[34]

Protestant Mission was successful, yet the majority of the Angolans became connected to the Roman Catholic Church. Estimates of the number of Roman Catholics after the end of Portuguese colonialism (1975) varied from 55 percent (1985) to 68 percent (1987). The proportion of Protestants in the Angolan population was estimated at 10 percent (1960s) to 20 percent in the late 1980s. The Angolan government recognised eleven Protestant denominations: the *Assemblies of God*, the *Baptist Convention of Angola*, the *Baptist Evangelical Church of Angola*, the *Congregational Evangelical Church of Angola*, the *Evangelical Church of Angola*, the *Evangelical Church of South-West Angola*, the *Our Lord Jesus Christ Church in the World* (Kimbanguist), the *Reformed Evangelical Church of Angola*, the *Seventh-Day Adventist Church*, the *Union of Evangelical Churches of Angola*, and the *United Methodist Church*.[35]

---

[32] Latourette, *Expansion* (vol.5), pp. 398-399.

[33] Du Plessis, *Evangelisation* (Central Africa), p.234.

[34] For a more recent survey of Protestant presence in Angola, see: Paas, *Het Protestantisme in Angola,* pp. 56-62.

[35] These data were derived from: *Library of Congress Country Studies*, February 1989.

Chapter 7

Southern Africa 1800-1900

1. The Dutch Speaking Settlers

In original missionary work in West Africa a crucial role was played by Africans educated in Europe or America. Before 1880 there was room for African initiative as the number of expatriates was relatively small. Unlike in West Africa, however, in South Africa the power of *white settler Christianity* and *white missionary presence* was much more substantial. The African scene was influenced by Dutch speaking settlers, and later also by an English speaking community.[1]

During the Napoleonic wars the British had begun to occupy the Cape, and in 1815 it was declared a British colony. Immigrants from Britain began to pour in, expanding the white community. They established branches of their own Anglo-Saxon churches. British missionary organisations, already active in West Africa, began to take an interest in South Africa. The new situation was increasingly unac-

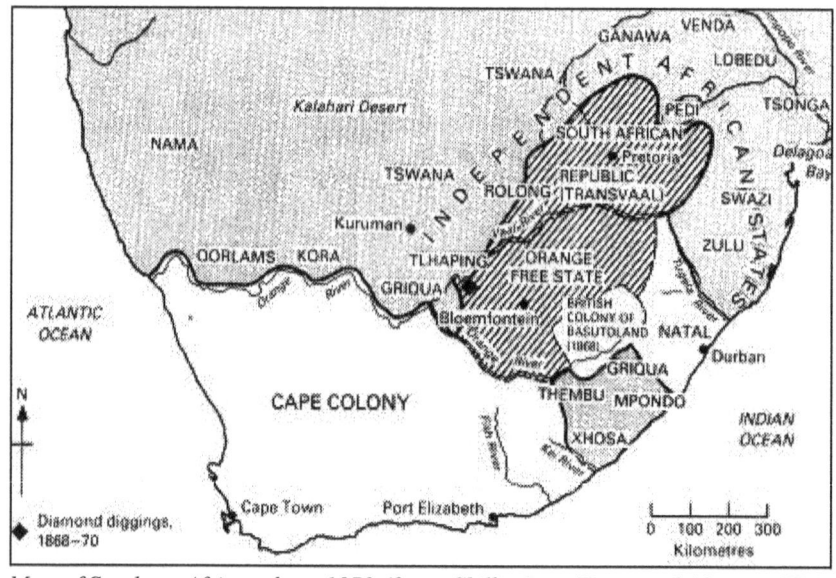

Map of Southern Africa, about 1870 (from: Shillington, History of Africa, p.274)

---

[1] Apart from this section, study also: Shaw, *Kingdom*, pp. 159-180; Baur, *2000 Years*, pp. 188-214, 412-440; Hastings, *Church in Africa*, pp. 250-252, 358-371; Ward, 'Africa', in: Hastings (ed), *World History*, pp. 209-214.

ceptable to the Boer population for various reasons. *First*, the Dutch at the Cape were congenial to their original homeland, The Netherlands, where there was a general mistrust against the British who had been competitors at sea and even enemies in a number of sea-battles. *Secondly*, the new arrivals created a growing need for more land. *Thirdly*, the newcomers criticised the way the Boers dealt with coloured and black Africans, treating them as slaves. *Fourthly*, the Boers had developed a feeling of nationhood, a sense of being preserved as the 'Afrikaander Volk' (Dutch: *volk = people*).

Many Boers decided to withdraw from British rule. In their *'Great Trek'* they migrated across the Orange river and into the interior beyond the Vaal river, where they established independent states. In this way they intended to defend their identity against British intrusion. The spirit of defence, often characterised as *'laager – mentality'*, was also strengthened at the Blood river in 1838 where a small number of Boers, after having pledged a *'Vow of the Covenant'*, defeated a large Zulu army under Shaka's successor Dingane.

The majority of the Boers were members of the *Nederduitsch Gereformeerde Kerk* (N.G.K.) originating from the main Protestant church in The Netherlands. In English literature this church is often referred to as the *Dutch Reformed Church* (D.R.C.). Not all N.G.K. church members at the Cape shared the sentiments of the Trekkers, which caused differences within the N.G.K.. Other differences were caused by the movements of the *Great Awakening* that did not fail to have their impact on the settlers in South Africa. Scottish Evangelicalism, revivalist secessions in Holland, and by the end of the century the Dutch neo-Calvinism of Abraham Kuijper, contributed to dissension in the N.G.K., and to the formation of separate churches among the Boers, the *Nederduitsch Hervormde Kerk* (N.H.K.) and the *Gereformeerde Kerk* (G.K.), also named *Dopper church*. The Coloured people, being from mixed Boer and African stock, were considered as part of Afrikaander national and religious identity, though later, when *apartheid* took shape, they formed their own churches.

Prior to 1843 the N.G.K. church was not very active in mission. Pauw mentions some reasons. First, up to that date the N.G.K. church was under the control of foreign ecclesiastical and political powers, first the Dutch until 1806, and then the British. The latter did not encourage mission work by the Boer churches. Secondly, there was a chronic shortage of ministers some of whom were liberals. Thirdly, the Boers felt threatened by the attitude of certain foreign missionaries, especially those of the *London Missionary Society*, who were critical of slavery.[2]

The arrival of a number of Scottish ministers and teachers did not lead to the intended anglicising of the Dutch, but it strengthened the struggle against *liberalism*, and it encouraged missionary efforts. Most of them belonged to the evangelicals in the *Church of Scotland* or to the *Free Church of Scotland*. Father and son Andrew

---

[2] Christoph Martin Pauw, *Mission and Church in Malawi: The History of the Nkhoma Synod of the Church of Central Africa Presbyterian, 1889-1962*, University of Stellenbosch, 1980, pp. 44,45.

Murray took the lead in the missionary enterprise. Decisions at the N.G.K. synod of 1857 signified the beginning of missionary work among the blacks of Africa. Mission stations were opened in Northern Transvaal (1863), Western Transvaal (1864), Botswana (1877), Malawi (1888), Zimbabwe (1891), Mozambique (1908), Nigeria (1911), Kenya (1944). In many aspects Andrew Murray Jr. († 1917) was the initiator of mission by the N.G.K.. He also took the initiative for mission in Malawi. His nephew A.C. Murray became the first N.G.K.-missionary to Malawi, and in the period 1886-1916 some fifteen other Murrays went to foreign mission fields, most of them to Malawi. Missionaries were also deployed in Lesotho, Swaziland, Zimbabwe, and Namibia. This missionary work has led to the creation of a Dutch Reformed family of autonomous churches spread over all of Southern Africa and elsewhere.[3]

2. The English Speaking Missions

For English speaking settlers the way to South Africa was paved by the British Empire which firmly established its rule in this part of the world. The first attempt was made in 1795 as a measure against France that had occupied the large parts of Europe including the fatherland of the Dutch speaking settlers. The British counteracted French aggression by snatching as many French colonies as they could. As The Netherlands had been incorporated in the French Empire, the British also tried to take Dutch colonies and settlements. In 1795 they conquered and occupied the Cape. However, when Britain at Amiens in 1802 concluded a peace treaty with the French, the Cape Colony was given to the *Batavian Republic*, a puppet regime, that was dependent on Napoleon. Four years later the British recaptured the Cape Colony, and during the *Congress of Vienna* (1814-1815) the Cape and its dependent regions was 'given' to Great Britain. British rule remained until the *Anglo-Boer Wars* of the end of the century, and the establishment of the *Union of South Africa* in 1910 which gave the country an autonomous dominion status in the British Empire.

In the first section of this chapter we noticed that British rule was not accepted by many of the Dutch speaking Afrikaanders or Boers. They withdrew to the north and established their own republics that for the time being were left untouched by the British. First the British subjugated the Zulu and Swazi peoples, and eventually they also destroyed the independence of the Boers. In the meantime, since about 1820 immigrants from England and Scotland began to enter the new colony. With the exception of the Scottish evangelicals indicated in the previous paragraph, the British settlers that came to South Africa as a result of British colonisation established their own churches, mainly Anglican, Methodist, Congregationalist Presbyterian, and Roman Catholic. Generally these churches had already formed missionary agencies. That is why their contribution dominated mission in Southern Africa

---

[3] Pauw, *Mission and Church in Malawi*, pp. 45-49.

Southern Africa 1800-1900

during the larger part of the 19th century. In 1792 the *Moravian Brethren* resumed their work among the Khoikhoi by re-opening the old settlement at Genadendal. A more important early contribution to mission, however, was made under the umbrella of the *London Missionary Society*, especially by: Van der Kemp, Philip, Moffat and Livingstone.

Johannes van der Kemp († 1811); he is going to be discussed in section 4 of this chapter. He was followed by others.

John Philip († 1851), a Scottish pastor, was sent to the Cape to be Van der Kemp's successor. He advocated the equality of blacks and whites, concentrating on the protection of Khoikhoi and Xhosa, wrote an influential book on these matters, *Researches in South Africa* (1828), and he supported the idea of tribal autonomy under British law.

Robert Moffat († 1883). For more than fifty years worked among the Khoikhoi and the Tswana, operating from his station at Kuruman at the southern edge of the Kalahari Desert. He had strong relations with the local Tswana king, and translated the Bible into Tswana. At Kuruman for the first time the whole Bible was printed in Africa.[4]

Robert Moffat (1795-1883) was a Scottish pioneer missionary to South Africa, for the London Missionary Society. He arrived in Cape Town in 1817. He and his wife settled at Kuruman in Bechuanaland and established a mission there. He translated the Bible into the language of the Bechuanas, Their oldest daughter Mary, married David Livingstone.

David Livingstone († 1873). He was a son-in-law of Moffat. He was less successful as a missionary than as a discoverer who paved the way for others to do missionary work. In 1840 he joined the L.M.S. and established stations at Mobatsa, Chonuane and Kolobeng. His only convert was Sechele, king of the Bakuena. His greatest fame was acquired when searching for the sources of the Nile. He journeyed across Africa in 1852-1856, which enabled him to give a first hand report on the extent of the slave trade. In his view this 'open wound' could be removed by introducing mission, trade, and commerce. In 1857 during a stay in England, Livingstone left the L.M.S. and devoted the rest of his life to the work of exploration and documenting of the slave trade and of useful waterways, propagating the combination of Christianity and commerce.

Livingstone inspired many missionary enterprises. He personally led the unsuccessful Makololo mission-

---

[4] The most recent study on Moffat's theological significance is: Bruce Ritchie, *The Missionary Theology of Robert Moffat*, Kachere: Zomba in 2006. Cf. John Smith Moffat, *The Lives of Robert and Mary Moffat by their son John Smith Moffat*, New York: Armstrong & Son, 1888; E.W. Smith, *Robert Moffat: One of God's Gardeners*, London: SCM, 1925; Cecil Northcott, Robert Moffat: Pioneer in Africa, London: Lutterworth, 1961; William Walters, *Life and Labours of Robert Moffat*, London: Walter Scott, 1882.

ary attempt through the Kalahari. The L.M.S. and the Roman Catholics followed his path to Zimbabwe's Matabele. Moreover, the L.M.S. penetrated into Zambia, where also the *Brethren* (Frederick Stanley Arnot), the *Paris Mission* (François and Christine Coillard) and the *Primitive Methodists* went. Livingstone's appeal to the Senate of Cambridge University in 1857 led to the formation by the Anglicans of the *Universities' Mission to Central Africa*. The news of Livingstone's death in 1873 'sent a wave of missionary zeal throughout Britain', and influenced the Church of Scotland and the Free Church of Scotland to take up missionary work in Malawi.[5]

The *Methodist Mission* was more successful, mainly through the work of William Shaw (†1854) at the Western Cape, where he established a settlement for freed slaves. Shaw was a missionary strategist. He developed a vision of founding stations throughout South Africa through which a general growth of the Methodist Church was assured.

Cartoon of John William Colenso (1814-1883), the first Anglican Bishop of Natal.

Presbyterian Missions. William Govan of the *Glasgow Missionary Society* made an important early contribution to the training of black and white evangelists and catechists by the opening of *Lovedale College* in 1841. One of its principals, James Stewart, in 1816 helped found *Fort Hare University*, a breeding ground for African leadership. James Stewart was instrumental in making the Free Church of Scotland begin work in Malawi, and in 1875/1876, together with Laws, he was to lead the initial search by the Livingstonia mission for a site on the shore of Lake Malawi.[6] Stewart also played a positive role in promoting cooperation between the Scottish Presbyterians and the N.G.K. of the Boers.[7] Later he worked as a missionary in Kenya.[8]

Anglicanism in South Africa had steadily grown since the beginning of British colonisation. In 1848 Robert Gray became bishop of Cape Town. He felt that his administration of the Anglican dioceses was undermined by John W. Colenso († 1883), who in 1853 was appointed the first Anglican bishop of Natal, and missionary bishop to the Zulu's. As an adherent of *Broad Church* principles Colenso propagated liberal ideas on ethical and doctrinal questions. In a study of Paul's letter to the Romans he rejected the doctrines of both substitutionary atonement and everlasting punishment. He also wrote a study

---

[5] There are many biographies of Livingstone, among them those by J. Simmons (1955, repr. 1962), G. Martelli (1970), T. Jeal (1973), and O. Ransford (1978). See also the recent study by Andrew C. Ross, *David Livingstone: Mission and Empire*, London: Hambledon & London, 2002; A brief but helpful survey is given by: Hildebrandt, *History of the Church in Africa*, pp. 111-119.

[6] Pauw, *Nkhoma Synod*, pp. 22, 23.

[7] Pauw, *Nkhoma Synod*, pp. 55, 56.

[8] On Stewart see chapter 8 section 2, and chapter 16 section 3.

on the Pentateuch and Joshua, in which he applied 'historical critical' methods to the text and challenged the historical reliability of Scripture. When Gray and other bishops wanted him to recant, Colenso refused. Then Gray excommunicated him. Another bishop was nominated in Natal, yet Colenso stuck to his rights and officially could not be deposed. By the end of his life Colenso became an able advocate of the interests of the Zulus, especially when the British started a war against them in the years 1878 and 1879.[9]

Lutheran presence in South Africa was strengthened by the arrival of the *Berlin Mission* in 1834, the *Norwegian Missionary Society* in 1843, the *Bauern Mission* from Hermannsburg in 1854, and the *Swedish Church Mission* in 1876. Together with the *American Lutheran Mission*, that arrived in 1927, these Missions are the origins of the churches that in 1975 established the *Evangelical Lutheran Church in Southern Africa*

Roman Catholicism at first was not welcome in South Africa, but in 1820 the colony was officially opened to Roman Catholics, and in 1837 a Vicariate Apostolic was established by the Dominicans. From 1852 there were missionary attempts among the Zulu, Sotho and the Indian immigrants. Prominent work was done from the missionary monastery of Mariannhil in Natal. Today the Roman Catholic Church has 27 Dioceses in South Africa with 3 million members.[10]

Throughout the 19th century the relationship between the Dutch speaking community and the English speaking community was bad. This harmed the Church and its mission to the unreached masses of Africans. Fortunately in both communities there were Christians whose visions and activities went beyond the boundaries of language and race. They contributed to the reconciliation between Boers and British. They were the founding fathers of mission in and from South Africa, and as such they were of great significance for the relationship between Whites and Blacks.

3. Andrew Murray

a. Scottish-Dutch descent

Andrew Murray (1828-1917) belonged to the Afrikaans-Dutch community in South-Africa.[11] Through his father and namesake, he was of Scottish descent, and through his mother he was of Afrikaans-German descent. The Murrays were incorporated in the Afrikaans-Dutch community. Their national loyalty was on the side

---

[9] Cf. Gerald Parsons, 'The Theology of Bishop J.W. Colenso', Open University Text.

[10] http://www.catholic-hierarchy.org/country/scza1.html

[11] Cf. Ben Conradie, *Andrew Murray na Honderd Jaar*, Stellenbosch: Christen Studenten Vereniging-maatskappij, 1951; For an extended biography, cf.:. J. Du Plessis, *From The Life of Andrew Murray of South Africa*, Marshall Morgan and Scott, 1919.

of the Boers. This played an important role during the *Anglo-Boer Wars*. After the Jameson raid that in 1881 led to the first war Murray published a protest against politics of imperialism. He addressed the English people pleading for peace and stressed that the Boers have just as much right as the British to freedom, national independence and use of their own language.

His loyalty did not prevent Murray from cooperating with ministers of the English churches in working and praying for peace. Murray realised that in due time the Boers and the English would have to reconciliate.

b. Missionary Strategist

Murray's influence was nation wide. His work affected the Dutch speaking community, but also the people of British descent. Through his efforts both communities became more conscious of their responsibilities towards the Blacks and Coloureds. This is particularly true for his missionary endeavours. In a time when mission did not seem a matter of course to the N.G. Kerk, Andrew Murray passionately tried to prepare South African Christians for missionary work in various ways. He tried to achieve his objective, since 1859, as a member of the Church's Committee for Mission. But after some time he concluded that the N.G. Kerk was too slow to finance the sending out of missionaries.

Andrew Murray (1828-1917), influential writer and preacher in the Dutch Reformed Church of South Africa, who inspired to mission.

That is why he took a personal initiative of organising a *Society of Ministers for Mission*. In 1886 at Cradock the Society was born. Members pledged personal financial support to mission. The Society, chaired by Andrew Murray himself, especially aimed at building up missionary work in Malawi. The Nyasa mission was started by the Chairman's nephew Andrew Charles Murray together with T.C.B. Vlok. Missionaries of the *Church of Scotland* and of the *Free Church of Scotland* had come to Nyasaland earlier, but they were unable to cover the whole region. That is why the Free Church had offered to the N.G. Church a wide mission field in the central part of Malawi. Encouraged and facilitated by Andrew Murray and his Society, the Murray family got increasingly involved in the work in Malawi; quite a number of them worked physically in the region, among them Andrew Murray's son Charles. In 1891 seven N.G. Church missionaries were in Malawi, in 1899 the number had grown to fourteen. In spite of the *Anglo-Boer War* of 1899-1902, missionary activities developed further. In 1903 there were 28 workers in the Malawian mission field. In the same year the N.G. Kerk Synod absorbed the Society and put the Nyasaland mission under its *General Committee for Mission* of which Andrew Murray became Chairman.

The scope of Murray's missionary vision was wider than the N.G. Church and the Dutch speaking community. He also affected English speakers, e.g. through his involvement in the *South Africa General Mission* (S.A.G.M.). Murray invited Spencer Walton to start organised mission in South Africa. In 1889 the *Cape General Mission* (C.G.M.) was established. Its two-fold objective was mission among the neglected and backsliding masses of South Africa and foreign mission. The C.G.M. cooperated with the yearly held Keswick conferences. Murray had copied these meetings from the movement of the *Keswick Convention* in England. They contributed to reviving church people and attracting outsiders. Foreign work started in 1890 with the establishment of a mission station in Swaziland, soon followed by stations in and outside South Africa, i.e. South East Africa, Zululand, Tembuland, Pondoland, Bomvanaland, Natal, Gazaland, Nyasaland and North Rhodesia.

Missionary consciousness was also promoted by the work of South African branch of the *Students Volunteer Movement* (S.V.M.), founded in 1890. Members promised to be 'ready and eager on God's will to become a missionary among the heathen'. The movement was soon re-shaped to the *Christian Students' Society of South Africa*. Donald Fraser and Luther Wishard were involved in its foundation. Murray remained the Society's guide until the end of his life.

In 1900 in New York a *World Mission Conference* took place. Andrew Murray belonged to the invited speakers. Because of the *Anglo-Boer War* he could not go. Yet, Murray made an important contribution to missiological thought after he received an account of the conference's dealings, by writing *Key to the Missionary Problem*. In this book he described the problem of mission as a personal matter.

> 'The Lord Jesus Christ is the Author and Leader of Missions. Whoever stands right with Him, and abides in Him, will be ready to know and do his will. It is simply a matter of being near enough to Him to hear his voice, and so devoted to Him and his love as to be ready to do all his will. ... He needs me for his service, and in love I gladly yield myself to Him'.[12]

This call contributed to growing missionary consciousness. An impressive example was given by ex-prisoners of war. The British victors in the *Anglo-Boer War* had put these people in camps in Ceylon. There a revival took place and some 150 pledged to give their lives to Christ and back in South Africa they were trained to spread the Kingdom of God in Africa. In the meantime the number of missionary organisations was growing. In a booklet, published in 1906, Murray described the work 31 missionary societies in South Africa. In 1911 he published *The State of the Church*, in reaction to the *World Mission Conference* in Edinburgh in 1910. In this book Murray showed how the impotence of the churches in the face of the unfinished task of world missions is the sign of common spiritual poverty and

---

[12] Andrew Murray, *Key to the Missionary Problem*, Fort Washington: Christian Literature Crusade, 1979 [first edition 1901], p. 134.

proof of the unrevived state of their members. He pleaded for more prayer and more sanctification.[13]

c. Writings

Andrew Murray's influence was not limited to South Africa. He received leading foreign evangelists and missionaries like Henry Varley, George Grubb, Donald Fraser and John Mott. His name was especially known in the Anglo-Saxon world, e.g. by his involvement in the *Keswick Convention* in England, he attended the one of 1883, and he personally addressed the one of 1895.

The main reason for Murray's lasting significance and fame in and outside Africa is the books he produced. They were spread widely, e.g. of *The Spirit of Christ* 53000 copies were sold in the period 1882-1888. Apart from articles, brochures and letters, Murray published about 250 titles. Later some 25 or 30 of them were published in one volume, *Collected Works*. Most of his writings were focused on sanctification and edification of believers. Originally Murray wrote in Dutch, later he also wrote books in English. His first published book was *Jezus de Kindervriend* (1858), later translated as *Life of Christ*. It dealt with the training of children, and was designed to assist the Christian mothers. For that matter all his Dutch writings were translated, mostly in English. We mention some examples using the English titles only. *Abide in Christ* (1992), *Like Christ*, *The New Life* (1885),[14] *With Christ in the School of Prayer* (1886), *The Holiest of All* (1895). In 1906 Andrew Murray retired, one year after the death of his wife. After this he intensified his work as a writer. From 1897 his daughter Annie helped him as a secretary.[15] In 1917 he died.

d. Theological Significance

In Conradie's view Murray's theology had three important aspects, which can be summarised in these words: prayer, holiness, evangelism.[16]

Prayer. Murray was convinced that 'prayer is the indispensable condition for anything that God wants to perform on earth'. This he preached, and this he practiced personally. He lived and died prayingly. He was called 'the Church's most prolific writer on the subject of prayer and deeper life'.[17]

---

[13] Andrew Murray, *The State of the Church*, Kempton Park: The Andrew Murray Consultation on Prayer for Revival and Mission, 1985 [first edition 1911].

[14] Murray's *The New Life*, was originally written in Dutch as *Het Nieuwe Leven* (1885). In 2002 it was published by Searchlight/ Christian Resource Ministries (Blantyre) in Chichewa, mistakenly entitled *Kubadwa Kwatsopano*, and in 2005 by Kachere (Zomba) as *Moyo Watsopano: Mawu a Mulungu kwa Ophunzira Ongoyamba a Yesu Khristu* (editor: Steven Paas).

[15] For Murray's writings, see: Du Plessis, *The Life of Andrew Murray*, pp. 460ff.

[16] Conradie, *Andrew Murray*, pp.14-150.

[17] Smithers, *Andrew Murray*, p.5

Holiness. He stressed that Christians should live holy lives. Sanctification shows justification. A person who is saved by the blood of Christ lives a life of obedience to God. The Cross of Christ is the centre of this. Believers who have progressed far on the way of sanctification, always are deeply conscious of their sin for which Christ had to give his life. Murray could perhaps be classified as a leading exponent of the European *Holiness Movement*, sometimes called *Third Awakening*, that was, in a way, channelled by the movement of the *Keswick Convention*.

Evangelism/ Mission. This aspect is a consequence of the previous one. Obedient Chistians necessarily are preachers of the Gospel to others. God wants more and more people to be converted to Him. That is why the Gospel has to be proclaimed. Make known to all: Become reconciliated with God through Christ.

4. Johannes van der Kemp

a. With the London Missionary Society

Because he was a Dutchman, Johannes Th. van der Kemp († 1811), should be classified with the Dutch speaking settlers.[18] While the *Moravian Brethren* before with Dutch help had made their contributions to the native evangelisation of South Africa, there came on the South-African scene in 1799 a different kind of Dutchman. He differed from other Dutch settlers, first because he worked for an English mission, the *London Missionary Society* (L.M.S.), and secondly because of his different social and political outlook. Both factors helped him to look wider and further than ethnic boundaries.

Van der Kemp was one of the Dutch pioneer missionaries, he was also the most remarkable of all. In 1792 he had been at the cradle of the first Dutch mission organisation in The Netherlands,[19] shaped after the example of the *London Missionary Society*. This happened after the history of his life has taken some sharp turnings. As a young man, Van der Kemp was a cavalry officer and womaniser. But soon after marriage he quitted the army and studied philosophy and medicine at Edinburgh, publishing works of originality in both fields. In 1791 he lost his wife and daughter in a sailing tragedy. This brought him to conversion to Christianity. After meeting the Moravians in 1792 his mind was set on the missionary direction. From the Moravians he learned about the establishment of the *London Missionary Society*. As the *Dutch Society of Missionaries* was not yet ready to send people, Johannes Van der Kemp joined the *London Missionary Society* who employed him for work in the Cape Colony.

---

[18] See for his life: L.H. Enklaar, *Life and Work of Dr. J.Th. van der Kemp 1741-1811: Missionary Pioneer and Protagonist of Racial Equality in South Africa*, Capetown – Rotterdam, 1988.

[19] *Nederlandsch Zendelingen Genootschap* (transl.: Dutch Society of Missionaries), founded in 1797.

b. Work among Khoikhoi, San and Xhosa

In 1799, at the age of fifty, Van der Kemp arrived at the Cape and somewhat later he started work among the Khoikhoi (Hottentots), identified himself with them. His living together with the Khoikhoi and his preaching of conversion and justice was not warmly greeted by the Boer settlers; it led to a growing hostility. [20]

Van der Kemp also worked among the San (Bushmen) and Xhosa tribes, though, because of the language barrier this work miscarried. His subsequent idea to achieve conversion of the Xhosa through war and force was resisted by the Khoi Khoi and by white settlers who had gathered round Xhosa king Ngika. Later he started learning the Xhosa language; he wrote an elementary grammar and word list entitled: *Specimen and vocabulary of the Kafree language* which he classified into 21 classes. Though his missionary attempts seemed to end in a failure, Johannes Van der Kemp made lasting impressions on King Ngika and the Xhosa. Among the Xhosa he was known by the name Yankanna or Nyengana. Later generations of converts were given this name as their identity. They were commonly called *ama – Yankanna* or *people of Johannes Van der Kemp*.

Drawing of Khoikhoi people worshipping the moon.

Hastings lists four characteristics that in his view set Van der Kemp apart among his contemporaries *First*, he was seen as a man of God, a man full of prayer, a spiritually powerful man, and a rainmaker. *Secondly*, he was a man of poverty. He went about walking bareheaded and barefooted unlike his fellow whites who often put on a hat and shoes. He fed on anything given to him and was contented to live under these poor conditions. *Thirdly*, he was a very intelligent person. For example, he struggled to know the Xhosa language and was anxious to explain the role of electricity in lightning to Xhosa King Ngika. *Fourthly*, Van der Kemp was noted for his sense of equality, behaving in a friendly, familiar manner to everyone in every way. Differences of colour, race, material level, culture and living conditions he did not recognise as divisive realities. That is why 'he touched more hearts than was immediately evident', so Hastings concludes.

The authorities gave him Betheldorp, a model community that he ruled as a missionary settlement. Due to bad conditions of the land, he found it increasingly

---

[20] L.A. Loetscher *A Brief History of Presbyterians*, Philadelphia: Westminster Press, 1978³ p. 34

difficult to realise his plans. Van der Kemp married a slave girl from Malagasy whom he had freed by buying her together with her parents. In 1807 slave trade at the Cape was abolished altogether, much to the relief of Van der Kemp. In general he disagreed with his fellow whites on matters of the treatment of the non-whites and slaves.

His influence among the Khoikhoi was considerable. He spread his missionary message to them, using the Dutch language too, teaching them some elementary Dutch, at the same time finding a written mode of the Hottentot language. The consequence of this was that most Khoikhoi after some generations, could hardly speak their native language. Apart from being Christianised, they spoke Dutch, and had Dutch names.

In a later stage many Khoikhoi became missionaries themselves, and they infiltrated the Gospel in non-Christian societies of South Africa. Some went outside South Africa, in most cases they helped European missionaries who worked in the interior of Africa. Some Khoikhoi missionaries were Waterboer, Afrikaner, Stoffels, Stuurman, and Jan Tshatshu. Besides, Van der Kemp influenced such very important religious figures in South Africa as Ntsikana.[21]

---

[21] Cf. Malikebu, 'Dutch Missionaries in Africa in the Period 1650-1950'; John De Cruchy, *The Church struggle in South Africa*. pp. 12, 13; Gray, *Black Christians, white Missionaries*. p. 87.

Chapter 8

Eastern Africa 1800-1900

1. Mozambique

Let us revisit Eastern Africa now.[1] In chapters 3 and 6, section 5, we referred to the comparative weakness of the early stage of Roman Catholic Mission in Africa. This also applies to Mozambique. Until the beginning of the 20th century the Portuguese administration and the Portuguese missionaries proved unable to establish lasting influence in the interior. Apart from the negative influence of their involvement in the slave trade, even until the end of the 19th century, the Portuguese had not much impact in the inland. This negatively affected the growth of the Roman Catholic Church and mainly limited it to the coastal regions. Another factor that hindered Roman Catholic progress was Portuguese paternalism and the lack of medical services and schools. Besides, the political situation in the European homeland sometimes turned against the missionaries, as was experienced by the Jesuits who worked in the Zambezi delta, but were driven out of the country as a result of an anti-clerical revolution in Portugal. Around 1850 the Portuguese had expelled all Roman Catholic missionaries for some time. In 1914 some Jesuits re-entered the country. Roman Catholic Mission in Mozambique was greatly stimulated in 1940 when Portugal's government under Salazar introduced a new mission policy.

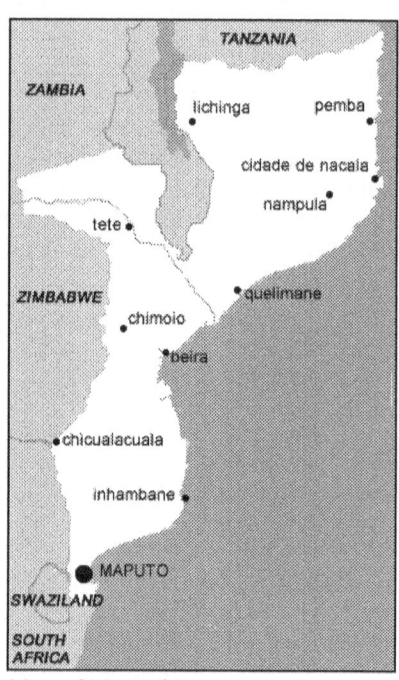

Map of Mozambique.

The relative weakness of Roman Catholic Mission made it easier for Protestant missions to make progress in Mozambique.[2] African initiative is apparent in the establishment of a church in Southern Mozambique by an African evangelist who had been trained at a Swiss mission station in Transvaal. This is another example

---

[1] Besides this chapter, study: Shaw, *Kingdom*, pp. 139-158; Baur, *2000 Years*, pp. 103-152; Hastings, *Church in Africa*, pp. 177-188, 338-358; Ward, 'Africa', in: Hastings (ed), *World History*, pp. 203-209.

[2] Sundkler and Steed, *A History of the Church in Africa*, pp. 482, 487

of the importance of the refugee factor. The Dutch Reformed missionary, F. Hofmeyer at Goedgedacht directed the Thonga known to him for their positive attitude to the Transvaal government. In 1879 the *American Board of Commissioners for Foreign Missions* sent a missionary to Mozambique but because of bad climate a permanent mission was not built until 1883.[3] Methodist, Pentecostals, Presbyterians, Anglicans, Episcopalians, Baptists, and African Independents followed and established churches.

The Boer wars created serious problems in South Africa, but indirectly they were a blessing in Mozambique because amongst the returning miners there were many Christians who helped to spread Christianity in their home villages.[4] In general Africans greatly contributed to the mission work. This is not to deny that 19th century Christian mission in Mozambique failed to reach many places.

2. Kenya

According to Ward, in Eastern Africa 'the figure of the missionary took on a greater importance' than it did in West Africa and Southern Africa. Whereas in the West and the South missionary work soon led to 'an actual African Christian Church', in the East for a long time the scene remained to be dominated by 'the missionary as explorer, as visionary of radical social transformation, as strategist'.[5]

The leading missionary organisation was the Anglican Church Missionary Society.. With permission by the Sultan of Zanzibar, C.M.S. missionary Ludwig Krapf, after the Ethiopian government had blocked the continuation of his work in Shoa Province, together with his wife established the first Protestant mission station in Kenya at Mombasa in 1544. The death of his wife very soon after this event was a hard blow for Krapf. In 1846 he was joined by colleagues Rebmann and Erhardt. Together they established mission stations in the interior. Dreaming of chain of mission stations across the African continent, they made journeys as far as Kilimanjaro and Mount Kenya. Krapf's main contribution is his book, *Travels, Researches and Missionary Labours* (1853) and his work in the Swahili language.[6] After 1885 other C.M.S.-ers tried to put part of Krapf's plans to practice, although they modified it from a chain of mission stations across Kenya to Uganda.

More successful than the idea of a 'chain of mission stations'[7] was the missionary concept of establishing cities for freed slaves (*othawa kwao*). The first one was opened in 1874 on the initiative of Bartle Frere, British emissary at the court of the Sultan of Zanzibar. Hence it was called Freretown. In these *'cities of refuge'* a

---

[3] Cf. Hildebrandt, *History of the Church in Africa*, p.176.
[4] Sundkler and Steed, *A History of the Church in Africa*, p. 487
[5] Hastings (ed.), *World History*, p. 209.
[6] Cf. Hildebrandt, *History of the Church in Africa*, pp. 122-126.
[7] Cf. Fiedler, *Story of Faith Missions*, 73-84.

The Faith Moves South

strong Christianity developed, often referred to as *'kitoro'* (= refugee) Christianity, which produced Kenya's first Christian martyr David Koi, beheaded by the Arabs in 1883,[8] and other influential Christians, such as William Jones.

By the end of the century the number of missionary organisations in Kenya had grown considerably. Again we meet James Stewart of Lovedale (see previous chapter), now as missionary of the *Church of Scotland Mission* (C.S.M.), pioneering in the interior of Kenya. These Scottish Presbyterians arrived in the Nairobi region in 1898, and they worked hand in hand with the Anglicans of the C.M.S. They were followed by the *Methodists* who moved from the coast into the interior in 1910, the *Neukirchener Mission* and others. Also a series of Faith Missions started work in Kenya, first was the *Africa Inland Mission* of Cameron Scott (1895).[9]

On the Roman Catholic side the *Holy Ghost Fathers* came to Kenya. They arrived in 1889, temporarily withdrew, and started work among the Agikuyu in 1899. They were followed by the *Consolata Fathers* in 1902 and then *Mill Hill Fathers* in 1903. The completion of the Uganda railroad in 1901 made it much easier for missionaries to enter the interior. In 1894 Kenya became a protectorate of Britain.[10]

Henry Bartle Frere (1815-1884), British diplomat who was sent to Zanzibar to negotiate a treaty with the sultan for the suppression of the slave traffic, and contributed to the establishment of refuges for ex-slaves.

3. Tanzania

Mount Kilimanjaro in North West Tanzania, its highest point is Uhuru peak (5,895 metres)

The routes of the slave trade and the traffic in ivory to Zanzibar ran through Tanzania. It was the Anglican *U.M.C.A.*, founded at Livingstone's appeal in 1857, that in 1861 under Bishop Mackenzie in Malawi had collided with the Yao slave traders.[11] This early attempt miscarried and under bishop Tozer the U.M.C.A. withdrew to Zanzibar in 1864, where they established St. Andrewes College

---

[8] Cf. Hildebrandt, *History of the Church in Africa*, p.183.
[9] Cf. W.B. Anderson, *The Church in East Africa 1840-1974*, Nairobi/ Dodoma/ Kampala, UZ.I.M.U/ CTP/ CPH, 1981 [1977]; R. Oliver, *The Missionary Factor in East Africa*, London: Longmans, 1965².
[10] Baur, *2000 Years*, pp. 257, 258.
[11] Hastings, *Church in Africa*, pp.268,286,293.

and a cathedral. In 1875 the U.M.C.A. moved to mainland Tanzania, establishing centres for freed slaves at Magila (1868), Masasi (1876) and Newala (1878).[12] The U.M.C.A. became one of the largest missionary organisations in that country. The Evangelical Anglican *Curch Missionary Society*, located mainly in Uganda, also entered Tanzania. In 1888 they opened a station in Nassa, on the east coast of Lake Victoria. But as it was difficult to administer this work from Uganda, the C.M.S transferred it to the *Africa Inland Mission*, in 1909.[13]

Also the *Holy Ghost Fathers* made a refuge for freed slaves, at Bagamoyo, a former collecting point of slaves on the Tanzanian coast, opposite Zanzibar. Schooling, manual work and rigorous discipline made the settlement self-supporting, but also led to a lack of freedom and protests by the inhabitants. The *Holy Ghost Fathers* were more successful in their new missionary stations along the coast and around Kilimanjaro. Christian communities of ex-slaves and others were also established by the *White Fathers* of Cardinal Lavigerie, who arrived at Lake Tanganyika in 1879.

Before the First World War German missionaries were already active for each of the four classical German Protestant missions in various parts of Tanzania. In the North Bruno Gutmann worked for the *Leipzig Mission* among the Chagga from 1902 to 1938, interrupted only by five years of exclusion (1920-1925) from the territory due to the Versailles Peace Treaty. The *Berlin Mission* was represented by Klamroth and Hermann Neuberg, working in the coastal areas. Ernst Johanssen was active for the *Bethel Mission*. There were also missionaries of the *Moravian Mission*, e.g. Traugott Bachmann, who worked among the Nyakyusa and the Nyiha.[14]

4. Uganda

From the 15th century there had existed the kingdom of Buganda, ruled by its sacred kings, the *kabaka*, who were most central figures in the traditional *balubaala* cult. The religious situation changed when Kabaka Mutesa I († 1884) and his court turned to Islam. However, Stanley, during his visit in 1875, explained to the king the advantages of Christianity, which made the king change again. Protests by Muslims at court were quenched in blood.

In witnessing the Gospel Stanley was ably assisted by one of his African employees, Dallington Muftaa.[15] When Stanley left Buganda Muftaa remained and continued to teach the people. His work prepared tha way for the evangelical An-

---

[12] Hastings, *Church in Africa*, p.257.

[13] Cf. Hildebrandt, *History of the Church in Africa*, p.181.

[14] Klaus Fiedler, *Christianity and Culture: Conservative German Protestant Missionaries in Tanzania 1900-1940*, Blantyre: Kachere/ Claim, 1999 (first published by Brill, Leiden, in 1996); cf. Hildebrandt, *History of the Church in Africa*, 181-183.

[15] Hildebrandt, *History of the Church in Africa*, pp.128,129.

glican C.M.S. They began to send missionaries in 1877. Alexander Mackay was the most successful. He began to translate the Scriptures into Luganda, and preached a Christian revival leading to the rule of Christ over individual, social, and national life.

In 1879 the Roman Catholic *White Fathers* entered Uganda. They rejected the suggestion of going to new mission fields, and started work near the Protestant stations. Competition between Protestants and Roman Catholics confused King Mutesa. He returned to the traditional *balubaala* cult. The bann on preaching and teaching was lifted in 1880. While Protestantism and Roman Catholicism grew, the new *kabaka*, Mwanga, who demanded freedom for his *homosexual* practices, became very hostile against Christianity. After having newly appointed bishop James Hannington murdered, he ordered the death of three African C.M.S. Christians in 1885. In 1886 he burnt 31 Roman Catholics and Protestants in the capital, and had many others killed in other parts of the country.[16] This cruel act against the *Ugandan Martyrs* was followed by three revolutions, the first one brought the Muslims to power, the second one gave power to the Christians in general, and the third one, the Protestants. In 1894 Uganda became a British protectorate.

5. Madagascar

a. First Roman Catholic Attempts

The island of Madagascar is populated by Bantu in the coastal regions mainly in the South, probably taken there as slaves by the Arabs from the 7th century onwards. The Arabs also started making notes on the island which can be considered as the beginning of written history of the island. The highlands in the centre are the homeland of the Hova (Merina and Betsileo peoples). They are of Malayan or Indonesian descent, and they immigrated from the 1st century onwards. This means that Madagascar's population is of Asian and African origin. Its main vernacular language is Malagasy.

The first missionary efforts in Madagascar were made by the Roman Catholics in the 16th century. European contact began after Diego Dias sighted the Island in 1506. Efforts by Portuguese Jesuits in the 17th century had no lasting

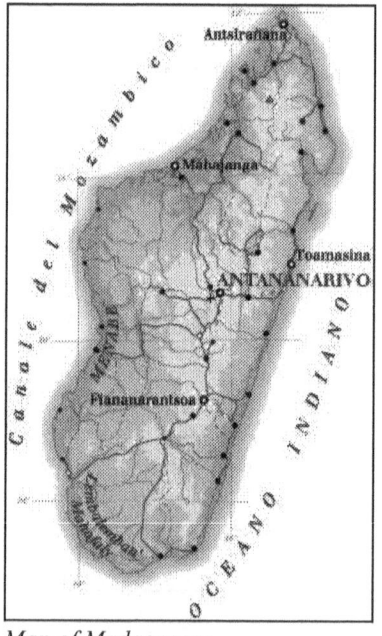

Map of Madagascar

---

[16] Louise Pirouet, *The Witness of the Ugandan Martyrs*, Kampala: Church of Uganda Literature Centre, 1969; cf. Hildebrandt, *History of the Church in Africa*, pp.187-189.

fruits.

Also in the 17th century the *French East Indies Company* established trading posts along the East coast, e.g. Fort Dauphin. In the period 1642-1674 they attempted to make these posts the basis of a French colony on the island. Members of the orders of the Carmelites and the Lazarists tried to start missionary work. They left in 1674 after many of them were murdered by local people. In the 18th century new attempts were made by French Lazarists, 'but the French Revolution put to an end all such work'.[17] About 1800 all traces of the early Roman Catholic efforts had vanished, leaving the Madagascar coast for some decades as a favourite hiding place for pirate ships.

b. Early work by the London Missionary Society

In the meantime the Merina rulers had started to establish power over almost the entire island, 'imposing on it a political as well as a linguistic unity'.[18] They looked for support from the British. In 1817 in a Treaty with Great Britain the Merina king promised to abolish slavery in exchange for British protection. British influence opened the island for Protestant missions.

The first Protestant missionaries were sent by the *London Missionary Society* (L.M.S.). On 18th August 1818 David Jones and Thomas Bevan arrived in Toamasina, the harbor at the Eastern coast of Madagascar. They enjoyed the protection of King Radama I (1810-1828). They opened a school and succeeded in attracting many young people from noble Malagasy families. In subsequent years many more schools were opened. Though all missionaries, with the exception of Jones, died soon after their arrival, the work went on. Until the death of King Radama I other L.M.S. missionaries were allowed to come to the island. One of their important achievements was reducing the Malagasy language into Latin script; the first translation of the Bible was published in Antananarivo in 1835. In the meantime, starting with the Merina court, hundreds of Malagasy people had converted to Christianity.

c. Persecution

Under Radama's widow and successor Ranavalona I (1828-1861) a period of brutal persecution began. In 1835, the same year as the Bible was published, the missionaries were forced to leave the country and many Malagasy converts suffered martyrdom. The Queen was put on the throne by a conspiracy of people who did not favour the modernisations brought by the missionaries. The Queen was led to maintain the royal protection of the missionaries but exercised stricter control over their activities because she was afraid of seeing Christianity become the focus of

---

[17] S. Neill, *A History of Christian Missions*, London: Watson and Vinely, 1964, p. 199.

[18] Neill, *Christian Missions*, p.318.

opposition. To obtain popular support and to make people forget the doubtful origins, of her power, the Queen relied on the soothsayers, and restored old institutions of monarchical power. Eventually she forbade missionaries to preach, and then banned the baptism of soldiers and children. Finally in March 1835 the Queen decreed that anyone would be put to death 'who practices the new religion'.

In 1836 the missionaries left the kingdom and took refuge on the East coast, at Tamatave. They left behind them a small group of about fifty dedicated Christians. Because these Christians kept in contact with the missionaries by letter, today this correspondence gives us direct evidence of this first wave of persecution and the way in which it was experienced. The corres pondence shows the central place occupied in the community, by the Bible and after that by Bunyan's *Pilgrim's Progress*. During the persecutions the number of Christians grew to almost 3000. Some went into exile beyond Madagascar when the threat became too strong, like Mary Rafaravary, daughter of a court dignitary, the first to organise prayer meetings in her home. Arrested in July 1836 and condemned to death, she escaped execution thanks to a providential fire which caused panic among the soldiers and allowed her to get to Tamatave. There she took a ship for Mauritius with a group of Christians. The whole adventure was immediately likened to the adventures of the 'pilgrim' in Bunyan's book with whom Mary is identified. She thought of Christians crossing the valley of the shadow of death, but recalled that it is through numerous tribulations they must enter the kingdom of heaven. During the same year, 1837, the martyrdom of another woman, Rafavavy Rasalana, became the symbol of answering and edifying determination.

Ranavalona I (1782-1861), Queen of Merina, Madagascar. After succeeding her husband, Radama I, she was also known as Ranavalo-Manjka I.

It was in 1849 that the persecution reached its height. After being interrogated, a group of Christians were condemned, some to fines and the confiscation of their goods, others to be flogged, and eighteen to be put to death, four to be burnt and fourteen to be hurled from a great rock and then burnt to ashes. Tertullian's adage 'The blood of the Martyrs is a seed' came true in Madagascar as it could be observed that the faithful attitude of Christians convinced others, at the end of the persecutions their number had grown to 3000 Christians and eleven years later to 27,000. The memory of this dark period plays a significant role in the life of the churches in Madagascar.[19]

---

[19] Cf. A.P. John, 'The Martyrs of Madagascar (1835-1861)', in F.J.Balasundaram (ed.), *Martyrs in the History of Christianity*, http://www.masombahiny.com/Martyrs-of-Madagascar.html Cf. Chenu Bruno, a.o., *The Book of Christian Martyrs*, London: SCM, 1990, p.143; E. Isichei, *A History of Christianity in*

d. Freedom Restored

Under the short reign of Ranavalona's son Radama II the situation changed again. He freed the imprisoned Christians, favoured mission, and sought to modernise the country. Neill cited how this wonderful experience was greeted by the persecuted Christians. Out of the recesses of the forests there came men and women who had been wanderers and outcasts for years. They re-appeared as if risen from the dead. Their brethren from the city went out to meet them, and to help them and as they saw their old city again, they sang the pilgrim song. 'When the Lord turned again the captivity of Zion, we were like them in our dream'.[20]

After the beginning of the new freedom, the *London Missionary Society* returned in the island, soon to be joined by Anglicans, Norwegians, Lutherans, Quakers, and Roman Catholics.

Again there was a brief period of danger to the Christians. An epidemic broke out, and some non-Christians misinterpreted it as revenge by the ancestral spirits. In 1863 King Radama II was overthrown and put to death. His wife Rasolerina became Queen. She supported those spirit worshippers who had threatened the Christians. She died in 1868. Her successor, Ranavalona II, was a daughter of the notorious Ranavalona I, but she did not follow her mother's and Rasolerina's examples. She was rumoured to have been a secret adherent of the Reformed faith, even while her mother was in power. She built a church alongside the palace and in 1869 she was baptised. Large numbers of the upper class followed her example.

e. French Colony

In 1883 the French started to colonise Madagascar. In 1885, the year of the *Berlin Conference* and the subsequent 'scramble for Africa' the British accepted the imposition of French influence in return for eventual control over Zanzibar and as part of an agreement on spheres of influence in East Africa and the Western Pacific. In the same year the French urged Queen Ranavalona III to conclude a Pact with them. In 1895 they occupied the capital Antananarivo and forced the queen to sign another Pact that made Madagascar first a *French Protectorate*, and then in the following year a French Colony. In 1897 the French exiled the queen of Madagascar.

The growing influence of France gave ample opportunities to Roman Catholic mission. As a result of its more favoured position Roman Catholicism spread rapidly, especially among the Bantu people in the coastal regions. This led to tensions between Roman Catholics and Protestants. To strengthen their work, the Protestant mission asked for the support of the *Paris Evangelical Missionary Society* in 1895. Throughout the colonial period the rivalry between Roman Catholicism and Protes-

---

Africa from Antiquity to the Present, University of Canterbury, 1995, p.151.
[20] Neill, *Christian Missions*, p. 319

tantism continued. Although the official separation of Church and State in France demanded equality of both denominations, French tradition made it difficult for the colonial authorities to treat them equally.

A nationalist revolution in 1947 was the beginning of the end of French colonialism in Madagascar. In October 1958 Madagascar became an autonomous republic within the *French Commonwealth*, adopting the name Malagasy, and in June 1960 it declared itself fully independent. Especially the Protestant churches had supported the movement that led to independence.

f. Independence

At the moment about half of the Madagascar people are members of Christian churches, divided almost evenly between Roman Catholicism and Protestantism. The *Malagasy Council of Christian Churches* (F.F.K.M.) comprises four denominations, the *Reformed Protestant Church of Jesus Christ in Madagascar* (F.J.K.M.), the *Lutheran Church*, the *Anglican Church*, and the *Roman Catholic Church*. The other half of the Malagasy are Muslims (less than 10%) or they still belong to traditional religions with much emphasis on cults of the dead, i.e. the custom of *famadihana*, or 'turning over the dead'. 'In this ritual relatives' remains are removed from the family tomb, re-wrapped in new silk shrouds, and returned to the tomb following festive ceremonies in their honour'.

The influence of traditional religious perceptions and customs has remained strong in the Churches and in the lives of many Christians. This together with the influence of liberal theologies seems to have diminished the once fervent spiritual life. Today, many who attend church seem to have little understanding of their faith and their churches make the impression of being spiritually dead. This challenges Christians to pray and work for revival within and without the mainline churches. *Africa Inland Mission* belongs to those who have consciously responded to this challenge by taking the initiative of evangelistic work amongst nominal Christians, students and non-Christians.

Chapter 9

Africa's Old Colonisers after 1885

1. The Scramble[1]

During most of the 19th century the majority of the missionaries in Sub-Saharan Africa were the guests of African rulers,[2] except for those who worked under British rule at the Cape and some other places, and for those who worked near the Portuguese colonial centres. However, this rapidly changed. Economical and other interests enticed countries like France, Germany and Belgium, preceded by Britain, to colonise the whole of Africa.

In the 1870s King Leopold II of Belgium had already claimed Congo, whereas Portugal had strengthened its grip on Angola and Mozambique. In 1882 Britain occupied Egypt. The *Berlin Conference* of 1885 made a plan of partition; this initiated the *Scramble for Africa*. Before 1880 only 10% of Africa was controlled by European Powers. Colonies dotted along the coast of West Africa from the defunct

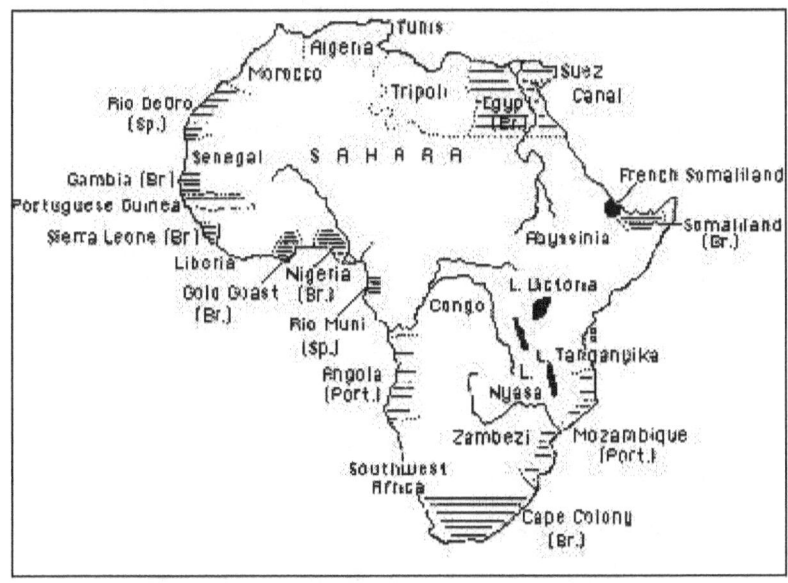

Map of Africa about 1880, at the time when the Scramble was to start.

The Faith Moves South

Berlin Conference of 1884-1885 of the foreign ministers of 14 Western states, to divide Africa. This pictures a meeting at the Berlin residence of Chancellor Otto von Bismarck in 1884 (from: The Horizon: History of Africa, American Heritage Publishing Co., New York, 1971, page 452).

slave trade, settlements in southern Africa by Dutch, English, and Portuguese, and Algeria in the north, conquered by the French.

Remaining African territories were taken by the Italians (Libya, Eritrea, and part of Somaliland), and by Spain (part of Morocco, part of the Western Sahara: Equatorial Guinea). By 1902 only Ethiopia and Liberia had remained free of European control. By this point in history, even the Dutch *Afrikaaner Republics* in South Africa were conquered by the English in the infamous *Boer War*. A history of 75 years of Western colonial rule over Africa had begun.

In this period 1885-1960 the number of Christians grew remarkably, from 4 million in 1900 to 34 million in the 1950s, being then about 20% of the population.[3] The missionary movement aimed at the conversion of Africans to Christianity emerged together with imperialism, followed by colonialism, but they were not necessarily partners. In the chapter 11 we will look at the relationship between mission and colonialism. But first we need to see how the events of the *Scramble for Africa* profoundly changed the political situation in the continent.

---

[1] Cf. Thomas Pakenham, *The Scramble for Africa 1876-1912*, London: Abacus, 1991.
[2] Cf. Ward, 'Africa', in: Hastings (ed) *World History*, pp. 216f.
[3] Cf. Shaw, *Kingdom*, p. 207, who quoted: R.Oliver, *The African Experience*, San Francisco: Harper/Collins, p. 207, and with: K.Fiedler, 'Christian Missions and Western Colonialism – Soulmates or Antagonists?' in: K.R.Ross, ed., *Faith at the Frontiers of Knowledge*, Blantyre: Claim, 1998 [Kachere Series no.6], p. 224, who quoted: D. Barrett, *World Christian Encyclopedia: A Comparative Survey of Churches and Religions in the Modern World AD 1900-2000*, Nairobi/Oxford/New York, 1982.

2. The British

Britain's imperialistic activities in Africa were aimed at finding new markets and raw materials, attaining world prestige, and spreading the English style of orderly government. They also wanted to safeguard their interests by protecting their overseas territories from German or French invasions.

a. Egypt and the Sudan

After the French completed the Suez Canal in 1869 the British began to take notice of Egypt. Britain realised that the Suez Canal would make travel to India faster and less expensive. The only problem the British had with the Suez Canal was that it was controlled by the French. After defeating Arabs and Egyptians who had risen against foreign intrusion, the British became the most powerful force in Egypt and France lost her claim for not helping put down the rebellion.

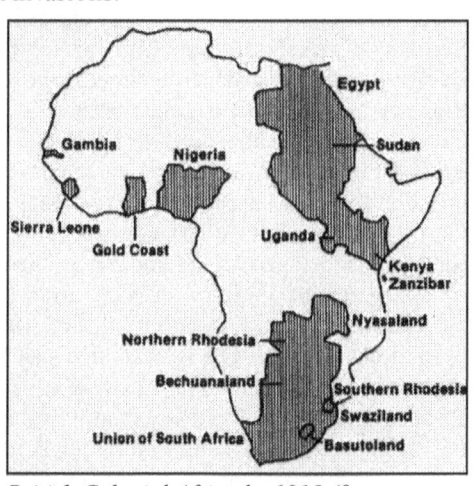

British Colonial Africa by 1915 (from: Hildebrandt, History, p.141)

In 1885 British troops pushing south from Egypt encountered resistance from a large Muslim Sudanese army which defeated the army of General Charles Gordon, killing the General himself, in a massacre at Khartoum. In 1898 the reconquest of the Anglo-Egyptian Sudan under General Horatio Kitchener ended with the Omdurman massacre. Later Kitchener's army at Fashoda almost clashed with a French force in the regions of the Upper Nile, one of the few unclaimed areas left by then. This almost led to a European war until the French pulled out.[4]

To secure the sea routes to India and the Far East the British considered it necessary to colonise Somalia. The first treaty was signed in 1827, and in the 1880's Somali tribes formed a British Protectorate. There were wars against Muslim fundamentalist Mohammed bin Abdulla, conveniently called the 'mad mullah' in the years before the *First World War*, and during the *Second World War* against Italian invaders. For their military campaigns the British not only used troops from Europe but also from the colonies. An example is the *King's African Rifles*,[5]

---

[4] N.R.Norman, *Africa and Europe: From Roman Times to National Independence*, Holmes and Meier, 1984[2]; P.Bohannan and P. Curtin, *African and Africans*, Waveland Press, 1995[4]; P. Curtin (ed.), *African History: From Earliest Time to Independence*, Addison Wesley, 1995[2].

[5] Clement A.D. Namangale, *A Brief History of the Origins of the Malawi Rifles to Mark the Centenary of the Formation of the King's African Rifles, 1902-2002*, Lilongwe: Malawi Defence Force, 2002; Cf.

mainly recruited from Malawi, an army unit that from 1902-1966 was active in Somaliland, Kenya, Tanzania, Ethiopia, and other parts of the British Empire.

b. South Africa

After the *Berlin Conference* British colonialism in Southern Africa intensified. The conflict between the British government, which claimed sovereignty over those areas, and the Boers culminated, after the discovery of gold in the Boer territories, in the *South African War* or the *Boer War* 1899-1902, which brought Transvaal and Orange Free State under British rule. Given self-government in 1907, they were formed, with Cape Colony and Natal, into the *Union of South Africa* in 1910. A very important role in British colonialism in Southern Africa was played by Cecil John Rhodes (1853-1902). He was a financier, statesman, and philosopher of mystical imperialism.

Charles Gordon (1833-1885), commander of the British army defeated and killed in the Battle of Khartoum.

Rhodes dreamed of a railway from the Cape to Cairo. His ideal was that the whole of Africa eventually would be under British control. He went to Africa in 1870, became a diamond miner, and in 1888 he started a very successful mining company, called the *De Beers*, that by 1891 owned ninety percent of the worlds diamond mines. Once he was elected to the Cape Parliament, and in 1890 as Prime Minister, he began to pursue his territorial dreams. However, resistance by the Boers and interference by German colonialism made it impossible for him to reach his objectives. In chapters 16-19 we will notice that, facilitated by the plans of Rhodes and of other empire builders, Botswana, Southern Rhodesia (later Zimbabwe), Northern Rhodesia (later Zambia), and Nyasaland (later Malawi) were added to the British Empire.

c. Sierra Leone

In chapter 6 we saw how Sierra Leone had become a free haven for returning slaves. In 1794 the French plundered the colony. In 1807 the private rights of the Sierra Leonean company were transferred to the British crown, the same year that the British Parliament declared the slave trade illegal. British warships that captured slave ships brought the freed slaves to the colony and thus the population grew. Internal exploration continued and an agreement with the French delineating the frontier was signed in 1895, shutting out Sierra Leone from its natural hinter-

---

Colin Baker, *A Fine Chest of Medals: The Life of Jack Archer*, Cardiff: Mpemba Books, 2003; For an extensive study of the K.A.R,, see: H.Moyse-Bartlett, *The King's African Rifles: A Study in the Military History of East and Central Africa, 1890-1945*, 2 volumes, Ridgewood: Naval & Military Press, n.d.

land. In 1896 it became a *British Protectorate*, which remained separate from the colony of Freetown until 1951.

d. Ghana

The West African 'Gold Coast' (later Ghana) since late 15th century had been the stage of Portuguese, Dutch, Danish and English activity. Trade in gold and slaves was the main interest. The slave trade was fed by the taking of prisoners of war, because of the continual conflict between the Ashanti and the Fante tribes. With the abolition of the slave trade in 1807 control passed from the merchants to the crown. British control gradually predominated on the coast and was recognised by the Ashanti. In 1824 after inciting the Fante to rise against the Ashanti, the British occupied the inland. In 1826 the Ashanti were defeated. Eventually treaties were worked out between the Fante and Ashanti. The Ashanti war of 1873-74 resulted in the extension of British influence. Further exploration north of Ashanti with various treaties secured the Northern Territories of the Gold Coast in 1897.

e. Nigeria

British influence in Nigeria began through the activities of the *National Africa Company* (the *Royal Niger Company* from 1886), which bought Lagos from an African chief 1861 and steadily extended its hold over the Niger Valley until it surrendered its charter in 1899; in 1903 the two protectorates of North and South Nigeria were proclaimed, and in 1914 they were merged to become Britain's largest African colony.

f. Kenya

Because of its height, East Africa was far more suitable for settlement by white colonists than the colonies in the west. Once again, private companies under charter from the British government pioneered the way, establishing their control over Kenya in 1888 and Uganda in 1890.

From the 8th century Arabs and Persians made settlements along the coast gaining some political supremacy leading to the formation of the so called *Zenj Empire*. The Masai pastoral people came into the area in the 18th century from the north and during the 19th century the agricultural Kikuyu steadily advanced from the south. In chapter 3 section 5 we saw that Portuguese traders operated in the region during the 16th and 17th centuries. Yet, control of the coastal towns was always under the Sultan of Zanzibar, until concessions were made to the British and Germans in the 19th century. British coastal trade began in the 1840s. In 1887 a trading company secured the lease of a coastal strip from the Sultan of Zanzibar. The Germans also courted concessions and soon agreements between Britain and Germany ratified British claims to the districts inland from Mombasa. With more concessions and agreements with the Germans, the company's lands spread from the coast up to Ethiopia in the north, and Lake Victoria in the west. In 1895 the territories became a *British Protectorate* and in 1920 Kenya became a Colony. From 1896 until 1903 the railway from Mombasa to Lake Victoria was built, thus linking Kenya with Uganda.

g. Uganda

In chapter 8 section 4 we noticed the importance of the Kingdom of Buganda that dominated the lands of Lake Victoria in the 18th and 19th centuries. Mutesa I, the kabaka or king of Buganda welcomed English explorers hoping for protection against Arab slave and ivory traders. Anglican and French Roman Catholic missionaries entered the country, as well as Muslim missionaries sent by the Arabs. Following Mutesa's death in 1884 tensions developed between his successor, Mwanga, and the Anglicans, Catholics and Muslims culminating in successively the killing of a number of Christians, and factional fighting (see chapter 8, section 4). In an Anglo-German treaty of 1890 Uganda was assigned to Britain. The British *East Africa Company* placed Buganda and the western states Ankole and Toro under its protection, and in 1894 these territories became a British Protectorate. After the Second World War the last Kabaka, Mutesa II backed the protectorate government in suppressing Buganda nationalist risings in 1945 and 1949. In 1953 he tried to secede his Kingdom from the protectorate but that was denied by the Ugandan High Court and he was deported, only to return in 1955 as constitutional monarch.

Edward Mutesa II, king of Buganda from 1924 to 1969 and President of Uganda from 1963 to 1966.

h. Zanzibar and Tanganyika

In 1890 Germany, which had already relinquished its interests in Uganda, ceded her interests in Zanzibar to Britain in exchange for Helgoland, an island off the German coast. The *First World War* ousted Germany from the African continent.
    i. Decolonisation
    Among the British African colonies Egypt was the first to become independent, in 1951. The Sudan followed in 1956. Then the Gold Coast followed, as Ghana in 1957. Then came Nigeria (1960), Sierra Leone (1961), British Cameroons (1961),

later to be divided among independent Cameroon and Nigeria, Tanganyika (1961), later to become Tanzania, Uganda (1962), Kenya (1963), Zambia (1964), Nyasaland (1964), later to become Malawi, The Gambia (1965), Botswana (1966), Swaziland (1968), Rhodesia, after a period of unilateral independence and guerrilla warfare (1980), later to become Zimbabwe.

3. The Portuguese

a. Extension

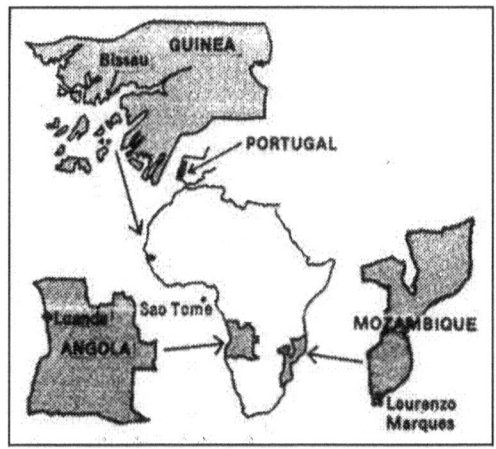

Map of Portuguese Africa by 1914 (from: Hildebrandt, History).

After 1885 the Portuguese increased their efforts to extend effective rule to the remote parts of the vast regions that they had claimed. In Southern Africa their aspirations even stretched beyond the boundaries of Angola and Mozambique. Whereas the British wanted to occupy an uninterrupted territory that would link the Cape and Cairo, the Portuguese wanted to connect their colonies in the West and in the East of Africa. That is why the Portuguese attempted to include the South of Nyasaland (present Malawi) and Northern Rhodesia (present Zambia) in their colonial empire. Portuguese intentions for Nyasaland were much disliked by Protestant missionaries, and finally they clashed with the British colonial Empire.

In Angola and Mozambique the extension of Portuguese administration also brought about a confrontation with the interests of Protestant mission. Nationalistic cultural pride (*Lusitanianism*) and a traditional preference for Roman Catholicism were the two important factors that hardened intrinsic anti-Protestant tendencies. In the early 20th century this began to make life difficult for Protestant missionaries and the churches they had established.

b. Lusitanianism

Portuguese cultural nationalism could not tolerate the Protestant way of using African vernacular languages in education and mission work. The use of the Portuguese language was demanded, especially for schools. In 1921 the colonial government decreed that all schools should teach only in the Portuguese language. They forbade teaching or printing of books in the African languages. Anything was to be communicated in Portuguese. This measure especially hindered Protestant missionary and educational work.[6] Protestant missionaries worked at learning the local languages, in part to communicate better with the people in the field, particularly to translate the Bible into the African tongues. The decree was followed by the *Colonial Act* of 1930 which advanced the view that Portuguese Roman Catholic Mission overseas were 'instruments of civilisation and national influence'

c. Between Concordat and World Council of Churches

The tendency of favouring Roman Catholicism, was emphatically confirmed by a *Concordat* concluded between the Portuguese State and the Roman Catholic Church on 7th May 1940. In this Pact the Portuguese State pledged to teach the Roman Catholic religion in state schools. It also included a missionary agreement that promised public money and other facilities to Roman Catholic missions in the overseas provinces. Protestant Missions were permitted to engage in educational activities, but without subsidy and on condition that Portuguese be the language of instruction.

The Portuguese colonial empire had started earlier and was disbanded later than other European colonial empires. Whereas the other powers, except for the Soviet Union, gave up their colonies around 1960, Portuguese overseas rule remained until 1974. In the meantime protests against Portuguese colonial presence grew stronger, not only inside Africa, but also in Europe and America. The *World Council of Churches* (W.C.C.), founded in 1948, contributed much to an almost universal outcry against Portugal. The W.C.C. to a certain extent was motivated by the desire to defend classical Protestantism that suffered under Portuguese nationalism and Romanism. In general, however, the W.C.C. supported religious liberalism and subsequently a kind of ecumenism that was less qualified by Scripture than by modern ideology.

d. Wars and Independence

This situation created room for the Portuguese to continue maintaining their colonial presence in and outside Africa. The Soviet Union tried to win influence in the 'third world' at the expense of the West by giving military support to liberation movements that had risen against oppressive regimes. The Portuguese in their propaganda of defending their colonial empire pretended to defend the interests of the West as a whole. Yet, the Portuguese increasingly clashed with public opinion in the West which coincided with growing resistance of Africans in the Portuguese colonies. Wars of liberation were started by Africans. The Portuguese reacted by

---

[6] Decree 77 of 17th December 1921, issued by the High Commission of the Portuguese Republic. A translation of the text is found in: Paas, *Het Protestantisme in Angola*, pp.53-56; cf. Hildebrandt, *History of the Church in Africa*, p. 135.

military and political action. In 1971, through issuing a special Law, they changed their religious policy. Full religious freedom was proclaimed. However, the law did not take away the main conditions of the old 'missionary agreement' that favoured Roman Catholicism.[7] Eventually Portuguese rule in Africa collapsed as a result of the combined effect of Western public opinion and African resistance. The Portuguese handed over power a decade later than most of the other colonisers. In 1975 Angola, Mozambique, Guinea Bissau, Cape Verde, Sao Tomé and Principe became independent.

A new era started. Yet, the newly won political and religious freedom was seriously undermined by the continuation of war. African liberation movements were deeply divided along the front between Western interests and Soviet-communist interests. That is why the ex-Portuguese countries became a stage where the competing world powers tried their weaponry. The Soviet Union and the United States each supported opposing parties in a series of devastating and cruel civil wars that continued for decades. In Angola the MPLA[8] and the UNITA,[9] and in Mozambique the FRELIMO[10] and the RENAMO[11] were the parties that tried to destroy one another. Some leaders of these former liberation movements continued fighting, long after they had lost in the competition for power. A notable example was Jonas Savimbi. As founder and leader of UNITA he once was a promising factor in Angola's struggle for political and religious freedom.[12] But gradually he deranged and got entangled in a cruel and useless struggle for personal victory and glory, until he was murdered in 2002.

Jonas Savimbi (†2002), leader of the UNITA liberation movement which later became a rebel army in independent Angola.

In the early 1990s the situation changed as a result of the collapse of the Soviet Union and of international communism. As power patterns in the world had become different, the opposing parties in the Angolan and Mozambican civil wars lost their allies. Gradually peace was restored under new governments. In the new era there were chances for development and freedom. The churches have profited from this. The Roman Catholic Church has been liberated from its very close ties with the State. It tries hard to reorganise and to make clear that the Church does not

---

[7] State Law no 4/71 of 21st August 1971 on religious freedom; for a translation, see: Paas, *Het Protestantisme in Angola*, pp. 48-52.
[8] Movimento Popular de Libertação de Angola.
[9] União Nacional para a Independência Total de Angola.
[10] Frente de Libertação de Moçambique.
[11] Resistência Nacional Moçambicana.
[12] Cf. Fred Bridgland, *Jonas Savimbi: A Key to Africa*, Edinburgh: Mainstream Publ., 1986; Sousa Jamba, *Patriots*, London: Penguin/ Viking, 1990.

The Faith Moves South

operate anymore on the side of the oppressor. These attempts have improved its image. Numerically the Roman Catholic Church in both countries is still the largest one. But Protestant Churches are growing, now that they acquired freedom for evangelism and mission. Old and new foreign missions are free to enter Angola and Mozambique.

Chapter 10

Africa's New Colonisers after 1885

1. The Belgians

a. Congo Free State

The *Congo Free State* was a private kingdom owned by Leopold II of Belgium between about 1877 and 1908. It included the area now known as the Democratic Republic of Congo. The kingdom was the scene of exploitation, greed, and mass killings and maimings of those who opposed Leopold's rule or who did not work hard enough as forced labourers in rubber plantations or other profit-making ventures.

At the *Berlin Conference* in 1885, King Leopold gained international support for his creation of the Congo Free State through proposals to end slavery in the Congo, protect the rights of the natives, and guarantee free trade. In the popular media he was often portrayed as a philanthropist who was selflessly devoting his efforts to rescue and civilise the peoples of Central Africa.

Leopold II (1835-1909), King of Belgium, until 1908 private ruler over Congo Free State.

Soon, however, reports from missionaries and merchants began to filter to Europe and the United States about slave labour, mutilations, and other forms of torture used to increase the collection of ivory, rubber, and other products. Most of the Missions were Protestant, mainly British and American Baptist and Presbyterian and Swedish Lutheran. The first one to start work in Congo was the *Livingstone Inland Mission*, led by Fanny Guinness. It started work in Congo in 1878.[1] Fiedler says that the first agitation against the atrocities was connected to the Guinness family, and that the first missionary to make them public was J.B. Murphy of *the American Baptist Missionary Union*.[2]

Leopold did prefer any religion, but he wanted Belgian missionaries in the first place, which practically excluded Protestants. To this end he even made an agreement with the Vatican, which gave way to the newly founded *Society of Scheut* and

---
[1] Fiedler,*Story of Faith Missions*, pp.37-39, 72.
[2] Fiedler, *Story of Faith Missions*, pp. 227, 228.

to Belgian Jesuits. However, the Belgian Roman Catholics were unable to fulfil the need for missionaries whereas the rapid spread of Protestant Missions could not be stopped.³ In general the early relations of Protestant missionaries with the Belgian rulers were not warm. During the existence of the *Congo Free State* often Protestant missionaries witnessed and publicised abuses against the population. Reports of atrocities were systematically countered by Leopold's sophisticated public relations efforts

In 1893, a young writer, inspired to adventure by the celebrated travels of Henry M. Stanley and believing the glowing reports of Leopold's rule, got a job on a steamer headed up the Congo River. Joseph Conrad turned his Congo experiences into *Heart of Darkness*, published in 1899, describing in fiction the horrors he saw.

Prisoners in the Congo Free State. This vast is territory, which was the private domain of King Leopold II of Belgium until 1908, experienced excesses of colonialism. Millions of people died as a result of pacification, forced labor, portage, indiscriminate slaughter, and slavery-like conditions.

Efforts to bring widespread public attention to atrocities in the Congo were largely unsuccessful until Edmund Dene Morel formed the *Congo Reform Association* in March, 1904. Morel's interest in the subject grew from hearing accounts of the Congo from merchants with whom he had contact as a clerk for a Liverpool shipping company. Born in France and speaking French fluently, he was often sent to Belgium on company business. He resigned from his job with the shipping company in 1901 to work full-time as a journalist, to highlight conditions in the Congo more directly. Morel was an able journalist being careful to provide documentation that would stand despite Leopold's denials. He was also able to organise a trans-Atlantic movement for reform in the Congo that included some of the leading political and cultural figures in Britain and the United States.

In September 1904 six months after he had founded the *Congo Reform Association*, Morel left for the United States to represent the Association at the *International Peace Conference* held in Boston. During the trip, Morel lobbied the American government, presenting a memorial on the Congo to President Theodore Roosevelt, and helped to solidify the organisation of an American branch of the *Congo Reform Association* based in Boston.

---

³ Hastings, *Church in Africa*, p. 416.

Both branches gained support from leading political and cultural figures in both countries, including Arthur Conan Doyle in England, and Mark Twain and Booker T. Washington in America. Reports of slave labor, mutilations and other forms of torture used to increase the collection of ivory and rubber were highlighted by this Association in efforts to end Leopold's rule of the Congo.

In 1908 King Leopold II formally relinquished personal control of the Congo Free State and the renamed Belgian Congo came under the administration of the Belgian parliament.

Joseph Conrad (1857-1924), whose original name was Joseph Korzeniowski, was a famous writer of short stories and novels. In Heart of Darkness (1902) he contributed to revealing the atrocities in the Congo Free State.

b. Congo Colony

The Belgian administration can be characterised as paternalistic colonialism favouring Roman Catholicism, though not excluding Protestant missions. The ruling elite consisted of the 'colonial trinity' of State, Roman Catholic Church, and the agro-industrial companies. Protestant missions did not belong to these institutions. That is why they did not enjoy the same degree of official confidence as was given to their Roman Catholic counterparts. For example, until after the end of the *Second World War* state subsidies for hospitals and schools, were in reserved for Roman Catholic institutions. In the period between the world wars the number of Protestant missions was more than doubled, with the arrival of e.g. the Norwegian Baptists (1919), the American Mennonites (1920), the Seventh Day Adventists (1921), the Belgian Protestants (1921), the Swedish Evangelical Free Church (1921), the Assemblies of God (1921), the Ubangi Evangelical Mission (1923), the Anglican Mission from Uganda (1926). Nevertheless the number of Roman Catholic missionaries remained the largest force, and 'it continued to receive money and advice from the Belgian government'. In 1926 the Belgian State and the Vatican agreed that all subsidies for education should be given to Roman Catholic Missions. Only in 1948 the law was changed 'to allow some Protestant Missions to receive government money'.[4]

The colonial state divided up the colony into spiritual franchises, giving each approved mission its own territory. Political administration fell under the total and direct control of the mother country; there were no democratic institutions. Native curfews and other restrictions were not unusual. Following the *Second World War* some democratic reforms began to be introduced, but these were complicated by ethnic rivalries among the African population.[5]

---

[4] Hildebrandt, *History of the Church in Africa*, pp. 212-217.
[5] This section leans on: J. Zwick: *Reforming the Heart of Darkness: The Congo Reform Movement in*

Protestant teaching was mistrusted, especially when it prepared for leadership by Africans. That is why Simon Kimbangu, a successful Baptist preacher, was put in prison, where he stayed until his death in 1951. Yet, his followers formed a very big Church, which was not allowed to exist by the authorities. The *Kimbanguist Movement* was instrumental in preparing Congo for independence. Kimbangu inspired nationalist leaders like Joseph Kasavubu.[6]

c. Independence

The Belgian Congo became independent in 1960, later to become Zaire, and after that the Democratic Republic of Congo. The Belgian colonies Rwanda and Burundi became independent in 1961.

At independence in 1960, in Congo some forty-six Protestant missions were at work, the majority of them North American, British, or Scandinavian in origin. The missions established a committee to maintain contact and minimise competition among them. This body evolved into a union called the *Church of Christ in the Congo* (l'Eglise du Christ au Congo). This united Protestant Church was established in 1935 by ten missions. In 1972 the government of Zaire decreed that all Protestant churches should either join the union or disband. The *Church of Christ* developed rules that permitted members of one evangelical congregation to move to and be accepted by another. This organisation of Protestant Churches is one of the four mainstreams of Christianity in Congo, beside the Roman Catholics, The Greek Orthodox and the Kimbanguists.

2. The French

a. Before Berlin 1885

To some extent France belonged to the old colonisers of Africa. At least two countries of Africa had met with French colonial power before the *Berlin Conference* of 1884/ 1885, Algeria and Madagascar.

With the French conquest of Algiers in 1830, the Ottoman rule ended, and Algeria became French. They occupied the North African nation and relentlessly pursued the objective of extending French sovereignty to Algeria. The French liked to consider Algeria as an ordinary province of France. That is why many French from Europe migrated to this region of North Africa. However, many Algerian Muslims expressed disagreement, either by armed and unarmed resistance, or by emigration to a Muslim territory. One of the results was a bloody guerrilla war

---

England and the United States; Wikipedia Encyclopedia, *Scramble for Africa*, and *Congo Free State*.
[6] A. Hastings, *A History of African Christianity 1950-1975*, Cambridge U.P., 1979, pp. 84, 85, 124, 131.

Africa's New Colonisers after 1885

waged by the Algerian people and the forced extirpation of French colonialism from Algeria in the late 1950s.

France's attempts to get a foothold on the island of Madagascar date from the 17th century. They were interrupted by the *French Revolution*, and resumed in the second half of the 19th century. Some years before the *Berlin Conference* the French began to rule the island as their colony. In 1960 Madagascar became an independent country. In chapter 9, section 5 Madagascar's history as a French colony, including the position of Mission and Church, is briefly described.

b. From Berlin 1885

In France's colonial history in Sub-Saharan Africa and the rest of North Africa a tradition of much military and political violence is continued. By the time of the *Berlin Conference* (1884/1885) the French had already claimed Senegal, Gabon and North Congo, and from Senegal they penetrated inland to the Niger River. They actually sought to expand their influence in the whole of North Africa and from West Africa to Eastern Sudan. They negotiated treaties with African leaders from a powerful military position. France focused on the military direction of the expansion, by going from fort to fort and taking over control. The French were harsh in their administration and in their attempts to increase economic footholds. They used forced labour and imprisonment of Africans to maintain and expand their interests. By 1900 France had occupied large territories of North West and Central Africa.

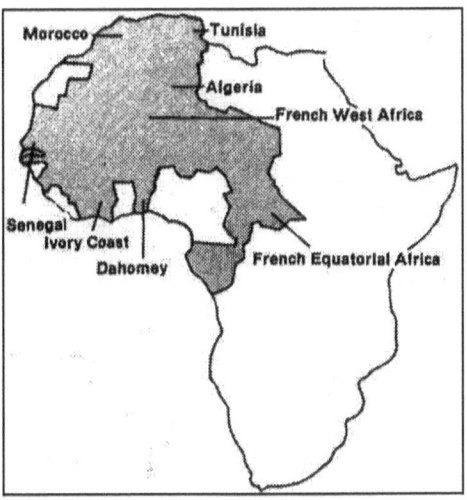

French Colonial Africa by 1915 (from: Hildebrandt, History, p. 140).

In the North the French extended their rule to the Muslim territories of Morocco and Tunisia. In West Africa they added to their empire: Dahomey, French Guinea, French Sudan, Ivory Coast, Mauritania, Niger, Senegal, and Upper Volta. These eight overseas territories were joined together in a Federation in 1895. The capital was Dakar. In Western Central Africa in 1910 they joined together four territories as the federation of *French Equatorial Africa*. It consisted of: Gabon, Middle Congo, Chad, and Ubangi-Shari. The capital was Brazzaville.

We conclude this sub-section with a few remarks on mission in the French colonies of Africa, focusing on West and Western Central Africa. The French colonial authorities favoured Roman Catholic missions, and in general they wanted missionaries who were French citizens. In Senegal Roman Catholic mission had already started before French colonial rule. Favour of the colonial government did not incule help in making converts among the Muslim majority with their history of almost 800 years. In Ivory Coast Roman Catholic Mission started in 1895. After the missionary campaign of Harris in 1914 the Wesleyan Methodists were allowed to enter and do some limited work, 'trying to consolidate people who had responded to Harris's message'. In Dahomey, present day Benin, the colonial government encouraged the Roman Catholic Society of African Missions, which about 1914 had become very large, and also permitted a small work by the Wesleyan Methodists. In Gabon the Roman Catholic Church was much helped by the government with money and guidance, so that it grew more rapidly than the small number of Protestant missions that were allowed to enter. This was in line with what happened in the whole of *French Equitorial Africa*. The Pope had assigned this region to the French *Holy Ghost Fathers* making it to a special Vicariate, heavily supported by French financial assistance.

c. Decolonisation

Of the French North African colonies, Morocco and Tunisia were the first to receive independence, in 1956. Algeria had to wait until 1962. In 1958 the territories of The West African federation became autonomous republics in the French Community, except for French Guinea, which became independent and withdrew from the French Community. The federation was dissolved in 1959. In 1960 the other territories became fully independent within the French Community, Dahomey became Benin, French Sudan became Mali, Upper Volta became Burkina Faso; the others, Ivory Coast, Mauritania, Niger, and Senegal did not change their names.

Also in 1960 the four territories of *French Equatorial Africa* became fully independent within the French Community: Gabon, Congo, later to become Republic of the Congo, Chad, and Ubangi-Shari, later to become Central African Republic.

This was followed by the independence of Cameroon (1960), Togo (1960), Madagascar (1960), Seychelles (1967), Mauritius (1968), Equatorial Guinea (1968).

3. The Germans

a. The German Scramble

Germany joined the Scramble for Africa quite late. The Germans followed the example of France and Britain, knowing that these powerful nations would not waste their time, resources, and energy on something that was not profitable. Otto Von Bismarck and the rest of Germany felt that colonisation in Africa would help Germany and force others to reckon with them.

Africa's New Colonisers after 1885

The German colonial presence in Africa basically concerned four territories. It began in 1884, just before the opening of the *Berlin Conference*, by taking control of the Cameroons. One week after the Conference ended, in 1885, Germany took possession of Tanganyika, hence called German East Africa, present day Tanzania. Then it claimed Togoland, a small strip between Dahomey and the Gold Coast. Finally Germany colonised South West Africa, present day Namibia. There were also periods of German colonial rule in Burundi, Rwanda, and Zanzibar.

b. The Cameroons and Togo

In the Cameroons the strict germanification programme made life difficult for the English *Baptist Mission*, started by Alfred Saker, in the Duala area (see chapter 6, section 4a). In 1886 they handed over the work to the *Basel Mission*, a Swiss organisation with Swiss and German personnel. The *Basel Mission* were followed by a German Baptist Mission in 1890. In the same year German Roman Catholics and American Presbyterians were welcomed by the German colonial rulers. Missionaries were not allowed to work in strong Muslim areas. In the *First World War* the France and Britain divided the Cameroons, a small portion in the north-west became British and the larger part became a French colony. The French wanted all German missionaries permanently out. Protestant work was taken over by the *Paris Missionary Society* and Roman Catholic work by the French *Holy Ghost Fathers*.[7]

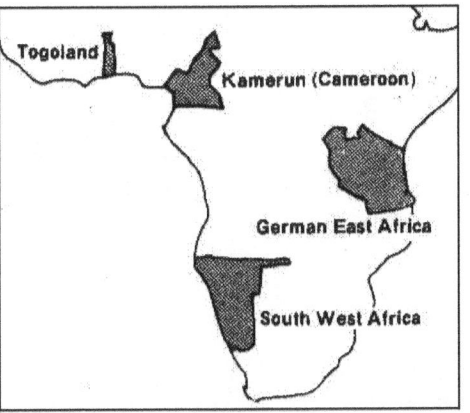

German Colonial Africa by 1914 (from: Hildebrandt, History, p. 143).

In Togo the arrival of the North German *Bremen Mission* preceded German colonial rule. They started work in the 1850s. After the establishment of colonial rule, the *Basel Mission* arrived, they left in 1902, only to return in 1912. The Roman Catholics started work in Togo in 1890. During the First World War the French and the British ended German rule over Togo, and in 1916 German missionaries were forced to leave. The work of the *Basel Mission* was taken over by the *United Free Church of Scotland*. The work of the *Bremen Mission* was handed over to African pastors, one of them was R.D. Baeta. In 1924 the British allowed the German Missions to return to British colonies, including the territories taken over from

---

[7] Hildebrandt, *History of the Church in Africa*, pp. 162-664, 211, 212.

German colonial rule. From then Germans and Scottish missionaries in Togo and Gold Coast cooperated for the establishment of one African Reformed Church.[8]

c. German East Africa

When German rule in Tanzania began, the *Roman Catholics*, the *Church Missionary Society*., the *London Missionary Society* and the *Universities Mission* had already established mission stations in the country. In chapter 8 section 3, we noticed that German colonial rule was followed by the arrival of German missionary organisations. Now German organisations were added, *Berlin III* (1887), the *Berlin Missionary Society* (1891), the *Moravian Mission* (1891), and the *Leipzig Missionary Society*, the *Bethel Mission*. In 1893 the C.M.S. withdrew to Kenya, handing over its work to the Leipzig Mission. Missionary work was weakened by the First World War. It took the Allied Forces four years to defeat the German army and its able commander Von Lettow-Vorbeck. German missionaries had to leave. The young Church was severly hit by this, although from Kenya the *Church Missionary Society*, and from Malawi the *Universities Mission* and the *Scottish Missions* tried to help out. In 1925 the German missionary societies began to return to their former regions.[9]

d. South-West Africa

In Namibia or South West Africa German presence had begun in the 1870s, before the colonial annexation, with the arrival of German missionaries. In 1842 the *Rhenish Missionary Society* started work beyond the Orange River. Later the *Finish Missionary Society* entered the North. After 1907 also the Roman Catholics made progress in Namibia.[10]

The establishment of colonial rule was followed by an increase of white immigrants, many of them Germans. These settlers moved inland, occupying land. They clashed with the local Herero people, who refused to give up their land. This led to a brutal attack by German troops under the command of General Lothar von Trotha, notorious for his cruelties in Tanzania (Tanganyika), Rwanda and Burundi. In the period 1904-1907 his army butchery exterminated some 65,000 Herero, that is about 80% of

Adrian Dietrich Lothar von Trotha (1848-1920), German military commander in Tanganyika, Rwanda Burundi and Namibia.

---

[8] Hildebrandt, History of the Church in Africa, pp.157, 200-202.
[9] Hildebrandt, *History of the Church in Africa*, pp. 226, 227.
[10] Hildebrandt, *History of the Church in Africa*, pp. 172, 173.

them.[11] Church and Mission had tried to protect the Herero. Yet the colonial war made it much more difficult to lead African people to Christ.

e. Defeat

The Germans were the first European power to abandon their colonies. This was not an example of decolonisation, but a change of colonial ruler. After their defeat in the *First World War* the Germans were forced to relinquish their colonies. Although it a long and tough war was required to defeat them in Tanzania (Tanganyika), they were easily displaced from the Cameroons, Togo and Namibia (South-West Africa). In 1921-1922 under the Treaty of Versailles the *League of Nations* gave temporary supervision of these territories to other countries. Tanganyika became a British mandate. Togoland was divided among the British and the French. The British joined their part to the Gold Coast. Burundi and Rwanda were mandated to Belgium. We saw that Cameroon was divided among the British and the French. Later the French part became the independent state of Cameroon together with the Southern section of British Cameroon. Northern British Cameroon was added to Nigeria (1972). South-West Africa was mandated to the *Union of South Africa* and became the independent state of Namibia in 1991.

---

[11] cf. Philip Ngunjiri, 'Germany Refuses to Apologize for Herero Holocaust' (through website).

Chapter 11

Missions and Colonialism 1885-1960

1. Protestant and Roman Catholic Missions

In the previous chapter we surveyed the way most of Africa was colonised by European powers after 1885. By this the question of the relationship between Missions and Colonialism arose.[1] We noted that Christian institutions from Europe had already started to send missionaries to Africa before that date. In general missionary presence preceded colonialist presence. Colonialist rule and Christian mission originated from different agencies in different times. Most European missionaries came from those countries that took part in the 'scramble for Africa', although quite a number of them did not work in regions ruled by their own people. In general they were motivated by the revivals and awakenings that had taken place since the early 18th century.

Here are the names of some of the missionary societies that started activities in Africa from about 1800. In 1792 the *Baptist Missionary Society* (B.M.S.) was founded by William Carey. In 1795 the *London Missionary Society* (L.M.S.) started as an interdenominational organisation (Anglicans, Methodists, Presbyterians, Congregationalists). In 1796 the *Edinburgh Missionary Society* (E.M.S.) and the *Glasgow Missionary Society* (G.M.S.) followed. Then in 1797, by Van der Kemp and others, the *Netherlands Society of Missionaries* was organised. The *Church Missionary Society*. (Evangelical Anglican) followed in 1799. In 1858 a society called the *Oxford and Cambridge Mission to Central Africa* was founded. The name was later changed to *Universities' Mission to Central Africa* (U.M.C.A.) and it first deployed activities in Malawi. In the 1870s the Free Church of Scotland and the Church of Scotland started organisations that were to work in Malawi as well.

In 1810 in the U.S.A. the American Board of Commissioners for Foreign Missions started to raise money for mission. The Baptist Foreign Mission Society (B.F.M.S.) followed in 1814, the American Bible Society in 1816, and the General Missionary Society (G.M.S.) in 1818, the F.M.B. of the Methodist Episcopalian Church, the F.M.S. in the Protestant Episcopalian Church (1820), the F.M.B. of the Presbyterian Church (1837).

---

[1] Besides this chapter, study: Shaw, *Kingdom*, pp. 139-158; Baur, *2000 Years*, pp. 103-152; Hastings, *Church in Africa*, pp. 177-188, 338-358; Ward, 'Africa', in: Hastings (ed), *World History*, pp. 203-209.

Missions and Colonialism 1885-1960

The Germans began to work in Africa in 1822 with various organisations, the *Rhenish Missionary Society* (1818), the *Berlin Missionary Society* (1824), the *Leipzig* and the *Bremen Missionary Societies* (1836), the *Bauern Mission*, of the *Hermannsburger Mission* (1853). The French started with the *Paris Missionary Society* (1824), the Swedish started in Africa in 1835, and the Norwegians in 1842.

The above mentioned missionary societies represent the majority of Protestant missions that started work in Africa before the *Berlin Conference* and the ensuing *Scramble for Africa*. These organisations were related to the mainline Protestant churches in Europe and America, and as such they could be named *Classical Missions*. Towards the end of the 19th century the classical missions slowed down in reaching out to new mission fields for reasons that we will see in chapter 15. However, other Protestant bodies took over the initiative of sending missionaries. In general they were private organisations, independent of denominational structures and clergy. As such they were sometimes called *Post-Classical Missions* or more often *Faith Missions*.[2] The first one to arrive in Africa (1878) was the *Livingstone Inland Mission*, founded by Fanny Guinness.

In the 20th century some classical denominations resumed the initiative by founding new missionary societies. To them belong some Dutch Missions, e.g. the *Reformed Mission League* who started work in Kenya in the 1960s and later in Malawi and other parts of Southern Africa, the *Christian Reformed Mission*, who work in Mozambique and South Africa, and the *Mission of the Reformed Congregations*, who work in Nigeria.

François Libermann (1802-1852), revived the Congregation of the Holy Ghost (Holy Ghost Fathers), which opened the new beginning of Roman Catholic mission in Africa.

The modern Roman Catholic Missions entered Africa later than most of the Protestant organisations. Actually there had been a lot of Roman Catholic missionary activity in the 16th and 17th centuries. But it had either aborted, or slowed down. Restoration of Roman Catholic influence in 19th century Europe eventually also affected Africa. Roman Catholic missions experienced a revival in the 1840s. To the old religious orders of the Benedictines, Dominicans, Franciscans, Jesuits, Augustinians, etc., a series of new orders and congregations were added. In the 19th century the *Holy Ghost Fathers* and the *White Fathers* were the first ones.

The Congregation of the Holy Ghost.[3] This Congregation was originally founded in 1703, for the purpose of preparing missionaries. Since 1765 the Pope entrusted it with direct care of mission in the French colo-

---

[2] Cf. Klaus Fiedler, *The Story of Faith Missions: From Hudson Taylor to Present Day Africa*, Oxford: Regnum, 1994.

[3] This religious order is also known as the *Spiritans*, or as the *Holy Ghost Fathers*.

nies. It suffered much from the French Revolution, and was threatened with extinction. In 1848 the dying Congregation was saved by François Libermann (1802-1852). Libermann was born in a Jewish family, but converted to Roman Catholicism in 1825. He opened a novitiate for the *Society of the Immaculate Heart of Mary* to send priests abroad, with a special interest in France's colonies. His order and the *Holy Ghost Fathers* merged. Libermann became superior general of the united Societies. The agreement included supervision of a seminary to train clergy for the French colonies, among them African black clergy. They started work on Africa's West Coast, and gradually spread to Angola, Senegal, Gambia, Sierra Leone, Gabon, Congo, Nigeria, Guinea, Spanish West Africa. They also started work on the East Coast, on Madagascar, Bagamoyo, and Kenya. Since the eventual downfall of Roman Catholic Mission in the 16th, 17th and 18th centuries, the *Holy Ghost Fathers* were practically the first Roman Catholic missionaries of the new era to arrive in Africa.

Secondly, the *White Fathers*. Charles Lavigerie (1825-1892), who was appointed by Pope Pius IX as the Archbishop of Algiers in 1867, used that position as a stepping stone to found the *Missionaries of our Lady of Africa of Algeria*, more popularly known as the *White Fathers*, since they dressed in flowing white Arab robes. Lavigerie's *see* included all of the Sahara and French Sudan; that is, all the nations bordering the Sahara, from the Atlantic Ocean eastward. In 1874 the work began to expand farther southward, to Equatorial Africa, Congo, Tanzania, and Malawi.

Charles Martial Allemand-Lavigerie (1825-1892), founder of the Missionaries of Our Lady of Africa (White Fathers), which started mission in various parts of Africa.

Other orders followed, like the Congregation of the Mission (Lazarists), the Oblates of Mary Immaculate, the Society of Mary, the Oratorians and Oblates of St. Francis de Sales, the Redemptorists, the Paulists, the Congregation of the Sacred Hearts of Jesus and Mary, the Priests of the Foreign Missions (Missions Etrangères). Among the Colleges of the regular orders for the training of missionaries may be mentioned: the College of St. Fidelis (Capuchin), the College of St. Anthony (Franciscan), the College of St. Isidore (Irish Franciscan), and the College of the Irish Augustinians, at Rome, the Seminary of Scheut, near Brussels (Congregation of the Immaculate Heart of Mary), the Veronese Institute and the Colleges of the Society of the Divine Word.[4]

---

[4] The Catholic Encyclopedia, Volume X, Online Edition 2000 by K. Knight, Nihil Obstat. Remy Lafort, Censor Imprimatur. +John M. Farley, Archbishop of New York

2. Competing Missionary Movements

Since the 16th century Protestantism and Roman Catholicism had been trying to counteract each other along the lines of Reformation and Counter Reformation. This religious struggle was continued in the African mission fields. It also was an important aspect of the relationship between the Colonialist State and the Mission organisations. In general Roman Catholic colonising countries favoured Roman Catholic Mission. Some of them even prohibited Protestant Missions to enter. On the other hand the culture of Protestant colonising powers would be more compatible with Protestant Missions. Yet, on both sides there were exceptions.

In the interest of their Lusitanian nationalism and because of the deeply rooted anti-clericalism the Portuguese often rejected interference by the Vatican and by other Roman Catholic nations. In some Portuguese colonies, especially Angola, but to a lesser extent in Mozambique, this created room for relatively relaxed relationships with the Anglo-Saxon world and for allowing missionaries from Protestant Europe and America.

King Leopold of Belgium deliberately prohibited non-Belgian RomanCatholic missionaries from entering the *Congo Free State*, though he permitted several Protestant missionaries to work there. The number of Belgian Roman Catholic missionaries did increase steadily after Belgium took over administration of the Congo in 1908, and their relationship with the Belgian administration was as close.

French colonial rule before 1900 prohibited Protestant Missions to enter, and was exclusively allowing Roman Catholic missionaries to work. In French West Africa the colonial administrators arrived in the interior before the missionaries, all of whom were French Roman Catholics. Most of these were *White Fathers*, supported by the French government in order to ensure their compliance in the work of colonial pacification. At the turn of the century the French government turned anti-clerical, ended diplomatic relations with the Vatican, and ended subsidies to the missionaries in the colonies. The missionaries were nevertheless permitted to remain.

Roman Catholic missionaries in Africa were loyal to the cult of Mary and more interested in obedience to the Church's teachings and authority than in literacy or access to the Bible, which they believed could easily be misunderstood its without proper filtering and interpretation by the church. Missionaries rarely addressed political or social issues out of that understanding.[5]

On the Protestant side there were many more exceptions. Protestant colonising powers did not make it impossible for Roman Catholic Missions to enter their territories. While generally the Protestant churches suffered in the French, Portu-

---

[5] Cf. on the many pages concerned: Hastings, *Church in Africa*; Hastings, *African Catholicism: Essays in Discovery*, London: SCM Press, 1989; Isichei, *A History of Christianity*. Bauer, *2000 Years of Christianity*;

guese and Belgian colonies 'because of opposition and lack of support, the Roman Catholic Church in British Africa got the same subsidies as the Protestants'.[6]

In a later stage the position of Roman Catholicism further improved. Protestant Missions turned critical to their own colonial governments as evidenced in their sympathy and support to African movements for independence. That is why colonial rulers began to mistrust Protestant missions. At the same time the rulers started to become friendlier to Roman Catholic missionary activities that seemed more in line with colonial paternalism and autocracy. Moreover governments of the Protestant countries of Europe and America have never prohibited their own Roman Catholic minorities to send missionaries overseas, or to receive them in their colonies. Here are some examples of Roman Catholic institutions organised in or from traditionally Protestant countries that trained missionaries for Africa: English, Irish, Scotch, American, and Canadian Colleges at Rome, Josephinum College at Columbus in Ohio, United States, American College at Louvain in Belgium, English Colleges at Valladolid in Spain and Lisbon in Portugal, Scotch College at Valladolid in Spain, St. Joseph's Seminary of the *Mill Hill Fathers* at London in Britain; St. Joseph's College at Rozendaal in The Netherlands.

The histories of Roman Catholicism and Protestantism in Africa contain many instants of mutual mistrust and a spirit of competition. The Colonial States often used this situation to their own political benefit. This pattern of negative relationship changed to a certain extent when, in the 1960's the colonial states were disbanded and replaced by African governmental systems. For Roman Catholicism the decolonisation process in Africa coincided with the *Second Vatican Council* (1962-65). Vatican II introduced a programme of *aggiornamento*, i.e. adaptation to the modern time. As a result of this the Roman Catholic Church in the Western homelands and in the former mission fields made a number of changes in its practical attitude towards Protestants. The Council opened the door to co-operation with Protestant Churches. The use of the vernacular, rather than Latin, in worship was prescribed. They also permitted, and even encouraged African Roman Catholics to read Protestant vernacular translations of the Bible, and strongly cooperated in joint Bible translation efforts.[7]

The scene has become much more African. By the early 1970s the European missionary priests and bishops began to leave Africa, voluntarily relinquishing their leadership positions to African churchmen. By the *African Synod* of 1994 ninety percent of the hierarchy was African.[8] The changes at least led to greater openness between Roman Catholics and Protestants. But Africanness and openness do not necessarily take away the fundamental differences in theology and ecclesi-

---

[6] Hildebrand, *History of the Church in Africa*, p.227.
[7] A product of such joint translation work is the new translation of the Bible into Chichewa, *Buku Loyera*, published by the Bible Society of Malawi in 1998.
[8] Cf. Thomas J. Reese (S.J.), *The Synod on the Church in Africa* (part 1), *The African Synod: You had to be there* (Part 2), America Press 1994.

ology. Sometimes Africans themselves contributed to reappearance of the old problems. As the missionaries left the African bishops often became more conservative than their white predecessors, and began to cut some of the reforms initiated by the missionary priests and bishops. This coincided with a political shift to an increasingly repressive series of regimes in the 1970s. In the 1990s a number of the more repressive African regimes were overthrown and a greater openness became possible again. Partly as a result of this, the African Church gathered in a great and important Synod, held in Rome, in 1994. This *African Synod* tried to list and solve some of the old and new problems that had risen. The Synod stressed the need to inculturate Christianity in the areas of liturgy, marriage, and reverence for ancestors.[9]

In general the Colonial States of the 19th and 20th centuries, either originating from Protestant Europe or from Roman Catholic Europe, were not very much interested in religion. They were very much the products of the *Enlightenment* and of *Secularism*, that did not have much use for the Church and for orthodox Christian beliefs. Christian Mission was not their first priority. The main focus was on an equilibrium of power and a maximum of economic profit. This they tried to reach through systems of *Indirect Rule* (the British), aiming at creating distance to the African, or *Direct Rule* (the French and the Portuguese), aiming at assimilation of the Africans. Christian Mission could disturb the equilibrium and diminish the profits. That is why British and French colonial officials often actively discouraged Christian mission work in Muslim areas. As a result of this Islam could consolidate its hold in certain African colonies. In this concern modern African political leaders do not seem to be much different from their colonial predecessors. Will the Church be able to challenge the State by redefining its Biblical call of mission to the Muslim masses?

Now we will have a closer look at this period in African history, especially highlighting the relationship or interaction between colonialism and mission.

3. Accusations

The unprecedented success of Christian missions in colonial Africa has been severely criticised from some quarters. Shaw mentions four major criticisms: (a) *collaboration* with the government, (b) cultural and religious *imperialism*, (c) *paternalism* in the church, and (d) *indoctrination* in education.[10]

The *first charge* is that 'missionary and colonial powers were allies in oppression ... partners in the crime of imperialism.' Missionaries and colonialists are seen as *soulmates*. Here Fiedler refers to the Marxist concept that reduces religion

---

[9] Hastings, African Catholicism: Essays in Discovery, pp. 128, 129. Aylward Shorter, 'The Roman Catholic Church in Africa Today', in: C. Fyfe et al. (eds) Christianity in Africa in the 1990s. Edinburgh: Centre of African Studies, University of Edinburgh, 1996, pp 22-38.

[10] Shaw, Kingdom, pp. 207-210.

to 'just a reaction to material deprivation'. In Marxist view Christianity was successful in Africa, because it was 'part and parcel of the colonial machinery of oppression', and the missionaries were collaborators in that machinery just as much as the explorers, traders, and soldiers. Missionaries 'had the important task of keeping the engine of colonialism from overheating and thereby destroying itself'. Not only did they lubricate the system by preserving its social relations, they also sweetened and softened the harsh impact of colonialism to the taste of the Africans, so that the Africans would be obedient subjects and useful workers. According to Marxist theory African Christianity would collapse at the end of colonialism. When the Marxists observed that their prediction did not come true, they labelled the period after 1960 as *neo-colonialism*, which enabled them to continue applying their theories to the growth of Christianity in Africa and elsewhere in the Third World.[11] The other accusations are closely related to this first one.

According to the *second charge* the missionaries were religious imperialists. They were intolerant of African culture and religion; to them there was nothing valuable in it.

The *third charge* is that missionaries demanded total control of the heart and the mind of the Africans. They ruled the church, even when Africans were capable of leadership. Paternalistically they addressed the African as if s/he were a child.

The *fourth of the charges*, mentioned by Shaw, is that the missionaries indoctrinated the Africans in a narrow pietistic way, emphasising spiritual and inward aspects, and neglecting political and social aspects.

4. Neither Soulmates nor Antagonists

Answering the main accusation, of *collaboration*, Fiedler says missions and colonialism cannot have been just soulmates, because of three indisputable facts. *First*, missions are older than colonialism. Christianity from its earliest beginning has been a missionary religion. As for Africa, missionaries reached 'a number of areas before any colonialist cast a coveting eye on them'. *Secondly*, the relationship between missions and colonial rulers was characterised by both cooperation and conflict. *Thirdly*, after the end of colonialism, neither church nor mission died. Church membership even grew considerably after the colonial period, to about 48% of the population by the end of the second millennium.

Fiedler admits that missionaries sometimes 'put the colonial system to their own use', profited from it, and cooperated with it. At the same time, however, missionaries resisted the cruelties and injustices of colonial rulers. Fiedler concludes that missionaries were neither soulmates nor antagonists of colonialism. Like the colonialists they were children of their times, but their agenda was older

---

[11] Fiedler, 'Soulmates', in: Ross (ed), *Faith*, pp. 218-221.

than and different from the agenda of colonialism. It was 'the agenda of the *Kingdom of Christ*, a kingdom not of this world, but with quite some effects on it'.[12]

Hanciles offers a more critical view. Regarding the charge of *cooperation* of missionaries with colonialists, he says that the abolition movement in a sense paved the way for colonialism, which he calls 'another more subtle and enduring form' of slavery. This leads him to the conclusion that 'Western missionaries, to a large extent, were conscious or unconscious agents' of colonialism.[13] Njoku follows this thought and lists various ways in which he thinks colonial governments have acted as a 'protective shield' or source of help for the missionaries.[14]

Shaw like Fiedler discerns two sides. He emphasises that colonialism was a mixed blessing for missions. Sometimes the 'colonial principle' distorted and undermined the Gospel message. Many missionaries realised the disadvantages, and though they cooperated, they also 'relished their role as leading critics of colonialism'. This 'double mindedness' was often rooted in the conviction of God's sovereign will that directs the nations, but also makes them morally and spiritually responsible.

Reacting to the accusation of *cultural and religious imperialism*, Shaw makes three observations:

First, missionaries often functioned as a bridge between Western culture and African tradition, making the collision between the two less damaging. *Further*, Africans became Christians voluntarily, and not as a result of some force of religious imperialism. Also, generally missionaries and not colonialists were the ones whose language work has helped African culture a lot. *Thirdly*, the strong conviction of the uniqueness and the saving power of Christ, did not bar missionaries from studying the traditional worldview of *African Traditional Religion*.

Regarding the accusation of colonialist *paternalism* Shaw admits that the policy of partnership by CMS's Venn and others was replaced by a *new paternalism* in the late 19th and early 20th centuries. Yet authoritarian patterns contributed to the fostering and empowerment of African leadership. Real understanding of their own discipleship gradually forced the missionaries to abandon paternalism. Anyhow, missionaries always have been dependent on African evangelistic zeal and expertise. As to the accusation of narrow pietistic indoctrination, Shaw admits that missionaries often equated modern thought with Christianity, as if Western technology and culture were Christian products. At the same time, however, he points to the fact that the mission schools produced the first leaders of African independence. Mission education implied the conviction that the coming Kingdom of Christ is more important than any Western colonial or African traditional power. This led to

---

[12] Fiedler, 'Soulmates', in: Ross: *Faith*, pp. 221-234.

[13] Hanciles, 'Back to Africa', in: Kalu (ed.), *African Christianity*, p.215.

[14] Njoku, 'The Missionary Factor in African Christianity 1884-1914', in: Kalu (ed.), *African Christianity: An African Story*, pp.246-252.

a conscious feeling for righteousness, both spiritually and also in the earthly structures. In agreement with Fiedler's view, Shaw concludes that missionaries were neither 'heroic angels', nor 'imperialistic devils'. Many were just 'fools of Christ', who worked paradoxically in this world, using 'foolish things to confound the wise'. Shaw is led to this conclusion by tracing developments in the history of colonialism and mission.

The era can be divided into three periods: 1885-1918, 1918-1945, 1945-1960.

5. The 'Hey Day of Missions', 1885-1918

After 1885, African Christianity changed. Missionary activities reached their climax, and the African church emerged. Shaw distinguishes three features (a) new *growth,* (b) a new kind of *cooperation*, (c) a new *aggressiveness*.

a. Growth

The number of converts grew enormously in the period after the *Berlin Conference* and the beginning of the scramble for Africa. Did Africans turn to Christianity because in many places they perceived the colonial power 'to exercise effective and beneficial control', or was it out of self-preservation, fearing the consequences of not being part of the new status quo? Probably Africans were not motivated by any of these two options. Colonialism as such was not perceived as a positive factor, and it cannot be seen as the cause of growth. Yet, Njoku thinks that the *Berlin Conference* indirectly contributed to growth, because 'it paved the way for stability and order in the missionary enterprise'. He says that 'the controlling and moderating presence of the colonial powers prevented' mission from becoming 'unduly disruptive and even explosive'.[15] Besides, the relative peace and order resulting from the *Pax Britannica* facilitated safe travel and communication by missionaries, and catechists. This helped the extension of religions. It supported the spread of the Gospel and the growth of the Church. Even Islam grew most under colonial rule.

Dramatic growth was seen: in Nigeria after 1888 in all places where the British colonial impact was strong; in Ghana after a British victory over the Ashanti in 1896; in South Africa after the *Union* of 1910 had brought Cape Colony, Transvaal and Orange Free State together; in Malawi after British rule was extended over the whole country in 1891; in Uganda after the British established a protectorate in 1894. Because of the apparent growth of Christianity, this period of early colonialism between 1885 (*Berlin Conference*) and 1918 (end of *World War I*) is sometimes indicated as the *'hey-day of missions'*.

---

[15] Chukwudi A. Njoku, 'The Missionary Factor in African Christianity 1884-1914', in: Ogbu U. Kalu (ed.), *African Christianity: An African Story*, University of Pretoria, 2005, p.220.

Missions and Colonialism 1885-1960

b. Cooperation

There was a kind of unofficial partnership between the missionaries and the colonialists, which benefited both, although their causes and aims differed. Roland Oliver calls this 'a happy accident'.[16] Mission was not just an extension of colonialism, but it profited from the 'law and order' brought by it. In most cases the Africans did not blame the missionaries for this. According to Ward for most Africans the colonial takeover belonged to a series of crises and changes that incorporated Africa into a global enlargement of scale, impinging on all aspects of life. The missionaries seemed to 'offer resources to cope with these radical changes'. Christianity, being the religion of the colonial powers, was 'equated with the modern, and modernisation was seen as essential for Africa, in material as well as intellectual and even spiritual terms'.[17] So, the colonial rulers and the missionaries were often enthusiastically welcomed.

George Grenfell (1849-1906), an English Baptist missionary, who worked in Africa for thirty-two years in Africa, the first three years in the Cameroons and then in the Congo.

As far as the imperialistic pride, the atrocities and the injustices of colonialism go, the attitude of missionaries had two sides. First, there are the historical facts of *missionary co-responsibility* for the beginning of colonial rule. The Scottish Missions in Malawi campaigned for the British government to colonise the country before the Portuguese would occupy the Shire Highlands. The British started to protect the Makololo in 1889, and finally, in 1891 the British Protectorate was proclaimed. The C.M.S. asked Britain to take over Uganda because of the disorder in the country and the threat by Germany. B.M.S.-missionary Grenfell in Congo advocated the advent of Belgian colonial rule because of the 'chaotic sway' of local chiefs. Cardinal Lavigerie of the White Fathers lobbied European powers to combat slavery by taking over political power in East Africa. Ndebele king Lobengula lost his land to Cecil Rhodes because L.M.S.-missionary Helm in 1888 on purpose wrongly translated a contract.

On the other side missions were *opponents* of aspects of colonialism. Ward says, they 'were predisposed to outspoken criticism of the perceived shortcomings or injustices of colonial rule'.[18] Missionaries disclosed the atrocities in the rubber plantation economy of the 'Congo Free State'.[19] In East Africa they protested against forced labour. C.M.S. missionary Miller was co-

---

[16] Roland Oliver, *The Missionary Factor in East Africa*, London: Longmans, 1965².

[17] Ward, 'Africa', in: Hastings (ed), *World History*, p. 218.

[18] Ward, 'Africa', in: Hastings (ed.), *World History*, p. 217; Hildebrandt, *History of the Church in Africa*, p. 228.

[19] Cf. Hastings, *The Church in Africa*, pp. 434-437.

responsible for the foundation of an organisation for political freedom in Northern Nigeria. In the German and Portuguese territories missionaries protested against administrative policies and mistreatment of people.

c. Aggressiveness

The early colonial period produced changes in the character of the missionaries and in the Africans who adopted the Christian faith. A different consciousness and attitude emerged, according to Shaw characterised by a 'new aggressivenes', intensifying the struggle for leadership between missionaries and African converts. Unlike the older missionaries like Henry Venn who had tried to *africanise* church leadership, the new missionaries wanted to keep leadership in their own hands.

The new attitude was inspired by various ideas: (a) the thought that a superior Western Christian civilisation was called to put the world under the Kingdom of God, (b) the belief that Christ's Second Coming was to be drawn near by the evangelisation of the world, (c) concentration on salvation of the individual. The consequences were that the shaping of africanised churches became less emphasised.

Most of the new missionaries were younger and less educated than the older type. Yet, their contribution to language work, converting and schooling Africans was considerable. The spirit of new self-consciousness also touched the African Christians. Most of them were converted through the work of fellow African catechists, teachers and evangelists. This is how they met with Christianity in their own vernacular languages. This is generally true for the classical 'mainline' churches, it is even more true for those churches who broke away from the missionary bodies and went on independently.

The 'new aggressiveness' sometimes led to outspoken protests against colonialism, and against white domination in the church and in the state. In Nigeria the Anglican assistant bishop James Johnson ('Holy Johnson') propagated an African version of Christianity. Charles Domingo in Malawi, after his clash with the *Livingstonia Mission*, came under the influence of Joseph Booth and Ethiopianism. He was convinced that European 'Christendom' had betrayed the Christian faith.[20] Much more radical was John Chilembwe, another pupil of Booth. In 1915 he initiated an armed rising against the British rulers in Malawi, thus becoming an early symbol of African nationalism.[21] The new consciousness of independency was encouraged during the *First World War* when many Western missionaries left

---

[20] Cf. Harry W.Langworthy (ed.), *Letters of Charles Domingo*, University of Malawi, Sources for the Study of Religion in Malawi No. 9, 1983.

[21] G.Shepperson, and Th. Price, *Independent African: John Chilembwe and the Origins, Setting and Significance of the Nyasaland Rising of 1915*, Edinburgh U.P., 1958, re-edited: Blantyre: Claim, 2000; Patrick Makondesa, *The Church History of Providence Industrial Mission 1900-1940*, Zomba: Kachere, 2006.

missionary work and church, leaving the leadership practically in the hands of Africans.[22]

6. Strained Partnership, 1918-1945

Although the First World War had left much of mission and church in African hands, after 1918 the returning whites, even more than before, took over the responsibilities. Shaw says, 'the control in Africa by colonist and missionary grew in size and scope'. Europeans took all the important initiatives. Yet, inwardly the structures of imperialism and colonialism weakened, as did the idea of the superiority of Western civilisation. Liberal thinking undermined the fundamental stance of classical churches. Gradually the European majority at international mission conferences gave way to the presence of non-Europeans. Missionaries began to question the validity of classical colonialism. In the meantime African Christianity and missionary presence continued to grow.

A new vision of colonialism led the colonial rulers to greater attention to *education*. In a process of education Africans had to be taught how to exist in the modern world, and how to govern themselves independently. Until reaching that point the African would be under colonial rule. With this educational aim in mind the *Phelps-Stokes Commission*, a missionary inspired and privately financed group, travelled about Africa in the early 1920's. One of its members was the Ghanaian educationalist and Ethiopianist church leader J.E.K. Aggrey.[23] The Commission saw many mission schools, but generally considered them insufficient. Yet, in 1924 the Commission 'called for partnership between missions and government, not separate development'. They advised the colonial governments to make use of the existing network of mission schools. In order to make them meet the educational requirements, the governments should subsidise, inspect and improve these schools.[24] Soon many mission schools worked under the new regulations. Generally the work of the Commission elevated and affirmed the 'school in the bush' and it underlined the importance of cooperation between black and white.[25] The advantage was great progress of education, stimulating new missionary initiatives.

However, for the missions and the churches there were also disadvantages. (a) The energy of mission and church sometimes was more directed at education than at the spreading of the Gospel. (b) Mission schools could easily become an exten-

---

[22] For the effects of the First World War on Livingstonia Mission, see: J. McCracken, *Politics and Christianity in Malawi 1875-1940: The Impact of the Livingstonia Mission in the Northern Province*, Cambridge U.P., 1977, pp. 266-276.
[23] Cf. Hildebrandt, *History of the Church in Africa*, p.203.
[24] The *Phelps-Stokes Commission Report* of 1924 was followed by a Colonial Office Memorandum of 1925, entitled, *Education Policy in British Tropical Africa*, in which these regulations were described. See also: Verstraelen Gilhuis, *A New Look at Christianity in Africa*, pp. 39-61 ['African Education as seen from Le Zoute 1926'], especially pp. 46-50.
[25] Ward, 'Africa', in: Hastings (ed), *World History*, pp. 218, 219.

sion of the colonial structure. (c) Government control could weaken the ties between church and schools and secularise the schools.

West Africa especially became the scene of widespread mission initiatives in education. In Nigerian Igbo land the Irish missionary Shanahan established many schools. In Ghana and Cameroon Christianisation programs through schooling were very successful, although there were problems when the German *Basel Mission* had to leave temporarily in 1916, and the work had to be taken over by British Baptists. In Togo the Presbyterians continued schoolwork that was started by the *Basel Mission*, after the latter's departure due to the *First World War*. The Liberian 'American Negro Bureaucracy' limited education to themselves, excluding the interior tribes. In Congo the Belgian government favoured Roman Catholic schools to the disadvantage of Protestant education.

In South Africa, Christianity flourished. Although the British colonial rule had practically ended by the establishment of the Union in 1910, colonial thinking was still alive in racialist legislation. Training of black leaders continued by e.g. the work of the *Paris Evangelical Mission Society* and by the University of Fort Hare, founded in 1916.

Especially in Kenya the tension between missions and the colonial government intensified. The bone of contention was the increasing number of white settlers occupying African land. There was tension between missionaries and Africans, for instance in the Kikuyu girls' circumcision crisis of 1929.[26] Missionary actions against this practice caused anger of the Kikuyu traditionalists and eventually resulted in the formation of African Independent Churches.[27] After the *Africa Inland Mission*, other missions too started moving into the interior of Kenya, e.g. the *Church of Scotland Mission* and the *C.M.S.*, and the *Seventh Day Adventists*. In 1890 the Roman Catholic *Holy Ghost Fathers* entered Kenya, first at Mombasa, by 1899 they had reached Limuru. Beside the white missionaries, there were also early black missionaries, e.g. Shadrack Mliwa who worked for the C.M.S. among the Kikuyu, and Yohana Mbila, one of the first *Church of God* workers at Kima.[28]

7. Final Period, 1945-1960

The defeat of Germany and the liberation of Europe contributed to a global desire for freedom. Africans saw the white man's divisions, and realised that whites could be defeated. In Africa winds of independence began to blow, even leading to the formation of liberation movements. De Gaulle's plan of 1958 for autonomous

---

[26] On this and related issues, see Klaus Fiedler, 'Bishop Lucas' Christianization of Tradtional Rites, the Kikuyu Female Circumcision Controversy, and the Cultural Approach of Conservative German Missionaries', in: Noel O. King, and Klaus Fiedler (eds), Robin Lamburn, *From a Missionary Notebook, The Yao of Tunduru and other Essays*, Saarbrücken: Breitenbach, 1991.

[27] Hildebrandt, *History of the Church in Africa*, pp.231, 232.

[28] Cf. Hildebrandt, *History of the Church in Africa*, p.186.

African states within a federal French community never became a reality, but in 1960 it changed to a plan for full independence which France's colonies received in the 1960s.[29] In 1957 colonial Gold Coast became the independent nation of Ghana. Its first leader Kwame Nkrumah promoted a pan-African movement of liberation. In 1962, after the Mau-Mau rebellion of the mid-1950s, Kenya became independent.

The *négritude* movement of Léopold Sédar Senghor was one of the African expressions of culture and literature that stimulated independence. The rediscovery of African culture had been anticipated in Tempel's book *Bantu Philosophy* (1945). The desire for a real African Christianity was gradually emerging, although most missionaries were not yet conscious of the necessity of indigenisation of faith and doctrine.

In the meantime the number of Christians kept on growing, for instance through the *East Africa Revival* climaxing in the 1950s. In this decade before political independence many mission-founded churches became autonomous in part or completely. Both missionaries and African Christians agreed to the training of leaders aimed at the transition from mission to autonomous church. Theological departments and colleges were shaped to that end. It was widely realised among whites and blacks that only in this way African Christianity could escape from secularism and syncretism. Examples in East Africa are the *Presbyterian Church* which became completely independent in 1961, John Gatu becoming its first General Secretary, the *Anglican Churches* in Kenya and Uganda, the *Africa Inland Church*, the *Lutheran Chuches* in Tanzania. In general the churches progressed, although Christianity was hindered by Mau Mau violence in Kenya and Muslim violence in Sudan. By 1960 mission and church in the colonial era had ended, because - as we have seen in chapters 9 and 10- most of the African states had begun their history of independence.

---

[29] Hastings, *History of African Christianity*, p. 132.

Chapter 12

African Instituted Churches

1. Two Traditions

The term *African Instituted Churches* (A.I.C.)[1] generally means 'churches founded in Africa, by Africans and for Africans'. There are alternative terms, such as *African Independent Churches*, *African Initiated Churches*, *African Indigenous Churches*, and *African International Churches*,[2] all maintaining the same abbreviation: A.I.C.[3] They refer to churches that emerged outside and independent from churches instituted as a result of the work by 'classical missions'. *'Classical missions'* then are the missionary organisations of 'mainline churches' from Europe and North America. The term *'mainline churches'* is often used for the Roman Catholic Church, and for the churches coming from the main-stream of the 16th century Reformation, excluding the off-spring of the more radical wings of the Reformation. These terms have relative significance, because often they can only partly define the real situation, which is rather more complex.[4]

We make four observations. *First*, all African churches, including the mainline churches, have become independent, at least autonomous, in the second half of the 20th century; they do not necessarily behave like the Western 'mother' churches. Besides, after the 1960s Africans have instituted churches similar to the established classical type, although classical missions were not instrumental in their foundation. *Secondly*, Western missions of Mennonites, Baptists, Pentecostals, Adventists and others, derived from the more radical wings of the Reformation, though dubbed as independent, generally did not behave differently from the missions of the established mainline churches. The most essential difference (although not in all cases) was that the former started mission work in Africa later. Although less than the classical missions, they too gave rise to African independency outside their 'daughter'-churches. *Thirdly*, Protestant mainline churches in Africa are not necessarily more faithful to the principles of Reformation Orthodoxy than African instituted churches. Neither being mainline classicist nor being African instituted guarantees that a church is more pure or true. *Fourthly*, right from the beginning of

---

[1] Apart from this section, study also: Shaw, *Kingdom*, pp. 239-257; Baur, *200 Years*, pp. 349-359; Hastings, *Church in Africa*, pp. 437-539; Ward, 'Africa', in: *World History*, pp. 221-226; Walls, *Missionary Movement*, pp. 85-89, 92-93, 111-118.
[2] Afe Adogame and Lizo Jafta, 'Zionist, Aladura and Roho: African Instituted Churches', in: Kalu et. Al. (eds) *African Christianity*, pp. 310-313.
[3] The abbreviation A.I.C. can be confusing, as it is also used for the churches established by the *Africa Inland Mission*, which do not belong to the African Instituted Churches.
[4] Cf. Walls, *Missionary Movement*, p. 114.

classical missions in Africa, there was the powerful factor of African initiative. Therefore, it is impossible to separate the history of African instituted churches after 1890, from early features of independency inside the main mission founded churches.

Ward stresses that 'it would be wrong to think too much of rigid contrasts between two conflicting traditions'.[5] Both the mainline mission founded churches and the *African Instituted Churches* are very diverse. Both demonstrate a wide spectrum of judgments about doctrine, church organisation, ethical behaviour, and the relation to African tradition. Walls comes to the same conclusion. He says the whole of African Christianity is likely to be a 'new religious movement' reworking old and newly found aspects of the Christian faith. Therefore the distinction between 'independent' and 'older' churches is of decreasing value, as both are 'new' manifestations of Christianity.[6]

2. Early African Initiatives

Apart from North Africa, Egypt, Nubia and Ethiopia, where African churches founded by Africans emerged and partly vanished, there is not much to tell about African Christian initiative prior to the end of the 18th century. Independent contributions were made by King Alfonso I in Congo and his successors, by the prophetess Beatrice (Kimpa Vita), who met her unhappy death in 1706, by Mother Lena who independently preserved and continued the work of the Moravian missionary Schmidt, by the ex-slave Ottobah Cuguano whose book was instrumental to the emergence of the anti-slavery movement, and others.

Yet, as Walls says, African Christianity 'is to a surprising extent the result of African initiatives'. The Evangelical Revivals of the 18th and 19th centuries not only put Europeans on the track of mission, they also directly ignited many Africans. The Sierra Leonean Church, founded by ex-slaves, was not a missionary creation. The settlers brought their own preachers with them, and in the course of years 'they supplied African missionaries in quantities for the rest of West Africa' and elsewhere. In Sierra Leone the *Church Missionary Society*. alone, 'over a 60-year period produced a hundred ordained men, in addition to countless catechists, teachers, and other mission workers'. Walls also points to the 'vital importance' of African evangelists and catechists in countries like Uganda and Nigeria. At a later stage there was the emergence of dynamic and influential preachers, whose effectiveness was recognised by the mission churches, although they did not easily fit into the organisational structures of those churches. Examples are William W. Harris in Ivory Coast, Sampson Oppong in Ghana, Joseph Babalola in Nigeria,

---

[5] Ward, 'Africa', in: Hastings (ed), *World History*, p. 223.
[6] Walls, *Missionary Movement*, pp. 112, 113.

Walter Mattita in Lesotho. Their work led to a 'massive expansion' of existent mission-led churches.[7]

Before the era of colonialism (1885-1960) the Christianisation of Sub-Saharan Africa, though in many aspects dependent on African initiative, was led by Western missions. Subsequently these missions, partly because of pressure by Africans, took the initiative of founding African churches under missionary tutelage. By the end of the colonial period missionary supervision ended.

Since about 1890, Africans had begun to institute churches, completely independent from the mission-led churches. The feature of *separatism* in the history of Protestantism may have been one of the causes, and also the dislike of missionary *authoritarianism* and the desire to keep something of *African tradition*. Shaw thinks that behind this there is a deeper cause. He points to the problem of evil and deliverance from evil. Westerners tend to look at it *philosophically*, whereas to Africans evil first of all is a *functional* problem. Africans saw evil in how the missionaries dealt with them, and they reacted to it. Successively this evil appeared to the Africans with different faces. That is why the reactions also were different.

In the movement of church independency before 1960, we discern three phases, (a) the *Ethiopianist* reaction, (b) the emergence of *Prophet-Healing churches*, (c) the East- and West African *Revivals*. These three phases were followed by a period of explosive growth of all kinds of *independency*. In the following sections we will look at these phases or waves.

3. The Rise of Ethiopianism, 1890-1910

The first wave of independency was a reaction against the evil of *'humiliation and shame'* caused by missionaries' disrespect or contempt. This reaction led to the movement of *Ethiopianism*, the separation of churches from the missionary churches.[8] The separations were motivated by the desire for having the leadership in African hands, and not so much by questions of doctrine and worship practice. Ethiopianism, triggered by the Ethiopian victory over Italian invaders in 1896, looked for an all African theocracy of racial justice and hope, anticipating - in Shaw's view - the *Black Theology* movement in the 1960s.

Ethiopianism was fed by Biblical notions or perceptions referring to connections between Africa and

J.E.K. Aggrey

---

[7] Walls, *Missionary Movement*, pp. 85-88.
[8] Cf. Hastings, *History of African Christianity*, pp. 35-38, 219-221.

African Instituted Churches

the Old and New Testament histories, like the stretched out hand of Ethiopia, rather Kush, in *Psalm* 68: 3, the Queen of Sheba's visit to Solomon and the 'Solomonic' dynasty of Ethiopian kings, the story of the Falasha linkage with ancient Israel, the flight of Jesus to Egypt, the African who carried Jesus' cross, the journey to and from Jerusalem by the Treasurer to the Queen Mother (Candace) of Meroe Afro-American returnees motivated by anti-slavery values were especially interested in searching for heroic roots of black Africa's past, and the heroic destiny of the Negro Race.

Hanciles characterises *Ethiopianism* as 'the most potent African Christian reaction', which 'epitomized anti-slavery, sowed the seeds of African nationalism, and enshrined alternative visions of African Christianity that found full expression in African independent church movements'.[9] Kalu, seems to position the beginnings of *Ethiopianism* In West Africa, and thinks it started in about 1860. He views it 'as an example of African response to colonial Christianity'.[10] In the descriptions by of Barrett[11] and Sundkler[12] *Ethiopianism* started in South Africa, a bit later. Let us now look at some phenomena of *Ethiopianism* in South-, South-Central-, and West Africa respectively.

In *South Africa* the Ethiopianist movement began in 1884, when Nehemiah Tile († 1891) left the white controlled Wesleyan Methodist Church in Tembuland, and founded the *Thembu National Church*.[13] This was followed by separations from Methodist, Presbyterian and Congregationalist churches. An important role was played by the Afro-American *African Methodist Episcopal Church* (A.M.E.C.) that had entered Africa. Wesleyan Methodist Mangena M. Mokone († 1936), in protest against racial segregation, first founded his *Ethiopian Church* in Pretoria,[14] which united with the A.M.E.C. of Bishop Henry M. Turner, who visited South Africa in 1898, contributed to the spirit of Ethiopianism. Turner befriended Mokone's assistant James M. Dwane († 1915), who had fiercely reacted against white church leadership. The famous song 'Bless, o Lord, our Land of Africa',[15] is a product of the Ethiopian movement, through its composer Mankayi Enoch Sontonga († 1905), who had studied at mission controlled *Lovedale Institution*, but had become a

---

[9] Hanciles, 'Back to Africa: White Abolitionists and Black Missionaries', in: Kalu (ed.), *African Christianity*, p. 215.
[10] Ogbu U. Kalu, 'Ethiopianism in African Christianity', in: Kalu et. al. (eds) *African Christianity*, p.262.
[11] David B. Barrett, *Schism and Renewal in Africa: An Analysis of Six Thousand Contemporary Religious Movements*, Nairobi: OUP, 1968.
[12] Bengt Sundkler, *Bantu Prophets in South Africa*, London: Oxford U.P., 1948.
[13] J.A. Millard, 'Tile, Nehemia, d. 1891: Thembu National Church, South Africa', Website: http://www.dacb.org/stories/southafrica/tile1.html
[14] Cf. Hildebrandt, *History of the Church in Africa*, p.175.
[15] M.E. Sontonga, *Nkosi Sikelel'i-Afrika*; in Chichewa: *Mbuye dalitsani Afrika* (Nyimbo za Mulungu/ Hymns for Malawi, no. 375).

member the African Presbyterian Church, founded by Pambani J. Mzimba who had similarly abandoned the Presbyterians of Lovedale.[16]

In *South-Central Africa*, the initiative to independency was taken by a white missionary. In *Malawi* the Australian missionary Joseph Booth (†1932) inspired the foundation of various independent churches. His book, *Africa for the African* (1897)[17] is also a straightforward protest against colonialism. His pupil John Chilembwe (†1915) was also directly influenced by Afro-American Baptists. Chilembwe's rising against British colonial power in 1915, belongs to the very rare cases of the Ethiopianists resorting to violence.[18]

Enoch Mankayi Sontonga (1873-1905), a Xhosa from the Eastern Cape, wrote the hymn Nkosi Sikelel'i Afrika.

Ethiopianism in *West Africa* started with the missionary activities of Afro-American returnees in Sierra Leone and with the vision of C.M.S. secretary Henry Venn's vision of African leadership. Through Sierra Leone it spread to Liberia, Gold Coast, and Nigeria. Leading figures in the movement were James Johnson (†1917), often named 'Holy Johnson' of Freetown and later of the C.M.S. mission among the Yoruba in Nigeria; the Methodist layman J.E. Casely Hayford († 1930), who adapted the African name Ekra-Agiman, and contributed to the emergence of an African literature. Then there was the Yoruba preacher David Brown Vincent († 1917) who also advocated a non-missionary version of African Christianity; he took on his original African name Mojola Agbebi, and in 1888 he seceded from the Baptist missionary work to found the *Native Baptist Church*. In 1913 Agbebi became the first president of the *African Communion of Independent Churches*.[19] In the field of africanisation of education, contributions were made by Henry Car, and especially by the Ghanaian J.E.K. Aggrey († 1927). Trained as a minister of A.M.E. Zion Church in America, Aggrey also was a leader of Ghana's model school at Achimota, established in 1924.[20] Generally, Ethiopianists remained within the boundaries of orthodox Christianity, but some adopted deviating ideas, like E.M. Lijadu († 1926), who meant that the Yoruba deity Orunmila was a pre-figuration of Jesus'.[21] Many Ethiopianists felt inspired by the Afro-American Liberian missionary and statesman Edward Wilmot Blyden (†

---

[16] Kalu, 'Ethiopianism', in: Kalu et. al. (eds), *African Christianity*, pp.274, 275.
[17] Joseph Booth, *Africa for the African*, 1897 [re-edited by Laura Perry and re-published as Kachere text no.6, Blantyre: Claim/ Kachere, 1996].
[18] See chapter 14.
[19] Robert C. Brockman, 'Agbebi, Mojola (David Brown Vincent) 1860 to 1917: Native Baptist Church, Nigeria', Website: http://www.dacb.org/stories/nigeria/agbebi.html
[20] Hildebrandt, History of the Church in Africa, p.203.
[21] Kalu, 'Ethiopianism', in: Kalu et. al. (eds), *African Christianity*, p.271.

African Instituted Churches

1912), who 'foresaw the coming shift in the centre of the gravity of Christianity from the north to the south Atlantic, and its import for African Christianity'.[22]

After 1910 the Ethiopian movement became Africa-wide. It also became more political, as can be seen in the activities of Reuben Spartas, in *Uganda*, who not only founded the *African Greek Orthodox Church* but also tried to realise nationalist and pan-african ideas. In *Kenya* there was a wave of independency, for example the 'Luo-schisms' resulting in the *Nomiya Luo Mission* cutting its ties with the Anglican Church in 1914. The *Mario Legio of Africa* split from Roman Catholicism.[23] By becoming political the Ethiopian movement lost its specific ecclesiastical characteristics and became part of a general movement for African independence from colonial rule. Kalu described the 'swan song' of Ethiopianism by summing up some reasons of its demise. It was absorbed in the period between the World Wars, by the emergence of a wider pan-african ideology and a shift from cultural to political nationalism.[24]

4. The Rise of Prophet-Healing Churches

William Wadé Harris, influential prophetic preacher in West Africa (from: A History of Christianity in Ghana, Waterville, through Hildebrandt, History)

The *Prophet-Healing Churches* not only address the evil of foreign leadership, they also react against the evil that 'destroys life', such as 'illness, infertility, pestilence, famine and sudden or inexplicable death'. According to *African Traditional Religion* these evils were caused by ancestral and demonic spirits and brought about by sorcery and witchcraft. Traditional healers had been unable to have victory over these powers, but the Christian prophets could, because their power originated in Christ.

Yet, religious leaders from the traditional context, like the Xhosa Nxele and Ntsikana, and the Igbo Dede Ekeke Lolo, could shift by adopting some aspects of Christianity and thus be successful as healers. In general the new prophets emerged from the newly established Christian churches. An example is the revivalist preacher and wandering Liberian prophet William Wadé Harris (†1929). Sundkler calls him the instigator of 'the greatest Christian mass movement on the West Coast.[25] Harris preached 'the bringing of all nations

---

[22] Kalu, 'Ethiopianism', in: Kalu et. al. (eds), *African Christianity*, p.272.

[23] Adogame and Jafta, 'Zionists, Aladura, and Roho: African Instituted Churches', in: Kalu et.al. (eds), *African Christianity*, p.315.

[24] Ogbu U. Kalu, African Christianity: From the World Wars to Decolonization', in Kalu et.al. (eds), African Christianity, pp. 333-341.

[25] Sundkler and Steed, *A History of the Church in Africa*, p.780.

under the political, peaceful rule on the earth of the Messiah Jesus of Nazareth'. His eschatological message was sometimes understood as politically subversive. He was accused of taking part in the rising of the Grebo people and was thrown into jail, where according to his own witness he was called as a prophet in a vision by the Archangel Gabriel. After being released, he itinerated in Gold Coast and Ivory Coast and Gold, preaching, and healing. He pointed at the imminent *Parousia*, and called people to immediate conversion to God in Christ, to destroy fetishes, to reject idols, to conquer traditional spirits, and to accept the authority of the Bible.[26] Perhaps between 60,000 and 100,000 people who had repented, were baptised by him. In Gold Coast he was only for three months, yet his preaching led to the growth of existing churches, like the Methodists and the Roman Catholics, and also in the Nzima distict to the springing up of four indigenous independent churches. In 1914 Harris was arrested in Ivory Coast, a country which at that time had not been touched by the Gospel, except for some work by Roman Catholics since 1895. Harris was accused of revolutionising the people. Later Harris told how the French administrators who interrogated him, mocked his prophetic ministry and the Bible. He was extradited to his homeland Liberia, where he was kept under house arrest until his death. Harris did not aim at starting new churches. His work led to the growth of mission churches in the region, among others the Methodist Church. Besides, after 1923 with the help of Methodist missionary Platt,[27] Harrist independent congregations arose where there were no established churches, for example in the *Church of the Twelve Apostles* in the Gold Coast. Hildebrandt calls Harris 'another one of the outstanding figures of African Church History'. He went where God directed him, without asking gifts or building a personality cult. In this way he 'was able to point thousands of people to Christ'.[28]

Another prophet of the faith-healing movement is Garrick Sokari Daketima Braide (†1918). He was of Igbo-Kalabari birth, originating from south-eastern Nigeria. After his conversion, in an Anglican church in New Calabar, he gradually started a very successful prophetic preaching, accompanied by healing, dreams and visions. He declared himself to be Elijah II. In 1916 he left the Anglican Church together with many followers, because he did not find sufficient recognition for his ministry. Suspicious because of his popularity, the authorities arrested Braide. In 1918 he died in jail. Followers founded *Christ Army Church*, an Ethiopianist type of church that 'still continues to this day'.[29]

---

[26] Graham Duncan and Ogbu U. Kalu, 'Bakuzufu: Revival Movements and Indigenous Appropriation in African Christianity', in: Kalu et. Al. (eds), *African Christianity*, pp. 285, 286.

[27] Hastings, *Church in Africa*, pp.505-507.

[28] Hildebrandt, *History of the Church in Africa*, pp. 153-155, 202.

[29] Duncan and Kalu, 'Bakuzufu: Revival Movements', in: Kalu et. Al. (eds), *African Christianity*, pp. 288,289; Hildebrandt, *History of the Church in Africa*, p.204.

West Africa was also the cradle of the *Aladura-movement* (aladura = praying people).[30] The earliest group was the *Cherubim and Seraphim* (C&S), originally it was an interdenominational society of men and women of prayer against magic, witchcraft and idols, but in 1925, as a reaction against 'intolerance by mission churches' an independent church was established. The wandering preacher Moses Tunolase Orimolade († 1933),[31] together with a young woman, Christiana Abiodun Emmanuel, née Akinsowon († 1994),[32] became the nucleus of the network of faith-healing communities of the C&S. The *Christ Apostolic Church* (C.A.C.) originated in an Anglican prayer group by three Nigerians, Joseph Babalola, Isaac Akinyele, and David Odubanjo. In the 1930s especially the revivalist preaching of Joseph Babalola did much to spread the *Aladura- movement* in Nigeria.[33] The *Church of the Lord-Aladura* (C.L.A.) was founded in 1930 by Josiah Ositelu, after the Anglican Church suspended him as a catechist. Another Aladura church is the *Celestial Church of Christ* (C.C.C.), founded in 1947 by Samuel Bilewu Oschoffa († 1985).[34]

In *eastern Africa* it was the *Arathi* and the *Abarohi* (= people of the Holy Spirit) that expressed the prophet-healing movement. Like in the Aladura there is an element of Pentecostalism in these movements (see chapter 19, section 5).

In *Congo* Simon Kimbangu († 1951) was the prophetic figure of independency. As a lay evangelist of the Baptist Church his preaching and healing had been very successful. But the Belgian colonial government and the Roman Catholic Church saw him as a threat. In 1921 he was condemned to 120 lashes and death. The Belgian king Albert changed the punishment into life imprisonment. In Lubumbashi (Elizabethville) he remained a prisoner until his death. However, his influence continued, and eventually led to the establishment of the flourishing *Church of Jesus Christ on Earth through the prophet Simon Kimbangu*, probably 'the biggest independent Church in Africa'. In 1971/1972, beside with the Roman Catholics, the Protestants and the Greek Orthodox, the Kimbanguists were allowed by President Mobutu to be one of the only

Simon Kimbangu (c.1889-1951) founded a numerous Church, although he himself spent most of his life in prison.

---

[30] Adogame and Jafta, 'Zionists, Aladura and Roho', in: Kalu et.al. (eds) *African Christianity*, pp. 316-318.
[31] Cf. 'Orimolade Tunolase, Moses 1879 to 1933: United Church of Cherubim and Seraphim, Nigeria', Website: http://www.dacb.org/stories/nigeria/orimolade.htlm
[32] Cf. Ebeye Boniface, 'Christiana Abiodun Emmanuel 1907 to 1994: Cherubim and Seraphim Society, Nigeria', Website: http://www.dacb.org/stories/nigeria/abiodun.html
[33] Hastings, *Church in Africa*, pp. 513-518.
[34] Cf. Elijah Olu Akinwumi, 'Oschoffa Samuel Bilewu 1909-1985: Celestial Church of Christ (Aladura), Nigeria', Website: http://www.dacb.org/stories/nigeria/oschaffa.html

four denominations in Congo. The Kimbanguist Church is one of the few African Independent Churches that are members of the *World Council of Churches*.[35] Kimbangu's successors and followers allowed the members of the Kimbanguist Church to keep many tradional beliefs, trying at the same time to keep up 'the appearance of being a type of Christianity'.[36]

In *South Africa* Zulu Zionism was an expression of the prophet-healing movement. Zionism was inspired by the American Pentecostal J.A. Dowie of Chicago and the South African N.G.K. missionary Le Roux, who promised complete spiritual and bodily healing in a newly established Jerusalem on the earth, before the speedy coming of the Messiah. Thousands of black Zion churches emerged, with a membership of 4 million (1990). One of the 'Zulu prophets' was Isaiah Shembe († 1935). He was very influential and controversial as well. In 1911 he founded the *amaNazaretha Church* and later the centres of Ekuphakameni near Durban as the New Jerusalem, and mountain top Inhlangakazi, calling himself the 'Promised One'. Stress was put on leadership, worship and hymns. There is a difference with the Zion movement in that the focus is on Jehovah of the Old Testament, and on the leader himself. His son Johannes Galilee Shembe († 1967) and grandson Londa Shembe († 1988) succeeded him as leaders of the church.[37] In chapter 21, under the heading of Pentecostalism, the account of Zionism will be continued.

Independent Churches among the Shona of *Zimbabwe* are profusely described by M.L. Daneel. In three volumes he deals with their history, and with the kind of 'messianic' leadership and the fissions that he observes in Independency, especially in the prophet-healing churches. Daneel looks positively at these characteristics. He understands independent 'messianic' leadership as a 'translation and interpretation of the work of Christ' and within the processes of fragmentation and fission of independent church groups he sees seeds for Christian unity. In 1972 Daneel founded the *Conference of Shona Independent Churches*, popularly referred to as *Fambidzano*.[38]

Prophet-healing churches have a mythical understanding of Biblical Zion, believed to have come from heaven in their own Zion mountain-top-centres. They show no interest in the Ethiopianists' idea of 'Africa for the Africans', being non-political in principle.

In this section we have seen that the prophet-healing movement led to a wave of *African Instituted Churches* all over Sub-Saharan Africa. They were sometimes very different from one another. Walls tried to describe some general characteristiscs. All of them were characterised by two urgent quests: (a) a desire for the

---

[35] Sundkler and Steed, *A History of the Church in Africa*, p. 967.
[36] cf. Hildebrandt, *History of the Church in Africa*, p. 214.
[37] Sundkler and Steed, *A History of the Church in Africa*, pp. 840, 841.
[38] M.L. Daneel, *Old and New Southern Shona Independent Churches,* volume 1: 'Background and Rise of the Major Movements', The Hague, 1971 (a), volume 2: 'Church Growth - Causative Factors and Recruitment Techniques', The Hague, 1974, volume 3: Leadership and Fission Dynamics, Gweru: Mambo Press, 1988.

demonstrable presence of the Holy Spirit, (b) a desire to directly address the problems and frustrations of modern African urban life. The prophet-healing churches in West-Africa arose from a revival prayer group after *World War One* that wanted to demonstrate God's power amid human misery. The movement came 'from an indigenous reading of Scripture and a lively apprehension of the priorities of many anxious people'. Church life is characterised by prophecy, healing, divination, and revelation. They have a strict and precise church order, with a detailed code of regulations, exhortations, and prohibitions, often under a charismatic leader and with much congregational participation. Members may wear uniforms, and there is much fasting and prayer. Combating witchcraft and sorcery, identifying witches, and curing witches are among the activities.[39]

5. The East Africa Revival

The *East Africa Revival* or *Balokole* (= saved ones)[40] is an example of a movement within the missionary church, seeking to transform the spiritual situation. It was an answer to lack of spirituality, decay, and deadness in the churches. Shaw calls this an answer to the evil of alienation, of being alienated from the power of God 'by attitudes like spiritual coldness and deadness'. The shedding of blood is necessary to do away with this evil. This makes the blood of Christ and His sacrificial death the central symbol of this new awakening. Through the movement many nominal Christians who had become church members without real conversion, for the first time in their lives were led to confession of sin and personal saving knowledge of Christ.

The revival started in Rwanda, at an Anglican mission station. Leading figure was Simeoni Nsibambi, a Baganda. After a deep religious experience he began to preach repentance and renewal. C.M.S. missionary Joe Church found himself in agreement with Nsibambi. He and Nsibambi together with Nsibambi's brother Blasio Kigozi went out to preach total surrender to Jesus Christ. In 1933/1934 Nsibambi and Church preached at Gahini, which the Holy Spirit used for a mass revival that spread widely with many converts (*abaka* = *those on fire*) which made sleeping churches awake (*zukuka* = *awake*). Meanwhile Kigozi and others spread the message to Uganda, and after Kigozi's death in 1936, also to Kenya, Sudan and Tanganyika. William Nagenda became Kigozi's successor as leader of the revival movement, soon called Balokole. In line with traditional Protestant revivals and perhaps influenced by the *Keswick Convention*, the Balokole preachers proclaimed

---

[39] Walls, *Missionary Movement*, p. 92.
[40] The Luganda word *bakuzufu*, meaning being re-awakened, renewed, resurrected, was used as a description for the English word *revival*, according to: Duncan and Kalu, 'Revival Movements', in: Kalu et. Al. (eds), *African Christianity*, p.278; the movement was also referred to as Rwandaism or Wandugu (Hildebrandt, *History of the Church in Africa*, p. 233).

salvation through faith in Christ and also 'spiritual renewal, commitment, uncompromising thruthfulness and moral integrity'.

The movement especially helped the work of the *Church Missionary Society*. in eastern Africa. It spread from Rwanda to Uganda, then southwards to the C.M.S. areas of Tanzania, north to Sudan and eastwards to Kenya. In Uganda the Anglican Bishop C.E.Stuart was very symphathetic to the Balokole. That was not always a matter of course, because there were also criticisms, mainly because of emphases on *second blessing* and potential *perfection* in the awakening movement. A breakaway-group even thought they could be free of sexual lust. The mainstream, however, rejected this doctrine of striving (*okufuba*), which implies that Christians through a second blessing can get to a state of near sinlessness. Mainstream leaders stressed that the greatest blessing is the cross of Christ, and being washed in the blood of Him, by faith alone. They also stressed that in this life Christians will never reach perfection.

William Nagenda (1912-1973) and his family. In a brief biography he was called 'Lover of Jesus'. This Ugandan preacher and teacher was a leader and a powerful witness in the East African Revival.

In 1941 the Balokole movement led to a conflict at Tucker Theological College at Mukono. A group of students, led by William Nagenda, resisted the warden's prohibition of their revivalist prayer group. The prayer group had emerged as a reaction against theft, immorality, theological liberalism, and High Church worship in this college. In the students' view the modernist spirit at Mukono 'minimizes sin, and the substitutionary death of Christ on the Cross, and mocks at the ideal of separation from the world to a holy and victorious life'. The revivalist students were dismissed. This almost led to a split. Eventually Bishop Stuart reconciled the Balokole with the college and the church by issuing guidelines for unity.[41] Waves of revival continued after the *Second World War*.

The movement harboured Ethiopianist elements, because it supported the principles of self-propagating, self-supporting and self-governing, and opened the way for recovery of African responsibility and leadership.[42] Some of the first African bishops in the Anglican Church belonged

---

[41] Hastings, *Church in Africa*, pp. 597,598.

[42] Duncan and Kalu, 'Bakuzufu: Revival Movements', in: Kalu et. Al. (eds), *African Christianity*, pp.289-293.

to the Bakolole, e.g. Erica Sabiti who was the first Anglican Archbishop in Uganda.[43]

There were also secessions. In 1948 Ishmael Noo formed his own church. In 1958 the revivalist Matthew Ajuoga and his *Johera* (= people of love) founded the *Churches of Christ of Africa*, breaking away from Anglicanism in western Kenya.[44]

6. The Golden Age of Independency

The age preceding political independence witnessed a rapid growth of the movements of ecclesiastical independency. *Ethiopianist* churches, *prophet-healing* churches, *revivalist* churches reached their height during the 1950s and early 1960s. All of them spread throughout Africa; independency was internationalising. Hastings says that the 1950s probably were 'the greatest decade for ecclesiastical independency in Africa'.[45] It was an age of expansion, consolidation, increasing self-confidence, and of expectations. Colonialism was weakening. There was an increasing tension between missionary church structures on the one hand and African initiative and ambition on the other hand. The foundation of independent churches was an important outlet for these feelings of tension. The movements of independency were not united. Ethiopianism aimed at combating inequality and racism; it saw nationalism as a means to reach this. The prophetic and revivalist movements stressed the spiritual side of evil and aimed at spiritual solutions.

Sometimes nationalist and spiritual interests clashed. New prophetic movements led by women-prophets like Alice Lenshina in Zambia, Gaudencio Aoko in Kenya, Mai Chaza in Zimbabwe, Miriam Ragot, Ma Nku and Ma Mbele in South Africa sometimes were even persecuted by African nationalists. Alice Lenshina († 1978) founded the independent Lumpa Church like a theocratic state with herself as queen. Her home village, the new Zion, was the centre of many other Lumpa-villages where her followers were gathered under her rule. Zambia's first president Kaunda banned this church, had the villages destroyed, killed some 700 of her followers, and had Lenshina imprisoned.[46] In Kenya the Balokole movement collided with the *Mau Mau* nationalists. Revivalists refused to take the Mau Mau oath that implied the repudiation of Christianity, and many paid with their lives. In Uganda Balokole followers clashed with dictator Idi Amin, which cost the lives of Archbishop Janani Luwum and other martyrs. In other cases, however, nationalist and spiritual expressions of independency could cooperate, like in Ghana and Swaziland.

---

[43] Cf. Hastings, *Church in Africa*, pp 598, 608, 609.
[44] Cf. Hastings, *Church in Africa*, p. 523.
[45] Hastings, *African Christianity*, pp. 121-130.
[46] Hastings, *Church in Africa*, pp.524,525.

7. Continuing Independency, after 1960

In the 1960s Africa received political independence and ecclesiastical autonomy. In the meantime, generally the mission instituted churches had become independent as well. They also tended to be partners of the new regimes, more or less similar to what the mission churches had been to the colonial governments. Some of the older independent churches, again in their diversity, gradually came to resemble the mission founded mainline churches. Thus, in many cases the differences have faded out, but the old problem of evil has not died. After the era of colonial mission Africans took over, giving way to new forms of misuse of power, mismanagement and corruption. Also now there is the need of integrating the Gospel into the African mode of being, so that salvation can really protect people against the destruction of life.

There is also the ongoing desire to react against spiritual coldness and deadness, and against *theological liberalism*. Very often the old evils have returned with new faces, but the old independency is often found to be unable to give the answers to the challenges. Critics of church government policies, advocates of Africanisation, and revival groups often feel strangers in their own churches. That is why movements of separatism and independency have continued.

However, we prefer not to classify all these newer movements by the historical term *African Instituted Churches*. Walls points to the new radical *charismatic churches*. Like the old prophetic-healing churches they derive from prayer and revivalist groups in the older churches. They also proclaim divine deliverance from diseases and demonic afflictions. But unlike the older independent churches their style of preaching and worship resembles the practice in American Charismatic and Pentecostal churches. Yet, they are very African in origin, leadership and finance. In their church services there are no African drums and uniforms, but there are the keyboards and the guitars, whereas the preachers wear business suits and the choir wears ties. It is western charismatism in an African way. A more aggressive type of charismatic churches was derived from Christian students' groups. They seek discipleship while protesting against the complacency, compromise and spiritual weakness of the established churches. They introduced a new African ascetism with emphases on 'prayer, fasting and readiness to suffer'.[47] Many of these young Christians met in the *Scripture Union*. Charismatic revivalism is also found in the *Students' Christian Organisation of Malawi* (S.C.O.M.). It stimulated the emergence of the *Born Again Movement* in the established churches, and it also led to the formation of independent churches. Yet, the characteristics of the *Charismatic Movement*, and of the earlier *Pentecostal Movement*, are not the same as those of the Ethiopianist churches, the prophet-healing churches, and the revivalist movements mentioned in the sections above. Pentecostalism and Charismatism

---

[47] Walls, *Missionary Movement*, pp. 92, 93.

were motivated by other theological challenges, often in a different political context. That is why we will deal with these movements separately, in chapter 19.

When evaluating the Christian witness of the movements for African Instituted Churches, and in a wider sense for African Independency, Shaw discerns three categories. The *first* group contradicted the Gospel of the Kingdom of Christ. This group, e.g. followers of Shembe and Kimbangu, obscured Christ by focusing mainly on the leader of the movement and by mixing the Christian witness with man-centred religion. Walls refers to the *'Hebraists'* who made a clear and conscious break with Christianity; in their schemes they took Christ away from the central place; a few like the Bayudaya of Uganda developed to a form of Judaism; The *second* category is characterised by a longing for and witness to the coming world order of Christ, of justice and righteousness. The *third* category points to the nature of the churches' spiritual warfare. The second and the third categories are indispensable for a church, provided they submit to the unique authority of Scripture. Much of the Harrist, Aladura and Balokole movements reflect this desire for re-orientation on the Bible. That is why they helped the Church in its quest for Reformation, that is for renewal or adjustment, and for reformulation of the Christian faith in African terms.[48]

---

[48] cf. Walls, *Missionary Movement*, p. 113.

Chapter 13

Church and Mission in Independent Africa

1. The Joy and the Pain of Change

The de-colonisation process that started about 1960 rapidly brought national independence to most African countries. It also brought a sense of African internationalism demonstrated in the formation of the *Organisation of African Unity* in 1963. De-colonisation also paved the way for a renaissance of African culture. All this contributed to the restoration of the dignity and respect of the African. However, the hopeful enthusiasm of the first years of independence soon was put to the test. The new ruling elites often resorted to repression and messianic nationalism.

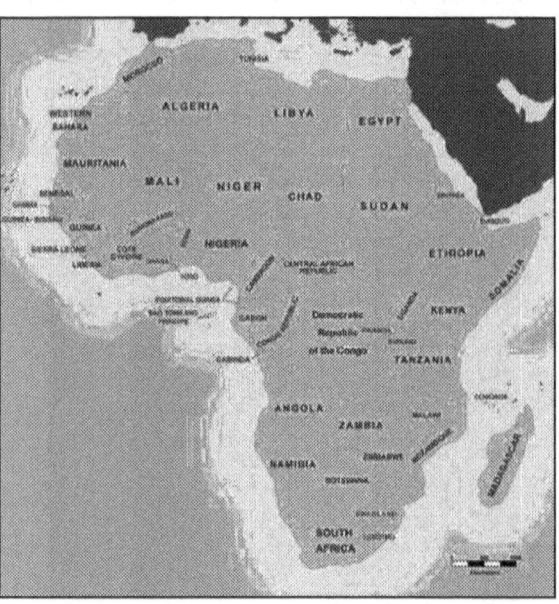
Map of Africa after regaining political independence.

Often this resulted in revolutions and military dictatorships. Africans suffered under ruthless African authenticity campaigns, under communism, and under Muslim oppression. Only in later years in many countries civil freedom was restored. Africa's attempt to establish democracy had begun. The position of the church during these stages of political independence varied from being persecuted to being an ally of the government, sometimes even co-responsible for the violence.[1]

---

[1] Together with this chapter, study: Shaw, *Kingdom*, pp. 259-282; Hastings, *African Christianity*, pp. 131-274; Ward, 'Africa', in: Hastings (ed), *World History*, pp. 226-233.

2. Churches Responding to Independence

In the new political situation the relationship between Church and State had shifted, which initially led to many problems. Here are some examples of Africa's first stages of political independence, and the church's response to it.

Angola, Mozambique and *Guinea-Bissau* continued to be under Portuguese rule until the 1970s. Especially the Protestant churches suffered because of this situation.

In southern *Sudan* the Arabs continued to persecute the Christians. Many fled to neighbouring countries. In *Somalia* the Muslim government expelled missionaries and forced the Church underground.

In *Liberia*, the patronising rule of Tubman was followed by the rule of Tolbert, and then power was seized by S.K. Doe in 1980.[2] Doe and his helpers killed Tolbert and almost the whole Liberian government. His regime was characterised by tyranny, manipulation and misrule. Some church leaders protested, but generally the church left politics alone not crying out against injustice. After Doe was assassinated in 1990 a civil war broke out and the country collapsed. Again the churches did not protest. Although they grew in the midst of chaos, according to Shaw the churches only tried to ameliorate the suffering.

In *Zaire* many Christians were killed during the rebellions of 1961 and 1964. Mobutu seized power in 1965. He established a one-party-state. He presented himself as kind of messiah, and introduced *'mobutuism'* as a replacement of other religions. In this period the churches adopted a low profile. By 1980 Mobutu backed away from his messianism, but after 1990 chaos returned and increased. Although the churches sometimes collaborated with the regime, there were also attempts to improve the political situation.

Statue of Janani Luwum (1922-1877), Anglican Archbishop of Uganda, killed by Idi Amin.

Nigeria is one of the countries where *messianic Islam* clashed with Christianity. In a civil war in the end of the 1960s many Christians were killed and many churches were destroyed. The Northern region, mainly Hausa, tended to be aggressively Muslim, although there were Protestant Christian minorities. The Western region, mainly Yoruba, and the Eastern region, mainly Igbo, were predominantly Christian. In 1966 Igbo army officers led by General Ojukwu rose against the central government and declared the Eastern region of Biafra to be an independent non-Muslim

---

[2] For a brief case study of church and state in Liberia in the period 1975-2000, see: J.W. Hofmeyr, 'Mainline Churches in the Public Space 1975-2000', in: Kalu et.al. (eds), *African Christianity*, pp. 367-372.

The Faith Moves South

Alice Auma in 1986 proclaimed herself under the orders of a Christian spirit named Lakwena. She raised an army in Northern Uganda, called the 'Holy Spirit Mobile Forces'. With it she waged a war against the Ugandan government and against internal enemies in the form of 'impure' soldiers, witches, and sorcerers.

state 'in a raging Islamic sea'. During the ensuing civil war, many western churches and missionaries tried to help Biafra, for instance by the organisation of relief flights. In 1970 the Biafran rising ended, and a rather successful campaign of reconciliation began. At the same time there was growing tension between Christians and Muslims, and an increasing pressure to bring Nigeria under Muslim law (*sharia*).

Also in *Uganda* the church faced aggressive Islam. In 1971 the dictatorship of Obote was replaced by the very cruel dictatorship of Idi Amin. Islam was promoted and churches were suppressed; some church leaders, among whom the Anglican Archbishop Luwum, and many other Christians were killed. In 1979 Amin was violently overthrown by Obote, who in his turn was overthrown, and in 1986 succeeded by Museveni. Suffering and bloodshed seemed to have ended, except for the activities of the *Holy Spirit Rebels* of prophetess Alice Lakwena (or: Lekwana) who violently tried to establish a Christian kingdom on Ugandan soil. This *Army of the Lord* was defeated by Museveni's troops, but a section of it, the *Lord's Resistance Army* remained active after 1995.

In *South Africa* the massacre of many participants in a protest demonstration at Sharpville in 1960, the prohibition of black political parties, and the banning of black leaders, led to an increasing consciousness of *apartheid* being against the Word of God. C.F. Beyers Naudé of the *Christian Institute*, Desmond Tutu leader of the *South African Council of Churches*, Allan Boesak and others in 1985 contributed to the *Kairos Document* that condemned apartheid. In 1990 Nelson Mandela was released from Robben Island. After De Klerk's government had dismantled apartheid, the elections of 1994 brought Mandela and the A.N.C. to power.[3]

Zambia belongs to the countries where the introduction of socialism was attempted. Kenneth Kaunda adopted this ideology, notwithstanding his professed personal faith in Christ, and when he became president he tried to make his country a socialist state. However, the attempt became a failure. In 1991, in multi-party elections, Kaunda was replaced by Frederick Chiluba, a professed Protestant Chris-

---

[3] For a brief case study of church and state in South Africa in the period 1975-2000, see: J.W. Hofmeyr, 'Mainline Churches in the Public Space 1975-2000', in: Kalu et.al. (eds), *African Christianity*, pp. 378-385.

tian as well, who had to answer accusations of the massive corruption during his regime, made by his successor President Mwanawasa.

In *Tanzania* President Nyerere, a Roman Catholic, tried to introduce his version of socialism (*ujamaa*), but also here it failed, at least economically. The challenge of Islam was increasingly felt after Zanzibar joined the *Islamic Conference Organisation*.

In *Ethiopia* the Marxist-Leninist version of socialism began to be forced on the people after Menghistu seized power in 1977. In 1991 he was overthrown after having brought intense suffering to the church and to many individual Christians.

Generally the initial criticism of Christianity during the de-colonisation process, was soon followed by powerful currents which served to reinforce Christianity. These currents especially helped the mission founded churches. Like of old in the colonial era - so Ward indicates - the majority of Africans expected more from churches coming from the West than from African Instituted Churches.[4] On the whole the growing churches contributed to (a) the *consolidation* of independence, (b) in some cases there was a *brave witness* against tyranny or barbarism, (c) and eventually churches helped the movements towards *democratisation*.

C.F. Beyers Naudé (1915-2004), minister in the Dutch Reformed Church in South Africa, who started a protest and reform movement, the Christian Institute, against the system of apartheid.

3. Theology Responding to Independence

In theology the church formulates and defends its position and message in response to the challenges from outside and inside the church. In the historical mainstream, Roman Catholic theology and Reformed theology, as well as the more modern theologies of

Julius Nyerere (1922 – 1999) known as Mwalimu or teacher, was President of Tanzania.

Liberalism and *Ecumenism* have had universal significance, though they have been coloured by their Western setting. In a way missionaries exported their theological convictions and differences to the mission fields outside Europe and America. At the same time missionary Christianity developed its own colours, theological ten-

---

[4] Ward, 'Africa', in: Hastings (ed), *World History*, pp. 229, 230.

dencies and even theological differences. We discern some expressions of theology in Africa after the beginning of independence.

a. African Theology

The term *African Theology* gives a face to a movement that attempts to indigenise and inculturate theology in Africa. Generally this movement 'has sought to demonstrate the value of the African religious heritage and to build bridges between that heritage and the Christian faith'.

In the *Roman Catholic* context, it began with Placide Tempel's book *Bantu Philosophy* (French: 1945, English: 1955) who said that *life-force* is the essence of African thought. In the wake of this a conference in Ghana in 1955 'defended the continuity between African culture and Christianity', exhorting the church to 'use African culture as the only language to proclaim the Gospel in Africa'. This inspired a 'generation of francophone Catholic scholars' such as Kagame (Rwanda), Mulago, Tshibangu (Congo). Kagame and Mulago belonged to a group of African students who, during their study in Rome, rethought the problem of 'African fundamental theology'. Tshibangu claimed that the seeds of authentic African Christian theology can be provided by African religion and philosophy. Vanneste criticised Tshibangu's thought by insisting that theology should be transcultural and international. Generally, the ideas of inculturation and indigenisation prepared the ground for wider acceptance of the reforms initiated by the *Second Vatican Council* in the 1960s. Expatriate missionaries still governed the church to a great extent, although the number of African priests rapidly grew, especially in the area of pastoral theology. Yet, the expatriates, not the locals, were the ones who pushed through the transformations suggested by Vatican II.[5]

On the *Protestant side* a milestone was the book *The Akan Doctrine of God* (1944) by the Ghanaian Joseph B. Danquah. He presented African traditional religion 'as basically monotheistic' and 'compatible with the Christian view of God'. More emphatic in this line is the Methodist missionary Smith who advocated 'a synthesis of African views of God and shaped it as a coherent, unified theology'. Following the same line was John S. Mbiti's book *African Religions and Philosophy* (1969). Another initiative was taken by the Norwegian Lutheran missionary Sundkler in his book *Christian ministry in Africa* (1960) which in 1966 led to a theological consultation in Nigeria of theologians such as Dickson, Mbiti, Sawyer, who published their findings in *Biblical Revelation and African Beliefs*. Some theologians believed traditional African culture and religion - similar to what Christianity was said to have - has a *'liberating dimension'*, which has to be rediscovered because colonialism had buried it.[6] Later, when it was experienced that

---

[5] Ward, 'Africa', in: Hastings (ed), *World History*, p. 231.
[6] Cf. Tinyiko Sam Maluleke, 'Half a Century of African Christian Theologies: Elements Emerging Agenda for the Twenty-First Century', in: Kalu et.al. (eds), *African Christianity*. pp. 469-485.

African independence could threaten the church, the original ideas of African theology began to be criticised. People like the Ugandan writer and anthropologist Okot p'Bitek (1931-1982) began to reject the idea that traditional African society is saturated with religion 'as basically consonant with Christianity'.[7]

b. Liberation Theology

In the 1970s a new emphasis was added to the emphasis on traditional religion and culture. Racial, political, economical and social justice came to be stressed as the starting point and as the aim of theology. Meetings by the *World Council of Churches* in Nairobi (1975) and by the *Third World Theologians* in Dar es Salaam (1976), advocating strongly the combat of *racism* and a just world order, contributed to the birth of the movement of *Liberation Theology* which professed to begin with the need of the poor and the oppressed, and to give them the hope of the coming kingdom. African theology was influenced by Liberation Theology and by some of its sub-movements.

Steven Bantu Biko was one of the founders of the Black Consciousness Movement in South Africa in the late 1960s. He was arrested and died in a prison cell in 1977.

Desmond Mpilo Tutu (born 1931), Anglican Archbishop, leader of the South African Council of Churches, influential figure in the struggle against apartheid.

Feminist theology (or: *Womanist Theology*) is a strand of Liberation Theology; it has affected the thinking of many male and female theologians in Africa.[8]

Another influential strand is the movement of *Black Theology*.[9] It originates from Afro-American writers like James Cone, and it developed particularly in the South African struggle for racial equality with representatives such as Boesak, Buthelezi, and Tutu; it directly influenced the *Black Consciousness Movement* and Steve Biko's *South African Students' Organisation*. The *Kairos Document* of 1985, made by black and white South African theologians, is seen as its major expression of protest against the apartheid's regime.

c. Evangelical and Reformed Theology

Evangelicalism aims at re-assertion of the final authority of Scripture as the only source of the central truths of the Christian faith. *Evangelical Theology*,[10] is rooted

---

[7] Cf. Ward, 'Africa', in: Hastings (ed), *World History*, p. 232.

[8] Cf. Tinyiko Sam Maluleke, 'Half a Century of African Christian Theologies: Elements Emerging Agenda for the Twenty-First Century', in: Kalu et.al. (eds), *African Christianity*. pp. 489-491.

[9] See a survey in: Verstraelen-Gilhuis, *A New Look at Christianity in Africa*, pp. 25-33

[10] Cf. Maluleke, 'Half a Century of African Christian Theologies', in: Kalu et.al. (eds), *African Christi-*

in the *Evangelical revivals* and *awakenings* of the 18th and 19th centuries. In a wider sense -as meant here- it does not differ from classical *Reformed Theology*. Unfortunately, to some the term *Reformed Theology* has been tainted negatively by a connotation to the South African Dutch Reformed churches which supported the apartheid system. Basically, however, *Reformed Theology* is a movement that emphasises the continuous importance of going back to the sources, i.e. to Scripture.[11] It recognises much in the Evangelical revivals and awakenings, in that they were a re-iteration of the theology of the great Reformers of the 16th century. That is why, especially in the Anglo-Saxon world the words 'evangelical' and 'reformed' basically covered the same tradition of thought and practice. The term *Presbyterian theology* is an alternative name for Reformed theology, although it reflects more of its ecclesiastical side. Reformed, Presbyterian, and Evangelical theological thought has stressed much the importance of the Christian Congregation, as such it could be called *Congregational Theology*.

The 20th century, however, saw the beginning and growth of movements of Neo-Reformed and Neo-Evangelical thinking that consciously deviated from the theology of the Reformation. This means that one can be confused by literature that refers to modern evangelical and reformed thought, without qualifying it in comparison to the theological heritage of the Reformation. Shaw for instance, does not define in this respect what he means by *Evangelical Theology* when he represents *African Evangelicalism* as one of the faces of African Christian Theology. Making the usual claim that Africa has many evangelicals, he mentions a number of theologians who, in his view, were formative for African Evangelical Theology: Kato, Imasogie, Olowala, Adeyemo, all from Nigeria, Bediako (Ghana), Tiénou (Burkina Faso). Some Evangelical theologians, like Byang Kato, emphatically rejected the optimistic idea that bridges could be built between African Traditional Religion and Christianity. They founded the *Association of Evangelicals of Africa*, and in 1982 they started a magazine, *Africa Journal of Evangelical Theology*.

Shaw has called Byang Kato (1936-1975) 'the founding father of modern African Evangelical Theology'.[12] In his doctoral thesis, *Theological Pitfalls in*

Byang Kato (1936-1975), Evangelical theologian of Nigeria, the first African General Secretary of the A.E.A.M. (From: Breman, The Association of Evangelicals in Africa, p. 41).

---

anity. pp. 487, 488.
[11] Cf. Steven Paas, 'Some Principles of Reformed Theology', paper at Workshop by Reformed Mission League, in Liwonde, Malawi, June 2004.
[12] Shaw, *The Kingdom of God*, p. 278.

Africa,[13] Kato was ready to contextualise the Gospel for Africans in the specific African cultures. At the same time Kato emphasised the Bible as the unique Word of God, 'the ultimate source and authority for all legitimate theological expression, including African'. Though appreciating the riches and inherent values of African traditions and cultures, Kato was of the opinion that *at their most fundamental level* they include a 'meaning and purpose of life' that is essentially incompatible with Christian faith. That is why he stressed the discontinuity between the Gospel and any traditional, non-Christian religion. There had to be a radical break with traditional beliefs, including *African Traditional Religions*. This view he also applied to Western cultures and all other cultures, stressing that the Gospel ultimately transcends and challenges all cultures. Kato was not à-cultural. In his thought the preachers of the Gospel should engage seriously with traditional culture. Domestication of the Gospel reveals and vitiates the essential integrity of African cultures. Kato responded to the universalism and syncretism which he observed in African churches and theologies, by the influence of liberal theologians like Mbiti and Idowu, and of the ecumenical movement, and also of the growth of politically inspired movements of opposition to the church in some post-colonial African states. Kato denounced all liberal theology and philosophy that deviated from the authority of the Bible as the Word of God. His adage was: 'Let African Christians be Christian Africans!'[14]

Shaw, although he appreciates the work of Kato and others, would have liked African Evangelical theologians to have achieved more, academically or in 'interaction with current African issues'. It is true that perhaps more could have been done, but African Christianity has maintained a strong classical Protestant, Evangelical tendency. By the end of the 20th century this tendency was still strong in Africa, and it showed signs of renewal. Shaw admits to this, and he thinks that contributions to new life were made by international Evangelical revivals in the wake of the *Lausanne Covenant,* formulated at the *Lausanne Conference* in 1974, where many Africans were present. He observes positive developments in *African Evangelical Theology*: (a) The formation of *Evangelical National Fellowships* in Zambia, Kenya, Nigeria and other African countries which stressed the uniqueness of Christ for salvation, thus counteracting the rampant ideas of religious pluralism that degraded Christianity to just one way of truth. (b) A new understanding of the positive relationship between Gospel and Culture. (c) The re-assertion of a Christ-centred view of the Kingdom of God at the end of time, 'that refused to be identified with human ideologies or programs' for a new political, social and economical world order. In Shaw's words, African Evangelical theologians are challenged to re-discover 'the lordship of the risen and returning Christ of Orthodoxy', who is the hope of the world. This re-discovery signifies the failure of (a) theological

---

[13] Byang Kato, *Theological Pitfalls in Africa*, Kisumu: Evangelical Publishing House, 1975.

[14] This paragraph is a summary of: Keith Ferdinando's well documented DACB article on Byang Kato, Website: http://www.dacb.org/stories/nigeria/kato.html

The Faith Moves South

liberalism, (b) escapist mainline traditionalism, (c) overspiritual charismatism, and of (d) the overrealised eschatology in the *charismatical movement* and in the various branches of *liberation theology*. In other words African evangelicals are different from liberals, traditionalists and charismatics.

d. Other Theologies

Besides these schools of theology in Africa, there are others. Maluleke mentions some of them. *Theologies of the A.I.C.'s* concentrate on the exposure of the significance of African Instituted Churches for African Christianity and Theology. Christian Baeta, David Barrett, Martinus Daneel, and Harold Turner are the leading theologians. *Translation Theologies*, with theologians such as Lamin Sanneh and Kwame Bediako, study the way the Gospel should be made to speak to the African situation. *Theologies of Reconstruction* reject the old approaches of African Theology, Liberation Theology etc. Their theologians like Jesse Mugambi and Charles Villa-Vicencio want to improve the quality of African life by engaging into dialogue with politics and economics.[15]

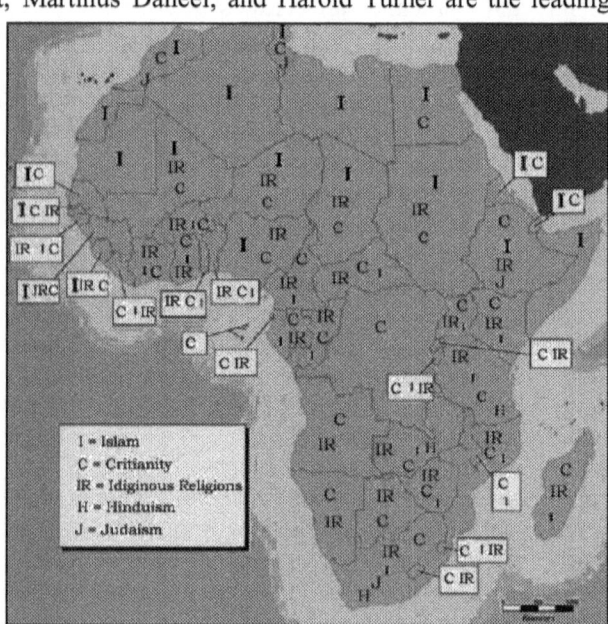

Map of the main religions in Africa.

4. Africa and Mainstream Theologies

Discussion will continue about the interaction between African Christianity and the mainstream theologies that came to Africa in and after the missionary era, e.g.: Reformed/ Evangelical theology, Roman Catholic theology (classical and post Second Vatican Council), Liberal theology (theological Modernism), Neo-reformed/ Neo-evangelical theology, Ecumenical theology, and Post Modern the-

---

[15] Maluleke, 'Half a Century of African Christian Theologies', in: Kalu et.al. (eds), *African Christianity*. pp. 485-487, 488-489, 491-492.

ology. These lines of theological thought may have originated in the West, yet they belong to global Christianity. Now , they are in the process of being inculturated in Africa. All continue to be challenged by Scripture, which is the touchstone of any theology either global, Western or African.

Chapter 14

Faith Missions

1. Pre-Classical Missions

Missions are as old as the Church, there is nothing new and strange in that. But in the first centuries after the Reformation the Protestants only concentrated on evangelising their own peoples. They did not do much mission overseas. The only major exception perhaps is the mission by the *Moravian Brethren*. For reasons that will be shown below, the *Moravian Mission* is called (by Fiedler[1]) a *Pre-Classical Mission*.

2. Classical Missions

Protestants became active in mission overseas by the end of the 18th century. According to Kenneth Scott Latourette this Protestant Missionary Movement summits in 'the great century of mission', 1792-1914, when it spread over the whole world. It is spiritually related to the *Great Awakening*, with people like Jonathan Edwards. The Methodists belonged to its exponents, with people like Charles and John Wesley. John Wesley declared: 'The world is my parish'. They strongly influenced the Anglo-Saxon area and prepared the ground for the Missionary Movement.

In 1792 William Carey was the first one to reshape the *Great Awakening* to a *Missionary Movement*. In 1793, after publishing his famous book *Enquiry*,[2] he started modern mission to India. To this aim he founded the *Baptist Missionary Society* (B.M.S.). Carey's initiative was fed by the idea that missionary societies instead of the churches themselves would be the agencies of mission. This is how *Classical Missions* started. The movement of Classical Missions was very successful. Through it Africa became Christian. It led to the foundation of Classical Churches, like C.C.A.P., Anglican Church, Congregationalists, Lutheran Churches, the Roman Catholic Church. They achieved a lot, but not enough. The *Classical Missionary Movement* did not reach all places, sticking to the coast. In general the inland was not reached, in China as much as in Africa. This was so in China and also in Africa. By 1880 inner Africa, e.g. the Sudan Belt and Congo, were not touched by Christianity. Even Roman Catholic efforts in Angola, Congo, that started in the 16th century, had stuck to the coast and were at a very low tide by 1880. Other initiatives were needed to reach the inlands. The *Classical Missionary*

---

[1] Klaus Fiedler, *The Story of Faith Missions: From Hudson Taylor to Present Day Africa*, Oxford: Regnum, 1994², pp. 32-111.
[2] William Carey, *An Enquiry into the Obligation of Christians to Use Means for the Conversion of the Heathen*, Leicester, 1792.

Movement could not fill the gap because their hands and money were bound by the new churches that they had to nurture.

3. Revival Ferment

In view of the need of mission to unreached lands, so Latourette says, the Holy Spirit pushed the Church forward through revivals that led to ever new organisations. Around 1800 some of the fervour of the *Great Awakening* had subsided, and the next great revival (the *Second Evangelical Revival* or the *Holiness Revival*) was still two generations ahead in time. In the early decades a new revival broke, which may be called the *Restorationist Revival*, which had the aim of restoring the primitive church once more before the end of the world.[3]

a. Brethren Movement

Of the movements brought about by the *Restorationist Revival*, the *Brethren* (also called 'Christian Brethren') became important for mission. They loved the Bible and discovered from it that there is no need for any clergy. All are Brethren and all share the missionary obligation, at home and world wide. The Brethren never became many, but with the exception of the Moravians a century earlier, no denomination ever was as missionary as they were.

The *Brethren* missionaries mostly work under the name *Christian Mission in Many Lands*, and they contributed greatly to the evangelisation of Africa, in Northern Angola, Northern Zambia and Eastern Congo from the Copperbelt to the north. Many Brethren also joined the Faith Missions, and Brethren played an important role for the early *China Inland Mission*. For the whole of Evangelical Christianity the *Brethren* were instrumental in changing the eschatology from postmillennial (as in the *Great Awakening*) to premillennial.

b. Prophetic Movement

Part of the revival ferment of those days was the *Prophetic Movement*. In it the Brethren were central, but it encompassed much of Evangelical Christianity. The *Prophetic Movement* stressed that the Scriptures, especially Daniel and Revelation, give a picture of the future of the Church in the end time. There was much concentration on and longing for the Second Coming of the Lord that was expected to happen soon. However, according to *Matthew* 24: 14, there is a pre-condition, the

---

[3] Klaus Fiedler, 'A Revival Disregarded and Disliked', Festschrift Käser, Bonn, VKW, 2004. Since the New Testament does not provide a clear and unified picture on how the primitive church was organised, the resulting restored churches differed greatly: the *Brethren* emphasised the breaking of bread in Biblical simplicity, the *Apostolic Movement* around Edward Irving emphasised the Apostles and spiritual gifts, the *Adventist Movement* emphasised the preparation for the soon coming of the Lord, and the *Churches of Christ* emphasised the independence of each local congregation.

Lord will not return until the Gospel has been preached to all nations. Therefore, they wanted to do their utmost to fulfil this pre-condition, until the last tribe will be reached.

One of the leading teachers of the *Prophetic Movement* was Grattan Guinness († 1910), whose wife Fanny started the *Livingstone Inland Mission* (1879), the first Faith Mission in Africa. Both together started in 1873 the *East London Training Institute for Home and Foreign Missions*, which became the first of many Bible Schools training Evangelical missionaries. The most famous of these is perhaps the Moody Bible Institute in Chicago. One of its students for some time was Daniel Malikebu, who later became successor to John Chilembwe as leader of the *Providence Industrial Mission* in Malawi.

c. Holiness Movement

The third element in the revival ferment of the first half of the 19th century was the *Holiness Movement*. It started with Phoebe Palmer in 1835. The aim was the promotion of sanctification in the lives of believers. This included great dedication and commitment, strengthening the power to serve, not in the least in mission, at home and abroad.

4. Faith Missions

On the strength of the spiritual energies of these three movements, and fuelled by the next major revival, the *Second Great Awakening* (or the *Holiness Revival* as Fiedler puts it), new missionary organisations emerged. The Sceond Great Awakening spread throughout the Anglo-Saxon world and the European Continent. Personal holiness and the power to serve were emphasised. In this movement the churches played no important role. The Faith Missions started with James Hudson Taylor. Deeply influenced by this

Phoebe Palmer (1807-1874) was a very influential Methodist woman in America. She was at the cradle of the American Holiness Movement, from which eventually emerged Pentecostal denominations, social reforms and also missions.

holiness revival he more or less personified the movement's disinterest in church affiliations. Hudson Taylor began as a Methodist, then he moved to the *Free Methodists*, then he joined the Brethren, subsequently he became a member of a Mission Hall Church, and he ended his life as a Baptist. This shifting of churches does not mean, however, that Taylor and his brethren were shaky in their beliefs. To them church affiliation was a matter of expediency. Moving freely from one church to another was typical for the whole movement.

Taylor's desire was to be a missionary in China, and he went there with the help of the *Brethren Movement*. He had a significant relationship with George

Müller, founder of an orphanage, who had been a disciple of Anthony Norris Groves, a one time missionary to Baghdad (1828) and India. Groves taught that there is no need for ordination, as the Bible does not mention it. God will supply the missionary with the necessary means. He mustnot beg or ask for money (except in prayer to God), and must not incur debts either. Müller followed this principle, and he transferred it to Taylor. When the *Brethren* forgot about him and left him in China without support, this principle became very important to Taylor. He became an independent missionary, who relied on God's help as the answer to private prayer. Often support came from George Müller, whom he had met only once before going to China.

James Hudson Taylor (1832-1905), founder of the China Inland Mission, which was an example for others to establish Faith Missions for Africa.

After working years as a pioneer not so far from the coast, Taylor became sick, and in 1861 he returned to England. But he continued to be consumed by the desire to spread the Gospel in Inland China. He travelled all over Britain trying to enlist support from various missionary organisations, but he had very little response. The *Classical Missions* had been so successful that they were unable to accept other commitments. There were other reasons too for their lack of extra capacity. In order to become a missionary you had to study theology first and be accepted and ordained as a minister. Not many other people were allowed to be sent out by the classical missionary organisations, so that much missionary capacity remained unused.

A.B. Simpson was the first to call for the use of *'neglected forces'* (non-clergy, women) and so reach the unreached at new places, and go to the last tribe. This led to the emergence of an innovative movement that encouraged the use of new forces, new types of missionaries, and new missionary ideas. The new (post-classical) organisations were not asking for money. They employed mostly missionaries that would not have been accepted according to traditional opinion. Being called was the most important thing that counted.

In 1865 the first organisation of the new type was formed, the *China Inland Mission*. The founders were James Hudson Taylor and his wife Maria. After Maria's death Taylor married Jennie Faulding who also played an important role in the C.I.M.[4]

---

[4] Cf. Howard Taylor (and his wife), *Biography of James Hudson Taylor*, London: China Inland Mission Overseas Missionary Fellowship, 1965; Peter Hammond, *The Greatest Century of Missions*, Howard Place: Christian Liberty books, n.d., pp. 101-109.

5. Special Characteristics of Faith Missions

The *China Inland Mission* and the other *Faith Missions* that followed its example differed in a number of ways from the *Classical Missions*. These different principles were not looked upon as a law for all missionary organisations, but as indicating how God had led this particular Faith Mission.

The *Faith Missions* accepted missionaries from all Protestant denominations. This was done on an individual basis, the aim was not corporal (denominational) unity, but individual unity in the common faith. Besides may be a reference from the local pastor, the churches where the candidates came from were not asked for permission or support. Most candidates for ordinary mission posts came from *Presbyterian, Baptist,* and *Anglican Churches*, whereas the leaders often came from *Free Churches*. In many cases candidates came from the *Brethren*, or they had been influenced by them. Many missionaries in their careers once or more often changed denominations.

People from different churches with different church orders and ecclesiological views could only cooperate if they considered the ecclesiological order to be of secondary importance. In some cases missionaries of a certain church were given their own field where they were allowed to establish a church of their own denomination, e.g. Anglicans working for the *Africa Inland Mission* in the West Nile Province of Northern Uganda were allowed to found an Anglican Church there.[5] In this way contradictions could be made acceptable.

The majority of the missionaries, however, did not much care for definite rules of church order. They did not consider different views of church order as dividing. In general this question was worked out *pragmatically* in the field. In most cases this resulted in the formation of churches that mixed a kind of *Presbyterian order* with the *Baptists' believer's baptism*, although the majority of the missionaries came from churches with *infant baptism*.

The *Classical Missions* were voluntary associations of people who contributed. Their missionaries were not members but employees, who were paid salaries according to a scale that allowed for differences in payment. Faith missions, however, were not based on (fixed) contributions. Their missionaries were *members*. They were the owners of the organisation, as such they did not get salaries. Instead of salaries they got support, based on needs and situations, not based on juniority, seniority, or education.

Classical and Post-Classical missionaries both lived and worked by faith. Post-Classical missions are called *Faith Missions*, not only because the missionaries were not paid salaries, but also because they did not ask for gifts or collections. Faith was to be the only guarantee that money would come in. Taylor's principle was never to take up a collection. He felt God did not allow him to do this. His adage was: *'God's work, done in God's way, will never lack God's supply'*. At the

---

[5] Fiedler, *Story of Faith Missions*, p. 83.

same time *Faith Missions* did not allow making debts or borrowing money. If no money would come in for a certain project, then it was concluded that the project did not have God's blessing and should be stopped. In Taylor's thinking, that was adopted by many others, the faith principle of funding was to be understood as a communal faith. This meant that God would supply *'us all'*, so that everything that came in would be *shared* in the field by all workers. In later times others have changed this communal faith principle into a principle of *individual faith*. The individual missionary would supply his/her own support. This change often made income rise considerably.

Spirituality, not intellectual training is decisive. God will enlist people from any class and with all kinds of qualifications. In order to prepare this great variety of workers for the mission field in 1873 the first *Bible School*, the *East London Training Institute*,[6] was founded, by Fanny and Grattan Guinness, which was strongly recommended by Taylor. (The term 'Bible School' was adopted, because the students did not know Greek and Hebrew, and used the Bible in the English vernacular). Taylor and other leaders of Faith Missions did not object to the ordination of ministers or of candidates for the mission. But he did not consider it necessary. In principle God ordains you.

In the *Faith Missions* the wives of missionaries were accepted as full missionaries in their own right. In the Classical Missions a wife was just the wife to the missionary. The Faith Mission's rule was that if one was accepted single, and wanted to marry later, then also the wife had to qualify before she would be accepted.

Especially the *Holiness Movement* paved the way for single women to various functions in the mission field. Many single women in their own right became evangelists, even heads of mission stations. The choice of women was not a matter of expediency because of the lack of male candidates, but Taylor wanted to use new people, new ideas, for new places. He could have found at least a few men for all missionary areas, but he consciously wanted to give a place to women too.

Faith missionaries were to live the life of the local people, using their language and accepting their living conditions. C.I.M. missionaries wore Chinese dress. Identification also meant: do not lean on your foreign power and privileges. Some missionaries who went far in the acculturation, were subjected to suffering, even to death, as was the case with the missionary martyrs in China around 1900. There is not a direct link between their acculturation and death, though. Acculturation made it possible for them to live in the interior, but they were killed as foreigners, and they would even have been killed if not acculturated.

---

[6] Perry, L. (ed.), *Joseph Booth: Africa for the African* (1st ed. 1897), Blantyre: Claim, 1997, pp. 73, 77, 105: Joseph Booth's son Edward attended this school before coming to Malawi, where he died soon after.

The Faith Moves South

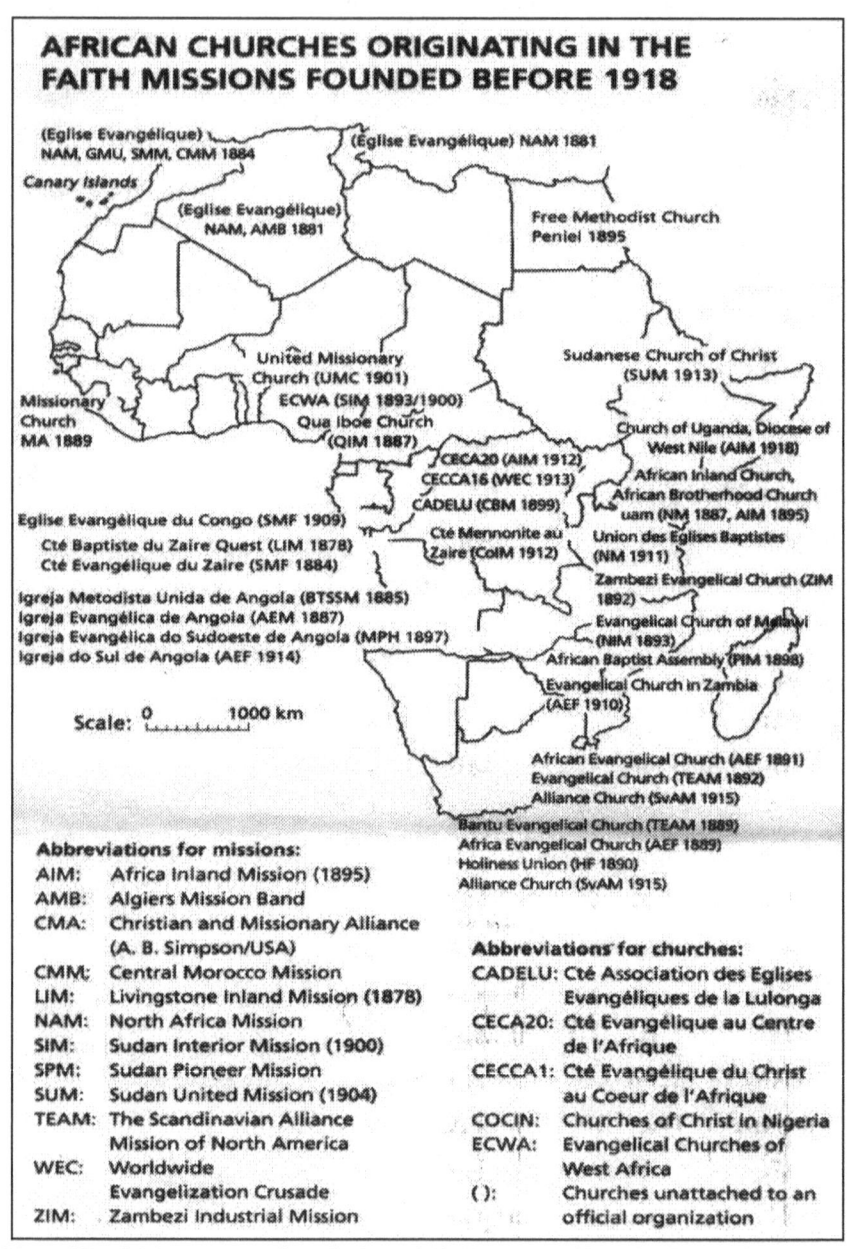

Map of Faith Missions in Africa before 1918 (From: Fiedler, The Story of Faith Missions, p. 82).

Other characteristics are acceptance of sacrifice and suffering, the principle that evangelism precedes the institution, stress on itineration of the missionary, acceptance of the international character of mission organisations, the principle that leadership of a mission is centralistic and field based.

6. Faith Missions in Africa

A map in Fiedler's handbook on the *Faith Missions*[7] shows the unreached areas in Africa and some of the Faith Mission organisations that filled up the inland gap. The Classical Missions had covered regions like South Africa, Madagascar, part of Ethiopia, Egypt, Southern Nigeria. But the advance had stopped because of the following reasons: (a) they had to consolidate their successes, (b) decline of the classical revival movement, (c) loss of spiritual power and (d) lack of cash, (e) lack of personnel.

Therefore the Classical Missions had little power to go into the inland. But the Post-Classical Missions provided new forces, personnel, spirituality, ideas, and money for the missionary enterprise in inland Africa. We mention the following *Faith Missions* in Africa.

a. Livingstone Inland Mission

The *Livingstone Inland Mission*, originally led by Fanny Guinness, was the first Faith Mission to start work at the mouth of the Congo River. In 1884 the work was handed over to American Baptists, but the Swedish L.I.M. members continued their work as a Faith Mission, entering also Congo-Brazzaville.[8]

b. Africa Inland Mission

Peter Cameron Scott was at the cradle of the A.I.M. He was born in Glasgow. The family emigrated to America. At first he was a missionary of the *Christian and Missionary Alliance* (C.M.A.) which was founded by A.B. Simpson. Simpson had been a minister of the Presbyterian Church in Canada and in the U.S.A.. He was dismissed because he accepted believers' baptism, and was privately 're-baptised', although he never became a Baptist. Then Simpson started his own church and in 1889, influenced by 'power for service' adage of the *Holiness Movement*, began the *Christian and Missionary Alliance* (C.M.A.). This evangelical and innovative mission organisation touched Africa in only a few places, like Congo and Sierra Leone.

In 1891 Simpson ordained Peter Cameron Scott who was sent to the west coast of Congo (border area of present Congo and Cabinda) to be a missionary there.

---

[7] Fiedler, *Faith Missions*, p. 53, cf. pp. 77, 83.
[8] Fiedler, *Story of Faith Missions*, pp. 37-39.

Scott's idea was to establish a *chain of mission stations* across Africa, first from the West (Congo) to the East (Kenya - Mombasa), and when this did not work out, from the East to the West, or even from both sides at the same time. However, Scott's preliminary attempts were not successful during his life time. After three years he fell ill and had to return. Moreover Simpson decided against his plans.

Peter Cameron Scott (1867-1896), founder of the Africa Inland Mission.

Then, in 1895, in line with the individualistic spirit of many faith missionaries, Scott quit the C.M.A., and started his own mission, the *Africa Inland Mission*, to work in inland Kenya. Scott's death at Kangundo in 1896 caused a serious crisis in the A.I.M. But the *Philadelphia Missionary Council* took over full responsibility, and the Principal of their Bible School, C.E. Hurlbert, accompanied by his wife and five children, and some other workers went to Mombasa, to become missionaries. The missionaries experienced many difficulties, but Scott's work survived. At Kijabe the A.I.M. centre in Kenya was established. The A.I.M. work in Kenya grew into a big church, the *Africa Inland Church*, with more than a million members. It is a Baptist type church, with somewhat Presbyterian structures. The work of the A.I.M. was extended to Tanzania where also a Baptist type church was established, and to North West Uganda where under the A.I.M. flag, an Anglican church came into being. With the intention of creating a 'chain of mission stations across Africa', beginning in Mombasa, the AI.M. headed for North East Congo, and in the direction of Lake Chad.⁹

A.B. Simpson (1843-1919), founder of the Christian and Missionary Alliance.

c. Sudan Missions

The founder of the *Sudan Interior Mission* was Roland V. Bingham. He was converted under the influence of the *Salvation Army*, which he joined. After his emigration to Canada he met with the leader of the C.M.A. in that country, and became a pastor in the C.M.A. Like many faith missionaries Bingham made several changes of denomination.

---

⁹ Fiedler, *Faith Missions*, p. 49, 53, 74, 75, 83; Hastings, *Church in Africa*, pp. 424,455; Hildebrandt, *History of the Church in Africa*, p.169.

Faith Missions

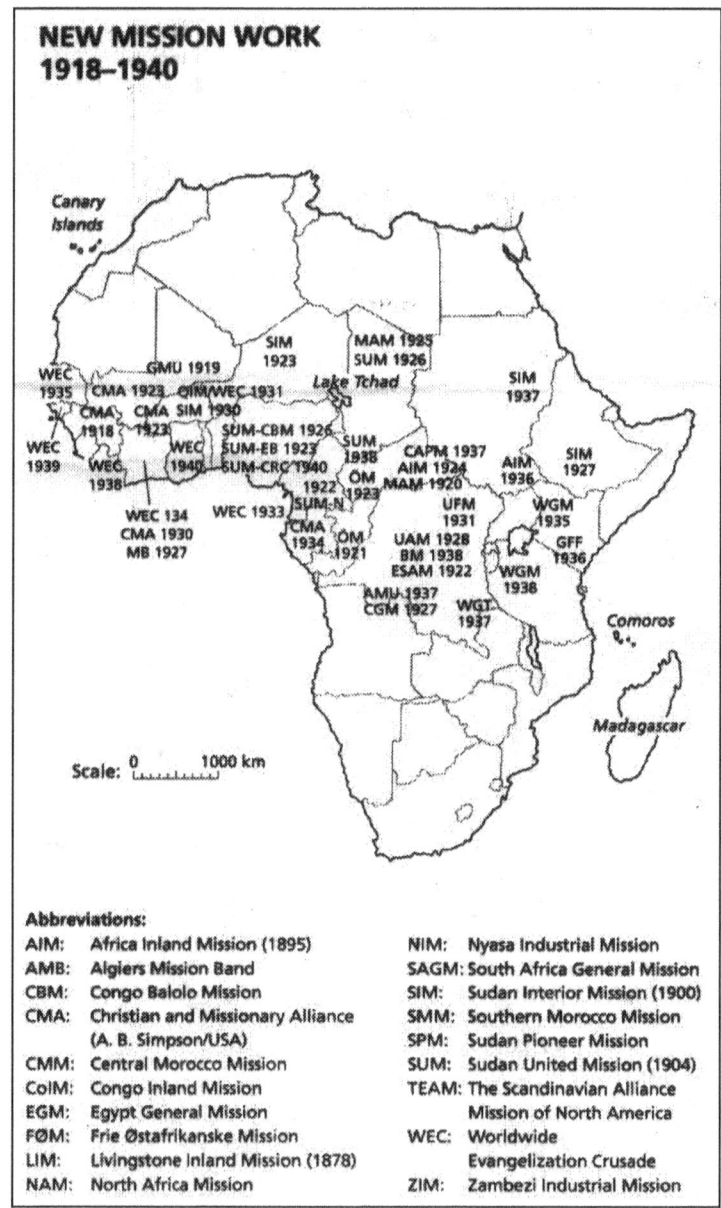

Map of Faith Missions in Africa in the period 1918-1940 (From: Fiedler: The Story of Faith, p.85).

He was influenced by the Brethren as well, and later he became a Baptist. In 1893, as independent missionaries, Bingham together with others went to the interior of Sudan, trying to reach Lake Chad. All except Bingham died due to problems of malaria, and lack of equipment.

A second attempt was made in 1900, by which time Bingham had formed his own society, the *Sudan Interior Mission*. The S.I.M. was successful in regions like Northern Nigeria, Niger, Southern Ethiopia, Sudan, Liberia, Somalia, and Ghana. The work led to the foundation of *Evangelical Churches of West-Africa* (E.C.W.A.), having now two or three million members, and its own missionary society with about a thousand missionaries.[10] The success of S.I.M. in Nigeria and other countries after the *Second World War* was partly due to its literature and radio work.[11]

In 1904 the *Sudan United Mission* was founded by Lucy Kumm-Guinness and her husband Karl Kumm. The mission began in Nigeria and from there it penetrated into the Sudan belt. The results were a church in Nigeria with millions of members,[12] and a church in Sudan, later heavily persecuted by the Muslim regime.[13]

In the North of the Sudan belt S.I.M. and S.U.M. worked in a border situation with Islam. They aimed at converting the remaining pagan tribes of Northern Nigeria before they would turn to Islam. Unfortunately most of the northern border tribes converted to Islam.[14]

Hospital of the Sudan Interior Mission in Galmi, Niger.

---

[10] Fiedler, *Faith Missions*, p. 50;

[11] Cf. Hildebrandt, *History of the Church in Africa*, pp.208, 209.

[12] Hildebrandt, *History of the Church in Africa*, p.205, describes a doubling of church attendance in S.U.M. areas in Nigeria and other places of West Africa between 1935 and 1940.

[13] Cf. Hastings, *Church in Africa*, p. 552.

[14] Cf. Hildebrandt, *History of the Church in Africa*, pp.159,160.

Chapter 15

Unity and Cooperation

1. What is Unity?

a. Diversity and Truth

The issue of unity and cooperation has attracted the attention of many people, especially the church leaders.[1] Unity, according to Scripture, is characterised by *diversity* and by *truth*. This applies to God and also to His creation.

First, in unity there is *diversity*. God is one. *Deuteronomy* 6: 4 (KJV) says: 'Hear o Israel, the Lord our God is one God'. In *Mark* 12: 29, 32, *Romans* 3: 30, and *James* 2: 19 this is repeated. But our God is also diverse. 'There are three that bear record in heaven, the Father, the Word, and the Holy Ghost, and these three are one' (1 *John* 5:7 KJV). God's diversity is an essential aspect of His character. It reflects His Tri-Unity, the Father who creates, the Son who recreates, and the Holy Ghost who quickens to life. Together the three are in all the works of our one God. Diversity in unity is a main characteristic of the created things, including man. In 1 *Cor.* 12: 12 ff. we are reminded of the human body's diversity. Yet, in its diversity the body is cohesive. The members of the body and the senses and functions of the mind are different, but there is no schism, for they are cooperating harmoniously, thus constituting the oneness and strength of the human being.

A Family: Unity in Truth and Diversity (from: web.syr.edu/~jrpierce/family.html).

Secondly, in unity there is *truth*. Being one, having unity is being true. This again is first of all shown in God. 'He is a God of truth, and without iniquity' (*Deut.* 32: 4). And Jesus Christ, through whom we know God in his oneness, says: 'I am the way, the truth, and the life' (*John* 14: 6). And again this is reflected in the created things. True unity, however divers it may be, is strong, healthy, and trustworthy. The bodily members and the spiritual functions of the human being can be trusted to cooperate in truth and faithfulness. The whole of nature is a composition

---

[1] Besides this chapter, study also: Shaw, *The Kingdom*, pp. 282-288; Sundkler and Steed, History of the *Church in Africa*, pp. 1018-1035; Hastings, *African Christianity*, pp. 159-162, 169, 292, and other pages; cf. Cairns, *Christianity through the Centuries*, pp. 468-500.

of endless variety that is composed to a faithfully working oneness of beauty and strength. In the true harmony of its parts the whole of nature gets its magnificence and glory. We see it also in marriage and family life. Husband and wife, their children, may be very different in character, but in their togetherness they are a strong and attractive unity, even reflecting the relationship between Christ and the congregation of believers (cf. *Eph.* 5: 22 ff). Thus, Scripture shows that there is unity in God and also unity in the things created by Him.

b. Analogy Qualified by Scripture

Depiction of Thomas Aquinas (from: The Demidoff Altarpiece by Carlo Crivelli).

There is an analogy between the unity of God and the unity of the created things. According to Thomas Aquinas (†1274) this analogy is an *analogy-of-being* (Latin: *analogia entis*). This opinion is a result of Thomas' view of the way in which the universal reality exists. He says that the structure of nature is similar to the structure of supra-nature. In principle there is comparability. Being in the eternal reality can be compared to being in the finite reality. This analogy enables natural reason to penetrate into the supra-natural knowledge of God, although with the help of God's grace. In Thomas' view the possibility of salvation for man depends on this. Salvation is only possible within the framework of *analogical togetherness* of human nature and divine grace. And this *analogical togetherness* leads to the possibility and the necessity of *cooperation* between human reason and divine revelation. 'Natural reason ascends from below above the knowledge of created things to God. And God descends from above meeting man'. In various ways Thomas tried to defend this idea which gives nature an upward power that can penetrate into the supra-natural. In his view the lower things support the higher ones, they even absorb part of them, which enables them to climb higher.[2]

But the analogy between Creator and created things cannot be explained in these terms of Thomist philosophy. Creatures do not harbour such a positive upward quality, because of the reality of *sin* and *death*. God is perfect but God's creation has lost its perfection. According to some, the fact of God's unity necessarily means that the diversity in nature is truly one in the same way. But this view denies the difference that is there between God and his creation. God is then sup-

---

[2] The analogy-of-being Thomas developed in the first part of his *Summa Theologiae* (I,q.45a.7, and I,q.47a.1); we used a survey in: H. Meyer, *Thomas von Aquin: sein System un seine geistesgeschichtliche Stellung*, Bonn: Hannstein, 1938, pp.152-167.

posed to be in everything, all things in nature would be divine, hence they would be one. This view also denies the awesome reality of the brokenness of created things by *sin*. Creation has fallen into sin. That is why the splendid unity in diversity and truth has been damaged utterly.

c. Restoration through Salvation by Christ

Restoration of the real unity in the God given diversity and truth cannot be achieved by man. The way to the regeneration of unity is the way of the Cross where Jesus Christ through his suffering and death restored unity by defeating the powers of Satan, death and sin. Only in Him is unity to be found. Through faith in Him man can go the way of the true and diverse unity that God has meant for His people. Faith in Christ comprises the acceptance of the Word of God as the highest and authoritative rule for all aspects of life. This applies to individuals and also to churches. Unity without being in Christ and without being obedient to the Word of God is no real unity. It can be even the *opposite* of it. Satan also pretends to seek unity. But this unity, however attractive it sometimes may seem, is a damaging unity that has no future but leads to eternal loss.

It is good to realise these things when we are discussing the pursuits for unity in the world in general, and in the churches in particular. Throughout history man has attempted to make his own unity in a way that distorted Christ and the Word, or even swept Christ and the Word aside. Real Christian unity is a spiritual and theological unity that is rooted in the Scripture, which through the Holy Spirit gives 'truth in love' (*Eph.* 4: 11, 15). However, attempts at unity that were labelled truly Christian, without being guided by the authoritative voices of the Word and the Spirit, have been no exception.

2. Syncretism

When Christian scholars and ministers lose confidence in the absolute divine authority of the Bible, they readily mix and combine elements which are contradictory in nature. Compromise is made in order to accommodate contemporary teachings and traditions. This has been done in Western theology by the liberal movements of Modernism and Post-Modernism. In an African context, liberalism also plays a role.

In some quarters of older African mainline churches Western liberalism has invaded. This has produced a mentality that it does not really matter what you believe, as long as there is some superficial connection to the Bible. This attitude in the African context paved the way for another consequence of liberal thought, syncretism, i.e. for the joining together of opposite beliefs of African Traditional Religions and Christianity.[3] Old examples of syncretism are the cults of the Nyau

---

[3] Wilbur O'Donovan, *Biblical Christianity in Africa Perspective*, Paternoster Press, 1992, p. 258.

Societies and the Mbona shrine in Malawi. After the missionaries arrived, members of these cults tried to combine their religious views with elements from Christianity.

Syncretism often operates under the disguise of *African Christian Theology*. By the end of the colonial era efforts were intensified to relate Christian theology to the African context. Although this process was started by white theologians, in a later stage it connected to the opinion of many Africans that the theology of the missionaries was too much a presentation of Western issues, and that it had failed to answer the important questions in African culture. Serious attempts were made to create a genuinely *African Christian Theology*. As such inculturation or incarnation of Christian teaching in Africa cannot be opposed by any Christian. But by mixing religious conceps the uniqueness and the absolute authority of the Word of God gets lost. Like the Israelites in the Old Testament who worshipped JHWH and also other Gods, African syncretists mix their vision of God with the traditional idea of the Supreme Being.[4] They fail to realise that God will not tolerate the worship of Himself to be joined with the practices of non-Christian religions as He is the jealous God. Many traditional rituals are related to non-Christian religions.[5]

It is not difficult to understand why Africans practise syncretism. People want to rediscover their African cultural past. Since culture and religion are so closely related, this has led to a return to traditional religions practices. Another important cause is emotional concern for the spiritual welfare of relatives who died before the Gospel came. Besides, many Christians have not distanced themselves from the traditional African perspective that God is distant and unapproachable. That is why they remain attached to a closely related pre-Christian perception of the nearness of lesser spirits and divinities who are said to help in the ordinary problems of life. Traditional African people find it difficult to address Christ directly. They are used to the idea of the ancestral spirits that play an intermediary role.[6] These are some of the reasons and backgrounds many people, including some leading theologians, try to justify pre-Christian traditional religions.

Many Africans think they are following Jesus Christ, without actually recognising Him as their only Saviour in all circumstances of life. In crisis situations they tend to go back to ancestral spirits or to mystical and magical powers. Then they resort to syncretistic practices by visiting the witchdoctor for assistance, or by indulging in the use of fetishes, magic, charms, divination and even sorcery.[7]

---

[4] R.J. Gehman, *African Traditional Religion in Biblical Perspective*, Nairobi: East African Educational Publishers, 1993³, p. 274.

[5] O'Donovan, *Biblical Christianity*, p. 257.

[6] O'Donovan, *Biblical Christianity*, p. 262;

[7] Maxford Blessings Chilindeni, 'Development of Syncretism in African Churches', Zomba Theological College, 2004, unpubl. Paper; M.F. Salanjira, *The North-Eastern Chewa: Response and Conversion to Christianity*, Zomba: Chancellor College n.d, [c. 1987].

3. Examples in Malawi

African history -similarly to European history- shows that Christianity took much time to ban *Traditional Religions* and in quite some cases has never fully succeeded to do that until today. Bregje de Kok studied the situation in Malawi. She noted that many Christians in Malawi 'are said to continue performing indigenous religious practices like funeral rites, birth rituals, and initiation ceremonies', and that 'many Malawians did not leave behind their traditional beliefs like witchcraft and ancestral spirits. De Kok looked into the backgrounds of 'devoted Christians' who at the same time can 'be involved in *African Traditional Religion* (A.T.R.)', against the pronounced will of their churches.[8] 'A.T.R. is to a large extent alive for different people from different strata of the population'. Yet, Christianity is the central religion of the country, and those who turn to A.T.R. do mainly so at *crisis-moments*, when death and sickness strike. Therefore De Kok thinks that A.T.R. and Christianity 'co-exist in the lives of many Malawians' in such a way that they separate the two, and 'consider the two as not obstructing each other'. In her opinion this situation does not reflect the mixing or fusion of religions that is generally meant by the concept *syncretism*, and as such 'has obtained negative connotations'. She thinks that Malawian Christians lead their dualistic lives 'in a skilful and unproblematic way'.[9]

Much of De Kok's interesting analysis of the religious situation in Malawi is likely to be true, but her conclusion is certainly not. The Christian faith cannot go side by side with other faiths in the lives of Christians. At all moments and especially face to face with death their allegiance is to Christ only. How can there be a living relationship with Christ as Saviour when at decisive moments one resorts to witchraft and magic?

Another example of syncretism concerns education. For a long time Mission and Church were the main organisers of education. However, after the *Second World War* 'the period in which the Church had been the most important contributor in education was drawing to a close',[10] first in West Africa and then also in other parts of Africa. The colonial governments and after them the national independent governments tightened their hold on education. In some countries officially room was given for anti-Christian feelings in schools, in other countries a policy of religious neutrality was developed.

Still others tried to operate from a position of religious plurality, offering pupils and students the idea of a general religious approach in which all religions to an extent would be taken together on the basis of equality. Of course this approach is apt to transgress the boundaries of faithfulness to Christ and Scripture. An example

---

[8] Bregje de Kok, *Christianity and African Traditional Religion: Two Realities of a Different Kind*, Zomba: Kachere Series, 2004, pp. 4-6, 20.
[9] De Kok, *Christianity and African Traditional Religion*, p.57.
[10] Cf. Hildebrandt, *History of the Church in Africa*, p.207.

of it is to be found in the new syllabus of *'Religious and Moral Education'* developed for Malawian Government Schools, issued in 1998 by the *Malawi Institute of Education* under the responsibility of the Ministry of Education, Sports and Culture.[11] Technical and financial support was given by the *World Bank* and by some *NGO*'s. The new syllabus says it is aimed at the addressing of certain problems, such as overpopulation, gender, pollution of the environment, AIDS, violence, drug abuse. It is thought that these problems could be addressed with the support of Malawi's three main religions, Christianity, Islam and African Traditional Religion. According to official opinion, the problems could be tackled through *multifaith instruction* in secondary schools. During three teaching periods a week, over 30 weeks in a year, certain religious themes are discussed from the angles of the three religions. Proselytising in favour of one of the religions is not allowed. There is the suggestion in this that one religion is as good as any other. Of course, the elements in a religion that exclude the other religions cannot be included in the syllabus. Only those elements that the religions are supposed to share, are highlighted. Everything that could annoy or anger the other is left out or played down. In the end comparisons between the three religions make them look like one another. For instance, when the syllabus deals with the causes of death, the three positions are almost similar. It is striking though, that the Christian view of sin acknowledging it to be the origin of death, is conveniently not discussed. The approach of the new syllabus inevitably leads to a denial of the main principles of the Christian faith.

4. Ecumenism and Christian Cooperation

There has always been a desire for Christian unity, as a consequence of Christ's admonition to *spiritual unity* in *John* 17: 11, 21. This desire is reflected in the *Apostolic Confession of Faith,* referring to the most basic characteristics of the Church, its *catholicity,* its *holiness*, and its *unity*. In these characteristics the Church expresses that it belongs to Christ. The Church is catholic, holy and one because it is the communion of people that are bound to Christ in faith. In a special way this is experienced by Christians when they recognise one another in Christ, beyond the boundaries of churches and denominations. They discover their *spiritual unity*.

Many considered spiritual unity as a preparation for *organisational unity*. Reformers in the 16th century like Luther, Zwingli, Calvin, Bucer and Cranmer tried hard to safeguard the organisational unity of the Church. Impressive attempts started in the 19th century as a consequence of the *Evangelical Revivals* and *Awak-*

---

[11] The new syllabus is widely discussed, for instance by: Jessica Olausson, *Christianity, Islam, Malawian Traditional Religion and the Malawian Culture: Possible Implications of the New Primary School Syllabus in Religious Education in Malawi,* Linköping University, 1996; S.W. Breton, 'Religious and Moral Education Syllabus', in *The Lamp*, Sept./Oct. 2000, no.25, p. 17;

enings, especially because of the desire to facilitate mission. People like Von Zinzendorf, Carey and Huntington led the way. Sometimes this led to *complete fusion* of old denominations into new ones. Even churches of unlike backgrounds fused, like the Presbyterians, Baptists, Congregationalists, and Methodists who fused into the *United Church of Canada* in 1925.

But earlier and more often it led to all kinds of *cooperation* between churches and denominations. The first organisation of cooperation was the *Evangelical Alliance* (London 1848, America 1867), which linked individuals rather than churches. In its wake other national and international bodies took shape mainly as a reaction against the emerging *liberalism* and *modernism*. Examples of this kind are: *World Christian Fundamentals Association* 1919, *American Council of Churches* 1941 (Carl McIntyre)[12], *International Council of Christian Churches* 1948, *World Evangelical Fellowship* 1951.

Nicholas Ludwig, Count von Zinzendorf (1700-1760), founder of the Moravian Mission at Herrnhut.

The 20th century 'ecumenical movement' aspired to organisational unity, even at the expense of spiritual unity. The term *'ecumenical'* was used first by the *Faith and Order Movement* at its conference in 1936. This *Faith and Order Movement*, and the *Work and Life Movement* joined together into an entirely new organisation the *World Council of Churches* (W.C.C.) in 1948. In 1961 the *International Missionary Council* was added to the pillars of this W.C.C, during its World Assembly in New Delhi. The word 'ecumenical' coined by the W.C.C. is derived from the Greek word *'oikoumene'* which was in use during the time of the Roman Empire as a secular reference to the inhabited world. Since 1948 in many countries *National Councils of Christian Churches* were formed with most of the mainline churches and often also the *Roman Catholic Church* as members. The majority of these national councils and mainline churches are affiliated to the W.C.C. The *Roman Catholic Church*, however, although having the status of observer, never joined the W.C.C. After the *Second Vatican Council* in the 1960s the Roman Catholic Church gave way to a more ecumenical attitude. Since then they have cooperated with the 'separated brethren' mainly in Bible translation and ethical issues. In 1961 in New Delhi many of the *Eastern Orthodox Churches* joined the W.C.C. Besides, international Protestant bodies representing churches with similar backgrounds, like the *Lutheran World Federation* (L.W.F.) and the *World Alliance of Reformed Churches* (W.A.R.C.) became affiliated to the W.C.C.

---

[12] The *American Council of Churches* should not be confused with its liberal counterpart the *Federal* or *National Council of Churches*.

But still a large number of churches and international church alliances have not joined because of the *liberal* and *(neo-) modernistic* tendencies in the ecumenical movement of W.C.C. Since the fall of *communism* and the Soviet Empire W.C.C. membership in the West has become less popular, because many realised that this liberal branch of ecumenism had done little to protect and defend the persecuted Christians in the former communist countries. Reformed and Presbyterian Churches have several national and international organisations of cooperation, like the *Reformed Ecumenical Synod*, based in Grand Rapids, U.S.A.

5. The Situation in Africa

In Africa various forms of cooperation, union and fusion took shape, some under the umbrella of the W.C.C. ecumenical movement, and others as a reaction against it or just as an expression of unity of churches with like background. Like in the West, in most African countries *National Councils of Christian Churches* have been formed, sometimes with combined Protestant and Roman Catholic membership. They originated in the thought that missionary societies could cooperate more. Early examples are the *Gold Coast Christian Council* and the *Christian Council of Nigeria* (1929). 'In Kenya the movement toward a joint missionary council was preceded by an attempt to form a single Protestant Church which would be built up by Protestant Missions'.[13] In 1913 a constitution was signed by representatives of the Africa Inland Mission, the Church Missionary Society., and the United Methodist Mission. However, immediately after that Anglicans of the C.M.S. began to oppose the process of full unification, and also the A.I.M. showed hesitations. A schism in the Anglican community on the issue of *Theological Modernism* complicated the relationship with other Missions and Churches. Attempts for a united Church in the period 1961-1967 failed too. Like other countries Kenya got its *National Christian Council*, in 1944. Later these *National Christian Councils* became *National Church Councils*. They were originally meant to promote evangelism and church growth. After the *Second World War* they often politicised, when liberal leaders tried to push them into the ecumenical movement.[14]

As for international bodies, most of the above mentioned universal organisations play roles in Africa. Besides, there are African international bodies. The pioneer international body in the line of the general ecumenical movement is the *All Africa Conference of Churches* (A.A.C.C.), founded in Kampala in 1963. Its Headquarters is in Nairobi. The first leader was Canon Burgess Carr of Liberia. In collaboration with the *World Council of Churches*, and financially supported by this ecumenical organisation, the A.A.C.C. developed various political, social and educational programmes. In the course of time it dealt with issues like reconciliation of warring peoples, and African self-hood. A controversial issue was Burgess

---

[13] Hildebrandt, *History of the Church in Africa*, pp. 229-231.
[14] Cf. Hildebrandt, *History of the Church in Africa*, pp.205, 206.

Carr's call at A.A.C.C.'s General Assembly in Lusaka 1974 for a *moratorium* on foreign mission, that is on 'external assistance in money and personnel'. The call was earlier aired by John Gatu, president of the *Presbyterian Church in Kenya* and by the Anglican bishop of Nairobi, Henry Okullo.[15] Some Western churches subsequently reduced their assistance. But the Roman Catholic Church, and the Evangelicals rejected the proposal. Continuing full strength Roman Catholic missionary presence, urbanisation, the resurgence of Islam, revived missionary interest in some Western churches and movements, and other challenges made the moratorium programme fail, and this also led to a new increase of mission agencies in Africa, and to the establishment of new *partnership structures* between Western and African churches.

On the Evangelical side in various countries *Evangelical Fellowships* were formed. Sometimes cooperation at a regional level led to the formation of new churches. An example is the the establishing in 1954 of the *Association of Evangelical Churches of West Africa*, resulting from the work by S.I.M. The Association has its own *African Missionary Society*.[16] From 1967 to 1973 its Secretary General was the Byang Kato (see chapter 13, section 3c).

In 1966 these fellowships founded the *Association of Evangelicals in Africa and Madagascar* (A.E.A.M.), also based in Nairobi. The second Secretary General and the first African to hold that position, was Byang Kato. Unfortunately this promising theologian died in 1975, at the age of 39. The danger of emerging liberalism in theology and church life was one of the reasons for the establishment of the A.E.A.M.. The constitution says that the Association is meant to 'alert Christians to trends and spiritual dangers which would undermine the Scriptural foundation of the Gospel testimony'.[17] The assemblies of the A.E.A.M. have mainly dealt with issues like evangelism and witness. Evangelical parachurch organisations have opened new ways for cooperation. An example is the *Accrediting Council for Theological Education* (A.C.T.E.A.), which works on upgrading the standards of theological training and providing new ways for church unity. Other organisations are *World Vision, World Relief, Tear Fund,* and *MAF*.

Theologically and ecclesiastically related to Evangelical orthodoxy are the organisations in which the more classically Reformed and Presbyterian Churches cooperate. An example is the *Reformed Ecumenical Synod* with members among the Reformed family of churches in South Africa and in regions where this family spread to, e.g. the *Reformed Church of East Africa* in Kenya and the *Nkhoma Synod* of the Malawian Presbyterians. Cooperation of Orthodox Evangelicals, Presbyterians and Reformed churches in the *International Council of Christian Churches* (I.C.C.C.) has spread to Africa. In 1975 the Ninth World Congress of the

---

[15] Cf. Ogbu U. Kalu, African Christianity: From the World Wars to Decolonization', in: Kalu et.al. (eds), *African Christianity*, pp. 359, 360.
[16] Hildebrandt, *History of the Church in Africa*, p. 209.
[17] Through: Hildebrandt, *History of the Church in Africa*, p.245.

I.C.C.C. took place in Nairobi's Yomo Kenyatta Conference Centre, some months before its liberal competitor and counterpart, the *World Council of Churches*, convened for its Ninth General Assembly at exactly the same place. Another important example of cooperation is *NetAct*, which is a network of theological institutions in the Presbyterian and Reformed tradition in Sub-Saharan Africa. In NetAct the Faculty of Theology of the University of Stellenbosch cooperates with sister theological institutions in Sub-Saharan Africa. It aims at promoting 'Congregational theology as practiced in the Christian Congregation as the body of Christ, discerning the will of God, in the process of interpreting the Scriptures and its own specific context, empowering the Congregation to address multiple problems, challenges and sufferings'.[18]

Independent churches also have their cooperative organisations. Some, like the Kimbanguists, are members of the W.C.C., others are not. Sometimes Independent churches profited from cooperation with Independents overseas, for example with Mennonite missionaries, who supported them in the field of theological education. In 1963 the *African Independent Churches Association* (A.I.C.A.) was formed, arranging an 'ambitious educational programme' for leaders and other members. Expert Western volunteers gave their support. Unfortunately the organisation collapsed because of financial troubles. Other independent churches cooperate in the Organisation of African Instituted Churches (O.A.I.C.). The O.A.I.C. has its origins in the work of Bishop Markos of the *Coptic Orthodox Church* of Egypt with A.I.C.'s since 1976 in Nairobi. In 1978 Pope Shenouda invited leaders of A.I.C.'s from various countries for a conference in Cairo where the O.A.I.C. was founded. The basic aims of the organisation were teaching and training.

The *Roman Catholic Church* in Africa has become more open for cooperation because of the influence of the *Second Vatican Council*, and also because of a strong desire to be African. In 1994 a special Synod of African bishops was held in Rome, which was considered as recognition of African Roman Catholic self-hood. Beside the mainline type of Roman Catholicism that generally is more traditional in Africa than in the West, in many Parishes.

Small Christian Communities (S.C.C.) have emerged. These groups function at the levels of prayer and Bible study, pastoral activities, social action, and also in ecumenical activities. Through the *Charismatic Movement* there is an interaction between these groups and charismatic groups in the Protestant churches.

A Session of the African Synod of the Roman Catholic Church in Rome in 1994.

---

[18] See Website: http://academic.sun.ac.za/theology/netact.html

Part Two

Focus on South-Central Africa

Chapter 16

The Church in Malawi

1. David Livingstone

The history of missionary developments that led to the foundation of the Church in Malawi[1] starts with the initiative and the work of David Livingstone. This Scottish missionary and explorer visited Malawi in 1856. In 1841 he had arrived in Cape Town as a worker of the *London Missionary Society* (L.M.S.). This society was in principle non-denominational but in practice congregational. Livingstone's first mission was among the Makololo, later he travelled northward and then across Africa, from Luanda on the Angolan Atlantic coast to Quelimane on the Mozambican Pacific coast, seeing the Victoria Falls on the way. On completing this journey he visited England in 1856 where he caused a great enthusiasm for the missionary enterprise. Livingstone expressed his own missionary aims as follows:

David Livingstone (1813-1873), through his travels contributed much to the preparations for Mission in Africa.

'Sending the Gospel to the heathen must include much more than is implied in the usual picture of the missionary, namely a man going about with a Bible under his arm. The promotion of commerce must be attended to, as this more especially than anything else, demolishes that sense of isolation which heathenism engenders, and makes tribes feel themselves mutually dependent on, and mutually beneficial to each other'.

In 1856 Livingstone addressed the Senate House of Cambridge University, appealing to the Church of England, represented by her two universities, Oxford and

---

[1] For the History of the Church in Malawi, study also: Christoph Martin Pauw, Mission and Church in Malawi: The History of the Nkhoma Synod of the Church of Central Africa Presbyterian, 1889-1962, University of Stellenbosch, 1980; John McCracken, Politics and Christianity in Malawi 1875-1940: The Impact of the Livingstonia Mission in the Northern Province, Cambridge, CUP., 1977 [reprinted by Kachere/ Claim in 2000]; Andrew C. Ross, Blantyre Mission and the Making of Modern Malawi, Blantyre: Claim, 1996; D.D. Phiri, History of Malawi From the Earliest Times to the Year 1915, Blantyre: Claim, 2004, pp. 111-199; Sundkler and Steed, A History of the Church in Africa, pp. 118, 415-416, 448, 457, 467-482, 646, 652, 795-799, 975, 978-981; Baur, 2000 Years Christianity, pp. 428-431; Hastings, The Church in Africa, pp. 210, 212-213, 257, 276, 406, 410, 411, 418, 422-423, 425, 427-229, 432-433, 455, 457, 475, 487-480, 483-484, 486-488, 504-505, 522, 528, 532, 543-544, 549, 557, 580, 584, 590-593, 603; M.S. Daneels, Mbiri ya C.C.A.P. Sinodi ya Harare 1912-1982, Harare: C.C.A.P., no date, pp.11, 12, 18, 19, 47;

Cambridge, to start mission work as well as commerce in Malawi. He finished his speech with these words:

> 'I go back to Africa to try to make an open path for commerce and Christianity. Do you carry on the work I have begun? I leave it with you'.

Swahili Arab ruler Mlozi and his slaveraiders, Karonga, Lake Malawi 1890 (from: Shillington: History of Africa, p.256).

As a consequence, in 1858 a society called the Oxford and Cambridge Mission to Central Africa was founded. The name was later changed to Universities' Mission to Central Africa (U.M.C.A.), including also the Universities of Durham and Dublin. Before his return to Africa in 1858 Livingstone resigned from the L.M.S. and was appointed royal consul for 'Exploration in East and Central Africa'.

His work led to the beginning of missionary activities by mainline churches from Britain and elsewhere in Central Africa. These missions sometimes are called *'classical'*, in order to distinguish them from later missions by younger denominations using different methods, called *'post classical'*.

2. Classical Missions

a. Universities' Mission to Central Africa[2]

The *Universities Mission to Central Africa* (U.M.C.A.), from which the present Anglican Church in Malawi grew, was the first classical mission to work in Malawi. The first U.M.C.A. party left England for Malawi in 1860. It was led by Bishop Charles Frederick Mackenzie. They were helped by Livingstone whom they met at the mouth of the Zambezi River. They found a suitable mission site in the Shire Highlands, at a place called Magomero, north-east of Blantyre, situated on a slave trading route. When seeing the plight of the slaves in a passing slave caravan, the missionaries decided to liberate them. Soon the mission site became a kind of refugee camp and the missionaries got entangled in an armed campaign against the slave traders and mixed up in inter-tribal disputes. This made their

---

[2] Study also: A.E.M. Anderson-Morshead, *The History of the Universities Mission to Central Africa,* vol. I 1859-1909, London: UMCA, 1953; A.G. Blood, *The History of the Universities Mission to Central Africa,* vol. II 1907-1932, London: UMCA, 1957; R.G. Stuart, *Christianity and the Chewa: the Anglican Case 1885-1950*, University of London, 1974.

position very difficult. Moreover Mackenzie got ill and died. Abashed by the setbacks the group withdrew, first to Chibisa (now Chikwawa), and then under the new Bishop, William Tozer, through Morambala to Zanzibar, where they arrived in 1864.

Many years later the Anglicans returned to their first love. After some soundings in Malawi by Edward Steere, it was William Percival Johnson who actually re-started the work in Malawi.[3] He arrived at the lake in 1881, and laboured in the area until his death in 1928. In 1885 a site on Likoma Island was given to the mission, and the steamer *Charles Janson* was launched. Likoma became the new headquarters. For some time the mission conducted its activities into the mainland from there. Charles Maples took charge of the work on the island, while Johnson worked on the mainland from the steamer. Johnson built schools and churches at many places along the shore, each one put under a teacher. Priests who visited these places by steamer could be left to work at villages along the coast.

On Likoma Island schools were started for boys and girls. Most of them formed the core of the new Anglican Church, though not all in the same way. One of the pupils was John George Phillips. At baptism he got the name of a local missionary. Phillips became known as a faithful evangelist among migrant workers to South Africa. Finally he left the Anglican Church and established the independent *Christian Catholic Apostolic Church in Zion*, of which he himself became bishop.

Yao slave trader in southern Malawi, c. 1860 (from: Shillington: History of Africa, p.248).

In 1897 the Diocese of Likoma was separated from Zanzibar. The second Bishop of the Diocese was Chauncy Maples. He drowned in 1895 on the way to Likoma after consecration in England.

b. Livingstonia Mission[4]

Livingstonia Mission was the second classical mission to set foot in Malawi. The beginning of this mission is linked with the history of the missionary-explorer David Livingstone, who had died at Chitambo village in Zambia on the 1st of May 1873. His servants, Chuma (Juma) and Suze (Susi), buried his heart there, but his embalmed corpse was brought to the coast, taken to Britain, and buried in West-

---

[3] For his life, see: Beryl Brough, *St. Johnson of Lake Malawi*, Zomba: Kachere [forthcoming].

[4] John McCracken, *Politics and Christianity in Malawi 1875-1940: The Impact of the Livingstonia Mission in the Northern Province*, Cambridge CUP., 1977 [reprinted by Kachere/ Claim in 2000]; Kenneth R. Ross (ed.), *Christianity in Malawi: A Source Book*, Gweru: Mambo/ Kachere, 1996, pp. 13-80; Bill Jackson, *Send Us Friends*, Claim, n.d., pp. 3-258.

minster Abbey in April 1874. After Livingstone's funeral James Stewart, a missionary of Lovedale in South Africa, proposed to the General Assembly of the Free Church of Scotland that a mission should be established at Lake Malawi. He said:

> 'I would humbly suggest as the truest memorial of Livingstone, the establishment by this church, or several churches together, of an institution at once industrial and educational, to teach the truths of the Gospel and the arts of civilised life to the natives of the country, and which shall be placed in a carefully selected and commanding spot in Central Africa, where from its position and capabilities it might grow into a town, and afterwards into a city, and become a great centre of commerce, civilisation, and Christianity. And this I would call Livingstonia'.

Stewart appealed to rich businessmen, mostly in Glasgow, for financial support. His request elicited immediate response, and on the 21st of May 1875 the first group of missionaries set off for Malawi, under the leadership of E.D. Young, a naval officer, who had previously visited Lake Malawi during the Livingstone search expedition in 1867. Robert Laws, a medical missionary, who was later to become the leading figure of the mission, was the only ordained minister of the six men who comprised this party.[5] At Cape Town the party added four Malawians to its number. Among them were Tom Bokwito and Sam Sambani whom Livingstone had freed from the Arab slave traders at Mbame village in 1861, and had eventually been sent to Lovedale for studies. These men proved to be very useful since they acted as interpreters.

On the 12th of October the party arrived in Malawi in the Mangochi area of chief Mponda, who allowed them to settle anywhere on his land. The party chose Cape Maclear as a suitable site because it had a good harbour, was sheltered from wind, and appeared to be a healthy place. On Sunday the 17th of October 1875 they opened the first station of the Livingstonia Mission.

The following year James Stewart brought four Xhosa missionaries from Lovedale: Isaac William Ntusane Koyi, Mapas Ntintili, Shadreck Ngunana, and Isaac Wauchope.[6] They played an important role in the development of the Livingstonia Mission. In 1876 Young returned to Scotland, and James Stewart took charge for fifteen months, until the end of 1877, when Robert Laws took over as head of the mission, a position which he held for fifty years.

Work at Cape Maclear

The missionaries used the method of establishing a 'Christian village'. They encouraged Africans to come and live at the mission, and by 1880 there were 590 of

---

[5] Hamish McIntosh, *Robert Laws: Servant of Africa*, Carberry: Handsel Press, 1993.

[6] T. Jack Thompson, *Touching the Heart: Xhosa Missionaries to Malawi 1876-1888*; McCracken, *Politics and Christianity in Malawi 1875-1940*, pp.68, 79, 232f; George H. Campbell, *The Lonely Warrior*, Blantyre: Claim, 1975 [A short biography of William Koyi, expected to be reprinted by Kachere in 2006].

them, mostly refugees fleeing from slave traders, but also Makololo sent there from Lower Shire for schooling. In terms of conversions, the work at Cape Maclear was not very fruitful. For the five years during which the mission laboured there, they had only one baptised convert, Albert Namalambe, baptised on the 27th of March 1881. Furthermore, by the end of the five years, five missionaries, including Shadreck Ngunana from Lovedale, had died at Cape Maclear. The site thus proved to be unhealthy, therefore Laws decided to transfer the mission to Bandawe, which happened in 1881. Albert Namalambe was left in charge of the old mission station.

Mission work was indirectly facilitated by the *Livingstonia Central Africa Company*, set up for industrial and commercial purposes, under the management of John and Alfred Moir. Later the name was changed to *African Lakes Company*, popularly known as *Mandala*.

Work at Bandawe

At Bandawe the missionaries were welcomed by the Tonga, a tribe of some 60,000 people, who had been raided by the Ngoni. Their fortified villages were not safe enough. That is why they wanted the protection of the missionaries. Discussions in 1887 by Laws with the Ngoni chief Mbelwa prevented the subjugation of the Tonga.[7]

Laws decided that no civil jurisdiction should be exercised by the mission. Consequently the 'Christian village' approach was abandoned and replaced by evangelisation and schooling in the Tonga villages. The Tonga were eager to take advantage of the educational opportunities provided by the mission. By 1894 there were 18 schools in Tongaland with over 1000 pupils; in 1906 the number of schools had increased to 107 with over 3000 pupils.[8] The people valued the mission because it gave them the techniques which were needed for dealing with the new western oriented world. But for a long time there were no converts. The growth of the number of converts was not similar to the educational response. Traditional Tonga religion kept its hold for a long time. The first Tonga baptism took place in 1889, and in the 1890s the number of baptisms increased.

Robert Laws (1851-1934), missionary of the Free Church of Scotland to Malawi.

---

[7] McCracken, *Politics and Christianity in Malawi 1875-1940*, pp. 16-112.
[8] McCracken, *Politics and Christianity in Malawi 1875-1940*, pp. 113, 114.

The Church in Malawi

Mission to the Ngoni

Although the Ngoni were political and military conquerors over the Tonga and others, they soon followed the Tonga in their turn to Christianity. In 1882 William Koyi and William Sutherland went to the Ngoni and set up a mission at Njuyu. Walter Elmslie joined the work in 1885. The mission had some influence through evangelistic services and through employing labour. Chief Mbelwa at first did not fully welcome the missionaries, but William Koyi, having a Zulu background and being able to speak the language of the Ngoni chief, opened communications. In 1886 Mbelwa wanted missions in all the divisions of the Ngoni area. This was impossible, but Laws promised a station as soon as possible at Mount Walos, where the mission station Ekwendeni was founded in 1889. Later Njuyu became a sub-station of Ekwendeni.

Isaac William Ntusane Koyi, Xhosa missionary to the Ngoni people.

Laws and Elmslie especially tried to convert the higher ranks, reaching first the patriarchal and aristocratic structure of Ngoni society. This elitist approach changed with the arrival of Donald Fraser.[9] In 1889 another station was opened at Hora which was moved to Loudon in 1902, and was called Embangweni. Donald Fraser was in charge of this station. Fraser had been inspired by the English *Holiness Movement* of Keswick. Right from the beginning of his work among the Ngoni (and the Tonga) he showed an interest in the conversion of the masses. From 1898 he led a series of mass meetings in Ngoni country for Baptism and the Lord's Supper. At these meetings thousands confessed sin and guilt, turned to Christ, and accepted forgiveness and peace. In the wake of these meetings many were sent as missionaries to Northern Zambia,[10] and other revivalist campaigns were organised giving room for the continuation of the work of the Holy Spirit. These were instances of religious excitement that were uncommon in Presbyterianism. The new religious climate opened up to African forms. Fraser encouraged the composers of vernacular hymns. Among the best known of these composers of hymns were Mawelera Tembo, Charles Chinula and Peter Thole.[11]

---

[9] T. Jack Thompson, *Christianity in Northern Malawi: Donald Fraser's Missionary Methods and Ngoni Culture*, Leiden: Brill, 1995.

[10] The best known of these missionaries was David Kaunda, the father of Kenneth Kaunda, later for many years President of Zambia (cf. Sundkler and Steed, A *History of the Church in Africa*, pp. 473, 974).

[11] For the hymns, see: Kenneth R. Ross (ed.), *Christianity in Malawi: A Source Book*, Gweru: Mambo/ Kachere, pp. 49-67 ('Hymns of Early Christian Converts').

Khondowe

Bandawe was not to be the permanent site of the Livingstonia headquarters. In 1894 the mission moved to Khondowe, and there it settled permanently under the name of *Livingstonia Mission Station*.

As a consequence of the great educational response from the Tonga, Tumbuka[12] and Ngoni, Laws set up the *Overtoun Institution* for training of artisans and clerks, teachers, evangelists and pastors. There was an industrial department that gave training to apprentices in such skills as carpentry, building, engineering and printing. The Central School taught regular schooling and trained certified teachers. Above this there was a one year theology course. Later were added four more post-primary courses, one for evangelists, one for store and office workers, one for dispensary and hospital assistants, and one in arts. Law's vision, that the Institution would one day develop into a University, was curbed towards the end of his career, and has only recently been taken up again.

Mission station at Livingstonia, Northern Malawi.

c. Blantyre Mission[13]

This was the third mission to arrive in Malawi. It was started by the Established Church of Scotland, and was called Blantyre Mission after David Livingstone's birth place in Scotland.

Its first worker, Henry Henderson, entered the country as a member of the first Livingstonia party. Henderson, accompanied by Tom Bokwito, set out from Cape Maclear and travelled to the Shire Highlands in the southern region to look for a suitable site. Chief Kapeni gave Nyambadwe Hill, between Ndirande and Soche Mountains as a place for the establishment of the mission. Around the site, eventually the city of Blantyre emerged. The first party of missionaries arrived in the country in 1876. They opened Blantyre Mission Station on the 23rd of October 1876. The site seemed so suitable because the population was numerous and of a friendly disposition. Henderson received instruction to act as the general director

---

[12] Tumbuka general and religious history is described in: Silas S. Ncozana, *The Spirit Dimension in African Christianity: A Pastoral Study among the Tumbuka People of Northern Malawi*, Blantyre: Kachere/ Claim, 2002, pp. 43-110; For a brief but helpful survey of Tumbuka history, see: D.D. Phiri, *History of the Tumbuka*, Blantyre: Dzuka, 2000.

[13] Andrew C. Ross, *Blantyre Mission and the Making of Modern Malawi*, Blantyre: Claim/ Kachere, 1996.

and as a Christian magistrate of the settlement. The aim of the mission was stated as follows:

> 'The mission is industrial and evangelical, designed to be a nucleus of advancing centuries of Christian life and civilisation to the Nyasa and the surrounding region'.

St. Michael's and All Angels, C.C.A.P. church in Blantyre, designed by David Clement Scott, and built by Africans.

In July 1878 Duff Macdonald arrived to take charge of the mission. He had to carry out the Home Board's intention to create 'mission villages' that is, settlements with missionaries exercising civil jurisdiction. In this Yao dominated area slaves and refugees would seek shelter in the mission village. There they were safe from slavery and persecution. At the same time they were withdrawn from traditional African law and rule. Not well acquainted with African tradition, the missionaries soon encountered conflicts with the people they had come to christianise. In 1878 this even led to severe disciplinary action and death of a black offender. When the situation was noted, the Home Board sent a special commission of inquiry. Duff Macdonald was charged with mismanagement, and in March 1881 he and the first staff were withdrawn.

A new start took place when David Clement Scott (1853-1907) was sent to take charge of the mission in October 1881.[14] Scott set himself the goal of concentrating more on promoting religious work. He defined his aim as follows:

> 'Our purpose we lay down as the foundation of our work, that we are building the African Church, not Scottish or English, but African'.

Scott laid great emphasis on local leadership and responsibility in the church. He encouraged people like Joseph Bismarck,[15] Harry Matecheta,[16] John Gray Kufa and Harry Mtuwa. Scott's Africanisation programme earned him mistrust by the colonial government. Long after his departure the investigators of the rising of John Chilembwe in 1915, would try to blame him. Scott also developed a school system. This led to the establishment of the *Henry Henderson Institute* offering training in various areas. Another achievement was the publication of the *Cyclopaedic Dictionary of the Mang'anja language*, produced initially in 1892.

---

[14] For an assessment of his life and work, see: Andrew C. Ross, 'Wokondedwa Wathu: The Mzungu who Mattered', in: *Religion in Malawi* 7:3-8 (1997).
[15] Joseph Bismarck, 'A Brief History of Joseph Bismarck', Occasional Papers of the Department of Antiquities, no. 7, Zomba 1968, pp. 49-54.
[16] Harry Kambwrir Macheta, *Blantyre Mission: Nkhani ya Ciyambi Cake*, Blantyre, Hetherwick Press, 1951.

His 'excellence as linguist and cultural specialist' enabled him to initiate and contribute to the translation of Scripture into the vernacular language. The entire New Testament in Mang'anja was published in 1886.[17] In Blantyre, Scott is best remembered as the architect of the church of *St. Michael's and All Angels*, built in a combination of Western and Eastern styles. Alexander Hetherwick joined him in 1883,[18] and the two did much to restore and promote the good name of the mission. By the time Scott left for Kenya in 1897, and was succeeded by Hetherwick, the mission was running well. More stations such as Domasi, Zomba and Mulanje had been opened. Hetherwick was head of the mission until his retirement in 1928. In 1929 he published a revision of Scott's Dictionary, entitled *Dictionary of the Nyanja Language*,[19] and he also made a comprehensive *grammar book of the Nyanja language*.

Harry Apika Mtuwa († 1949), one of David Clement Scott's pupils who were trained and encouraged by him to be pastors and leaders of the young African Church. Mtuwa became a minister of the CCAP church in Zomba in 1916 (cf. Zomba C.C.A.P. Congregation, Then and Now: A Centenary Booklet, Zomba, 1998, pp. 7-10), and the picture has a place in its vestry.

d. Dutch Reformed Church Mission[20]

The *Dutch Reformed Church Mission* (D.R.C.M.) or *Nederduitsch Gereformeerde Kerk Sending* (N.G.K.S) from South Africa was the fourth mission to join in the evangelisation of Malawi. In 1886 the Synod of the Cape Province of the *Dutch Reformed Church* was looking for a new field for missionary work. Andrew Charles Murray, a nephew of Andrew Murray, the instigator and leader of South African mission work (see chapter 7 section 3), then a student of theology, made contact with Robert Laws through James Stewart of Lovedale.

Consequently Andrew Charles Murray became the first missionary of the South African *N.G.Kerk Mission* in Malawi. He arrived in the country in July 1888, and was welcomed at Bandawe by Laws. On a visit to a Nkhonde chief at the north of the Lake, Murray suffered from sunstroke. He went to Njuyu to recover. While he

---

[17] Ernst R. Wendland, *Buku Loyera: An Introduction to the New Chichewa Bible Translation*, Blantyre, Claim/ Kachere, 1998, pp. 20-23.

[18] For his memoirs, see: Alexander Hetherwick, *The Romance of Blantyre: How Livingstone's Dream Came True*, London: James Clarke, n.d. [1931].

[19] David Clement Scott and Alexander Hetherwick, *Dictionary of the Nyanja Language: Being the Encyclopaedic Dictionary of the Mang'anja Language*, London: Lutterworth Press, 612 pages, 1929 [reprints in 1951 and 1957].

[20] Christoph Martin Pauw, *Mission and Church in Malawi: The History of the Nkhoma Synod of the Church of Central Africa Presbyterian, 1889-1962*, University of Stellenbosch, 1980; A.L. Hofmeyr, *Het Land langs het Meer*, Stellenbosch, 1910; K.J. Mgawi, *CCAP Nkhoma Synod: Mbiri ya Mpingo ndi Mudzi wa Nkhoma 1896 mpaka 1996*, Nkhoma: Nkhoma Synod n.d.

was there Elmslie explained to him the policy and the experiences of the Livingstonia Mission. Since the Livingstonia Mission was operating in the north and the Blantyre Mission in the south, it appeared appropriate for the Dutch Reformed mission to operate in the centre.

In 1889 Murray together with Theunis C. Botha Vlok, who joined him that year, explored central Ngoni land, and decided to settle in the area of Chief Chiwere. They opened their first mission station at Mvera on the 28th of November 1889. Murray saw two particular needs. One was a good translation of the Bible, and the other was an institute for the training of teachers and evangelists. As soon as the work had started, in 1890 a school and medical services were opened at Mvera. The school was run by Tomani whom Murray had fetched from Cape Maclear.

During its early days the mission was regarded as part of the *Livingstonia Mission*. In 1894 a division was made between the area of the Livingstonia Mission and the area of the *Dutch Reformed Mission*. The dividing line was a little north of Kasungu. Shortly afterwards, more workers came from South Africa, including William Hoppe Murray, who remained in Malawi until 1937. W.H. Murray took over as head of the mission when A.C. Murray returned to South Africa in 1901. W.H. Murray's ideal was to expand the mission by means of outposts, schools and mission stations. By 1899 the number of missionaries had increased to eighteen, and by 1903 there were stations at Mvera, Kongwe, Livulezi, and Nkhoma. A network of schools was established, with Albert Namalambe, as the first African inspector. In 1904 a Normal School was opened at Mvera for the training of teachers. By 1914 there were 2000 African helpers, preaching to 60,000 people in 200 villages. J.L. Pretorius wrote that the Dutch Reformed mission made its greatest contribution at the village level. Its aim was always to establish a local church which would be self-supporting, self-governing, and which would expand from its own inner strength. The other emphasis of the mission was rural development. The mission stressed the need to set up village industries, and to promote agriculture. Until 1909 they issued their own money, a coin punched with two holes and stamped 'MM' (Mvera Mission).

The priority of the Dutch Reformed Church Mission was always the ingathering of souls for the Kingdom of God, followed by the building of the local church, schooling, and improving the medical and material conditions of the people. The Mission stressed the Bible as the highest authority for the life and the teaching of the Church and of individual Christians. It was strongly opposed to the Roman Catholic Church that was supposed to put the authority of Tradition and Church higher than the Bible.

Another notable aspect of the mission was the emphasis it placed on working with women and girls. Boarding homes for girls were opened at most of its stations. These girls were instructed in Christian matters, including various practical subjects which would help them to be good wives in their future marriages. Further the mission introduced pastoral or advisory activities among the girls, called *Chi-*

langizo, in order to impress upon them a more Christian life. At a later stage a Women's Guild (*Amayi a Chigwirizano*) was formed to coordinate all the activities of women's work.[21]

One of the most valuable contributions of the mission was the great role it played in translating the Bible into Chichewa, especially by the efforts of W.H. Murray. Together with Hetherwick and two African teachers, Murray worked on the New Testament and they published a new translation in 1906. The translation of the Old Testament by Murray and a team of African and European assistants took much longer. Eventually, in 1922, with the help of the *Scottish Bible Society* and the *British and Foreign Bible Society* the full Bible was published, entitled *Buku Lopatulika* (Holy Book).[22]

e. Church of Central Africa Presbyterian

Many of the early Scottish missionaries had been intent on the founding of a local church. Laws was of the opinion that the mission church should not merely be a Presbytery of the Home Church. He wanted to 'work towards a Central African Presbyterian Church which should include Blantyre and the Dutch'.

In 1899 the Livingstonia Presbytery was founded. This was seen as the first step towards a Central African Presbyterian Church. In 1902 the Blantyre Presbytery was set up as a Presbytery of the Church of Scotland. A meeting took place in 1904 with a view to uniting Blantyre and Livingstonia in a single church. It was decided not to use any existing confession of faith from the home churches as the doctrinal basis of the union, but to draw up a simple statement of Christian faith, and to have the *Apostles' Creed* as the sufficient confession of faith for the church.

In 1910 a *General Missionary Conference* was held at Mvera between representatives of Blantyre and Livingstonia. Dutch Reformed missionaries L. Hofmeyr and William H. Murray were present as observers on behalf of their mission. They were hesitant to join, because they feared that modernistic teaching would be brought into the C.C.A.P. by certain missionaries from Scotland, as some of their missionaries, working in South Africa, were accused of denying the Atonement and various other doctrines.

On the 27th of September 1924 the two Presbyteries of Blantyre and Livingstonia, held a united session. The motion to unite in one common Synod was unanimously approved, and Robert Laws was unanimously elected the first moderator. Thus came into being a united indigenous African Church. The next step was for the *Dutch Reformed Mission Church* with their centre at Nkhoma to join. Nkhoma joined in 1926 after being satisfied that the conditions and safeguards the *Dutch Reformed Mission Church* desired were included in the constitution.

---

[21] Isabel Apawo Phiri, *Women, Presbyterianism and Patriarchy: Religious Experience of Chewa Women in Central Malawi*, Blantyre: Claim/ Kachere, 2000², pp.73-93, and many other pages.

[22] Wendland, *Buku Loyera*, pp. 23-25.

f. The Roman Catholic Mission

Portuguese claims

The penetration of Central Africa by the Roman Catholic missions was started through the efforts of Charles Lavigerie (see chapter 11 section 1), founder of the order of the *White Fathers*, who in 1887 became Archbishop of Algiers. Apart from the White Fathers, an important role was played by the *Montfort Missionaries*.

In the beginning Lavigerie in his campaign in Central Africa cooperated with the Portuguese. In 1888 a Portuguese official, Antonio Cardobo, contacted chiefs in the area south of Lake Malawi about the possibility of starting a Roman Catholic Mission, to counteract the Scots. He made treaties with several chiefs, including Mponda and Matipwiri. Meanwhile two explorers, Serpa Pinto and Henry de Macedo, approached Lavigerie, because the Portuguese had no missionary orders of their own to occupy the area. Lavigerie would have liked the mission to be under his control, but the Portuguese claimed that the ecclesiastical jurisdiction in that part of Africa had been given to them by the Pope in the early 16th century.[23] Lavigerie was in no position to argue. The mission was to teach in the Portuguese language. The mission stations were to be Portuguese property, and spiritual authority was to be exercised by the Bishop of Mozambique. The Portuguese promised financial assistance to the mission until it should be self-supporting. The Portuguese wanted it to be a national mission. However, it was agreed that any Portuguese priest who joined the mission should undergo training with the White Fathers.

The White Fathers and the Montfort Fathers

In June 1889 Lavigerie sent *White Fathers* from Algiers to Malawi. This was part of Lavigerie's plan for Sub-Saharan Africa. The *White Fathers* everywhere were to establish a series of mission stations. Lavigerie laid down detailed instructions for the community life of the *White Fathers*, in each one of these stations, and for their missionary work. Each station must have at least three members. Their life was to be centred on prayer, meditation, and spiritual reading. They had to study and record details of religious, political and economic life of the people amongst whom they lived. The *White Fathers* placed great emphasis on religious instruction of the people. New converts had to undergo a four year preparation for baptism, and the examinations were taken very seriously. They tended to concentrate on the intensive cultivation of a limited area rather than on rapid expansion. The funds of the mission were limited, and so it was necessary for them to become, as far as possi-

---

[23] Under the *Padroado Agreement* between the Pope and the Portuguese, missionary priests in Portuguese colonies were directly responsible to the Portuguese Government.

ble, self-supporting. Vegetable gardens were planted at the stations, cash crops were developed and herds of cattle were started. The missionaries were practical men; many of them had been brought up as farmers.

The three lonely missionaries who stayed in Malawi for two years were not very successful. From 1889 to 1891 these *White Fathers* were at Mponda, south of Lake Malawi. Political difficulties arising between Great Britain and Portugal on the question of demarcation of colonial territories, contributed to the failure of this first attempt.[24]

Permanent settlement of the Roman Catholic missions dates from 1901 and 1902, when successively the *Montfort Fathers* and again the *White Fathers* started their work.[25] The *Montfort Fathers* were of French and Dutch background.[26] In 1901 they sent their first missionaries including Pierre Bourget, who was leader of the group, Antoine Winnen, and Auguste Prezeau. These men started work among the Ngoni. Sundkler says that they 'understood the authoritarianism of the Ngoni more readily than the Chewa system which had more indeterminate authority'.[27] On the 25th of July 1901 the party reached the area of Njobvuyalema, a sub-chief of the Maseko Ngoni paramount chief Gomani. Without much preparation a number of Ngoni were baptised.[28] The Montfortian missionaries in the first four years are said to have baptised seventy-six people.[29] The *Montfort Fathers* also associated with the Lomwe-people, a weak and vulnerable group, who had arrived in southern Malawi as refugees from Mozambique. Through the work of the *Montfortians*, the Roman Catholic Church in the south has a strong Lomwe majority.[30]

Edel Mary Quinn (1907-1944), planted the work of the Legion of Mary in Malawi and in other countries of East and Central Africa.

In June 1902 *White Fathers* under the leadership of Guyard and Perrot opened their first mission at Chiwamba. In September a second station was opened at Mua

---

[24] Cf. Ian Linden, *Mponda Mission Diary 1889-1891*, Lilongwe: White Fathers, 1989. Extracts in: K.R. Ross (ed.), *Christianity in Malawi: A Source Book*, pp.15-22.
[25] Cf. Roland Vezeau, *The Apostolic Vicariate of Nyasa: Origins and First Developments 1889-1935*, Rome: Archives, Missionari d'Africa, 1989 [re-edited by Kachere, 2006];
[26] Hubert Reijnaerts, Ann Nielsen, and Matthew Schoffeleers, *Montfortians in Malawi: Their Spirituality and Pastoral Approach*, Blantyre: Kachere/ Claim, 1997. A note on p. 137 says that the *Montfort Fathers* are often confused with the *Marist Brothers*, who also work in Malawi.
[27] Sundkler and Steed, *A History of the Church in Africa*, p. 479.
[28] Reijnaerts, et.al., *Montfortians in Malawi*, pp. 32-34.
[29] Reijnaerts, et.al., *Montfortians in Malawi*, p.123.
[30] Cf. Sundkler and Steed, *A History of the Church in Africa*, p.797.

on the Southern Lake shore, and a year later Kachebere was founded. In 1912 the *White Fathers* opened a seminary at Mua, which was transferred to Kasina in 1927. In 1939 the seminary was moved to Kachebere. The *White Fathers* also started a leprosarium at Mua, in 1927. In 1932 they opened a printing press at Bembeke, and shifted it to Likuni in 1949.

Founder of the *Legion of Mary*, in Malawi was Edel Quinn. The Legion of Mary was an organisation for lay apostolate originating from *Catholic Action*. Edel Quinn was based in Nairobi from 1936 until her death in 1944. She visited Malawi in 1940-1941, and recruited the first organisers of the Legion of Mary.[31]

Roman Catholic secondary school teaching was helped by the arrival of the *Teaching Brothers*, the *Marists*.

Conflict with the Nyau Societies

There was a continual struggle between the Roman Catholic missions and the *Nyau societies*. The missionaries especially objected especially to certain dances and ritual practices, and the introduction of masks. The Nyau sometimes used masks that distorted the Christian message by representing Mary, Joseph and Peter. They presented themselves as the guardians of traditional society that was said to be disrupted by the missionaries.[32] In order to combat mission influence the Nyau rules were changed, so that children of school age were able to join. Thus the *Nyau Societies* were a powerful force in reducing school attendance.

3. Post-Classical Missions

In 1891 Malawi became a British Protectorate. In the new colonial situation the classical missions had to re-orientate themselves as to the state-church relationship. At the same time colonial rule gave room for a type of missions that deviated from the classical ones. Some of the characteristics of these Post-Classical Missions or Faith Missions are mentioned in chapter 14.

a. Joseph Booth and the Industrial Missions

Unlike the Faith Missions in general, those in Malawi did not come to an unreached area. By 1890 there were missionaries in all regions of Malawi. Yet, many people of Nyasaland had never heard the Gospel.

Joseph Booth was a main founder of several Post-Classical Missions in Malawi.[33] He was also one of the first missionaries who pleaded for the rule of Church

---

[31] Cf. Reijnaerts, et.al., *Montfortians in Malawi*, pp.238,239, 247.
[32] Cf. Orison Chaponda, *Gule Wamkulu in the Catholic Church, Lilongwe Rural: A Cultural Phenomenon and a Pastoral Problem*, Zomba: University of Malawi, 1998 [unpublished MA module].
[33] H. Langworthy, *Africa for the Africans: The Life of Joseph Booth*, Blantyre: Claim, 1996;

and Society by Africans themselves.[34] Booth was a British, but he had worked in Auckland (New Zealand) and Melbourne (Australia) as a businessman, selling milk products for ten years. After a dream by his wife Mary Jane, in which she saw a Chinese calling them to become missionaries, the couple applied with organisations like the *China Inland Mission* and the *Baptist Missionary Society*. But being considered too old, they were not accepted. Mary Jane Booth died three weeks before departure. In the meantime they had founded their own organisation. Booth came to Malawi in 1892 to establish missions that would be interdenominational, whose missionaries should earn their living by their industry.

The idea of industrial missions was new to *Faith Missions*, although it had been applied by *Classical Missions* like Livingstonia, Blantyre, and Nkhoma. However, there was a difference. Whereas these Classical Missions used the idea for training people in industrial skills like agriculture, carpentry, or laundry, for Booth industry was the means for the missionaries to support themselves, independently from any overseas donor. He would accept money from donors, but basically the missionaries were to live on their own industry. That is why he started to grow cash crops, mainly coffee. As he needed the vicinity of people and markets where he could sell the goods, he settled near the *Blantyre Mission*. Allegedly he 'stole' John Chilembwe from Blantyre Mission. Chilembwe had been to school there, but was not yet baptised.

In 1892 Booth opened the *Zambezi Industrial Mission* (Z.I.M.) at Mitsidi near Blantyre. Z.I.M. is now called *Zambezi Evangelical Church* (Z.E.C.). It is a kind of Baptist church, although its organisation is Presbyterian like. In 1893 Booth founded the *Nyasa Industrial Mission* at Likhubula, now *Evangelical Church of Malawi* with its centre at Ntambanyama.

Elliot Kamwana (second from the left) and Joseph Booth, 1909 (from: Chakhanza, Voices, p. 28).

Elements of Booth's varied message were taken over by others, who followed ways that were not necessarily Booth's own. Examples are Elliot Kamwana and Charles Domingo, alumni of Livingstonia's *Overtoun Institution*. Kamwana turned to Booth when he was at the Cape in 1907. He was especially attracted by Booth's fascination for the Watchtower message.[35] The movement of *Jehovah Witnesses* started with the thousands that were baptised

---

[34] Cf. Joseph Booth, *Africa for the Africans*, 1897 [edited by Laura Perry, reprinted by Claim/ Kachere in 1996]; Kenneth Ross, *Christianity in Malawi*, pp. 181-194; Hildebrandt, *History of the Church in Africa*, p.219, misunderstands Booth's defence of African selfhood, by accusing him of teaching 'racial intolerance' towards the whites;

[35] George Shepperson and Thomas Price, *Independent African: John Chilembwe and the Origin, Setting and Significance of the Nyasaland Native Rising of 1915*, Blantyre: Claim/ Kachere, 2000, pp.153-159.

by Kamwana.[36] Charles Domingo was one of the foremost of Livingstonia's students and teachers and also was at Lovedale at the Cape. Between 1907 and 1910 Domingo broke with Livingstonia, to set up his own independent African *Seventh Day Baptist Church*.[37]

In 1895 Booth began the Scottish *Baptist Industrial Mission* at Gowa in Ntcheu, since 1929 *Churches of Christ*.[38]

Another branch of Baptism in Malawi, was founded by Booth's disciple John Chilembwe, under the name *Providence Industrial Mission* (P.I.M.). Although P.I.M. indirectly is one of Booth's churches, we deal with it separately in the next section.

In 1901 the *Seventh Day Baptists* sold *Plainfield Mission* to the *Seventh Day Adventists* (S.D.A.) from America, who named it Malamulo. The first missionary was Joseph Booth together with the Branch family, black Americans. The daughter Mable Branch, founded and taught the first school at Malamulo. Booth did not stay long. In 1907 they were replaced by Cyrill Rogers. Mark Chakachadza started the S.D.A. Church at Matandani. Rogers gave the permission and bought the mission plot in 1908, the Koenigmachers built it up.[39] Also beginnings were made of the development of medical services at Malamulo and Matandani.[40] By now the S.D.A. Church has become the third largest denomination in Malawi.

But these Missions are missing a specific characteristic of the *Faith Missions*, as they are denominational.

b. Africa Evangelical Church of Malawi

The *South Africa General Mission*, whose headquarters was in London with a regional office in Cape Town, came to the Lower Shire at Nsanje in 1898, and later moved its centre to Chididi. At Luriwe Mission a school for the blind was established. In 1996 the name of the mission was changed to *Africa Evangelical Fellow-*

---

[36] Cf. J.C. Chakanza, *Voices of Preachers in Protest: The Ministry of two Malawian Prophets, Elliot Kamwana and Wilfred Gudu*, part 1 'From Preacher to Prophet: Elliot Kenan Kamwana and the Watchtower Movement in Malawi 1908-1956', Claim/ Kachere, 1998, pp. 12-54;

[37] Shepperson and Price, *Independent African*, pp.159-164; Cf. Kenneth Ross, *Christianity in Malawi*, pp.131-144.

[38] Literature on the Churches of Christ in different denominational groups, include: Ernest Gray, 'The History of the Churches of Christ Missionary Work in Nyasaland, Central Africa 1907-1930', in: *Churches of Christ Historical Society Occasional Paper*, no. 1, Cambridge, 1981; Anne Thiessen, *The Warm Heart of Africa*, Winona: Choate Publ., 1998; C.B. Shelburne, 'History of the Church of Christ in Malawi', n.p., n.d. [A brief factual account of the history of the Church of Christ in southern Malawi].

[39] Mvula and Lwesya, *Flames of Fire*, p. 66f; cf. Stefan Höschele, *From the Ends of the World to the Ends of the Earth: The Development of Seventh Day Adventist Missiology*, Zomba: Kachere, 2004.

[40] Cf. Yonah Hisbon Matemba, *Matandani: The Second Adventist Mission in Malawi*, Zomba: Kachere, 2003.

ship (A.E.F.),[41] and later joined S.I.M. International.[42] The church's name that resulted from its work is *Africa Evangelical Church of Malawi*..[43]

c. Providence Industrial Mission[44]

The *Providence Industrial Mission* was started by a Malawian, John Chilembwe. He was a Yao, born in Chiradzulu, who went to a Scottish mission school in Blantyre for his early education. In 1892 Chilembwe joined the work of Joseph Booth. In 1897 Booth took him along to the United States. There he studied at a black Baptist institution, *Virginia Theological Seminary* in Lynchburg. In 1900 Chilembwe returned to Malawi. Supported by the *National Baptist Convention Inc.* in America, now in Malawi known as *African Baptist Assembly*, Chilembwe started his own mission, called *Providence Industrial Mission*, at Mbombwe, in his home district Chiradzulu.

John Chilembwe (†1915) and his Family.

Chilembwe aimed at running his mission by involvement in industrial enterprise. His policy was not to depend on whites but upon his own people, whom he encouraged to take up farming and other industries. Chilembwe himself started farms of coffee and cotton. By 1910 he is said to have organised 'a well dressed and drilled community'.[45]

The mission had a serious setback when an uprising broke out in January 1915. The rebellion started as a revolt against the bad and cruel treatment of African labourers by white planters, traders and other settlers during the period of famine in 1912-1914. People also resented the hut tax and forced participation of Africans in the *First World War*. After failing to obtain satisfaction by stating his grievances peacefully, Chilembwe and his followers decided 'to strike a blow and die'. Thus on the evening of the 23rd of January 1915 the uprising started, between Chilembwe and his followers on the one side and the planters and the government on

---

[41] Cf. Hildebrandt, *History of the Church in Africa*, p.175.
[42] SIM = *Society of International Missions*, the former *Sudan Interior Mission*.
[43] Mvula and Lwesya, *Flames of Fire*, p. 66.
[44] Patrick Makondesa, *The Church History of Providence Industrial Mission 1900-1940*, Zomba: Kachere, 2006; Shepperson and Price, *Independent African*, pp. 165 ff, etc.; D.D. Phiri, *Let us Die for Africa: An African Perspective on the Life and Death of John Chilembwe of Nyasaland/ Malawi*, Blantyre: Central Africana, 1999; Kenneth Ross, *Christianity in Malawi*, pp. 145-154.
[45] Shepperson and Price, *Independent African*, pp. 142-147

the other side. Chilembwe was captured and shot dead on the third of February 1915.⁴⁶

The present P.I.M. church in Chiradzulu.

But the mission did not die on account of the loss of its founder. Chilembwe's leadership was taken over by Daniel Malikebu (c.1890-1978).⁴⁷ In 1905 Malikebu had gone to the United States to study, invited by Emma De Lany, one of the early American missionaries with the P.I.M.. In 1917 he qualified as a medical doctor, and after that he continued to study theology with a hope of serving the church as a medical missionary. Malikebu returned to Malawi in 1926. He re-opened and re-organised the mission Chilembwe had founded. He only reopened the mission, the church had been re-opened with government permission in 1924. Malikebu led it for almost 30 years. In 1971 he was succeeded by Leonard Muocha who was P.I.M. chairman until 1987.⁴⁸

4. From Mission to Church⁴⁹

a. Forms of Cooperation

The uniting of three strands of Presbyterianism in 1926 was influential to further forms of cooperation between Missions and Churches in Malawi. The C.C.A.P. partly resulted from a wider form of cooperation that had started earlier. From 1900 to 1949 a series of six *General Missionary Conferences* took place, which aimed at bringing Protestant Missions together to discuss and plan matters like recognition of one another's membership, education, Bible translation, and issues concerning the relationship with the government. Except for the Anglican U.M.C.A., the P.I.M., and the *Seventh Day Adventists*, all Protestant Missions were represented at these conferences.

In 1910 during their Conference at Mvera, representatives of almost the whole of Malawian Protestantism decided to establish a Consultative Board of Federated Missions and Churches. Eventually six Missions joined: the *Livingstonia Mission*, the *Dutch Reformed Church Mission*, the *Blantyre Mission*, the *Zambezi Industrial Mission*, the *Nyasa Industrial Mission*, and the *South Africa General Mission*.

---

⁴⁶ Hildebrandt, *History of the Church in Africa*, p.220, misrepresents or at least oversimplifies the *Chilembwe Rising* by reducing Chilembwe's motivations to hatred against enemies.
⁴⁷ Shepperson and Price, *Independent African*, pp. 391, 412, 440, 455, 509.
⁴⁸ Patrick Makondesa, *Moyo ndi Utumiki wa Mbusa ndi Mai Muocha wa Providence Industrial Mission*, Blantyre: Claim/ Mvunguti, 2000.
⁴⁹ Pauw, *Mission and Church in Malawi*, pp. 37-43.

These Missions pledged to recognise one another's membership and discipline, promised to devise a common standard of religious instruction and knowledge required for (full) members, and agreed to respect one another's sphere of work. The *Consultative Board* further functioned as a mouthpiece to the government, and it paved the way for the formation of an indigenous African Church in Malawi. In it there was close cooperation in matters such as Bible translation and the composition of a hymn book (*Nyimbo za Mulungu*). In 1949 the Board agreed on full African membership. In 1962 it adapted its name to be a Fellowship of Churches. In 1967 the *Consultative Board* was disbanded.

In the meantime, since 1939, a wider and more general body of ecclesiastical cooperation had emerged, the *Nyasaland Christian Council*. All Missions and Churches, including the U.M.C.A., the Seventh Day Adventists and the Roman Catholics were invited to join, of which the latter two declined. Since independence it has operated under the name *Christian Council of Malawi*. As such it continues to coordinate aspects of the work of different Churches in the country.

b. Machona Churches

Over all the 20th century many Malawians went to Tanzania, Zambia, Zimbabwe and South Africa as migrant workers.[50] Sometimes, where they went, they founded Malawian churches, like the P.I.M. in Soweto, and the C.C.A.P. Harare Synod. Others joined existing churches at the places where they went, and when they returned home, brought these churches with them, like John George Phillips, who brought the *Catholic Apostolic Church in Zion*,[51] Hannock Phiri who brought the *African Methodist Episcopal Church*,[52] Robert Chinguwo who brought the *Apostolic Faith Mission* (1933),[53] Moses Phiri who brought the *Free Methodist Church*,[54] John Wesley Dingswayo who brought the *Zion Church*,[55] whereas the *Evangelical Lutheran Church* was brought from Tanzania to Malawi.[56] Another branch of Lutheranism, the *Lutheran Church of Central Africa* (L.C.C.A.) was brought from Zambia to Malawi by Richard Mueller and Raymond G. Cox, and started among Malawian workers returning from the Copperbelt.[57] The *Evangelical*

---

[50] For an example of such migration, read: Masiye Tembo, *Touched by His Grace: A Ngoni Story of Tragedy and Triumph*, Zomba: Kachere, 2005.
[51] Cf. Shepperson and Price, *Independent African*, p. 412, who quote Sundkler.
[52] Cf. Devlin Chirwa, 'The History of the African Methodist Episcopal Church in Malawi, The Karonga Branch (1943-2000)'.
[53] Ulf Strohbehn, *Pentecostalism in Malawi: A History of the Apostolic Faith Mission 1931-1994*, Zomba: Kachere, 2005., pp. 44-52.
[54] Henry Church, *Theological Education that Makes a Difference*, Blantyre: Claim/ Kachere, 2001.
[55] Cf. Smart Y.J., Msinkhu, 'Zionism in Malawi: The History and Theology of 'Zion City Church' in Ntcheu District' [University of Malawi, 2005].
[56] Cf. H.Z. Mwimba, 'The Establishing of the Evangelical Lutheran Church in Malawi', Tanzania, Makumira, 1992 [unpublished B.Div. paper of Makumira Lutheran Theological College].
[57] This church is born out of the mission work by the Wisconsin Evangelical Lutheran Church in the

Brethren Church was brought in from South Africa by Joshua Monjeza.[58] Some of these Machona churches later also attracted Western missionaries, like the *Apostolic Faith Mission*, and the *Assemblies of God*. They will be further discussed in chapter 19, together with other Pentecostal Churches.

5. Independent Malawi

a. Church and State

In 1964 Malawi changed from colonial rule to independence.[59] The new government led by Hastings Kamuzu Banda soon turned the country into a dictatorial one-party-state. In the new situation the relationship between the state and the various denominations changed.

This was most apparent in the state's attitude towards Roman Catholicism and Protestantism. Because of the *Chilembwe Rising* in 1915 the British colonial government generally had come to mistrust the educational success of the Protestant churches, as it aimed at the Africanisation of leadership. The Roman Catholic Church with its training of obedience to the leading hierarchy of priests, was found more fitting to the colonial system. Baur says: 'Soon the marked difference between Catholics and Protestants was that between the critical and the obedient mind'. The Presbyterians in particular had produced an elite of leaders. Some of them later underwent radical influences, and became independent activists, like Elliot Kamwana, Charles Domingo, and John Chilembwe. Emerging African nationalism looked upon Roman Catholicism as a supporter of the status quo. That is why Chilembwe not only attacked the colonialist establishment, but also the Roman Catholic Church, destroying the church at Nguludi. This made the Roman Catholic Church more respectable in the eyes of the colonial rulers than the Protestant churches.

For the independent government after 1964, however, this was reason to trust the Protestants more than the Roman Catholics. The movement towards independence was a Protestant affair till the last moment. Native Associations and the Malawian African Congress were Presbyterian enterprises. President Kamuzu Banda († 1997) liked to present himself as a Presbyterian elder, and his first cabinets mainly consisted of Presbyterians. That is how Malawian independence took away the Roman Catholic Church's position as much trusted partner of the government. Protestant churches took over this favoured place.

United States. Cf. Harold R. Johne, and Ernst H. Wendland, *To Every Nation, Tribe, Language and People: A Century of WELS World Missions*, Milwaukee: Northwestern Publ. House, 1993², pp.206-221; Ernst H. Wendland, *A History of the Christian Church in Central Africa: The Lutheran Church of Central Africa 1953-1978*, Wisconsin: Mequon, 1980.

[58] Joshua Monjeza, 'Distinctives and Polity of the Evangelical Brethren Church in Malawi, including Church History', n.d. [about 1995].

[59] For a missionary witness, see: Jackson, *Send Us Friends*, pp.233-396

However, the pattern of state-church loyalties would change again by the end of the Banda regime.[60] The publication of the *Lenten Pastoral Letter* by the Roman Catholic bishops in 1992[61] was instrumental in the downfall of the one-party-government and the transition to a multi-party democracy in 1994. Whereas the C.C.A.P., especially the Nkhoma Synod, was looked upon as the Banda-government-comrades-in-prayer,[62] the new government led by Bakili Muluzi cherished its contacts with the Roman Catholic Church. Whether the new situation has led to a growth of Roman Catholicism in Malawi is uncertain.[63] The C.C.A.P. Livingstonia and Blantyre strongly supported the struggle against one party rule, and cooperated with the Roman Catholic Church, Islam, The Law Society and the Chamber of Commerce, in P.A.C. to bring about the desired change.

Hastings Kamuzu Banda, President of Malawi from 1964 to 1994.

In spite of their support for the new dispensation, the churches have grown increasingly worried about corruptive and dictatorial tendencies in the new administration.

Roman Catholicism and Protestantism have differed as to the degree and the pace of Africanisation. In 1966 there were only 75 Malawian priests in the Roman Catholic Church. The Africanisation of the hierarchy began with Cornelio Chitsulo, who later became a bishop. He was succeeded by James Chiwona in 1956, who became Archbishop of Blantyre in 1967. The third was Patrick Kalilombe, who in 1972 became bishop of Lilongwe.[64] In the Presbyterian churches

---

[60] Cf. Matthew Schoffeleers, *In Search of Truth and Justice: Confrontations between the Church and the State in Malawi: 1960-1994*, Blantyre: Kachere/ Claim, 1999, pp. 121-354.; Kenneth R. Ross (ed.), *God, People and Power in Malawi: Democratisation in Theological Perspective*, Blantyre: Kachere/ Claim, 1996; Matembo S. Nzunda and Kenneth R. Ross, *Church, Law and Political Transition in Malawi 1992-1994*, Gweru: Mambo/ Kachere, 1997²; Kenneth Ross, *Christianity in Malawi*, pp. 203-236.

[61] *Living our Faith* [Pastoral Letter of the Catholic Bishops of Malawi to be read in every Catholic Church on 8 March 1992]; later reprinted in: Kenneth R. Ross (ed.), *Christianity in Malawi*, pp.203-216. For much detail, see: Matthew Schoffeleers, *In Search of Truth*, pp. 116ff, 181ff.

[62] The Blantyre and Livingstonia Synods joined the struggle against Kamuzu not long after the Lenten Letter, supported by the W.A.R.C.

[63] In line with publications on spectacular growth numbers of Roman Catholicism in Africa as a whole it is suggested that the relative popularity of Roman Catholicism after the *Lenten Letter* could have led to recent increase of the number of converts in Malawi, although no local evidence is found (cf. Bryan T. Froehle and Mary L. Gautier, *Global Catholicism: Portrait of a World Church*, Maryknoll: Orbis Books, p. 5; Baur, *2000 Years*, p. 431).

[64] Baur, *2000 Years*, p. 430, 431.

the Africanisation had largely taken place before the beginning of independence in 1964.[65] Developments in the Anglican Church were slower. The first Malawian bishop. Josiah Mtekateka (1903-1996), was ordained in 1965.[66]

Anglicans and Presbyterians decided to cooperate in training, by establishing a joint institution at Chilema in 1974, and joint theological training in Zomba in 1976. In 2005 it seemed that such a cooperation in *Zomba Theological College* is going to end, because of plans of withdrawal by the Anglicans. In the *Christian Council of Malawi*, churches cooperate in the *Christian Hospitals Association of Malawi* (C.H.A.M.).

Banda's regime clashed with the *Jehovah Witnesses*. The *Watchtower Movement* had been banned in Zambia and Malawi at an early stage in its history after the *First World War*. They would not cooperate with the governments. Many considered them not to be Christians, as they do not believe in the divinity of Jesus.[67] After independence the *Jehovah's Witnesses* refused to become members of the omnipotent *Malawi Congress Party*. They were exposed to very harsh treatment, including killing, burning, captivity in concentration camps, and banishment. Many were chased to Zambia, only to be chased back to Malawi and then deported to Mozambique to new persecution and suffering.[68]

b. New Missions after the 'End of Missions'

When around the time of independence the mainline churches received Malawian leaders, the missions supporting them stepped aside, so to say, and the daughter churches now became sister churches. While this marked the end of established missiological strategy, many Malawians happily welcomed new missions. Several *Pentecostal Churches* enriched Malawi's Christian diversity.[69] The *Baptist Convention* was set up in 1960 by American Southern Baptists from Zimbabwe.[70] The

---

[65] For an example, see: Silas Ncozana, *Sangaya: A Leader in the Synod of Blantyre Church of Central Africa Presbyterian*, Blantyre: Claim/ Kachere, 1999, pp.19-21.

[66] Cf. Henry Mbaya, *Josiah Mtekateka,* http://www.dacb.org/stories/malawi/mtekateka_josiah.html

[67] Cf. Hildebrandt, *History of the Church in Africa*, p.222, who mistakenly says that *Jehohah's Witnesses* 'do not believe that Jesus is the Son of God'.

[68] K. Fiedler, 'Power at the Receiving End: The Jehovah's Witnesses' Experience in One-Party-Malawi', in: K.R. Ross (ed.), *God, People and Power in Malawi – Democratization in Theological Perspective,* Blantyre: Claim/ Kachere, 1996, pp. 149-176;

[69] There are in Blantyre alone, more than 120 denominations of Pentecostal and Charismatic character [Ulf Strohbehn, PhD Module, University of Malawi, 1998].

[70] Cf. Judy Garner, *History of the Baptist Mission in Malawi: A Rambling Remembrance of Some People and Events in the History of the Baptist Mission in Malawi*, Lilongwe: Baptist Publications, 1998; Rachel Nyagondwe Fiedler, *Women of Bible and Culture: Baptist Convention Women in Southern Malawi*, Zomba: Kachere, 2005; D.L. Saunders, *A History of Baptists in East and Central Africa*, Southern Baptist Seminary 1973 [unpublished PhD thesis]; Harry Longwe, 'The History of BACOMA', Zomba: Kachere [expected in 2006].

Lutheran Church of Central Africa[71] came from Zambia, Moses Phiri brought the *Free Methodists* from Zimbabwe,[72] The *Reformed Presbyterian Church* of Malawi was born out of a Biblestudy group in Ndirande consisting of Ephraim Tembo and Edward Mwase, Justin Gonakumoto later also Wyson Chitsulo Phiri. These people from Baptist and S.D.A.and Nazarene backgrounds had developed a special interest in the Westminster Catechism and Confession of Faith, and had an informal relationship with the Free Presbyterian Church (F.P. Church) of Scotland, especially its extension in Zimbabwe. Contacts grew, and in 1988 the F.P. Church sent a missionary, Dick Vermeulen, a Dutch immigrant in New Zealand. The F.P. Church Mission withdrew in 1995, but a Dutch interest in the R.P.C. remained, mainly through *Stephanos Foundation*, fed by a recent schism among Reformed Christians in The Netherlands.[73]

c. Revival

While the decade of transition to independence may have seen some slackening of religious interest, the 1970s and the 1980s were decades of revival, centred in the cities, especially Blantyre, and with much influence among middle and upper class and among the educated. Whereas the 1970s revival mainly strengthened the evangelical element in the church,[74] the 1980s revival gave strength to the *Charismatic Movement*, which may now comprise more than 5% of all Malawian Christians,[75] with the *Living Waters Church*, led by Apostle Stanley Ndovi being the biggest church.

d. Women's Organisations

In all churches in Malawi women outnumber men, and often women provide much of the strength of a local church. In addition, almost every church has its own women's group, often distinguished by a specific uniform and a specific name, like *Mvano* (C.C.A.P. Blantyre Synod, P.I.M.), *Chigwirizano* (C.C.A.P. Nkhoma Synod),[76] *Umanyano* (C.C.A.P. Livingstonia Synod), *Mpingo wa Azimayi* (Anglicans), *Umodzi* (Baptists), *Amayi a Dorika* (S.D.A.), *Otumikira mwa Chikondi* (Assemblies of God), *Chiyanjano cha Azimayi* (Churches of Christ). On the Roman Catholic side, in addition to the *Amayi a Chifundo*, *Amayi a Tereza*, and the

---

[71] Ernst H. Wendland, *A History of the Christian Church in Central Africa*, op. cit.
[72] Henry Church, *Theological Education that Makes a Difference: Church Growth in the Free Methodist Church in Malawi and Zimbabwe*, Zomba: Kachere, 2002, pp. 44-46.
[73] Cf. Ephraim Tembo, 'History of the *Reformed Presbyterian Church of Malawi*', n.p., n.d.
[74] Cf. J.C. Selfridge, *Jack of All Trades Mastered by One*, Fearn: Christian Focus, 1989.
[75] For an overview see: Klaus Fiedler, 'The Charismatic and Pentecostal Movements in Malawi in Cultural Perspective', in: *Religion in Malawi*, 9 (1999). In all the country there are about 150 different Pentecostal and Charismatic denominations.
[76] Phiri, *Women*, pp.71-90 and other pages.

Legio Maria, there are the Religious Orders of the Malawian Sisters, like the *Daughters of the Blessed Virgin Mary*[77] and the *Sisters of our Lady of Africa*.[78]

---

[77] Nelly Michongwe, *Meet the Daughters of the Blessed Virgin Mary in Malawi Africa*, Zomba: Kachere, 2005².
[78] Reijnaerts, et. al., *Montfortians in Malawi*, refers to the *Sisters of our Lady of Africa* (p.65), and also to the *Daughters of Wisdom* (pp. 65,314), and to others.

Chapter 17

The Church in Zambia

1. East Zambia

Our survey of Zambia[1] starts in the East. In Eastern Zambia the *Dutch Reformed Church Mission* (D.R.C.M.) of South Africa was active. Reformed missionaries entered Zambia from two directions. One group came from the central region of Malawi where the West Cape Synod of the D.R.C. had established many stations and congregations.

The other group came directly from South Africa, and was sent by the Orange Free State Synod of the D.R.C. Reformed missionary influence also came from the north of Malawi, where the Livingstonia Mission of the *Free Church of*

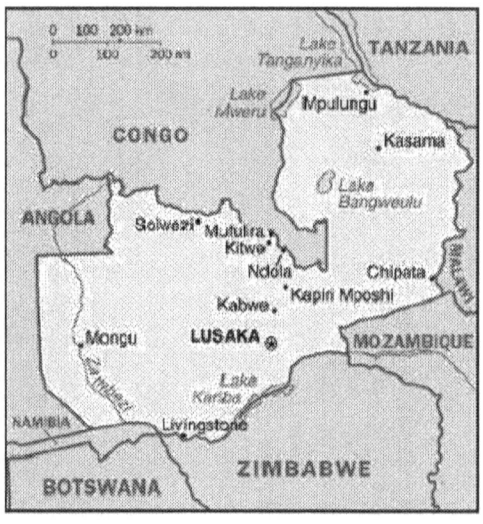

Map of Zambia.

Scotland worked among the Tonga, Tumbuka and Ngoni. A mass movement among the Tonga led to mission campaigns beyond the Malawian boundaries. Scottish Free Church missionaries even went to the Bemba people in the north of present-day Zambia, and also to the centre. To the early converts belonged two fathers of later presidents, the Tonga evangelist David Kaunda, father of Kenneth Kaunda, and the Chewa John Afwenge Banda, father of Kamuzu Hastings Banda. In their turn the Bemba spread the Gospel to neighbouring tribes. Zambian Christians adopted the Livingstonia idea of 'welfare organisations' and Zambian churches had their leaders trained at Malawi's *Overtoun Institution*.

2. South Zambia

By the end of the 19th century the south and the west had been invaded by two foreign powers. First, by the *Chartered Company* of Cecil Rhodes that eventually

---

[1] Study also: Sundkler, and Steed, *A History of the Church in Africa*, pp. 449, 459-467, 473, 609, 786-795, 974-981; Baur, 2000 Years, pp. 432-437.

would secure British hegemony over Zambia. The presence of European power was a challenge to the loyalty of European missionaries. Generally African leaders offered various degrees of resistance, except for King Lewanika and his Lozi people, who adjusted to the situation. Lewanika represented the other invasion, namely by the Kololo, a Sotho-tribe, who had subjugated and enslaved various other tribes, thus establishing in Barotseland the kingdom of Lozi. King Lewanika of the Lozi only allowed missionaries who would accept and honour his supremacy. Initially this led to problems with Evangelical, Methodist, Baptist and Jesuit missions.

We follow the attempts by the evangelical *Paris Mission* in Barotseland, which was led by François Coillard. Coillard had worked in Lesotho and assumed that knowledge of the Sotho language might give him an easy entry among the Sotho speaking elite of the Lozi kingdom. However, the king got angry because in his view the *Paris Mission* had entered his kingdom through a wrong route. Consequently Coillard and his Sotho co-workers had to leave, only to be received and accepted seven years later. In 1889 the first convert was baptised, Nguana Ngombe, a slave boy. In 1894 Coillard opened a Bible school. After that there was a continual growth of the number of Christians. The king never converted to Christianity, although he let himself be influenced by Coillard for almost twenty years. His main interest remained the economical, technical, and educational side of the missionaries' activities. The introduction of various trades as well as a literacy movement gradually changed life in the Lozi kingdom, especially of the elite. At grass root level the pace of social and economical change was slower. At the same time the new faith rooted in the hearts and lives of many. Even Siwi, an influential priest of the local cult, turned to Christ. Also Litiya, the king's son, and Mokamba, his chief minister, became Christians. These conversions contributed to the formation of the new self-conscious mission-educated elite that during the rise of the *Ethiopian Movement* tended to independency and disagreement with the missionaries.

Mainly through Methodist missionaries, Christianity also spread among the Lomba and Ila-speaking peoples, although they were slow to accept because they tended to identify the Christian faith with the interests of the Lozi who dominated them.

3. The Copperbelt

The London Missionary Society (L.M.S.) were the first to start, in 1878. They established churches, schools, industrial training and medical services.[2] The discovery of copper in the North West changed much of the social and economic position of many Zambians. Changes were also induced by Zambia's becoming a British Protectorate in 1924. Like South Africa at the Rand and Zaire in Shaba, the new colony opened mines, and cities emerged with Ndola as important centre.

---

[2] Cf. Hildebrandt, *History of the Church in Africa*, p.178.

These urban communities, classed together as the *Copperbelt*, consisted of a majority of black labourers who had migrated from the Bemba country or from great distances, quite often from Malawi, and a minority of whites mainly from South Africa.

Before the mission organisations entered the Copperbelt, an African Christian movement had already prepared the ground. In the country as a whole a second generation of missionaries became active. The missionary organisations started the formation of various denominations. In this Copperbelt region of Zambia's West Anglicans, Methodist, Paris Mission, Roman Catholics, Brethren, and others formed their churches.

4. Unity and Dissent

Common concern about the needs of the masses in the Copperbelt led to some cooperation between missionaries of various backgrounds. Among some missionaries this also stimulated debate on Church union, which by 1965, led to the formation of the *United Church of Zambia*, a combination of Congregationalist, Methodist, and Presbyterian-Reformed Churches. Plans for church unity in Zambia were greatly stimulated by the *Mindolo Ecumenical Institute* in the Copperbelt. Here also the *All Africa Church Conference* was stationed before it was removed to Nairobi. For various reasons a considerable number of churches and missions in Zambia did not join the Union: the Roman Catholics, Anglicans, the *South Africa General Mission*, the *Plymouth Brethren*, the Baptists, and the Dutch/African Reformed Church. Generally the Zambian proceedings to union were inspired by a specific white theological thinking in bodies like the *International Missionary Council* and later the Geneva based *World Council of Churches*. Kenneth Kaunda, Zambia's first president, was one of the advocates of the ecumenical programme. The United Church of Zambia has spread to nearly all parts of the country and is relatively big, yet much of Zambia's church life continued to develop outside this 'Genevan' ecumenical climate.

In 1891 the Roman Catholics started work in Zambia. On their side there were the *White Fathers*, who worked in the extreme north, establishing stations near those of the L.M.S., and had much response among the Bemba people.[3] The later spreading of Bemba about the whole country helped a nation wide growth of Roman Catholicism. Although at Mindolo the Africa expert Adrian Hastings served as a representative of Rome, his church has kept itself outside the ecumenical structure, like it always does. This does not mean that the Roman Catholic Church in Zambia found it easy to identify with the Roman world church in all aspects. Lusaka's Archbishop Emmanuel Milingo resisted Rome when he began healing sessions in 1982. Immediately the Archbishop was called to Rome. The Pope tried to use him because of his popularity. But Milingo did not fit nicely in the Euro-

---

[3] Vezeau, *The Apostolic Vicariate of Nyasa*, pp. 19-45.

Roman system. Even in his 'exile' he went on with prayer-healing meetings and found acceptance in charismatic Roman Catholic circles. From Roman Catholics in Zambia complaints reached the Vatican about the absence of their leader. Two decades later Milingo created a new crisis by marrying a member of the Moon sect. Unlike the Protestant missions who mainly concentrated on urban areas, Roman Catholicism especially developed in the countryside. Baur's suggestion that the Roman Catholic Church in Zambia is 'twice as large as all Protestants together',[4] seems to have no foundation when compared to the 2004 figures of the Website of *Catholic-Hierarchy*.[5]

In the north west there was the successful *Open Brethren* Kalene Hill mission among the Lunda, started by Walter Fisher in 1906. This work initiated great spiritual and social change among the Lunda. Although the Brethren do not recognise an ordained ministry, the work in Zambia has led to the church-like formation of hundreds of 'assemblies' of baptised believers shepherded by elders.

The *Seventh Day Adventists* started their presence in Zambia in the south at Rusangu in 1903. Under the control of missionaries a thriving farming community developed. Later an African group, under the influence of Ethiopian thought, withdrew from the missionaries at Rusangu and settled at the Kemba Hills under African leadership. The Adventists contributed

Emmanuel Milingo (born 1930), R.C. Archbishop of Lusaka.

much to the formation of the *Northern Rhodesian African Congress* in 1937 and therefore to the ensuing nationalist movement in Zambia.

In the 1950s, initiated by black American missionaries, the *African Methodist Episcopal Church* (A.M.E.C.), one of America's largest black denominations, started a branch in Zambia. The church had close links to the nationalist Congress Party. Sundkler claims that even the party's general secretary and later state president Kenneth Kaunda was a local preacher and choir leader of the Lusaka A.M.E.C., before he joined the *United Church* in 1965.[6] Although the A.M.E.C. claimed to be African and black, it still depended on American leadership. This led

---

[4] Baur, *2000 Years*, p. 432.
[5] Of the 11.7 million inhabitants 3 million are said to be Roman Catholics, i.e. 26 percent (www.catholic-hierarchy.org/country/zm.html)
[6] Sundkler and Steed, *A History of the Church in Africa*, p. 795. Kenneth Kaunda may have had some connection with the A.M.E.C. during his years in Lusaka, but he is of Presbyterian descent. He was raised at Lubwa mission in North Zambia, where his father worked as a Presbyterian missionary. Father David Kaunda came from North Malawi. He was sent to Zambia by the *Free Church of Scotland* which had already established the *Livingstonia Mission* in Malawi, which developed into the Livingstonia Synod of the Church of Central Africa Presbyterian (C.C.A.P.).

to a break, and consequently to the establishment of an independent parallel church (*African Methodist Independent Church*).

5. Reformed and Presbyterian Churches

There are three denominations of Reformed - Presbyterian character in Zambia.[7] First, there is the Zambian Synod of the *Church of Central Africa Presbyterian* (C.C.A.P.). The other C.C.A.P. Synods are in Malawi and Zimbabwe; there are also congregations in Mozambique. The Zambian C.C.A.P. originates in missionary activity under the responsibility of the *Free Church of Scotland*. The Free Church began its work in Malawi by the end of the 19th century. Later the work was extended to Zambia, where a mission was established at Lubwa, with congregations in the north and the centre of the country. The *Zambian Free Church* that was produced by this mission had its members mainly among the Bemba speaking people, whereas there are also Chitumbuka and Chinyanja (Chichewa) speaking members, the main vernacular languages of neighbouring Malawi. In church services these languages are used alternatively. In 1965 this *Zambian Free Church* joined the *United Church of Zambia*. At that time especially the Bemba in the North felt more at home in that church. Later, however, the United Church grew less popular. Some of its members together with immigrants from Malawi formed congregations and established the Zambian Synod of the C.C.A.P., thus joining the General Synod of the C.C.A.P. and through this the three main Presbyterian churches in Malawi. Its congregations are to be found in the Copperbelt, the Eastern Province and in Lusaka. Ministers are trained either at Justo Mwale Theological College in Lusaka or at Zomba Theological College in Malawi.

Secondly, there is the *Presbyterian Church in Zambia*. This church originated from groups of Malawian C.C.A.P. immigrants who were not accepted by the United Church in 1965, because their leader, Khowani, was a suspended minister. This denomination and the Zambian C.C.A.P. are two equally strong churches, each having about 9 Presbyteries and some 45 congregations. The Presbyterian Church in Zambia has its congregations mainly in Lusaka; it also has some membership in the Copperbelt and in the Eastern Province. The majority of the members speak Chinyanja (Chichewa), the rest are Chitumbuka or Chibemba speaking. The Presbyterian Church in Zambia is not independent, but a part of the *Uniting Presbyterian Church in South Africa*. It has two Presbyteries under the Synod of that church, and students for the ministry are sent to Justo Mwale Theological College and to South Africa.

---

[7] For the information in this paragraph I owe to: G.Verstraelen-Gilhuis, *From Dutch Mission Church to Reformed Church in Zambia: The Scope for African Leadership and Initiative in the History of a Zambian Mission Church*, Franeker, 1982, and to Mr. Burnett Muwowo's study of this book.

Thirdly, there is the *Reformed Church in Zambia*.[8] It originated in missionary work by the Orange Free State Synod of the Dutch Reformed Church of South Africa. It is the largest of the three denominations discussed in this paragraph. The earliest Dutch missionary arrival in Zambia was in the 1890s through the Orange Free State Synod which opened stations at Fort Jameson, Madzimoyo, Nsanje, Nsadzi. The station at Magwero station was established in 1908.[9] These days congregations of the Reformed Church can be found in Lusaka the Copperbelt, and in the Eastern Province, especially in the Chipata region. A great majority of the members are Chinyanja (Chichewa) speaking. Future ministers are trained at Justo Mwale Theological College in Lusaka and in South Africa.

6. Independent Zambia

Memorial of Alice Mulenga Lenshina (1953-1991) at Chinsali.

The British inspired and dominated federation of Zambia, Malawi and Zimbabwe met with much African opposition, and was a prelude to these countries' independence. In 1964 Kenneth Kaunda became president of independent Zambia. He wanted to introduce a humanism with socialist characteristics, coloured by Christianity. These ideals were put to the test by the movement of the prophetess Alice Mulenga Lenshina, and by the *Jehovah's Witnesses*.

Lenshina came from Lubwa-Chinsali, the same district as Kaunda. She went through a death-and-resurrection-experience in 1953. Then according to Sundkler she was baptised in the Presbyterian Church by Paul Mushindo, a Bemba minister who had worked at Lubwa mission where Kenneth Kaunda had grown up.[10] She started a millennarian preaching sharply focussed against sorcery, witchcraft, and beer drinking. At a later stage she and her movement were accused of using the evils that they condemned, like mobilising the power of magic and the condoning of sexual orgies. In the beginning the prophetess cooperated with nationalist leaders because of their joint hatred of the British founded federation. Until 1959 her movement, called Lumpa, attracted many followers, even Presbyterians, Roman Catholics and Traditionalists. Then the tide turned. Many left the movement when the announced return of Christ did not

---

[8] Cf. Verstraelen-Gilhuis, op.cit.
[9] Cf. Jonathan Hildebrandt, *History of the Church in Africa* p. 178 also J. Du Plessis. *The Evangelisation of Pagan Africa*, p. 308.
[10] Sundkler and Steed, *A History of the Church in Africa*, p. 790.

take place. Lenshina's attitude towards the outside world changed. In 'another Bible' given to her by Jesus – so she said- the remnant of her followers were called upon to flee the world and go to Zion, i.e. to Lenshina's villages that tended to behave as a separate state. The movement lost much of its voluntary character as the inhabitants of her closed settlements were sometimes forced to join and to remain. Lenshina was said to behave like a traditional sorcerer who pushed her followers into things like murder and having people eat faeces. From 1963 there were violent clashes between her Lumpa-movement and Kaunda's United National Independence Party. Lenshina's movement was crushed by the troops of Kaunda in the months before the day of Independence, 24 October 1964. The bloodshed took the lives of many of Lenshina's followers and would not easily be forgotten.

The beginnings of the *Jehovah's Witnesses* were in Malawi. The movement was started by Elliot Kenan Kamwana, who was educated at the Overtoun Institution of the Livingstonia Synod of the C.C.A.P. Kamwana left Overtoun and Presbyterianism and was drawn to the *Watchtower Movement* through Joseph Booth. In 1908 migrant workers brought the movement to Zambia. In a later period influences from the south were added. Labour migrants from the Southern Rhodesian (Zimbabwean) mines carried the Watch Tower teachings with them when they returned to their homes in Zambia. In 1968 the Watch Tower movement was violently attacked by the youth wingers of Kaunda's party. The president stopped the persecution, but agreed to the expulsion of foreign *Jehovah's Witnesses*.

In 1972 Malawian *Jehovah's Witnesses* entered Zambia as refugees, after the regime of Kamuzu Banda had started to persecute them. More than 20,000 of these refugees were placed in a camp at Sindamisale. Again the Zambian state did not show much of its humanist or Christian ideals. Although according to Sundkler the churches provided help through a combined committee[11], Fiedler reports on miserable circumstances in the camp.

> 'Nsindamisale (or: Sindamisale – S.P.) was a place of refuge but also of death. The camp was ill-equipped, the number of people was too large, and the sanitary conditions terrible. Hundreds died of waterborne diseases'.

The Zambian state only very reluctantly allowed refugees to enter. Inspite of responsibilities given by the United Nations, Kaunda's government did not like to keep them. Some were humiliated and beaten, and finally all were forced to go back to Malawi and to new persecution.[12]

---

[11] Sundkler, *A History of the Church in Africa*, p.975
[12] Klaus Fiedler, 'Power at the Receiving End: The Jehovah's Witnesses' Experience in One Party Malawi', in: K. R. Ross (ed.), *God, People and Power in Malawi – Democratization in Theological Perspective*, Blantyre: Claim, 1996, pp. 163, 164

Chapter 18

The Church in Zimbabwe

1. Jesuit and Dominican Attempts

The earliest history of Zimbabwean Christianity[1] is written in blood. It began with the successful missionary work of the Portuguese Jesuit Gonzalo da Silveira in December 1560 and January 1561. It took him little time to baptise King Mwene Mutapa, the king's mother and hundreds of his courtiers and other subjects. However, this victory soon changed into disaster. A witchdoctor saw his influence increase, and he told the king that Da Silveira was a spy for the Portuguese army, and that the water of baptism was a magic poison. This made the king turn round, and decide to have Da Silveira strangled. Because of the findings of gold the Portuguese state tried indeed to establish its power in Mwene Mutapa's territory. At the same time the order of the Dominicans succeeded Da Silveira in attempting to spread Roman Catholicism. In the years 1628-1633 the Dominican Luis do Espirito Santo combined the political and the religious aims by militarily interfering in favour of one of the contenders for the throne of the Mwene Mutapa kingdom. He organised an army headed by armed Dominicans and eliminated the army of the other contender. After this action the successive kings of the Mwene Mutapa Kingdom were Christians. They depended on the power of the Portuguese who soon shared out large portions of land to landlords and started using slaves.

Part of the Ruins of Great Zimbabwe, built by Bantu people from 11th to 14th century.

In the 19th century the circumstances for spreading the Gospel in Zimbabwe were much more favourable than before. Sundkler says that 'there was a preparedness on the part of marginal people or leading men and women to break with the guardians of the ancient cult'. He refers to different kinds of 'territorial cults' in Central Africa that were relating 'to what is seen as a High God' or to 'divinised human beings'. These cults, like the Mwari cult and the Mhondoro cult in Zimbabwe and the Mbona cult in Malawi and Zimbabwe, un-

---

[1] For the History of the Church in Zimbabwe, study also: W.J Van der Merwe, *From Mission field to Autonomous Church in Zimbabwe* (A Publication of the Institute for Missiological Research of the University of Pretoria, NG Kerkboekhandel, 1981; cf. Sundkler, and Steed, *A History of the Church in Africa*, pp. 68-69, 93-94, 398, 402, 408, 445-449, 800-816, 981-983; Baur, *2000 Years*, pp. 417-428.

derwent important changes that made them seem parallel to Christianity or a stepping stone to it. The central figure in the Mbona cult, a martyred prophet, is even said to be the 'Son of God' or the 'Black Jesus'

2. Mission before 1890

In the 19th century Zimbabwe was opened up for mission through various routes from the south to the north. Even in the pré-colonial period before 1890, there was much missionary activity in the country. The main route ran from Kuruman to Bulawayo. Through it hunters and explorers approached the north. It was called 'the missionary road' because it was originally used by missionaries like Moffat, Livingstone and MacKenzie. Mzilikazi and Lobengula, the Ndebele kings, only allowed those strangers who had travelled through 'the missionary road', to enter their kingdoms. There were also other routes. The eastern route was especially used by African Evangelists. The Dutch, Paris and Swiss missions organised many expeditions to Zimbabwe using almost exclusively African personnel. Some expeditions started in Lesotho.

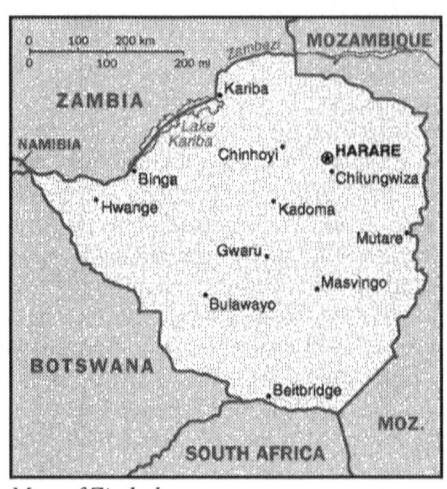
Map of Zimbabwe.

A permanent mission station was started in 1859 when Robert Moffat from Kuruman led a group of missionaries into the region.[2] Missionary expeditions from North Transvaal are also connected with the name Stephanus Hofmeyr, a Dutch Reformed missionary. Hofmeyr had successfully worked among the Buys people, a group of coloured half-casts at Goedgedacht in North Transvaal, and was ready to extend his work beyond the Limpopo River. In the period 1872-1887 he trained not less than seven groups of Africans, especially from the Buys clan, to enter the land that now is known as Zimbabwe, effectively carrying and spreading the Gospel. After Hofmeyr's death his work was continued by J.W. Daneel, his son-in-law. Likewise, hundreds of Zimbabweans who had become Christians while working in the mines at the Rand, returned home as missionaries of various denominations.

Among those who crossed the Limpopo were Wesleyan Methodist preachers at the Rand, including David M. Ramushu. On their way they established new Methodist centres in Zimbabwe.

---

[2] Cf. Hildebrandt, *History of the Church in Africa*, pp.176f.

From their centre Tshakoma in Vendaland the Lutheran *Berlin Mission* organised mission to Zimbabwe. Missionaries Schwellnus and Knothe had trained Africans, among whom Johannes Madima, who himself together with other Africans made several expeditions to Zimbabwe.

Not all missionaries were welcomed. François Coillard of the *Paris Mission*, who had planned to work among the Shona, was refused and sent back by Lobengula because he had not travelled through 'the missionaries' road' and because the king considered the Sotho people who accompanied Coillard as his enemies. Later Coillard returned to the north, but then to Zambia.

3. The Era of Colonialism

Cecil Rhodes (1853-1902), an Architect of British Colonialism.

In 1889 King Lobengula had to submit to Cecil Rhodes' *Chartered Company*. In 1890 this was followed by Rhodes' military invasion of Mashonaland and the hoisting of the British flag at Fort Salisbury (now Harare). In the wake of this invasion many settlers and also missionaries entered the country. Two risings against the British, the Matabele war in 1893 and wars by the Shona and the Ndebele in 1896-1897, sometimes called the *First Chimurenga* (First Liberation War), could not change the situation of complete British military supremacy.[3] Baur explains the violent character of the beginnings of colonialism in Rhodesia. 'Everywhere else in tropical Africa European powers entered into some contracts with chiefs before they occupied a country, but Mashonaland was invaded by settlers abruptly without any previous notice'.[4] The integrity of the missionaries, especially of the British among them, was put to the test. On which side was their loyalty? In 1923 Southern Rhodesia became a colony. The relationship between colonialism and mission would continue to be a problem. Although the first years of colonialism saw many new missionary groups, who were offered large plots of land, the number of conversions slowed down, especially among the Ndebele.

However, the above mentioned Dutch Reformed and Lutheran missions successfully continued their evangelisation among the Southern Shona. Methodism also continued its progress after 1890. Beside the British Wesleyans with centres in e.g. Harare, in 1898 the American United Methodists entered and started work mainly in the east of the country. The United Methodist missionaries were blacks. Both branches started early to Africanise the leadership of the church. The Meth-

---

[3] Cf. D.N. Beach, *War and Politics in Zimbabwe 1840-1900*, Gweru: Mambo Press, 1994².
[4] Baur, *2000 Years*, p.417.

odists produced important figures in the movement for independence, like Abel Muzorewa, Canaan Banana, Joshua Nkomo, and Ndabaningi Sithole.

The Anglican Church in Zimbabwe was established after the beginning of the Protectorate. Its first bishop was George Knight-Bruce. It progressed considerably in the period when Edward Paget was bishop in Salisbury (1926-1957). After independence Africans were nominated (1981) as archbishop and as bishops in the dioceses of Gweru and Mutare.

After earlier attempts in the 16th and 17th centuries the Roman Catholic Church entered Zimbabwe again in 1890 together with Cecil Rhodes' expedition. The first mission workers were German Dominican Sisters from South Africa. Soon the Jesuits followed. After 1927 English Jesuits were responsible for Roman Catholic Mission in the whole of Southern Rhodesia (Zimbabwe). Their method of Christian villages seemed to fit to the situation. They were active in agriculture and education.

King Lobengula of the Matabele who was misinformed about the meaning of the Tati Concession, by which he was disowned.

Abel Tendekayi Muzorewa (born 1925), a Methodist Bishop who was prime minister of a coalition government of Zimbabwe in 1979 for a few months.

4. The Reformed Church of Zimbabwe

Its origin is in the mission of the *Dutch Reformed Church* of South Africa which had reached Zimbabwe (Mashonaland) in 1891.[5] Its first establishment was at Morgenster near the Great Zimbabwe court building of Mwene Mutapa, the King, where in 1894 a first minister was ordained.[6] The founder was Andrew Louw. Right from the beginning he cooperated with African evangelists.[7] Jozua Masoha, Lukas Mokoele, Jeremia and Petrus Morudu, David Molea and Izak Kumalowho were trained by Stephanus Hofmeyr. They contributed much to the missionary work of the D.R.C. in Zimbabwe. Louw and his wife Cinie Malan translated the Bible into Karanga. They started theological courses for evangelists. This work was later developed into a full training of ministers at Morgenster, Murray Theo-

---

[5] Van der Merwe, *From Mission Field*, 47-57; cf. C.M. Pauw *Mission and Church in Malawi* p. 48.
[6] Adrian Hastings. *Church in Africa*. p. 455; Jonathan Hildebrandt, *History of the Church in Africa* p. 177.
[7] Cf. Louw's biography: A.A. Louw, *Andrew Louw van Morgenster*, 1965.

logical College. New centres were opened in Dete in 1995 and in Binga among the Tonga people in 1996. There are plans for evangelising the Shonga and Venda peoples near the southern border of Zimbabwe. At present the *Reformed Church of Zimbabwe* has about 85,000 members, and 50 ministers. It has 47 congregations subdivided into smaller units to suit pastoral work.[8]

5. The C.C.A.P. in Zimbabwe

Although the *Church of Central Africa* (C.C.A.P.) is mainly a Malawian church, offshoots of it took root in Zimbabwe. The imposition of hut tax in Malawi forced many to go abroad and seek work. Soon groups of Malawians were found as far away as Harare[9] and Johannesburg. Regular labour migration from Malawi to Zimbabwe dates from 1903. In the same year the Mission Council consisting of various Protestant missions in Malawi, emphasised the urgent necessity to begin work in Harare in conjunction with the work in Malawi. They saw the need of providing for the spiritual welfare of the large number of Malawians who went to Harare. In 1905 a delegation of these migrants walked from Zimbabwe to Mvera mission in central Malawi to ask for a missionary who would minister to their spiritual needs in Zimbabwe. The delegation comprised Joseph Mandovi from Livingstonia, Yonamu from Nkhoma, Yeremiya Mwalo from *Zambezi Industrial Mission*, and a person from Blantyre whose name has remained unknown.

Five years later a general Missionary Conference at Mvera decided to send a European missionary to Zimbabwe[10] for the purpose of looking after and ministering to Malawian migrants. Because none of the missions indicated a person, finally T.C.B. Vlok of the Dutch Reformed Mission, by then a veteran of 23 years experience in Malawi, offered to go, and he started this work in November 1912. The following year Vlok began to employ African evangelists to enlarge the scope of the activities. This marked the beginning of the C.C.A.P. in Zimbabwe. Actually Vlok was sent by the Synod of the Western Cape of the D.R.C. through the Nkhoma Synod of Nyasaland. Vlok, also called Foloko or Voloko by the migrant population, travelled all over Zimbabwe meeting zealous Nyasas who agreed to establish a separate Reformed Church branch in Zimbabwe.

The first Nyasa affiliated church was established in 1935 operating under the Nkhoma Synod and after the number of congregations had grown, they were divided into several Presbyteries. The Synod of Rhodesia gained autonomy in 1965. After the Civil war the name of the capital city changed from Salisbury to Harare. The Rhodesia Synod also changed to be called the Harare Synod.

---

[8] Enos Chomutiri during a workshop in Liwonde, Malawi in June 2004.
[9] At that time named: Salisbury.
[10] At that time named: Southern Rhodesia.

In 1965 the Harare Synod became a fourth constituent synod of the Church of Central Africa Presbyterian CCAP.[11]

6. Independence

Right from the beginning white settlers in Southern Rhodesia (Zimbabwe), Northern Rhodesia (Zambia) and Nyasaland (Malawi) expected economical advantages from a federation of these regions. In general the Africans, however, resisted the idea, because a federation would strengthen white domination, and would consequently lead to more discrimination. Despite the opposition by emerging African nationalism, and resistance by Garfield Todd, ex-missionary and Rhodesian prime-minister, the federation was forced through, in 1953.

In Rhodesia this event led to a sharp division between the blacks in the *African National Congress* and the whites in the *Rhodesian Front*. In 1964 the white minority led by prime-minister Ian Smith, challenged Britain and the West and the African majority by announcing a *Unilateral Declaration of Independence*. The Roman Catholic Church and the Ecumenical Protestant bodies clashed with the white minority regime. The ensuing civil war, also called the *Second Chimurenga* (Second War of Liberation) aimed at majority rule for the Africans ended in 1978 by a provisional agreement, which made the Methodist bishop Abel Muzorewa president. However, this *Internal Settlement* did not work. In 1980 the *Lancaster House Agreement* gave Rhodesia complete independence under majority rule. Robert Mugabe was elected prime-minister. The division of land belongs to the difficult problems that the new government has never adequately solved. The invasion of white farms by 'war veterans' by the end of the millennium, dubbed by the government the *Third Chimurenga*, was universally criticised, and has damaged Zimbabwe's economical and social stability.

Although Mugabe moderated his Marxist-Leninist stance, he and President Canaan Banana tried to introduce a kind of socialist Christianity with a church for and of the proletariat. Generally the new government had a policy of 'forgive and forget'. However, this reconciliatory attitude did not apply to the relationship between the Shona and their pre-colonial overlords, the Ndebele. Mugabe's Shona security forces caused tremendous bloodshed and suffering among the Ndebele. Yet, Zimbabweans have been voting him into power for 21 years. Reconciliation between the Shona and the Ndebele was achieved in 1987 when the parties of Mugabe (largely Shona) and Joshua Nkomo (largely Ndebele) joined to form one party. However, with the death of Nkomo the relationship became uneasy again.

---

[11] cf. Isabel Apawo Phiri, *Women, Presbyterianism and Patriarch*, Zomba: Kachere, 2000, p. 50.

Chapter 19

Pentecostals and Charismatics

1. Five Streams

In African Protestant Christianity there are (a) *Classical* mainline churches, (b) *Post-Classical* churches, (c) *Pentecostal* churches, and the groups and churches of the (d) *Charismatic Movement*. Besides there are the (e) *Independent* churches who directly or indirectly derive from the above mentioned types.

The *Classical* churches originated in the missionary movement, which was a product of the 18th and 19th century evangelical revival or awakening in the mainline churches in Europe and America bringing them in line again with the 16th century Reformation. In Malawi there are the *Presbyterian*, *Lutheran*, and the *Anglican* churches.

The *Post-Classical* churches have their roots in the evangelical awakening of the mid 19th century holiness revival that led to the formation of interdenominational faith missions and denominational evangelical missions. Examples in Malawi: *Zambezi Evangelical Church*, *Nyasa Industrial Mission*, *Africa Evangelical Church*, *Providence Evangelical Church*, *Seventh' Day Adventists*, *Free Methodists*, and *Baptists*.

In this chapter we will deal with the Pentecostal Movement, and with the Charismatic Movement.[1]

2. Beginnings of Pentecostalism

Pentecostalism is a distinct variant of Protestantism, born out of the 16th century *Reformation*. As such it is a relatively young phenomenon. It started in America and soon touched Africa. In some cases there was an interaction between Pentecostalism and Independency, but the two movements remained distinct. After its American beginnings, Pentecostalism spread to Africa. There were various ways.

First there were the 'solo entrepreneurs', such as Clyde Miller who founded the Nyang'ori Mission in Western Kenya.

Secondly there were the sponsored missionaries from Pentecostal groups, such as the Azusa Street ministry, who sent Lucy Farrow and Henry M. Turner to South Africa in 1908. Generally Pentecostal Churches are rooted in the Pentecostal re-

---

[1] Apart from this chapter, study also: A. B. Anderson, *African Pentecostals in South Africa*, Pretoria, 1991; A. Anderson, *Zion and Pentecost – The Spirituality and Experience of Pentecostal and Zionist/Apostolic Churches in South Africa*, Pretoria, 2000; K.Fiedler, 'The Charismatic and Pentecostal Movements in Malawi in Cultural Perspective', in: R.I.M. 9, (1999). Fiedler, *The Story of Faith Missions*, 116-121; K.Ward, 'Africa', in: Hastings, *World History*, pp. 234, 235.

vival that began in Azusa Street in the Californian city of Los Angeles in 1906. Soon the movement spread to other parts of the world. The missionaries that arrived in 1908 founded the *Apostolic Faith Mission*, at first mainly among the whites. Instrumental in this cross-ocean movement were the South Africans David du Plessis, called 'Mr. Pentecost', and P.L. le Roux.

Thirdly, there is the influence of the radical American-Scottish/ Australian Pentecostal preacher J.A. Dowie († 1907) of the *Christian Catholic Apostolic Church*. He was at the cradle of many Pentecostal Churches in Africa, especially in South Africa. Near Chicago he founded a *New Jerusalem* which he called *Zion City* and a *Zion Tabernacle* where healings and miracles took place. Dowie considered himself 'Elijah the Redeemer', the last prophet before the coming of the Messiah. At the time of his death his church had spread to South Africa. Dowie's message was taken over by P.L. le Roux who was a missionary to the Zulus, and had left the D.R.C. Le Roux re-established the *New Jerusalem* among the Zulus. Soon the *Zion Apostolic Faith Mission* was formed, consisting of blacks.[2] One of the original leaders was Edward Lion from Lesotho. By 1990 the Zion movement claimed to have more than 2000 black churches with about 4 million members in South Africa alone. A distinctive variant of the Zionists is the *amaNazaretha Church* of Isaiah Shembe († 1935), who unlike other Zionist leaders developed a personality cult by calling himself the new David and a black messiah, even the 'Promised One' himself. The Zionists featured healing, speaking in tongues, purification rites and the handling of various taboos. Like the contemporary Ethiopianist movement, the Zionists operated an 'Abyssinia-theology' that is a mythical conception of Biblical Zion (*Hebrews* 12: 22), which was drawn near into African reality. At the same time the Zionists differed from the Ethiopians because they did not exclude non-African from leadership.[3] There was also a Pentecostal breakthrough among the Indian community in Natal,

David Du Plessis, an Afrikaner of South Africa who was a traveller for the Pentecostal Movement.

Isaiah Shembe (1867-1935), founder of the amaNazaretha Church; he combined Traditional African Religion with Christianity.

---

[2] Gregory Chawanangwa Mvula and Enson Mbilikile Lwesya, *Flames of Fire: A History of the Assemblies of God in Malawi*, Limbe: Assemblies of God in Malawi, 2005, pp. 360, 361.

[3] Sundkler and Steed, *A History of the Church in Africa*, pp.426, 427.

mainly through the work of J.F. Rowland. In 1931 in Durban a centre was founded, called 'Bethesda'.

In Southern Africa there was a flowering of Zion churches. Only a few can be mentioned. A Malawian migrant worker from Likoma Island, J.G.Phillips, settled at the Rand, where he founded the *Christian Catholic Apostolic Church in Zion*. In 1925 the Zion movement split because Legkangane formed his own Zion Christian Church. His follower Samuel Mutendi, a Shona from Zimbabwe, founded the church in his home country. Mutendi's Zion Church experienced many schisms. Other famous Zimbabwean Zion leaders were Yohane Masowe and Yohane Maranke. They travelled extensively. That is why their influence was not limited to Zimbabwe. In the 1920s the *South African General Mission* at Rusitu in Zimbabwe witnessed Pentecostal enthusiasm, often induced by Western preachers, like Rees Howells. There was also a Pentecostal awakening in the Methodist Episcopal Church at Mutare.[4]

Fourthly, Africa was also reached by a Pentecostal wave from the Swiss Herisau community, led by Johannes Buchler, who founded his own Zion church in Johannesburg. To his disciples belonged Edgar Mahon, an ex-Salvation Army officer.

Let us look at important events in the history of Pentecostalism some parts of Africa. In 1914 the majority of American Pentecostals joined together in the denomination of the *Assemblies of God* (A.O.G.) under leaders like James Mullan Africa, and Nicolas Bhengu (†1985) with his influential *Back-to-God-Crusade*. The A.O.G. started its ministry in Sierra Leone in 1914, Burkina Faso in 1920 and Dahomey in 1947. In the meantime, in 1939, missionary W.L. Shirer and his wife had started work in Eastern Nigeria. The road for Pentecostalism was paved by Apostolic preachers, first whites from the *Bradford Apostolic Church*, like the brothers Daniel P. and William J. Williams, and George Perfect, and then by African preachers like Joseph Babalola, whose work extended the *Christ Apostolic Church*.[5] Since 1964 the American *Assemblies* have formed a separate organisation with branches in Africa as well. Other denominational brands of Pentecostalism established in various parts of Africa, beside South Africa, especially in Western Kenya, Burkina Faso, and Benin. They include the *Church of God in Christ*, the *Pentecostal Holiness Church*, and later the *Foursquare Gospel Church*.[6]

Sundkler refers to the Swedish Pentecostal influence in Burundi, which coloured Burundi Protestantism. When ethnic clashes forced Hutu refugees to 'settle in their hundreds of thousands in South Central Tanzania', they brought with them their Pentecostal enthusiasm, and established 'an intense Pentecostal community'. Earlier the Swedish Pentecostals had already started work in Tanzania, among the

---

[4] Sundkler and Steed, *A History of the Church in Africa*, pp. 809, 813.
[5] Duncan and Kalu, 'Bakuzufu: Revival Movements', in: Kalu et. al. (eds), *African Christianity*, pp.295, 296.
[6] Kalu, 'African Christianity', in: Kalu et.al. (eds), *African Christianity*, pp.346, 347.

Sukuma, and about 1960, they were represented all over the country.[7] At an early stage the Swedish Pentecostals also sent missionaries to South Africa, e.g. Mary Johnson and Ida Andersson to Durban in 1904 and in 1915, they opened stations in Congo and Egypt.

Interacting with the historical *Pentecostal Movement* were some ecstatic or charismatic movements most of whom we discussed before. They were revivals within or outside existing churches, like the *Aladura Movement* in West Africa, the revival in the *Qua Iboe Mission* among the Ibibio people in Southern Nigeria (1925-1947), the one among the *Quakers* in Kaimosi in Western Kenya in 1927 and 1928, referred to as *Abarohi* (= people of the Spirit), and the one that started at Swedish mission centres in Kimpese in Belgian Congo and Ngouedi, near Brazzaville in 1946, the *Jamaa Movement* among the Roman Catholics in the Congo, the *Balokole Movement* in Eastern Africa, the *Ngunza* (= prophetic) movements of Kibongi, Kimbangu and Matswa in the Congo region. These groups are sometimes very different from one another. In them there was some indirect influence by Pentecostalism, but even more they are expressions of the movements of *African Instituted Churches*, or of *Evangelical Revival* in Classical churches, whereas some are heralding the modern *Charismatic Movement*.[8]

3. Pentecostal Churches in Malawi

In 1923 the *Zionist Churches* reached Malawi via South Africa. They were not conscious of their affinity to the Pentecostal Churches which would reach Malawi by the same route. In other words, the Zionists behaved as independent or African Instituted Churches.[9] Malawian workers in South Africa brought the two oldest Pentecostal Churches to Malawi. After having founded their 'native controlled missions', foreign missionaries followed.

First there was the *Apostolic Faith Mission,* originating in the Azusa Street revival, founded in Zomba near Jali by Robert Chinguwo in 1933.[10] Later it spread considerably in the Lower Shire area, where the work was begun by Jim Phiri. Early missionaries were Erasmus, Cooksey and Wendland. Foreign missionaries played a role, the A.F.M. in Malawi, with its African style of worship and emphasis on healing. That is why - according to Fiedler – it qualifies as an African Church, but not as an A.I.C.[11]

---

[7] Sundkler and Steed, *A History of the Church in Africa*, pp. 878,911,1015

[8] Duncan and Kalu, 'Bakuzufu: Revival Movements', in: Kalu et. Al. (eds), *African Christianity*, pp. 296-300.

[9] There are now 33 different Zionist denominations in Malawi [Ulf Strohbehn, PhD dissertation, University of Malawi, forthcoming].

[10] Mvula and Lwesya, *Flames of Fire*, pp. 362-365.

[11] Cf. Chapter 16, section 4b; Ulf Strobehn, *Pentecostalism in Malawi*, op. cit.

The *second* Pentecostal Church to reach Malawi, also through returning migrants, was the *Assemblies of God*. It started in Igali in Tanganyika where Paul Derr, a missionary of the Assemblies of God, had worked since 1928. Derr 'influenced Noah Siwale, an itinerant evangelist who went back to his home, Kameme, Nyasaland and influenced a group of people who relocated and followed him'.[12] In 1934 Lyton Kalambule started in the Misuku Hills (Mubulu) and Elliot Nkunika in Dedza (Gilbert Village). Later they moved to Lilongwe, where there is now also a Seminary. Foreign missionaries from Tanzania and South Africa followed. In the following decades several other Pentecostal Churches settled in Malawi.

Generally the new Pentecostal Churches are more thriving than the older ones, a phenomenon that is also apparent in the (faith mission) Evangelical churches. Their comparative growth might be explained by their ability to answer certain African needs. According to Ward:

> 'The *Pentecostal Movement* tends to be even more condemnatory of compromise with paganism than the old established Churches, and consequently more hostile to those *African Instituted Churches* which are arrogantly dismissed as pagan. On the other hand the Pentecostal Movement does focus on, rather than shy away from, the realm of spiritual powers, and so (like the older Independent Churches) can be seen as dealing with this important area of life in more honest and direct ways, helping people to cope with the struggle which defines and circumscribes day-to-day-life for so many'.[13]

In comparison to Pentecostals and Evangelicals, the Classical (mainline) churches are declining worldwide. Fiedler might be mistaken in his opinion that this process 'does not show clearly in Malawi yet'. There is hope, though, that new revivals including rediscovery of the spiritual riches of the *Reformation* will reverse their decline, at the same time strengthening the orientation on the Word and the Spirit in Pentecostalism and Evangelicalism.

4. Features of Charismatism

The *Charismatic Movement* as such is much less a variant of the churches that go back on the Protestant *Reformation* of the 16th century, although like the Pentecostals it is related to some characteristics of the Radical or the Left Wing of the Reformation.[14]

In African Christianity there are early examples of *charismatism*. Enthusiast expectations of the speedy outpouring and miraculous working of the Holy Spirit can be noticed in the 2nd century movement of *Montanism* of which North African church father Tertullian was a follower later in his life. Early Christianity in Sub-Saharan Congo witnessed the enthusiastic utterances of prophetesses like Maffuta

---

[12] Mvula and Lwesya, *Flames of Fire*, pp. 72-76.

[13] Ward, 'Africa', in: Hastings, *World History*, p. 234.

[14] Cf. Paas, *From Galilee to the Atlantic*, pp.235-240.

and Kimpa Vita (Donna Beatrice, † 1706).[15] Some African Charismatics in the first half of the 20th century are Simon Kimbangu in Congo, Isaiah Shembe in Natal (South Africa), William Wadé Harris in Liberia and Ivory Coast, George Khambuli in Johannesburg (South Africa), Ma Nku in Evaton (South Africa). In the end of section 2 we referred to ecstatic and charismatic phenomena in Africa that heralded the modern *Charismatic Movement*.

The modern *Charismatic Movement* is a loose worldwide 'network' that began in California in 1960, by Dennis J. Bennett, an Episcopalian priest. The movement was not affected by missionaries or by a worldwide organisation. Charismatic groups began to emerge in the 1960s as a reaction against secularisation in the Western countries. Charismatism started in the Protestant, Roman Catholic and Eastern Orthodox mainline churches in America, then it spread to Europe and the other continents. Initially it remained a movement inside existing churches, but after a time 'independent' charismatic churches came into being.

Dennis J. Bennett an Episcopalian priest in California who started the Charismatic movement in 1960.

Although the modern *Charismatic Movement* in Africa was connected to previous ecstatic stirrings and movements, it entered Africa from abroad, by external spiritual forces in the white western Christian community. The kind of external origin is one of the reasons why the movement is different from the movements for African Independent Churches or African Instituted Churches. Modern Charismatic churches are not just 'New African Independent Churches'.[16] Duncan and Kalu point to the *Scripture Union* (S.U.) as a 'signifier' demonstrating the start and the early history of the *Charismatic Movement* in Africa. The S.U. began as an interdenominational agency for Bible study and prayer in British Protestant Schools in the 1950s. It spread to Africa, first to the West, and radicalised under the influence of social, political and economic challenges. In this process it influenced existing organisations and churches. Other igniting agencies were the *Hour of Freedom* ministry, the work of Benson Idahosa, founder of *Church of God Mission International*, and Welsh missionary Pa G. Elton of the *Apostolic Church*, movements within the *Student Christian Movement*, especially a break-away group, the *Christian Union*. More recent groups like the *Rhema Bible Church* of South Africa like to use for-

---

[15] Sundkler and Steed, *A History of the Church in Africa*, pp. 59,60.
[16] The term 'New African Independent Churches' is used by: Kibutu Ngimbi, *Les Nouvelles Eglises Indépendantes Africaines (NAIC): Un phénomène ecclesial observe au Congo/ Kinshasa et auprès de ses extensions en Europe occidentale: Approche historico-missiologique*, Heverlee (Louvain/ Leuven): Faculté de Théologie Evangélique (Evangelical Theological Faculty), 2000, although he admits that 'all those New Churches came from the Charismatic Movement and could all be dated from 1980 and not earlier' (English Summary, p.2).

eign preachers and televangelists, e.g. Kenneth Hagin, Oral Roberts, Morris Cerullo, and Rheinhard Bonnke. The foreign white origin of these groups and churches is apparent, which makes them different from the older movements for *African Instituted Churches*. Asamoah-Gyadu points to other differences between these charismatic movements and the *African Instituted Churches*. In comparison to the A.I.C.'s, charismatic groups are said to be more Spirit centred, less hierarchical, more 'Afro-optimistic', more involved at all levels of society including education, more friendly to ruling politicians, more open to supernatural possibilities. Charismatics stress the possibilities for empowerment against evil powers, leading to transformation and freedom, including health and prosperity.[17]

Benson Idahosa (1938-1998), founder of Church of God Mission International, based in Benin City, Nigeria.

Re-evangelising the mainline churches and winning new souls is the charismatic goal. The charismatic objectives were adopted by representatives of the youth and of the leadership of some mission churches.

The *Charismatic Movement* undoubtedly became part of African Christianity. Whether it really changed the character of African Christianity -as Duncan and Kalu claim- remains to be seen. According to them the *Charismatic Movement* has been so much Africanised that it shows 'continuity with the traditional past, embedding African Christianity into the deep structures of all *African Traditional Religions*'.[18] If it is true that in a way the *Charismatic Movement* is a continuation of African traditional religions, then critical questions on its Biblical orthodoxy could be rightfully asked. The features of the *Charismatic Movement* can be defined in comparison to those of the *Pentecostal Movement*.

Charismatism is related to *Pentecostalism*, but at the same time it strongly differs from it 'in terms of origin, social context, and spiritual appeal'.

(a) Charismatism started within mainline churches. Pentecostalism started at the fringes of historical Protestant Christianity.

(b) Charismatism started in middle and upper classes. Pentecostalism started in poor and lower classes.

(c) Charismatism was started by whites. Pentecostalism was started mainly by blacks.

(d) Charismatism generally did not start its own churches. Pentecostalism soon separated from mainline churches and established its own churches.

---

[17] J. Kwabena Asamoah-Gyadu, 'Born of Water and the Spirit: Pentecostal/ Charismatic Christianity in Africa', in: Kalu et. al. (eds), *African Christianity*, pp.403-406.
[18] Duncan and Kalu, 'Revival Movements', in: Kalu et. al. (eds), *African Christianity*, p. 306.

(e) Charismatism was to a degree accepted by Evangelical interdenominational agencies. Pentecostalism was rejected early by Evangelical churches and missions.

(f) Charismatism mixes Protestants and Roman Catholics. Pentecostalism is conscious of differences from Roman Catholicism.

(g) Charismatism is open to Theological Modernity. Pentecostalism is historically connected to Protestant Orthodoxy.

Apparently the historical, social, and ecclesiastical and theological features of the *Charismatic Movement* and the *Pentecostal Movement* differ considerably, although at the same time they interact and run parallel in aspects of Pneumatology. Charismatics are not just *New Pentecostals*.[19]

5. Charismatic Movement in Malawi

Mark Kambalazaza, founder of the Charismatic Renewal Ministry, who broke away from the Roman Catholic Church in Malawi.

The *Charismatic Movement* started in Malawi in the 1970s. Some interdenominational para-church organisations, like *Scripture Union, Students' Christian Organisation of Malawi* (S.C.O.M.), *New Life for All* provided a breeding and teaching ground. Further developments have left S.U. and S.C.O.M. with an internal struggle between Charismatics and Evangelicals. From abroad Malawian charismatism was stimulated by people like Barbara Tippet, who in 1980 founded *Blantyre Christian Centre* in Blantyre. Although the Charismatic Movement has 'no inbuilt intention to start new denominations', and many groups remained in the existing churches, these beginnings also led to the formation of charismatic churches, like: *Agape* (1982, Mgala), *Faith of God* (1984, Matoga), *Living Waters* (1985, Ndovi),[20] *Glad Tidings* (1986), *All for Jesus* (1993, Zalimba), *Flames of Victory* (1993, Katchire), *Calvary Family Church* (1994, Mbewe),[21] *Vineyard* (1994, Gama), and the *Charismatic Renewal Ministry* (1997, Kambalazaza). Their membership comprises about 250,000, according to Fiedler, which would indicate that the Charismatic Movement is stronger on that side than in the established churches.

Originally these groups were *fellowships* of active members of existing churches, but they consolidated themselves into denominations over the years. The

---

[19] Asamoah-Gyadu, 'Born of Water and the Spirit', in: Kalu et. al.(eds), *African Christianity*, pp. 389-409, in general classifies both movements together as 'Pentecostal/ Charismatic Christianity', and uses the term 'New Pentecostal' for newer phenomena of Charismatism.

[20] Cf. Mvula and Mbilikile, *Flames of Fire*, pp.373, 374.

[21] Cf. Mvula and Mbilikile, *Flames of Fire*, pp. 375-378.

fellowships organised themselves around a *'ministry'* group consisting of a leader and helpers. Members are recruited on an interdenominational or even nondenominational basis. Gradually the fellowship is meeting at the times of worship of existing churches, members calling themselves 'born agains'. Formalisation of this new status takes place as the sacraments are being administered, to which is added the baptism with the Holy Spirit and the sacramentalisation of weddings.[22] Fellowships started *outside* existing churches, and later they developed into separate denominations. Generally the fellowships that started *inside* the structures of the existing churches, remain there, but in some cases, like that of the *Presbyterian Church of Malawi* (P.C.M.), and the *Charismatic Renewal Ministries* there have been secessions.

Stanley Ndovi, founder of the Living Waters Church, in Malawi.

The *Charismatic Movement* has been interpreted in sociological, economic, and political terms, which -according to Fiedler- do not take it seriously. Fiedler sees the *Charismatic Movement* as a 'quest for a deeper Christian life' going beyond attending catechism classes, church services, and behaving properly. As such the Charismatic fellowships and churches are a necessary challenge for the older churches, although he does not expect them to replace the mainline, evangelical and independent churches.[23]

Charismatism generally does not thrive in rural areas, it mainly reaches the urban and middle class. To which extent, it still is a Western phenomenon, remains to be seen.[24] Charismatic Churches are less African than the Pentecostal churches, although their African leaders might develop them into the direction of more 'Africanness'.

6. Politics

Generally *Pentecostals* and *Charismatics*, just like many *Evangelicals*, do not mix themselves in politics. They define their vision of the Kingdom in eschatological terms as a future hope. This can lead to condoning oppression and social injustice. Shaw mentions the example of Liberia in 1980 where 'charismatic preachers and

---

[22] Cf. R.A. van Dijk, *Young Malawian Puritan Preachers in a Present-Day African Urban Environment*, University of Utrecht, 1992, who gives a sociological interpretation of the emergence of the 'born again' movement.

[23] K.Fiedler, 'The Charismatic and Pentecostal Movements in Malawi in Cultural Perspective', in: R.I.M. 9, (1999); See also: Rhodian G. Munyenyembwe, 'The Church and Socio-cultural Issues: An Evaluation of the Charismatic Movement's Contribution towards the Centralisation of the Gospel in Malawi', 2006 [unpublished MA dissertation of the University of Malawi]

[24] Munyenyembe, 'The Church and Social Structures, op. cit., stresses the Africanness of the movement.

evangelists avoided any confrontation with the oppressive regime of S.K. Doe, 'by blaming poverty and injustice on territorial demons that hovered above Liberia'[25] He says, sometimes Charismatics restrict themselves to casting out demons, 'while their nation goes to the devil'.[26] However, Pentecostals in South Africa took their stance against 'apartheid'. Parallel to the *Kairos Document* (1985), produced by the South African Council of Churches, and the *Evangelical Witness* by 'concerned Evangelicals', the Pentecostals issued their *Pentecostal Witness* (1986). Charismatics in Malawi seem to be 'invariably apolitical' tending to support the ruling powers of the country.

---

[25] Shaw, *The Kingdom of God*, p. 265.
[26] Shaw, *The Kingdom of God*, p. 292.

Chapter 20

The Position of Africa's Women

1. Biblical Pattern

a. Together with Man

A description of the position of Christian women in Africa[1] needs a wider perspective than Africa alone. Christians believe that the Word of God has the final say in teaching and life. That is why the normative for the position of women in Africa and anywhere is to be found in the Bible.[2] Scripture pictures the position of the woman within the relationship between man and woman. Men and women are one another's counterparts. They are partners. In a very special way this is true in marriage and in family life. In a more general way it is also true in the Church and in society as a whole. One cannot get a bal-

One of the many ways the African woman tries to sustain herself and others.

---

[1] Here is a selection of recent titles that can be helpful in studying the subject in a Central African setting: Isabel Apawo Phiri, *Women, Presbyterianism and Patriarchy: Religious Experience of Chewa Women in Central Malawi*, Blantyre: Kachere/ Claim, 1997; Isabel Apawo Phiri, Devarakshanam Betty Govinden, Sarojini Nadar, *Her-Stories: Hidden Histories of Women of Faith in Africa*, Pietermaritzburg: Cluster, 2002; Janet Y Kholowa, and Klaus Fiedler, *In the Beginning God Created them Equal*, Zomba: Kachere 2003; Helen E.P. van Koevering, The Lakeshore Nyanja Women of the Anglican Diocese of Niasa, Zomba: Kachere, 2005; Rachel Nyagondwe Banda, *Women of the Bible and Culture: Baptist Convention Women in Southern Malawi*, Zomba: Kachere, 2005; Rachel Nyagondwe Fiedler, *Coming of Age: A Christianized Initiation among Women in Southern Malawi*, Zomba: Kachere, 2005; Clara Henderson, *They rolled away the Stone* [to be published by Kachere]. See also: Seodi Venekai-Rodo White et. al., *Dispossessing the Widow: Gender Based Violence in Malawi*, Blantyre: Kachere/ Claim, 2002; Klaus Fiedler, *The Story of Faith Missions*, pp. 292-309; C.M.Pauw, *Mission and Church in Malawi – The History of the Nkhoma Synod of the Church of Central Africa Presbyterian, 1889-1962*, 1980, pp. 199-204; T.O. Ranger & J.Weller (eds), *Themes in the History of Central Africa*, London: Heineman, 1974, pp. 256-268.

[2] Among the many Bible studies on this issue I recommend here: George and Dora Winston, *Recovering Biblical Ministry by Women: An Exegetical Response to Traditionalism and Feminism*, Xulon Press, 2003; Alexander Rattray Hay, *The Woman's Ministry in Church and at Home*, Audubon: New Testament Missionary Union, 1962; Cf. C. den Boer, *Man en Vrouw in Bijbels Perspectiegf: Een Bijbels-Theologische Verkenning van de Man-Vrouw Verhouding met het oog op de Gemeente*, Kampen: Kok, 1987².

anced and truthful vision of the position of women without realising how they relate to men. In the same way the position of men becomes clear when we see how it is situated within the framework of men's interaction in partnership with women. In some Philosophies or Theologies either women or men are looked at as independent entities, disconnected from this partnership. They are doomed to distort the positions of either women or men in married life, in the Church and in society.

b. Equal to Man

African woman pounding maize.

In Biblical thought, God created man and woman in close relationship to one another and to Himself. He created them in His own image. That is why they are equal[3] and to a great extent similar. In their equality and relative similarity they reflect their Creator to Whom they are related. This togetherness as equal and relatively similar beings dependent on their Creator and reflecting Him, is one of the most central thoughts in Scripture. This togetherness in equality is meant by God as the basic structure of any human relationship. Divisions of responsibility including labour and family care, or positions of leadership, power and authority are to fit in the pattern that relates woman and man to one another and both to God. The threads that hold its elements harmoniously together are made by the supreme authority of the Word of God. In faithful acceptance of that Divine authority, man and women are called to cooperate when performing the tasks of life, sharing one another's burden and challenges.

c. Different from Man

Man and woman have many characteristics in common. In this relative similarity they are images of God. At the same time they are not uniform. They are not similar in an absolute sense. There are

African women, carrying water.

---

[3] Cf. Janet Y Kholowa, and Klaus Fiedler, *In the Beginning God Created them Equal*, Zomba: Kachere 2003.

distinct differences. In this they are also images of God. Their differences from one another are parallel to the differences between the three Persons in God. In marriage, church and society man and woman have many similar roles and responsibilities, but at the same time they represent different aspects of life and act in different role patterns.

2. Cultural Patterns

a. Philosophy

Of course African Christianity is a product of the Word of God, and so is the position of women in marriages, churches and societies that have fully accepted the authority of the Bible. However, the reality of daily practice is more complicated than this. Unfortunately, there is the reality of sin that corrupts or even obliterates Biblical patterns. Even Christians have no perfect understanding of God's will, neither are they perfectly obedient to Him.

Moreover, like societies anywhere on this globe, African societies, including churches and Christians, are being influenced by culture. The term culture comprises the way in which humanity builds up life, using the means given by human capacities and by surrounding nature. Traditions and customs belong to it, also traditional religions. The term culture is closely related to the term philosophy, referring to man's love of wisdom. Philosophy is the rationalising power of man. It enables human beings to reflect on their own being and existence. Through philosophy human beings can organise their thinking on culture and their knowledge of it in an orderly way.

The perception that African Christians have on the position of women is influenced both by Western Culture and by African Culture.

b. Western Culture

In Western Culture at least two different strands can be discerned. There is the Biblical line, focusing on God, which led to the plantation of God's Church, through Paul, Augustine, the Reformation, and the Evangelical or Reformed and Jansenist Revivals and Awakenings in modern times. This line leads from and to the Cross of Jesus Christ, through Whom there is salvation for anyone who believes in Him. Sometimes pharaseistic and heterodox Jewish Culture weakened this line, e.g. by its onesided emphasis on perfect obedience to the Law, presented as a feasible way for mankind to be saved. Another strand is the wisdom of pre-Christian Greek and Roman Cultures, focusing on man and nature. On the one hand, through Humanism, Enlightenment, Industrial Revolution, Positivism, and Emancipation, it contributed immensely to the development of science and technology. On the other hand it undermined Christian life. Gnostic ideas distorted the relationship between matter and spirit, body and soul, which wronged the view of

Western man on his own life, including his sexuality. It also led to the replacement of God by the mistaken faith in the power of human progress. This blinded man to the limitations of economical and technical development. In post-modern thought there is again a realisation that man cannot live by bread alone. By the end of the 20th century transcendental religiosity took the place of unlimited materialism. However, in general, this has not led people back to Christ and to acceptance of salvation through his work.

The position of women in Western Culture has changed as history continued. In the Jewish-Biblical climate women were respected and were not always completely dependent on men. In general they were under the leadership and authority of men, particularly in marriage. The New Testament shows that discriminatory differences between men and women fade out when people are living near to Christ. In the classical Greek and Roman Cultures women were positioned at a very low level. They were not much different from slaves, assigned to act as workers and sex tools. Only as religious prostitutes and priestesses at the pagan temples, and sometimes in related queenship positions some of them could have independent power.

The arrival of Christianity fundamentally changed the position of women. The number of women among the first Christians was disproportionately large. Consequently many played an important role in the Church, especially in prophetic and charismatic ministries. In the *Middle Ages* the position of women deteriorated. Their influence did not fit well in the male oriented feudal organisation of society and hierarchical rule of the Church. At best they were given honour by noblemen, through the courtesy songs of bards, or by the Church, by elevating them to a special religious position as inhabitants of a convent. A Gnostic view of marriage and sexuality was maintained.

The *Reformation*, as a back-to-the-Bible-movement, tried to restore the Biblical pattern of the relationship between men and women. The Reformers re-appraised family life as the cornerstone of society. In the family the wife played a key role, so indirectly her position in society was elevated. In the churches of the *Reformation* women received room for various activities, especially diaconial work. In marriage, church and society, men were considered to be the leaders, having final authority. However, a Biblical reform of man-woman relationships, taking into account equality, similarity, and difference, did not take place. Gradually the promising perspectives of the *Reformation* on real christianisation of the man-woman relationship patterns grew dim, and later developments were less inspired by Biblical thinking than by cultures that had started outside and before the birth of Christianity.

Changes in the position of women in the *Modern Era* were mainly the result of views that had revived in the periods of *Renaissance* and *Humanism,* then taken over by the movements of *Enlightenment, Romanticism* and *Positivism.* These movements were not necessarily anti-Christian, yet they took their criteria from earthly realities considered without the Bible or God. In this way much of Western society was secularised. Also the view of the relationship between men and women was secularised to a high degree. In the Modern Era of Western history, as a result of philosophical revolutions, the position of women changed in two directions.

First, there was the ever growing tendency of emancipation. This tendency got momentum, especially after the French Revolution, and it summitted after the *Second World War*, getting to extremes in movements of feminism and women's lib. Its ultimate objectives are beyond reaching equality, it aims at removing all differences between the two sexes.

The second tendency seems to go against the first one. In the agrarian and early capitalist societies, that had started to erode before 1800, to a certain extent women could be economically independent from men, because they had access to land and commerce. This strengthened women's influence in a culture that for the rest was dominated by men. Man's overlordship was balanced by the fact that in rural family life, wife and husband only could survive by being one another's cooperating partners.

This situation began to change by the technological and industrial revolutions of the 19th century. The heartbeat of economical life shifted to the cities, where factories, ports and civil service attracted many people that thus far had lived in the country side. As a result farm life and home industry reduced, together with the relatively independent position of women. More and more the kitchen and the delivery room were the only areas where women could be of significance. In general the churches did not try to counteract this tendency of diminishing the space in which a woman could operate. Absolute male dominance seemed a matter of course.

In the meantime, mainly from the secular world outside the churches, movements for women's emancipation grew stronger. To many Christians, the campaigns for women's emancipation seemed to aim at anti-Biblical objectives. In this polarised situation, although in theory accepting women's equality, the churches would defend the contemporary situation in which there were practically no similar responsibilities for women and men. Yet, sometimes in the church there was a powerful wave of influence by women. The evangelical revivals and awakenings of the 18th and 19th centuries had revived the churches, and had given more room to women in various activities.

European and American missionaries who came to Africa were very much products of the cultural situation in their home countries. They brought with them not only Biblical views, but also Western cultural perceptions of the relationship between women and men. Among them there was a wide spectre of views, some were on the progressive side, most of them were conservatives. Some were under the influence of liberal thought, most of them were children of the evangelical revivals and awakenings. That is why there was no uniformity in their ideas on the position of women. Missions of the mainline churches (classical missions) did not send women as missionaries in their own right. But the post-classical missions did. (See chapter 14).

c. African and Islamic Cultures

African Culture. In the traditional African context women have always been subordinated to men. Women obey, men are in command.[4] Besides, they were considered as a segregate group, because of their specific female roles, e.g. in pregnancy and childbirth.[5] There was total submission to the husband. Girls were taught not to argue with the husband and treat him as king. They were prepared to live with a man at a very young age. Initiation ceremonies for girls were considered very important as they were regarded as moral and religious education. However, sexual rites have been performed between the initiates and unknown men, called in Chichewa *afisi*,[6] to mark the end of puberty initiation. Widows have been forced into the custom of *kuchotsa fumbi*,[7] which means that they have to sleep with a brother of the deceased husband.[8]

On the other hand there have been areas where women dominated. Like in classical Greek Culture, certain women dominated-fields were often related to religion, fertility (including rain making), prophecy and priesthood.

Here is an example of the Chewa women in Malawi, described by Phiri. Women known as spirit-wives were the controllers of the territorial rain shrines. When in ecstasy they were said to receive messages from god. The shrine for Chisumphi in Central Malawi was served by a succession of women known as Mangadzi or Makewana.. In the south there was the shrine of the Mbona cult. There a human woman was provided as wife for the spirit who was believed to visit the shrine. The woman was known as Mbona. Makewana

Literacy project for African women (Mariotschool).

had female attendants. These were young virgins between the age of five and eight. At a shrine, it was believed that god would not be present if the woman was producing menstrual blood. Makewana and her female attendants were not allowed to marry or to become pregnant. Yet Makewana was involved in ritual sexual intercourse at the shrine with a special functionary, called Kamundi, as a way of marking the end of the initiation ceremony for girls.[9] The example shows that women

---

[4] Cf. Phiri, *Women*, p.17.
[5] Rachel Banda, *Women of the Bible and Culture,* pp.169-189.
[6] Paas, *Chichewa/ Chinyanja – English Dictionary*: the word *afisi* is plural for *hyena*:
[7] Paas, *Chichewa/ Chinyanja – English Dictionary*: 'kuchotsa fumbi' literally means: *to remove dust.*
[8] Phiri, *Women*, etc. pp.38-40.
[9] Phiri, *Women,* etc., pp. 23-33.

could have complete control of religious shrines, and that their position was connected to cultic prostitution.

As priesthood and kingship were closely related, women could also be leaders in a wider political sense. Traditionally quite a number of Chewa chiefs are female. In a matrilineal situation women could also be in a stronger position because of the marriage arrangements that forced the husband to move to the village of the wife, thus making him dependent on the family of the wife. Economically the wife used to have independent access to land and commerce, adding to her relative independency.

On a negative note, a number of women would enlarge their power by witchcraft. Most witches are female,[10] and with their manipulations they definitely influence many people, including men.

Islamic Culture. The arrival of Islam in Africa did not improve the status of women. Islamic tradition puts the woman lower than the man. A man is allowed to marry four wives, and room is created for extra marital sex by men. Islam offers perceptions that are offensive to women, for example the expectation that in heaven man 'enjoys' the presence of virgins ready for him. On the other hand Islamic law regulated the position of women, giving them probably more protection than unstable structures of *African Traditional Religions*.

d. Christ is more than Culture

We have noted that philosophy is a consciously designed system of principles of wisdom for reasoning on our way of life, i.e. on our culture. This applies to any culture, including Western, African, and Islamic Cultures. Cultures and religions that preceded the arrival of Christianity or cultures and religions that operate outside the scope of Biblical faith may harbour some august philosophical insights and noble ethical values that confirm Scripture. Yet, they do not focus Christ.

Now the question is what value do we attach to our philosophy, our culture, our system of thought, our tradition, our wisdom? If compared to the faith in Jesus Christ, which position does our natural wisdom take? We cannot completely separate the two. They are related. But there is a certain order. What is the order of these things in our lives? There are basically two positions. In the first position our wisdom and culture dominate our faith. In the second position wisdom and culture are dominated by faith. In the first position faith in Jesus Christ is the first thing in our lives and everything else is second. In the second position our culture and philosophy are first. They are dearer to us than Jesus and the faith in Him. In this case our own wisdom and the wisdom of the world want to rule over our faith in Jesus. Here we have to make a choice. This choice has great consequences. When you put your wisdom higher than your faith, then in the end you'll find that your wisdom

---

[10] R.J.Gehman, *African Traditional Religion in Biblical Perspective*, Nairobi: East African Educational Publishers, p. 73.

fails you, and that you have no faith at all. When you put your faith first, then it will 'colour' everything in your life, also your wisdom.

Only those who believe in Him, will find real wisdom. They find real understanding of sin and grace and of the ways of the Lord. Being in the faith produces a culture, customs, a philosophy that are Christ oriented. Faith precedes philosophy and produces it. Because of the faith in Christ wisdom becomes real wisdom. Faith produces a wisdom that is both disciplined by the Word of God and derived from the Word of God. The centre of the Word of God is the Cross of Jesus Christ. That is why we can say that Jesus Christ is the wisdom of God. Christ's saving work on the Cross is the ultimate wisdom.

3. Christian Women Today

a. Situation before Independence

It is apparent that today's position of Christian women in Africa has been influenced from various sides. First, by the work of the sovereign God himself through his Word and Spirit. Secondly, by the effects of the Jewish-Biblical, the Western, the Traditional African and the Islamic Cultures. At some point all these cultures show a break with the Word of God, although many of their phenomena may run parallel to it.

In general, missionaries from the West were sincere Christians, ignited by revivalist movements. They professed the final authority of the Bible in all issues, including man-woman relationships. As such they looked at African society, and made comments on it. Often they did not favour African traditions, and they wanted to bring the lives of African men and women in line with the Biblical patterns.

Religious Sisters in an African Independent Church in Zimbabwe.

Yet, at the same time they were influenced by their own Western Culture which means that unconsciously they may have defended views that do not necessarily agree to Scripture. They may also have condemned certain features of traditional African gender features too rigidly or in the wrong way. In a way Phiri could be right when she says that the coming of the missionaries and the colonial governments did not create a favourable environment for improvement of the position of women. According to Phiri the missionaries attacked traditional female cults, matrilineal privileges for women, and royal positions for women. In the vision of the missionaries, defined by a 19th century rural tradition in Europe and America, women particularly belonged to the spheres of housekeeping and childcare.[11]

There may be truth in this, yet it cannot be denied, that there is an important other side. Missionaries realised that women should participate fully in developments in family, church and society. That is why they had to be educated. Western missions included women and girls in their education programmes.

On the other hand, attempts for uplifting women were hindered by factors of change due to the effects of Western economical and social influence. There was a parallel here with 19th century Europe and America that experienced the effects of the industrial revolution. The social and economical infra-structure of African family and village life changed when traditional barter economy in an agricultural environment were replaced by a cash economy depending on an urban environment. The new economy had not much use for women participating independently in the economical process.[12]

b. Present situation

What is the Greatest Problem? Today African women operate in societies and churches that are independent of Western rule. Yet forms of dependence on the West have continued ever since the end of colonialism. Moreover, modern Africa has become part of the global community. How have these changes affected the position of African women? A description of the present situation was offered on a conference in Dakar in 1994 and more especially in 1995 at the *Fourth Women's World Conference* in Beijing.[13] In a report made by Takyiwaa Manuh, the growing recognition of the contributions of women is noted, but also the enormous obstacles that they face. The report exclusively deals with social, economic and political aspects of the position of women. According to the World Conference the greatest problem of African women is that they were not given sufficient access to resources, and decision-making powers. This is said to have affected their general position in a negative way. Here is a summary of the main parts of the report.

Three Developments. The report says that in recent decades women's lives have been profoundly affected by three main developments: *First*, the structural adjustment programmes. By placing greater emphasis on export crops, which usually are grown by men, the domestic terms of trade have tended to shift against food production, where women predominate. *Secondly*, there has been increased civil strife and conflict. The majority of refugees, displaced persons and post-conflict returnees were women and children. *Thirdly*, many African countries are grappling with

---

[11] Cf. Phiri, *Women,* etc., p.23.

[12] Cf. Fiedler, *The History of the Faith Missions*, pp. 292-298.

[13] Takyiwaa Manuh, 'Women in Africa's development: Overcoming Obstacles, Pushing for Progress', *Africa Recovery Briefing Paper*, Number 11, April 1998.

the AIDS crisis, high and increasing rates of HIV infection and the costs in human lives. Just over half of the estimated 20 million cases of HIV in Africa are female.

Marriage and Family Life. In the country side and in the cities women perform all domestic tasks, while many also farm and trade. They are responsible for the care of children, the sick and the elderly, in addition to performing essential social functions within their communities. While today women rarely have the same access to resources as men, in the past some resources were available to them, especially land. Wives in many societies were not fully economically dependent upon their husbands. Women's power and spheres of influence largely disappeared under the impact of colonialism and external religions, which upset existing economic and social complementarity between the sexes. Women have profited from improved education, employment, health care, nutrition, but in general their position has deteriorated. Development plans were made and executed without an adequate understanding of women's contributions to African economies. That is why they have tended to be marginalised. New marriage laws transformed the previously fluid and negotiable relations between them into rigid duties and obligations of wives and women. Women came to be regarded as primarily dependent on men, making it unnecessary to plan and provide for their needs; they were to work in the fields and home to produce food and other crops to support their men, who worked in visible, documented activities. About half of all women in Africa are married by the age of 18 and one in three women is in a polygamous marriage. Estimates of average total fertility rates in Africa were 5.7 children per woman in 1995. Women head about 31 per cent of households in urban and rural areas across Africa, often with no working resident males.

Labour. In many rural areas, women contribute unpaid labour to the household's agricultural production and spend up to 50 hours a week on domestic labour and subsistence food production, with little sharing of tasks by spouses or sons in the household. Studies have documented that women work 12-13 hours a week more than men, as the prevalent economic and environmental crises have increased the working hours of the poorest women. In some areas, women may have separate access to land and work independently in farming or in some other income-generating activity. But in general they have fewer opportunities to earn income. They combine their unpaid labour with independent production to meet the needs of their families and to attain some measure of autonomy and self-reliance. Their income is indispensable for family survival regardless of the presence of men, since the system of allocation and distribution within many African households usually imposes individual responsibilities on men and women to meet their personal needs.

Women provide the backbone of the rural economy in much of Sub-Saharan Africa. About 80 per cent of the economically active female labour force is employed in agriculture and women comprise about 47 per cent of the total agricultural labour force. Food production is the major activity of rural women and their responsibilities and labour inputs often exceed those of men in most areas in Africa. Women also provide much of the labour for men's cultivation of export crops, from which women derive little direct benefit. Food security in Africa cannot be assured without improving the situation of women producers.

Education and training. Although a number of women profited from education, for very many there is still a lack of access to formal education and training. This has been identified as a key barrier to women's employment and advancement in society. In Africa, female illiteracy rates were over 60 per cent in 1996, compared to 41 per cent for men. In many African countries, parents still prefer to send boys to school, seeing little need for education for girls. In addition, factors such as adolescent pregnancy, early marriage and girls' greater burden of household labour act as obstacles to their schooling. In 1993, only about 40 per cent of school-age girls were enrolled in primary or secondary schools.

Health and sanitation. For women, as for men, inadequate potable water, sanitation and waste disposal in urban and rural areas in Africa leave populations vulnerable to water-borne and other environmental diseases. Malaria, lung and other respiratory diseases are still major killers in Africa.

Maternal and infant mortality remain high. Up to 40 per cent of pregnant women in many countries have no access to antenatal care, while the percentage of births attended by trained personnel has declined. In 1994 the infant mortality rate in Africa was estimated at 92 deaths per thousand. High rates of infant mortality, the opposition of male partners and religious and cultural factors result in levels of contraceptive use of only around 15 per cent.

The health of women and girl-children is also jeopardised by female genital mutilation (F.G.M.). It is estimated that about 2 million girls are subjected to the practice each year.

The high and growing incidence of AIDS also highlights women's lack of power over their own sexuality. Research in West and Central Africa has shown that because of cultural and economic reasons, many women feel unable to refuse the sexual advances of partners even when they know they risk infection.

Issues of rape, sexual assault and domestic violence also are beginning to receive due attention in discussions of women's health.

In situations of conflict, refugee and displaced women and girls often have been sexually assaulted.

Political power. Many governments have been negligent in enacting women's rights into national law. Moreover, many women are ignorant of the existence of laws that recognise their rights and which can be invoked for their protection. Traditional women leaders have not been given the same recognition as male chiefs who after independence have been co-opted into new positions of power in their societies.

4. The Way Forward

This report of the *Beijing Conference* reflects the views of many African leaders in Church and Society. They like to depict the problems of Africa's women mainly from an economical and social angle. This general acceptance is also true for the solution suggested in the *Beijing Report*. It boils down to one demand. Give to women the same access to resources, and decision-making powers as to men. In other words, remove the gender bias and realise gender equality. The philosophical starting point for this description of problems and solution is not explicitly given, but reminds of a Western or globalist approach in the line of the *Enlightenment*. Possession of economical means and power is supposed to solve all women's problems.

Can this thought determine the vision of Church and Christians? I think it can't. Christians have more to say, and they have to say it differently. In the conclusion of the *Beijing Report* the reality of the Biblical patterns of relationship between men and women to God and men and women to one another are not taken into account. Secular thought pays no attention to the fact that the similarity of men and women is limited, and that differences between them necessarily play an important and positive role. Realising this biblical reality is required when Church and Christians want to fathom the the economical and social misery of so many women in Africa. Christians should prophetically encourage political leaders to develop their economies and social structures for the benefit of the people, giving also to women their rightful place.

In the light of Scripture, Church and Christians in Africa have to make a diagnosis of the deepest causes of the crisis. Secularist approaches are blind for spiritual dimensions. The basic Biblical lines for marriage, for sexuality, for family life, and for role patterns of men and women in church and society mean to prevent problems and to heal relationships that got broken and lopsided. Having found the spiritual diagnosis of the problem, the Church and the individual Christians should also derive from Scripture the method of healing. They are called to proclaim and apply the Gospel of Jesus Christ, and show that He is able to touch and heal in any broken relationship.

What does this mean for the Church? Traditionally in the African churches women are conspicuously present, often more than men. Women were among the first to receive the message and they were very influential as local evangelists. Mwaura explored how the planting and growth of Christianity in Africa has been facilitated by female agency. She concludes that especially in *African Instituted Churches* women played an essential role as spirit-filled initiators of revival, as church founders, as prophetic figures, as healers, as evangelists.[14] In *Classical Churches* too women have played pivotal roles in initiating, upholding and extend-

---

[14] Philomena Njeri Mwaura, 'Gender and Power in African Christianity: African Instituted Churches and Pentecostal Churches', in: Kalu et.al. (eds), *African Christianity*, pp. 410-445.

ing the life of faith in family and congregation. In the light of this situation and by the influence of female oriented and feminist theologies the role pattern for Christian women in the church has become an issue for renewed discussions.[15] Like Christian men, female Christians are kings, prophets and priests in Christ (1 *Peter* 2: 9). What does this mean for the position of women concerning the leadership in the Church? This challenging question has to be answered with an open mind, in obedience to Scripture.

Members of the Women's Guild (Amayi a Mvano) of Mulunguzi C.C.A.P., Malawi.

---

[15] Cf. Nyambura J. Njoroge, 'A New Way of Facilitating Leadership: Lessons from African Women Theologians', in Kalu et.al. (eds), *African Christianity*, pp.446-468.

Chapter 21

Conversion

1. Conversion in Context

The Expansion of Christianity and *The Planting of Christianity*. Under these headings Latourette and Groves wrote their extensive accounts of *African Church History*. They made their books during the three decades before, in and after the *Second World War*. It was visible to them that much of Sub-Saharan Africa was in the process of conversion from *Traditional Religions* to Christianity. However, at that time they could not know that the most spectacular increase of the number of Christians in Africa was still ahead of them. The growth of Christi-

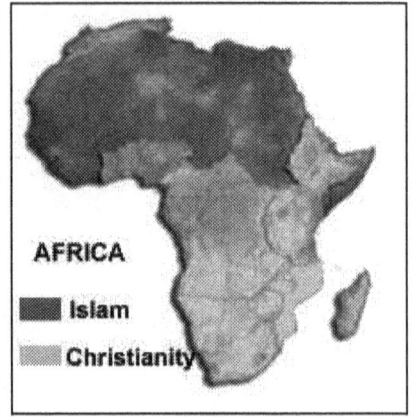

anity in Africa is called by Bonk 'one of the most astonishing phenomena of the 20th century'. He quotes figures from recent publications showing that during the 40 years since the beginning of independence, about 1960, the 'number of Christians in Africa has multiplied by six to nearly 380 million', that is nearly fifty percent of the total population of Africa. The numerical progress of Christianity has overtaken the growth of Islam, to which another 41 percent of Africans are said to belong.[1]

There are many reasons why Africans would become Christians. According to Walls[2] an important reason is that becoming a Christian is a means of access to the desirable things of Europeans, especially to *power*. The writer thinks it a mistake to call this reason secular. He uses the example of Igboland, where 'religion always was directed at the acquisition of power'. When the British came and subdued them, for the Igbos there was every religious reason to abandon traditional religion, because it had shown not to be of any value for the acquisition of power. There were two movements in Igbo Christianity. First, vigorous adhesion to Christian

---

[1] Jonathan J. Bonk, 'The Dictionary of African Christian Bibliography: Ecclesiastical Cartography and the Invisible Continent', 2004 [http://www.dacb.org], who quotes: Lamin Sanneh, *Whose Religion is Christianity: The Gospel Beyond the West*, Grand Rapids: Eerdmans, 2003, p. 15, Patrick Johnstone and Jason Mandryk, with Robin Johnstone, *Operation World: Twenty-first Century Edition*, Carlyle: Paternoster, 2001, pp. 20, 21; cf. Isichei, *History of Christianity*, p. 31.
[2] Walls, *Missionary Movement*, pp. 89-93.

worship, understanding it as a kind of *Deuteronomic Theology*, and secondly in a later generation a new emphasis on the cross and the taking up of the cross. So, first they 'accepted Christianity in terms of traditional world view' and then, 'it entered deep into the traditional system and interacted with it'.

Generally, Western influences contributed to the many changes in African society. If tradition has no answer to the changes, then there is the danger of disintegration, disturbance, and confusion, unless a new *rule* of life, a *key* to conduct, can be found. Evangelical preaching can provide such a key, but sometimes it got stuck in the attitudes of *legalism*.

A Diviner leaving a religious shrine in Burkina Faso.

2. God and the African Past[3]

Unlike African converts, the old Greek Christians did not give God a personal name; for them he was just *ho Theos* (= the God), who replaced their polytheism. The Africans, however, generally recognised a creator god, the moral governor of the universe, a supreme being. They tended to use the name of this being for the God of the Bible.[4]

Early baptisms in Lake Malawi.

The question is: Was God thus part of the African past? Can God be found in the African heritage? Or is this Christianising African traditional religion? Okot p'Bitek, a non-Christian, says: 'the process of seeking God in the African past will render the Christian revelation unnecessary'. But the other side is: no one can have an identity without his or her past. Kwame Bediako, who paralleled ancient Hellenistic and modern African identity questions, says: the first question on the African theological agenda is: Where was God in Africa's past? He answers: The Supreme Being of Africa's past with its many names is the God of Scripture, Zeus and Odin never were! But is this answer true according to Scripture? And if so, does this help Africans to get saved?

---

[3] Walls, *Missionary Movement*, pp. 94-97.

[4] NB 1: Muslims were very reluctant to do this. NB 2: Sometimes this practice contributed to neglecting God the Son.

3. New Perspectives on an Encounter[5]

Some approach these questions from a nationalistic and political angle, stressing the usefulness of Christian mission for modernisation and political independence of Africa. This approach neglects the deeper religious reasons why Africans found Christianity 'appropriate or useful in their campaign with the new and wider world that was intruding upon them'.

Horton observed a change in the way Africans appreciated their traditional religious hierarchy of the *Supreme Being* as the highest level, together with subordinate deities, and the lower local spirits. He says that of late the cult of the *Supreme Being* became more important, whereas the lesser *spirit cult* declined. Modern developments drew people more into the realm of the *macrocosmos* of the *Supreme Being*, whereas the realm of the *microcosmos* with its spirits became less important. This development would have facilitated the acceptance of the Christian God who was considered to give power for coping with the advancing macro-world of modern life. Horton thinks that African Christianity borrowed features of these two levels of *African Traditional Religion*. This would mean that to some Mang'anja and Sena Mbona woshippers of Southern Malawi Mbona became a black Christ,[6] and that to some even anti-witchcraft cleansing would be identified as an aspect of Christian sanctification. Whether Horton observed rightly, remains to be seen. On the ground, the worship of territorial cults and spirits, like the Mbona cult, may still be active, but they have declined and have a limited appeal only. Moreover, there are examples of remaining Mbona worshippers, who are far from mixing with Christianity, and even publicly advert hostility towards the Christians and their 'alien god'.[7] At the same time it cannot be denied that in the perception of many people the 'lower' spirits, acestors etc. still play important roles.

According to Horton, the change in African religious concepts was not only brought about by the advent of Christian mission, but also by changes in African traditional religious systems that had begun before the coming of the missionaries and by which these systems retained their vitality. Vitality of African traditional religion, as expressed in the new emphasis on super-natural healing, witchcraft cleansing, and spirit-possession (often denounced and neglected by the missionaries), partly assimilated into Christianity, and partly it expressed itself in anti-mission protest, as can be seen in the ridiculing of Christianity by the *Nyau Societies* and their *Gule Wamkulu* by adopting pseudo Christian forms like *Mpingo wa Aroni* in Malawi.[8]

---

[5] R. Strayer, 'Mission History in Africa: New Perspectives on an Encounter', in: B. Carmody, *African Conversion*, Ndola: Mission Press, pp. 1-15.

[6] Cf. J.M. Schoffeleers (ed.), *Guardians of the Land: Essays on Central African Territorial Cults*, Gweru: Mambo, 1992, pp. 147-186.

[7] Cf. Deogratias Mmana, 'Asking for Rain through Libations at Khuluvi', and 'Otsatira Chipembedzo cha Makolo apempha mvula kwa Mbona ku Khuluvi', in: Malawi News, October 1-7, 2005

[8] Steven Paas, *Chichewa/ Chinyanja – English Dictionary*, Zomba: Kachere, 2005^2, p. 127: The main

Many became disappointed with the inability of mission Christianity to meet with African needs for explanation, prediction, or control and practical problems like life-healing, unemployment, sterility, and casting off evil as a real and personal power. This disappointment contributed to an ongoing interest in aspects of traditional religion and to the growth of independent separatist churches that gave room to traditional approaches. On the other hand, however, Christian mission in Africa was extremely successful, and churches grew in influence and number, at the expense of traditional religion and independent churches. There are a number of reasons for this:

a. Adaptation

There was an adaptation of Christian mission to the African situation and needs, which did not provoke schism.

First, the missionaries often expressed their message as instruments to overcome 'this-worldly-problems', like praying for rain, reading as a magic art, the power of modernisation. In the changing and secularising world of Africa, to many, the missionaries seemed more instrumental than traditional religion and later independent churches.

Secondly, the missionaries, especially the Roman Catholics, allowed adaptation in African religious and cultural terms. Examples are Roman Catholic leniency in matters of polygamy, bride wealth, and the veneration of ancestors. This gave them an advantage over Protestantism. In working among the southern Shona the *Dutch Reformed Mission* was less successful than the *Roman Catholic Mission*. There are few separatist churches in Tanzania probably because of strong adaptation by Roman Catholic missionaries. Acceptance of female circumcision by the Anglicans gave them more influence among the Kikuyu than the Presbyterians and the *Africa Inland Mission*.

Thirdly, missionary absolutism from above by the foreign missionaries was often balanced by pragmatism from below by the African helpers, catechists and clergymen. In practice, room was created for the wearing of protective charms, consulting traditionalist religious specialists, and interaction with traditional religious communities.

Fourthly, in the mission churches there was reinterpretation of Christian rites and practices in terms of traditional belief within mission, for example Dominican sisters as the equivalent of the *Mbonga-Virgins* at the shrine of the Mwari, the Shona high god, baptism became a healing rite, and miraculous healings and exorcism were incorporated.[9]

---

ceremony of the *Nyau* is the *Gule Wamkulu* (Big Dance) which can admit persons into the *Mpingo wa Aroni* (Church of Aaron, derived from the idolatrous golden calf religion in the Old Testament, *Exodus* 32, including old pagan practices, and connotations to satanism); Cf. J.W.M. van Breugel, *Chewa Traditional Religion*, Zomba: Kachere, 2001, pp. 125-168.

[9] Cf. Isabel Mukonyora, *Women and Ecology in Shona Religion*, Harare: Univ. of Zimbabwe, 1999.

b. Functions in Society

Mission churches came to perform important functions in society. Acceptance of Christianity was strengthened when these functions helped to underline valued traditional views. Examples: The Roman Catholic mission especially underlined male dominance. Mission churches gave expression to political and economical aspirations of peoples and tribes.

c. Mediators of Modernity

Mission churches came to be viewed as important mediators of modernity, both progressive and consonant with tradition, whereas their members of mission churches sometimes regarded independent churches as backward and ignorant. Mission schools played a very important role in this view.

d. Position towards the State

In the colonial era the mission communities functioned as linkage between the culture of subordinate groups and the rulers. In some cases missions were instruments of the colonial administration. At the same time there were contradicting interests, and ensuing struggles between mission communities and the colonial establishment. There was a cleavage that rooted in class, education, values and Evangelical convictions. Generally missions tried to avoid close association with the state. As children of their time missionaries were imperialists, but they aspired to a different empire than the colonialists. They resented increasingly strong government control, because they feared the secularising effect of government policy, for example in the field of education, where the colonial governments gradually opted for secular schools free from mission influence. Missions often clashed with governments on the issue of defending African interests. The linkage between mission communities and the colonial state weakened to the extent of disengagement when the nationalist mass movements challenged the missionaries to choose for independence of African states against colonial rule.

e. Agents of Cultural and Social Change?

The alleged Westernisation as a result of the work of the missions has been both damned and praised by Africans. Were the missions agents of Westernisation?

Missionaries cannot be considered as friends of contemporary Western Culture, simply because they denounced some aspects of African Culture. Strayer points to 'a deep missionary ambivalence regarding modern Western Culture'. Many missionaries wanted to safeguard Africa from the secularising effects of rationalism, materialism and urbanisation that were undermining Christianity in the West.[10]

---

[10] For examples from Tanzania and how Tanzanians reacted to such missionary attempts, see: Fiedler,

Strayer quotes Horton who claims that the process of cultural and social change was not at all brought about by missions, and that the process of religious change only partly originates in the activities of missions. Further Strayer points to 'recent studies' suggesting that Roman Catholic and Dutch Reformed Mission in Malawi 'simply did not generate anything akin to a modernising elite'.[11]

Missions did not always disrupt the existing political, social, and psychological patterns of society. Christians were not separated from other members of their communities. Christianisation did not break political unity and it did not lead to 'detribalisation'. Of course there were instances of conflict and discontinuity, but often they were in a 'subtle relationship with continuity'.

4. African Conversion[12]

Horton describes the 'typical traditional cosmology' or worldview of Africans, originating in pre-modern life, that is in pre-Christian and pre-Islamic times. It is a two-tiered system of ideas about unobservable personal beings which provides an instrument for explanation, prediction, and control of ordinary daily events.

(a) The lower level of the *microcosmos*: lesser spirits, who are concerzned with local things. Most events are attributed to them. There are many ideas about their modes of action. Some deal with human morality. There are many ideas about approaching and manipulating them.

(b) The higher level of the *macrocosmos*: a Supreme Being, who is concerned with the world as a whole, and who controls the lesser spirits. Ideas about his modes of action, the events that he controls, the techniques to address him, are much vaguer and less developed.

In a pre-modern situation the *microcosmos* of the lesser spirits plays a much bigger role than the *macrocosmos* of the *Supreme Being*. The former are constantly approached, whereas the latter has no direct association with daily events and morality, hence he is rarely addressed. In Horton's view this religious system has persisted in modern times. It has continued to be the basis of the African worldview, irrespective of the presence of Christianity and Islam. It has been able to adapt itself to the cultural and social changes in modern times. Instead of abandoning it, African people remoulded it, so that it still is an instrument of explanation-prediction-control. In the situation of modern change the macrocosmos of wider life becomes more important to people than the microcosmos. This means that the lesser spirits are being regarded irrelevant or even evil, whereas the *Supreme Being* is taking over control. New techniques of addressing him are being developed. As daily life is becoming more and more part of the macrocosmos, the *Supreme Being*

Christianity and African Culture, esp. pp. 136ff.
[11] Strayer, 'Mission History', in: *African Conversion*, p. 13.
[12] Horton, 'African Conversion', in: *African Conversion*, pp. 19-26.

is becoming the direct controller of morality. In the traditional setting man's relationship with the spirits already differed greatly from man's relationship with the *Supreme Being*. This difference becomes much bigger in the modern situation. Depending on the degree to which individuals have left their *microcosmos*, the rudimentary cult of the *Supreme Being* has been expanded in response to cultural and social change. The more an individual lives 'modern', the more the cult of the spirits is likely to be overshadowed by that of the *Supreme Being*. Even diviners and other 'philosophers of traditional religion' tend to adapt themselves to this new religious situation.

Horton concludes that the acceptance of Christianity (and Islam) is *'as much'* due to this development in *African cosmology* as it is to the activities of the missionaries. He says that Africans in accepting Christianity both *added* their own cosmology and *omitted* those elements in mission Christianity that are not fitting to this African cosmology. Consequently this acceptance was 'highly conditional and selective'. Christianity (and Islam) were accepted because of the adaptation of traditional religion to modern cultural and social challenges. This view reduces Christianity (and Islam) to the role of *catalysts*, 'stimulators of changes that were in the air anyway'. In Horton's view, missions who refuse to accept this humble role, produce 'very meagre results'. Having added Christianity to the adapted traditional cosmology, Africans reject the other-worldliness of Christianity, they use Christianity as an instrument for explanation-prediction-control, just as they used religion in the pre-modern situation. They accept the monotheism, and the moral concern of Christianity, just as they valued the *Supreme Being*. In Horton's view, the 'so called converts' in church (or mosque) form a *'continuum'* with the cult of spirits and the *Supreme Being*.

Because Islam has been 'fairly content' with this role of catalyst, it has expanded without having many breakaway sects. Missionary Christianity, however, has never been content to play this role. Therefore many members of its churches are dissatisfied which, results in many breakaway sects.

5. The Character of the 'Continuum'

What can we learn from what the writers summarised above? In comparing pre-modern society, modern society, and mission Christianity, they see continuity. In our opinion this view is onesided. Christianity did more than continuing African tradition. There is *continuity*, and there is also *discontinuity*.

Scripture characterises the position of heathen peoples, whether they are pre-modern or modern, in two different ways. On the one hand the *demonic character* of their existence is stressed:

> They follow 'the ways of this world and of the ruler of the kingdom of the air, the spirit who is now at work in those who are disobedient'. They are 'gratifying the cravings of our sinful nature and following its desires and thoughts'. They are 'objects of wrath' (*Eph*.2:2,3).

They are 'without hope and without God in the world' (*Eph*.2:12).

They are 'darkened in their understanding' (*Eph*.4:18).

They have 'lost all sensitivity, they have given themselves over to sensuality so as to indulge in every kind of impurity, with a continual lust for more' (*Eph*.4:19).

On the other hand, it is admitted that the non-Christian cultures have elements of *knowledge of the Law* of God:

'When Gentiles, who do not have the Law, do by nature things required by the Law, they are a Law for themselves, even though they do not have the Law, since they show that the requirements of the Law are written on their hearts, their consciences also bearing witness, and their thoughts now accusing, now even defending them' (*Rom*.2:14,15).

This natural knowledge of God that is planted in the hearts of people, does not lead them spontaneously to Christ. Something else is done by it to men. It stresses their personal responsibility for their own iniquity. The Reformer John Calvin says:

'In the human mind there is a certain consciousness of God, that is to say through natural inspiration. God himself has laid in everyone a certain understanding of his Divinity, so that no one could resort to the pretense of his ignorance ... because all without any exception understand that there is a God who is their Creator, and they would be condemned by their own witness, because they have not served Him'[13]

John Calvin (1509-1564), the most influential representative of the 16th century Reformation.

People do not come to Christ *spontaneously* or *voluntarily*. They come because God calls them. Mission work is not done because missionaries are invited. Mission work is done in obedience to a command. Neither is the missionary message an invitation to people of good will. The message is the proclamation of God's command, although the hearers themselves bear the responsibility for their reaction to it. They are chosen, *not because of* their continuity with the past, but *notwithstanding* their continuity with the past. The old creature, including his cultural or religious 'sparks' of divine light, is called to new birth, so that it is renewed to be a new creature in Christ.

---

[13] John Calvin, *Institutes of the Christian Religion*, Grand Rapids: Eerdmans, 1998 [Translated from the first edition in 1559 by Henry Beveridge in 1845], Book I, chapter 3, section 1 (p. 43); cf. Dutch transl. by Sizoo, volume I, p.8.

6. Lessons from History

God's call to turn to Christ for salvation is the basic reason for conversion in Africa, or in any other part of the world. This call created the Church, and it is proclaimed by the Church through the spreading of the Word, and the answer to it is worked by the Holy Spirit. Only by being faithful to this command the Church can be established, survive and expand. This is what Hildebrandt means when he sums up some lessons from history for the Church in Africa. First, the history of persecutions and attacks by heresy has taught that loyalty to Christ and the Scriptures is a necessity for the Church and for all individual Christians. This implies that the Scriptures be made available to all people in their local languages. Secondly, the Church needs faithful pastors and elders; by their care and by their example they build and continue the Church. Fourthly, evangelism and missionary outreach have been priority, otherwise the Church could not continue to deploy. Fifthly, the Church has to 'be careful about how much it adapts itself to the national culture in which it is practiced'.[14] In history many have mixed the Gospel with their traditional religion. This has weakened or taken away the witness of the Church. We can use good aspects of our culture for the expression of our faith in Christ, but glorification of humanity, superstitions, magic and witchcraft cannot be part of that.

Finally, the writing and learning of *Church History* reflects the teaching of a lesson, the conveying of a message, the stressing of a reality. Because it is part of Theology, the lesson or the message or the reality of *Church History* is Christ. In the *Covenant* of his Grace ultimately expressed in the sending of his Son, God planted the Church and commanded it to spread the Good News and to being deployed unto the ends of the earth, so that anyone who surrenders to Christ in faith, will have eternal life in his Kingdom. Proclaiming the Good News of the King and his Kingdom that saves and changes people's lives, is the best contribution which the Church and the Christians can give to Africa and to the world. In the realisation of the Kingdom, the history of the Church finds it goal and its end.

---

[14] Hildebrandt, *History of the Church in Africa*, pp.38-42.

Bibliography

a. Historiography

Barnes, H.E., *History of Historical Writings*, University of Oklahoma Press, 1937.
Barrett, D., *World Christian Encyclopedia: A Comparative Survey of Churches and Religions in the Modern World AD 1900-2000*, Nairobi/ Oxford/ New York, 1982.
Bediako, K, *Christianity in Africa – The Renewal of a Non-Western Religion*, Edinburgh University Press, 1995.
Bediako, Kwame, *Jesus in Africa: The Christian Gospel in African History and Experience*, Akropong-Akuapem: Regnum Africa, 2000.
Bradley, J.E. and R.A. Muller, *Church History – An Introduction to Research, Reference Works, and Methods*, Grand Rapids: Eerdmans, 1995.
Cairns, E.E., *God and man in Time*, Grand Rapids: Baker, 1979.
Case, S.J. (ed.), *A Bibliographical Guide to the History of Christianity*, Chicago University Press, 1931.
Collingwood, R.G., *The Idea of History*, Oxford University Press., 1956².
Davidson, B., *Africa in Modern History – A Search for a New Society*, London: Penguin, 1978.
Denis, Ph., *Orality, Memory and the Past – Listening to the Voices of Black Clergy under Colonialism and Apartheid*, Pietermaritzburg: Cluster Publ., 2000.
Guilday, P. (ed.), *Church Historians*, New York: Kennedy, 1926.
Jewsiecki, B., and D.Newbury (eds), *African Historiographies: What History for which Africa?*, Beverly Hills: Sage, 1986.
Kalu, O.U. (ed.), *African Church Historiography – An Ecumenical Perspective*, Bern: Evangelische Arbeitsstelle Oekumene Schweiz, 1968.
Kalu, Ogbu, U., 'The Shape and Flow of African Church Historiography', in: O.U. Kalu et. al. (eds), *African Christianity: An African Story, University of Pretoria*, 2005, pp.2-23.
Livingstone, E.A. (ed.), *The Concise Oxford Dictionary of the Christian Church*, Oxford U.P., 1977².
McIntyre, C.T.,*God, History, and Historians – An Anthology of Modern Christian Views of History*, 1977.
Olubumehin, O.O., *Issues in Historiography*, College Press Publ., 2001.
Oyemakinde, W., *An Introduction to Church Missionary Society Manuscripts*, College Press Publ. (Nigeria), 2001.
Paas, Steven, *Chichewa/ Chinyanja – English Dictionary*, Zomba: Kachere 2005².
Paas, Steven, *Digging out the Ancestral Church – Researching and Communicating Church History*, Zomba: Kachere, 2006³ [This book includes a chapter and a bibliography on Oral History].
Paas, Steven, *English – Chichewa/ Chinyanja Dictionary*, Zomba: Kachere, 2004³.
Smith, Ken, *The Changing Past: Trends in South African History Writing*, Athens: Ohio University Press, 1989.
Sykes, N., *The Study of Ecclesiastical History*, Cambridge, 1945.
Verstraelen, Frans J., 'Southern Perspectives on Christian History', in: *Neue Zeitschrift fur Missionswissenschaft*, 53-1997.
Verstraelen, Frans J., *History of Christianity in the Context of African History – An Assessment*, Gweru: Mambo Press, 2002.
Verstraelen, Frans J., Kenneth R. Ross, P. Gundani, and I. Mukonyora, *The Teaching of Church History and Ministerial Formation,* ATISCA Bulletin no 2 (1993).
Verstraelen-Gilhuis, Gerdien, *A New Look at Christianity in Africa*, Gweru: Mambo Press, 1992, pp. 77-98 ('Rewriting the History of Christianity in Africa').
Verstraelen-Gilhuis, Gerdien, *From Dutch Mission Church to Reformed Church in Zambia: The Scope for African Leadership and Initiative in the History of a Zambian Mission Church*, Franeker: Wever, 1982, pp. 13-21 ('Recovering the African Perspective of Mission History', and 'Written and Oral Sources').

b. Africa in General

Adams, W., *Nubia: Corridor to Africa*, Princeton University Press, 1977.
Adeyemo, Tokunboh (ed.), *A Christian Mind in a Changing Africa*, Nairobi, 1993.
Adeyemo, Tokunboh, *The Making of a Servant of God*, Nairobi, 1993.
Adeyemo, Tokunboh, *Is Africa Cursed?*, Nairobi, 1997.
Adeyemo, Tokunboh, *Salvation in African Tradition*, Nairobi: Evangel Publ., 1997 (first ed. 1979).
Adeyemo, Tokunboh, *Deliver us From Evil: An Uneasy Frontier in Christian Mission*, Nairobi, 2002.
Ajayi, F.F.A., 'Henry Venn and the Policy of Development', in: O. Kalu (ed.), *The History of Christianity in West Africa*, London: Longman, 1980.
Ajayi, J.F.A., *Christian Missions in Nigeria 1841-1891*, London: Longmans, 1965.
Anderson A., and O.S. Tumelo, *The Faith of African Pentecostals in South Africa*, Pretoria: Unisa, 1993.
Anderson A., Bazalwane, *African Pentecostals in South Africa*, Pretoria: Unisa, 1992.
Anderson, A., *Zion and Pentecost – The Spirituality and Experience of Pentecostal and Zionist/ Apostolic Churches in South Africa*, Pretoria: Unisa, 2000.
Anderson, D., *We felt like Grasshoppers – The Story of Africa Inland Mission*, Nottingham: Crossway, 1994.
Anderson, W.B., *The Church in East Africa 1840-1974*, Nairobi/ Dodoma/ Kampala, UZ.I.M.A/ CTP/ CPH, 1981 [1977].
Ayandele, E.A., *The Mission Impact on Modern Nigeria 1842-1924 – A Political Analysis*, London: Longmans, 1966.
Baëta, C.G. (ed.), *Christianity in Tropical Africa*, Oxford U.P., 1968.
Bane, M.J., *The Popes and Western Africa: An Outline of Mission History 1460-1960s*, New York: Alba House, 1968.
Barret, D.B., World Christian Encyclopedia: A Comparative Survey of Churches ad Religions in the Modern World AD 1900-2000, Nairobi/ Oxford/ New York, 1982.
Barrett, D.B., *Schism and Renewal in Africa - An Analysis of 6000 Contemporary Religious Movements*, Nairobi: Oxford U.P., 1968.
Barrett, David B., 'AD 2000: 350 million Christians in Africa', in: *International Review of Mission*, 59 (1970).
Barrett, David B., *Schism and Renewal in Africa: An Analysis of Six Thousand Contemporary Religious Movements*, Nairobi: OUP, 1968.
Baur, J., *2000 Years of Christianity in Africa: An African History 62-1992*, Nairobi:1994.
Beachley, R.W., *A History of East Africa 1592-1902*, London: Tauris, 1995.
Becken, H.J. (ed.), *Relevant Theology for Africa*, Durban: Lutheran Publ., 1973.
Bediako, Kwame, *Christianity in Africa – The Renewal of a Non-Western Religion*, Edinburgh: Orbis, 1995.
Bediako, Kwame, *Jesus in African Culture – A Ghanaian Perspective*, Accra: Asempa Publ., 1990.
Bediako, Kwame, *Theology and Identity – The Impact of Culture upon Christian Thought in the Second Century and Modern Africa*, Oxford: Regnum Books, 1992.
Beidelman, T.O., *Colonial Evangelism*, Bloomington: University of Indiana Press, 1982.
Beinart, William, *Twentieth Century South Africa*, Oxford University Press, 1994.
Birmingham, David, *The Decolonization of Africa*, London: University College of London Press, 1996.
Blyden, E.W., *Christianity, Islam and the Negro Race*, Edinburgh, 1967.
Boahen, A.A. (ed.), *Africa under Colonial Denomination*, vol. 7, *General History of Africa*, Paris: UNESCO, 1990.
Boesak, A., *Farewell to Innocence*, Maryknoll: Orbis, 1977.
Bowers, P., 'Nubian Christianity: The Neglected Heritage', in: *East Africa Journal of Evangelical Theology* 4, no 1 (1985), pp. 3-23.
Brain, J.B., *Catholic Beginnings in Natal and Beyond*, Durban: Griggs, 1975.

Breman, Christina M., 'A Portriat of Dr. Byang Kato', in: *Africa Journal of Evangelical Theology* 15, no.2 (1996), pp. 135-151.
Breman, Christina M., *The Association of Evangelicals in Africa – Its History, Organization, Members, Projects, External Relations and Message*, Zoetermeer: Boekencentrum, 1996.
Brown, P., *Augustine of Hippo – A Biography*, London: Faber and Faber, 1967.
Brown, P., *Religion and Society in the Age of Augustine*, London, 1972.
Bujo, B., *African Theology in Its Social Context*, Maryknoll: Orbis, 1992.
Carey, William, *An Enquiry into the Obligation of Christians to use Means for the Conversion of the Heathen*, London, 1792.
Chirenje, J.M., *Ethiopianism and Afro-Americans in Southern Africa 1883-1916*, Baton Rouge: Louisiana State U.P., 1987.
Church, J., *Quest for the Highest – An Autobiographical Account of the East Africa Revival*, Exeter: Paternoster, 1981.
Colenso, J.W., 'A Sermon Preached in the Cathedral Church of St. Peter, Pietermaritzburg', Yale Divinity School Archives, 1879.
Dachs, A.J. (ed.), *Christianity South of the Zambezi*, Gweru: Mambo, 1973.
Danquah, J.B., *The Akan Doctrine of God*, Lutterworth, 1944.
Davidson, Basil, *Africa in Modern History – A Search for a New Society*, London: Penguin, 1978.
Davidson, Basil, *Old Africa Rediscovered: The Story of Africa's Forgotten Past*, London: Victor Gollancz, 1959.
Davidson, Basil, *The African Past: Chronicles from Antiquity to Modern Times*, Boston: Brown, 1964.
Davidson, Basil, *The Black-Man's Burden: Africa and the Curse of the Nation-State*, London: Currey, 1992.
De Gruchy, J.W., 'From Cairo to the Cape: the significance of Coptic Orthodoxy for African Christianity', in: *Journal of Theology for Southern Africa*, no 99 (November 1997), pp. 24-39.
De Gruchy, J.W., *The Church Struggle in South Africa*, Grand Rapids: Eerdmans, 1979.
De la Haye, S., *Byang Kato: Ambassador for Christ*, Ghana: Africa Christian Press, 1986.
Dickson, K., *Theology in Africa*, London: Darton, 1984.
Donovan, V., *Christianity Rediscovered – An Epistle from the Masai*, New York: Orbis, 1978.
Duminy, Andrew, and Charles Ballard (eds), *The Anglo-Zulu War: New Perspectives*, Pietermaritzburg: University of Natal Press, 1981.
Ejofodomi, L.,'The Missionary Career of Alexander Crummell in Liberia 1853-1873'; unpublished PhD thesis, Boston University, 1988.
Elphick, R., *KhoiKhoi and the Founding of White South Africa*, Johannesburg: Ravan, 1985.
Enklaar, L.H., *Life and Work of Dr. J.Th. van der Kemp 1741-1811: Missionary Pioneer and Protagonist of Racial Equality in South Africa*, Capetown – Rotterdam, 1988.
Fage, J.D., *A History of Africa*, London: Hutchinson, 1988².
Fage, J.D., and R.Oliver (eds), *The Cambridge History of Africa* (8 vols), Cambridge U.P., 1975-1986.
Falk, P., *The Growth of the Church in Africa*, Grand Rapids: Zondervan, 1979.
Faupel, J.F., *African Holocaust: The Story of the Uganda Martyrs*, New York: Garland, 1990.
Fiedler, K., 'Christian Missions and Western Colonialism: Soulmates or Antagonists?', in: K.R. Ross (ed.), *Faith at the Frontiers of Knowledge*, Blantyre: Claim, 1998, pp. 218-234.
Fiedler, K., *Christianity and African Culture – Conservative German Protestant Missionaries in Tanzania 1900-1940*, Blantyre: Claim/ Kachere, 1999².
Fiedler, K., P. Gundani, Hilary Mijoga (eds), *Theology Cooked in an African Pot*, ATISCA Bulletin, no 5/6, Zomba, 2000².
Fiedler, K., *The Story of Faith Missions – From Hudson Taylor to Present Day Africa, Regnum International*, Oxford et.al., 1998.
Fiedler, Klaus, *The Story of Faith Missions From Hudson Taylor to Present Day Africa*, Oxford: Regnum International, 1998.
Fitts, L., *Lott Carey: First Black Missionary to Africa*, Valley Forge: Judson, 1978.
Frederiks, Martha, *We have Toiled all Night: Christianity in The Gambia 1456-2000*, Zoetermeer: Boekencentrum, 2003.

Frend, W.C.H., *The Donatist Church – A Movement of Protest in Roman Northern Africa*, Oxford University Press, 1985[2].
Gehman, R., *African Traditional Religion in Biblical Perspective*, Nairobi: East African Educational Publishers, 1993[3]. \
Glover, R., *The Progress of Worldwide Missions* (revised by Herbert Kane), New York: Harper, 1960.
Gray, R., *Black Christians and White Missionaries*, New Haven: Yale U.P., 1990.
Groves, C.P., *The Planting of Christianity in Africa* (4 vols), London: Lutterworth, 1948-1964.
Gschwandtner, Walther, 'The Church in East-Africa Encounters the Challenge of Islam - A Historical Perspective', in: Thomas Schirrmacher und Christoph Sauer(Hg.), *Mission verändert - Mission verändert sich: Mission Transforms - Mission is Transformed: Festschrift für Klaus Fiedler*, edition afem mission academics 16, Nürnberg: Verlag für Theologie und Religionswissenschaft, 2005, pp. 193-210.
Guy, Jeff, *The Destruction of the Zulu Kingdom: The Civil War in Zululand 1879-1884*, London: Longman, 1979.
Hadfield, P., *Traits of Divine Kingship in Africa*, Watts, 1949.
Haliburton, G., *The Prophet Harris*, New York: Oxford U.P., 1973.
Hamilton, Carolyn, *Terrific Majesty: the Powers of Shaka Zulu and the Limits of Historical Invention*, Cambridge Mass.: Harvard University Press, 1998.
Hamilton, J. Taylor, *Twenty Years of Pioneer Missions in Nyasaland: A History of the Moravian Missions in German East Africa*, Bethlehem (Pa): S.P.G., 1912.
Hargreaves, J.D., *Decolonization in Africa*, London: Longman, 1988.
Harrison, C., *France and Islam in West Africa 1860-1960*, Cambridge University Press, 1988.
Hastings A., and Godwin Tasie, *Christianity in Independent Africa*, Bloomington: Indiana University Press, 1978.
Hastings, A. (ed.), *A World History of Christianity*, London: Cassel, 1999.
Hastings, A., *A History of African Christianity 1950-1975*, Cambridge University Press, 1979.
Hastings, A., *African Catholicism: Essays in Discovery*, London: SCM, 1989.
Hastings, A., *African Christianity: An Essay in Interpretation*, London: Chapman, 1976.
Hastings, A., *The Church in Africa: 1450-1950*, Oxford: Clarendon Press, 1994.
Hildebrandt, J., *History of the Church in Africa, A Survey*, Achimota (Ghana): African Christian Press, 1990 (first edition: 1981].
Hilton, A., *Kingdom of Congo*, Oxford: Clarendon, 1985.
Hincliff, P., *Cyprian of Carthage*, London: Chapman, 1974.
Hincliff, P., *The Church in South Africa*, London: SPCK, 1968.
Hofmeyr, J.W., and J. Pillay (eds), *A History of Christianity in South Africa*, Haum Tertiary, 1994.
Idowu, E.B., *African Traditional Religion*, London: SCM, 1973.
Idowu, E.B., *Toward an Indigenous Church*, London: Oxford U.P., 1965.
Isichei, E., *A History of Christianity in Africa From Antiquity to the Past*, London: SPCK, 1995.
Jahn, J., *Muntu*, Faber, 1961.
Jenkins, P., 'The Roots of African Church History – Some Polemic Thoughts' in: *International Bulletin of Missionary Research*, vol. 10, no 2, April 1986, pp. 67-71.
July, R., *The Origins of Modern African Thought – Its Development in West Africa during the 19th and 20th Centuries*, London: Faber and Faber, 1968.
Kairos Document. Challenge to the Church: A Theological Comment on the Political Crisis in South Africa, Braamfontein: The Kairos Theologians, and London: CIIR/BBC, 1985.
Kalem'Imana, J.B., 'Christianity and Socialism in Tanzania', unpubl. PhD thesis, Drew University, 1986.
Kalu, O.U. (ed.), *African Christianity: An African Story*, University of Pretoria, 2005.
Kalu, O.U. (ed.), *African Church Historiography: An Ecumenical Perspective*, Bern: Evangelische Arbeitsstelle Oekumene Schweiz, 1968.
Kalu, O.U., *History of Christianity in West Africa*, London: Longman, 1980.
Kamill, J., *Coptic Egypt*, Cairo: American U.P., 1987.
Kanya-Forstner, A.S., *Conquest of the Western Sudan*, Cambridge University Press, 1969.

Kaplan, S., *Monastic Holy Man and the Christianization of Early Solomonic Ethiopia*, Wiesbaden: Steiner, 1984.
Kato, Byang H., *Limitations of Natural Revelation*, Master's Thesis, Dallas Theological Seminary, 1971.
Kato, Byang H., *A Critique of Incipient Universality in Tropical Africa*, Doctoral Dissertation, Dallas Theological Seminary, 1974.
Kato, Byang H., *African Cultural Revolution and the Christian Faith*, Jos: Challenge Publ., 1976.
Kato, Byang H., *Biblical Christianity in Africa*, Achimota: Africa Christian Press, 1985.
Kato, Byang, *Theological Pitfalls in Africa*, Kisumu: Evangelical Publ. House, 1975.
Kessel van, Ineke, *Merchants, Missionaries and Migrants*, Sub-Saharan Publ. 2002.
Killingray, David, and R.Rathbone (eds), *Africa and the Second World War*, London: Macmillan, 1986.
Klingberg, F., *The Anti-Slavery Movement in England*, Hamden: Archon, 1968.
Krapf, J.L., Travels, Researches and Missionary Labours During an Eighteen Years' Residence in Eastern Africa, London: Frank Cass, 1968 [1st edition 1860].
Kwabena Asamoah-Gyadu, J., 'Born of Water and the Spirit: Pentecostal/ Charismatic Christianity in Africa', in: Kalu et. al. (eds), *African Christianity*, pp.403-406.
Lagerwerf, L., *They Pray for You: Independent Churches and Women in Botswana*, Leiden: IMO, 1982.
Langat, R., 'Western Evangelical Missionary Influence on East African Culture', unpubl. PhD thesis, Denver: Iliff School of Theology, 1991.
Latourette, Kenneth Scott, *A History of the Expansion of Christianity*, volume 4 (out of 7 volumes), New York: Harper, 1943 [bibliography].
Law, Robin, *The Oyo Empire, c.1600- c.1836*, Oxford University Press, 1977.
Le May, G.H.L., *The Afrikaners: an Historical Interpretation*, Oxford: Blackwell, 1994.
Lovejoy, Paul, E., *Transformation in Slavery: A History of Slavery in Africa*, Cambridge Un iversity, 2000^2.
Manning, Patrick, *Francophone Sub-Saharan Africa, 1880-1985*, Cambridge University Press, 1988.
Manning, Patrick, *Slavery and African Life: Occidental, Oriental, and African Slave Trades*, Cambridge University Press, 1990.
Manus, U.C., *Christ is the African King*, Frankfurt: Lang, 1993.
Mbiti, J., *African Religions and Philosophy*, London: Heinemann, 1969.
Mbiti, J., *Bible and Theology in African Christianity*, Nairobi, 1986.
McLynn, N.B., *Ambrose of Milan – Church and Court in a Christian Capital*, Berkeley/Los Angeles, 1994.
Miers, Suzanne, and Richard Roberts (eds), *The End of Slavery in Africa*, Madison: University of Wisconsin Press, 1989.
Molyneux, G., *African Christian Theology – The Quest for Selfhood*, San Francisco: Mellen Research U.P., 1993.
Murray, Andrew, *Key to the Missionary Problem*, Washington: Christian Literature Crusade, 1979 [first published in 1901].
Murray, Andrew, *The State of the Church*, Kempton Park: Andrew Murray Consultation, 1985 [first published in 1911].
Neill, S., *Christianity and Colonialism*, New York: McGraw-Hill, 1966.
Neill. S., *A History of Christian Missions* (revised edition by O. Chadwick), Harmondsworth: Penguin, 1986 [1964].
Newitt, Malyn, *A History of Mozambique*, Bloomington: Indiana University Press, 1993.
Ngimbi, Kibutu, Les Nouvelles Eglises Indépendantes Africaines (NAIC): Un phénomène ecclesial observe au Congo/ Kinshasa et auprès de ses extensions en Europe occidentale: Approche historico-missiologique, Heverlee (Louvain/ Leuven): Faculté de Théologie Evangélique (Evangelical Theological Faculty), 2000.
Njeri Mwaura, Philomena, 'Gender and Power in African Christianity: African Instituted Churches and Pentecostal Churches', in: Kalu et.al. (eds), *African Christianity*, pp. 410-445.
Northcott, Cecil, *Christianity in Africa*, London: SCM, 1963.
Noshy, I., *The Coptic Church*, Washington: Sloan, 1955.

Nyamiti, C., *Christ as our Ancestor – Christology from an African Perspective*, Gweru: Mambo Press, 1984.
O'Donovan, Wilbur, *Biblical Christianity in African Perspective*, Paternoster Press, 1992.
Ofori, P.E., *Christianity in Tropical Africa: A Selective Annotated Bibliography*, Nedel: KTO Press, 1977.
Ojo, Matthew A., 'The Charismatic Movement in Nigeria Today', in: *International Bulletin of Missionary Research*, July, 1995.
Okot p'Bitek, *African Religions in Western Scholarship*, Kampala: East African Literature Bureau, 1970.
Oliver, R., *The African Experience*, San Francisco: Harper/Collins, 1991.
Oliver, R., *The Missionary Factor in East Africa*, London: Longmans, 1965[2].
Oosthuizen, G.C., *The Birth of Christian Zionism in South Africa*, KwaDlangezwa: University of Zululand, 1987.
Oosthuizen, G.C., *The Healer-Prophet in Afro-Christian Churches*, Leiden: Brill, 1992.
Paas, S., *A Conflict on Authority in the Early African Church – Augustine of Hippo and the Donatists*, Zomba: Kachere, 2003[2].
Page, J., *The Black Bishop: Samuel Ajayi Crowther*, London: Hodder and Stoughton, 1908.
Pakenham, Thomas, *The Scramble for Africa 1876-1912*, London: Abacus, 1991.
Parrat, J., *A Reader in Africann Theology*, London: SPCK, 1987.
Parrat, J., *Reinventing Christianity: African Christian Theology Today*, Grand Rapids: Eerdmans, 1995.
Parrinder, G., *African Traditional Religion*, Hutchinson, 1954.
Pauw, B.A., *Christianity and Xhosa Tradition*, cape Town: Oxford U.P., 1975.
Pearson, B., 'Earliest Christianity in Egypt', in: Pearson and Goering (eds), *The Roots of Egyptian Christianity*, Philadelphia: Fortress, 1986.
Phiri, I.A., D.B. Govinden, and S.Nadar, *Her-Stories: Hidden Histories of Women of Faith in Africa*, Pietermaritzburg: Cluster Publ., 2002.
Pillay, G.J. and J.W. Hofmeyr (eds), *Perspectives on Church History: An Introduction for South-African Readers*, Pretoria, De Jager – HUM, 1991.
Pirouet, Louise, *The Spread of Christianity in Uganda 1891-1914*, Collings, 1978.
Pirouet, Louise, *The Witness of the Uganda Martyrs*, Kampala: Church of Uganda Literature Centre, 1969.
Pobee, J., *Toward an African Theology*, Nashville: Abingdon Press, 1979.
Présence Africaine (two volume account of early African writers/artists) in: *Le Monde Noir*, special issue of nos 8-9, Paris, 1950; see also: *Des Prêtres Noires s'interrogent*, Paris: Du Cerf, 1956.
Rapozoh, I.B. and Malemu Bambo Dirkx, *Ulendo Wathu monga Mbumba ya Mulungu*, Limbe: Popular Publ., 1992.
Roberts, C., *Manuscript, Society, and Belief in Early Christian Egypt*, London: Oxford U.P., 1979.
Robertson, Claire C., and Martin Klein (eds), *Women and Slavery in Africa*, Madison: University of Wisconsin Press, 1983.
Sanneh, Lamin, *Whose Religion is Christianity?: The Gospel Beyond the West*, Grand Rapids: Eerdmans, 2003.
Shank, D., *A Prophet for Modern Times: The Thought of William Wadé Harris, West-African Precursor of the Reign of Christ* (2 vols), unpublished PhD thesis, Aberdeen, 1980.
Shaw, Mark, *The Kingdom of God in Africa – A Short History of African Christianity*, Grand Rapids: Baker, 1996.
Shelburne, G.B., *Mbiri ya Mpingo*, Thondwe: Namikango Bible School, 1994[2].
Shenk, D.W., *Peace and Reconciliation in Africa*, Nairobi: Uzima, 1983.
Shillington, K., *History of Africa*, London: Macmillan, 1995[2].
Smith, E., (ed), *African Ideas of God*, Edinburgh, 1959.
Smith, Robert S., *Warfare and Diplomacy in Pre-Colonial West Africa*, Madison: University of Wisconsin Press, 1989[2].
Stott, J., *Christian Mission in the Modern World*, London, 1975.
Sundkler, B., and C. Steed, *A History of the Church in Africa*, Cambridge University Press, 2000.
Sundkler, B., *Bantu Prophets in South Africa*, London: Oxford U.P., 1948.

Sundkler, B., *The Christian Ministry in Africa*, London: SCM, 1962².
Sundkler, B., *Zulu Zion and Some Swazi Zionists*, London: Oxford U.P., 1976.
Tamrat, T., *Church and State in Ethiopia 1270-1527*, Oxford: Clarendon, 1972.
Tasie, G.O.M., *Christian Missionary Enterprise in the Niger Delta 1864-1918*, Leiden: Brill, 1978.
Taylor, J.V., *Christianity and Politics in Africa*, London: Penguin, 1957.
Taylor, J.V., *The Growth of the Church in Buganda*, London: SCM, 1958.
Taylor, J.V., *The Primal Vision: Christian Presence amid African Religion*, London: SCM, 1963.
Tempels, Fr. Placide, *La Philosophie Bantoue*, Elizabethville: Lovania, 1945.
Temu, A.J., *British Protestant Missions*, London: Longman, 1972.
Thompson, Leonard M., *A History of South Africa*, New Haven: Yale University Press, 1985.
Turner, H.W., *African Independent Church* (2 vols), Oxford U.P., 1967.
Vantini, G., *Christianity in the Sudan*, Bologna: EMI, 1981.
Walker, S., *The Religious Revolution in the Ivory Coast – The Prophet Harris and the Harrist Church*, Chapel Hill: University of N. Carolina Press, 1983.
Walls, A.F., 'The Gospel as a Prisoner and Liberator of Culture', in: *Faith and Thought*, vol. 108, 1981.
Walls, A.F., *The Missionary Movement in Christian History*, Edinburgh: Clark, and New York: Orbis, 1996.
Walls, A.F.,*The Significance of Christianity in Africa*, Edinburgh: Church of Scotland Centre, 1989.
Walvin, J., Black *Ivory: A History of British Slavery*, London: Fontana, 1993.
Ward, K., 'Tukutendereza Yesu - The Balokole Revival Movement in Uganda', in: Zablon Nthamburi (ed.), *A Handbook of Christianity in East Africa*, Nairobi: UZ.I.MA, 1991.
Worden, N., and C.Crais, *Breaking the Chains: Slavery and its Legacy in the 19th Century Cape Colony*, Wit Watersrrand University Press, 1994.
Wright, Marcia, *German Mission in Tanganyika 1891-1941: Lutherans and Moravians in the Southern Highlands*, Oxford: Clarendon, 1971.
Wyse, Akintola, *The Krio of Sierra Leone: An Interpretive History*, Madison: University of Wisconsin Press, 1989.

c. South-Central Africa

Alpers, E.A.,'The Role of the Yao in the Development of Trade in East-Central Africa 1698-c.1850', unpublished PhD thesis, London University, 1966.
Anderson-Morshead, A.E.M., *The History of the Universities Mission to Central Africa*, London: U.M.C.A., 1953.
Baker, Colin, *A Fine Chest of Medals: The Life of Jack Archer*, Cardif, Mpemba Books, 2003.
Banda, Kelvin, N., *A Brief History of Education in Malawi*, Blantyre: Dzuka, 1982.
Banda, Rachel Nyagondwe, *Women of Bible and Culture: Baptist Convention Women in Southern Malawi*, Zomba: Kachere, 2005.
Beach, D.N., *War and Politics in Zimbabwe 1840-1900*, Gweru: Mambo Press, 1994².
Bilima, J., *The Life of K.M. Malinki*, D. Min., Andrews University, 1993.
Bilima, J., *The Seventh-Day Adventist Church in Malawi 1900-1980*, M.Div., Andrews University, 1987.
Birmingham, David, and Phyllis Martin (eds), *History of Central Africa*, vols I and II, London: Longman, 1983.
Bismarck, Joseph, 'A Brief History on Joseph Bismarck', Occasional Papers of the Department of Antiquities, no. 7, Zomba, 1968, pp. 49-54.
Blood, A.G., *The History of the Universities Mission to Central Africa*, (3 vols), London: U.M.C.A., 1962.
Bolink, P., *Towards Church Union in Zambia*, Franeker: Wever, 1967.
Bone, D.S. (ed.), *Malawi's Muslims: Historical Perspectives*, Blantyre: Claim/ Kachere, 2000.
Booth, J., *Africa for the African*, Baltimore, 1897 (reprinted: Blantyre: Claim, 1998).
Breugel, J.W.M., *Chewa Traditional Religion*, Blantyre: Claim/ Kachere, 2001.
Brough, Beryl, *St. Johnson of Lake Malawi*, Zomba: Kachere [forthcoming].

Campbell, G.H., *Lonely Warrior*, Blantyre: Claim/ Kachere, 1975 [a short biography of William Koyi].
Carmody, B. (ed.), *African Conversion*, Ndola: Mission Press, 2001.
Chadwick, Owen, *Mackenzie's Grave*, London: Hodder and Stoughton, 1959.
Chakanza, J.C. and K.R. Ross, *Religion in Malawi: An Annotated Bibliography*, Blantyre: Claim/ Kachere, 1998.
Chakanza, J.C., *Voices of Preachers in Protest – The Ministry of Two Malawian Prophets: Elliot Kamwana and Wilfred Gudu*, Blantyre: Claim/ Kachere, 1998.
Chaponda, Orison, *Gule Wamkulu in the Catholic Church, Lilongwe Rural: A Cultural Phenomenon and a Pastoral Problem*, Zomba: University of Malawi, 1998 [unpublished MA module].
Chimulu, F.M. (ed.), *The Universities' Mission to Central Africa: A Bibliography in Progress*, Zomba: University of Malawi, 1980.
Chiphangwi, Saindi D., *Why People Join the Christian Church: Trends in Church Growth in the Blantyre Synod of the Church of Central Africa Presbyterian 1960-1975*, University of Aberdeen, 1978 [PhD].
Chirwa, Devlin, 'The History of the African Methodist Episcopal Church in Malawi: The Karonga Branch (1943-2000)'.
Church, Henry, *Theological Education that Makes a Difference*, Blantyre: Claim/ Kachere, 2001.
Conradie, Ben, *Andrew Murray na Honderd Jaar*, Stellenbosch: Christen Studenten Verenigingmaatskappij, 1951 [an extended biography].
Crosby, C.A., *Historical Dictionary of Malawi*, Metuhen and London: The Scarecrow Press, 1980.
Dachs, A.J. (ed), *Christianity South of the Zambezi*, Gweru: Mambo, 1973.
Daneel, M.L., *Old and New Southern Shona Independent Churches*, volume 1: 'Background and Rise of the Major Movements', The Hague, 1971 (a), volume 2: 'Church Growth - Causative Factors and Recruitment Techniques', The Hague, 1974, volume 3: Leadership and Fission Dynamics, Gweru: Mambo Press, 1988.
Daneel, M.L., *Quest for Belonging*, Gweru: Mambo, 1987.
Daneels, M.S., *Mbiri ya C.C.A.P. Sinodi ya Harare 1912-1982*, Harare: CCAP, no date.
Denis, Ph., *Orality, Memory and the Past – Listening to the Voices of Black Clergy under Colonialism and Apartheid*, Pietermaritzburg: Cluster Publ., 2000.
Du Plessis, J., *Evangelisation of Pagan Africa: A History of Christian Missions to the Pagan Tribes of Central Africa*, Cape Town, 1919.
Du Plessis, J., *From The Life of Andrew Murray of South Africa*, Marshall Morgan and Scott, 1919.
Elmslie, W. A., *Among the Wild Ngoni: Being Some Chapters in the History of the Livingstonia Mission in British Central Africa*, Edinburgh/ London: Oliphant Anderson & Frerrier, 1899.
Fiedler, Klaus, 'Christian Missions and Western Colonialism: Soulmates or Antagonists?', in: Kenneth R. Ross (ed), *Faith at the Frontiers of Knowledge*, Blantyre: Claim/ Kachere, 1998, pp. 218-234.
Fiedler, Klaus, 'Power at the Receiving End: The Jehovah's Witnesses' Experience in One-Party-Malawi', in: K.R. Ross (ed.), *God, People and Power in Malawi – Democratization in Theological Perspective*, Blantyre: Claim/ Kachere, 1996, pp. 149-176;
Fiedler, Klaus, 'The Charismatic and Pentecostal Movement in Malawi in Cultural Perspective', in: *Religion in Malawi*, no 9 (1999).
Fiedler, Klaus, 'The Charismatic and Pentecostal Movements in Malawi in Cultural Perspective', in: *Religion in Malawi*, 9 (1999).
Fiedler, Klaus, *Christianity and African Culture: Conservative German Protestant Missionaries in Tanzania 1900-1940*, Blantyre: Claim, 1999[2].
Fiedler, Rachel Nyagondwe, *Women of Bible and Culture: Baptist Convention Women in Southern Malawi*, Zomba: Kachere, 2005.
Fraser, A.R., *Donald Fraser of Livingstonia*, London: Hodder and Stoughton, 1934.
Garner, Judy, *History of the Baptist Mission in Malawi: A Rambling Remembrance of Some People and Events in the History of the Baptist Mission in Malawi*, Lilongwe: Baptist Publications, 1998;
Gray, Ernest, 'The History of the Churches of Christ Missionary Work in Nyasaland, Central Africa 1907-1930', in: *Churches of Christ Historical Society Occasional Paper*, no. 1, Cambridge, 1981.
Hetherwick, A., *The Romance of Blantyre: How Livingstone's Dream Came True*, London: James Clarke, n.d. [1931].

Hinfelaar, Hugo, *History of the Catholic Church in Zambia 1895-1995*, Bookworld Publ., 2004.
Jackson, Bill., *Send us Friends*, Blantyre: Claim, n.p., n.d.
Jeal, T., *Livingstone*, New York: Putnam, 1973.
Johne, Harold, R., and Ernst H. Wendland, *To Every Nation, Tribe, Language and People: A Century of WELS World Missions*, Milwaukee: Northwestern Publ. House, 1993^2, pp.169-221;
Kalilombe, P.A., *Doing Theology at the Grass Roots: Theological Essays from Malawi*, Zomba: Kachere, 1999.
Kamnkhwani, H.A., *An Evaluation of the Historiography of Nkhoma Synod, Church of Central Africa Presbyterian*, D.Th., University of Stellenbosch, 1990.
Kaplan, S., 'The Africanization of Missionary Christianity – History and Typology', in: *Journal of Religion in Africa* (16), pp. 166-186.
King, M. & E., *The Story of Medicine and Disease in Malawi: The 130 Years since Livingstone*, Blantyre: Montfort, 1992^2.
Kishindo, J.H.A., *Mbiri ya Ecclesia Anglicana ku Nyasaland 1860-1960*, Cape Town: Oxford U.P., 1960.
Koevering, Helen E.P., *Dancing their Dreams: The Lakeshore Nyanja Women of the Anglican Diocese of Niassa*, Zomba, Kachere, 2005.
Langworthy, H., *Africa for the Africans: The Life of Joseph Booth*, Blantyre: Claim, 1996.
Laws, R., *Reminiscences of Livingstonia*, Edinburgh/ London: Oliver and Boyd, 1934.
Lehmann, D., and J.V. Taylor, *Christians of the Copperbelt*, London: SCM, 1961.
Linden, Ian, *Catholics, Peasants and Chewa Resistance in Nyasaland 1889-1939*, London: Heinemann, 1974.
Linden, Ian, *Mponda Mission Diary 1889-1891*, Lilongwe: White Fathers, 1989.
Livingstone, D., *The Last Journals – David Livingstone in Central Africa* (vol. 1), Westport: Greenwood, 1970 [first edition 1874].
Longwe, Harry, 'The History of the Baptist Convention of Malawi', Zomba: kachere [expected in 2006].
Lwanda, J., *Politics, Culture and Medicine in Malawi*, Zomba: Kachere, 2005.
Macheta, Harry Kambwrir, *Blantyre Mission: Nkhani ya Ciyambi Cake*, Blantyre: Hetherwick Press, 1951.
Macpherson, F., *North of the Zambezi – A Modern Missionary Memoir*, Edinburgh: Handsel, 1998.
Makondesa, Patrick, *Moyo ndi Utumiki wa Mbusa ndi Mai Muocha wa Providence Industrial Mission*, Blantyre: Claim/ Mvunguti, 2000.
Makondesa, Patrick, *The Church History of Providence Industrial Mission 1900-1940*, Zomba: Kachere, 2006.
Mandivenga, E.C., *Islam in Zimbabwe*, Gweru: Mambo Press, 1983.
Matemba, Yona Hisbon, *Matandani: The Second Adventist Mission in Malawi*, Zomba: Kachere, 2003.
McCracken, J., *Politics and Christianity in Malawi 1875-1940: The Impact of the Livingstonia Mission in the Northern Province*, Cambridge U.P., 1977.
McIntosh, H., *Robert Laws: Servant of Africa*, Carberry: Handsel & Blantyre: Central Africana, 1993.
Merwe Van der W.J, *From Mission field to Autonomous Church in Zimbabwe* (A Publication of the Institute for Missiological Research of the University of Pretoria, NG Kerkboekhandel, 1981.
Mgawi, K.J., *Mbiri ya Mpingo ndi mudzi wa Nkhoma 1896 mpaka 1996*, Nkhoma Press, n.d. [1996].
Mbiri ya Atumiki a Maria Virgo Woyera 1925-1975, Limbe: Montfort, 1975.
Michongwe, Nelly, *Meet the Daughters of the Blessed Virgin Mary in Malawi Africa*, Zomba Kachere, 2005^2.
Moffat, John Smith, *The Lives of Robert and Mary Moffat by their son John Smith Moffat*, New York Edition: Armstrong & Son, 1888.
Moir, Fred, *After Livingstone: An African Trade Romance*, no details.
Monjeza, Joshua, 'Distinctives and Polity of the Evangelical Brethren Church in Malawi, including Church History', n.d. [about 1995].
Msiska, S.K., *Golden Buttons: Christianity and Traditional Religion among the Tumbuka*, Blantyre: Claim, 1997.
Mukonyora, Isabel, *Women and Ecology in Shona Religion*, Harare: University of Zimbabwe, 1999.

Munyenyembwe, Rhodian G., 'The Church and Socio-cultural Issues: An Evaluation of the Charismatic Movement's Contribution towards the Centralisation of the Gospel in Malawi', 2006 [unpublished MA dissertation of the University of Malawi]
Murray, Andrew, *Moyo Watsopano: Mawu a Mulungu kwa Ophunzira Ongoyamba a Yesu Khristu*, Zomba: Kachere, 2006 [transl. of *The New Life*, ed. by Steven Paas; first published 1885].
Murray, Andrew, *The State of the Church*, Kempton Park: The Andrew Murray Consultation and Prayer for Revival and Mission, 1985 (first edition, 1911).
Murray, Andrew., *The Key to the Missionary Problem*, Fort Washington: Christian Literature Crusade, 1983 (first edition, London: Nisbet, 1901).
Mvula, Gregory Chawanangwa, and Enson Mbilikile Lwesya, *Flames of Fire: The History of the Assemblies of God in Malawi*, Lilongwe: Assemblies of God in Malawi, 2005.
Mwimba, H.Z., 'The Establishing of the Evangelical Lutheran Church in Malawi', Tanzania, Makumira, 1992 [unpublished B.Div. paper of Makumira Lutheran Theological College].
Ncozana, S.S., *Sangaya: A Leader in the Church of Central Africa Presbyterian*, Blantyre: Claim, 1996.
Ncozana, Silas S., *Sangaya: A Leader in the Synod of Blantyre Church of Central Africa Presbyterian*, Blantyre: Claim/ Kachere, 1999.
Ncozana, Silas S., *Spirit Possession and Tumbuka Christians*, Ph.D, University of Aberdeen, 1985.
Newell, J., 'Not war but Defence of the Oppressed? - Bishop Mackenzie's Skirmishes with the Yao in 1861', in: K.R. Ross (ed.), *Faith at the Frontiers of Knowledge*, Blantyre: Claim, 1998, pp. 129-143.
Northcott, Cecil, *Robert Moffat: Pioneer in Africa*, London: Lutterworth, 1961.
Nthara, S.Y., *Mbiri ya Achewa*, Limbe: Malawi Publications and Literature Bureau, 1965.
Nthara, S.Y., *Namon Katengeza*, Nkhoma Synod, 1964.
Nthara, S.Y., *The History of the Chewa*, Wiesbaden: Steiner, 1973.
Nursg, G.T., *The Physical Characters of the Maravi* [PhD Thesis], 1974.
Nzunda, M.S. and K.R. Ross, *Church, Law and Political Transition in Malawi 1992-1994*, Gweru: Mambo Press, 1997^2.
Oliver, R., and G.Matthew (eds), *A History of East Africa*, New York: Oxford University Press, 1963.
Pachai B. (ed.), *Early History of Malawi*, London: Longman, 1972.
Parrat, J.K. (ed.), *A Bibliography of Traditional Religion in Malawi*, Zomba: University of Malawi, 1983^2.
Pauw, C.M., *Mission and Church in Malawi: The History of the Nkhoma Synod of the Church of Central Africa Presbyterian 1889-1962*, PhD, University of Stellenbosch, 1980.
Perry, L. (ed.), *Joseph Booth: Africa for the African* (1st ed. 1897), Blantyre: Claim, 1997.
Phiri, D.D., *From Nguni to Ngoni – A History of the Ngoni Exodus from Zululand and Swaziland to Malawi, Tanzania, and Zambia*, Limbe: Popular Publ., 1982.
Phiri, D.D., *History of Malawi: From Earliest Time to the Year 1915*, Blantyre: Claim, 2004.
Phiri, D.D., *History of the Tumbuka*, Blantyre: Dzuka, 2000.
Phiri, D.D., *Let Us Die For Africa: An African Perspective on the Life and Death of John Chilembwe of Nyasaland/ Malawi*, Blantyre: Central Africana, 1999.
Phiri, I.A., *Women, Presbyterianism and Patriarchy: Religious Experience of Chewa Women in Central Malawi*, Blantyre: Claim, 1997.
Phiri, Kings M., 'Wealth and Power in the History of Northern Chewa Chiefdoms 1798-1895', [MA Thesis].
Phiri, Kings M., *Chewa History in Central Malawi and the Use of Oral Tradition 1600-1920*, [PhD Thesis], 1975.
Phiri, Kings M., and K.R. Ross (eds.), *Democratization in Malawi – A Stocktaking*, Blantyre: Claim, 1998.
Pike, J.G., *Malawi: A Political and Economic History*, London: Pall Mall, 1968.
Ranger, T.O., and J. Waller (eds.), *Themes in the Christian History of Central Africa*, London: Heinemann, 1975.
Reijnaerts, H., and A. Nielsen, and M. Schoffeleers, *Montfortians in Malawi, their Spirituality and Pastoral Approach*, Blantyre: Claim/ Kachere, 1997.
Retief, M.W., *William Murray of Nyasaland*, Lovedale Press, 1958.
Ritchie, Bruce, *The Missionary Theology of Robert Moffat*, Zomba: Kachere, 2006 [PhD Thesis].

Ross, Andrew C., 'Wokondedwa Wathu: The Mzungu who Mattered', in: *Religion in Malawi* 7: 3-5 (1997).
Ross, Andrew C., *Blantyre Mission and the Making of Modern Malawi*, Blantyre: Claim, 1996.
Ross, Andrew C., *David Livingstone: Mission and Empire*, London: Hambledon and London, 2002.
Ross, Kenneth R. (ed.), *Christianity in Malawi – A Source Book*, Gweru: Mambo/ Zomba: Kachere, 1996.
Ross, Kenneth R. (Ed.), *Faith at the Frontiers of Knowledge*, Blantyre: Claim/Kachere, 1998.
Ross, Kenneth R. (ed.), *God, People and Power in Malawi: Democratization in Theological Perspective*, Blantyre: Claim/ Kachere, 1996.
Ross, Kenneth R., *Here comes your King – Christ, Church and Nation in Malawi*, Blantyre: Claim, 1998.
Rowley, H., *The Story of the Universities Mission to Central Africa from its Commencement under Bishop MacKenzie to its withdrawal from the Zambezi*, 2nd ed., London: Saunders, 1867.
Saunders, D.L., *A History of Baptists in East and Central Africa*, Southern Baptist Seminary 1973 [unpublished PhD thesis].
Schoffeleers, M., 'The Meaning and Use of the Name Malawi in Oral Traditions and Precolonial Documents', in: B. Pachai (ed.), *The Early History of Malawi*, London: Longman, pp. 91-103.
Schoffeleers, M., 'The Religious Significance of Bush Fires in Malawi' in: *Cahiers des Religions Africaines*, no 10, pp. 271-287.
Schoffeleers, M., and I. Linden, 'The Resistance of the Nyau Cult to the Catholic Mission in Malawi', in: Ranger and Kimbambo (eds), *The Historical Study of African Religion*, London: Heinemann, 1972.
Schoffeleers, M., *In Search of Truth and Justice – Confrontation between Church and State in Malawi 1960-1994*, Blantyre, Claim, 1999.
Schoffeleers, M., *Pentecostalism and Neo-Traditionalism: The Religious Polarization of a Rural District in Southern Malawi*, Amsterdam: Free University Press, 1985.
Schoffeleers, M., *Religion and the Dramatisation of Life – Spirit Beliefs and Rituals in Southern and Central Malawi*, Blantyre: Claim, 1997.
Scott, D.C., and A. Hetherwick, *Dictionary of the Nyanja Language: Being the Encyclopaedic Dictionary of the Mang'anja Language*, London: United Society for Christian Literature, Lutterworth Press, 1929 (reprinted 1951, 1957).
Selfridge, J.C., *Jack of All Trades Mastered by One*, Fearn: Christian Focus, 1989.
Shelburne, C.B., 'History of the Church of Christ in Malawi', n.p., n.d. [A brief factual account of the history of the Church of Christ in southern Malawi].
Shepperson, G. and Th. Price, *Independent African: John Chilembwe and the Origins, Setting and Significance of the Nyasaland Rising of 1915*, Edinburgh U.P., 1958, re-edited: Blantyre: Claim, 2000.
Smart, Y.J., Msinkhu, 'Zionism in Malawi: The History and Theology of Zion City Church in Ntcheu District', [University of Malawi, 2005].
Smith, E.W., *Robert Moffat: One of God's Gardeners*, London: SCM, 1925.
Strohbehn, Ulf, *Pentecostalism in Malawi: A History of the Apostolic Faith Mission 1931-1994*, Zomba: Kachere, 2005.
Stuart, R.G., *Christianity and the Chewa: the Anglican Case 1885-1950*, unpublished PhD thesis, University of London, 1974.
Tembo, Masiye, *Touched By His Grace: A Ngoni Story of Tragedy and Triumph*, Zomba: Kachere, 2005.
Thiessen, Anne, *The Warm Heart of Africa*, Winona: Choate Publ., 1998;
Thompson, T.J., 'African Leadership in the Livingstonia Mission 1875-1900', in: *Malawi Journal of Social Science*, vol.2 (1973), pp. 76-91.
Thompson, T.J., 'Xhosa Missionaries in Late Nineteenth Century Malawi: Strangers or Fellow Countrymen?', in: *Religion in Malawi*, no 8 (1998), pp. 8-16.
Thompson, T.J., *Christianity in Northern Malawi: Donald Fraser's Missionary Methods and Ngoni Culture*, Leiden: Brill, 1995.
Thompson, T.J., *Touching the Heart: Xhosa Missionaries to Malawi 1876-1888*, Pretoria: Unisa, 2000.
Tindall, P.E.N., *History of Central Africa*, London: Longman, 1997 (first publ. 1968).

Van Dijk, R.A., *Young Malawian Puritan Preachers in a Present-day African Urban Environment*, PhD, University of Utrecht, 1992.
Verstraelen-Gilhuis, G., *From Dutch Mission Church to Reformed Church in Zambia: The Scope for African Leadership and Initiative in the History of a Zambian Mission Church*, Franeker, 1982.
Vezeau, R., *The Apostolic Vicariate of Nyasa: Origins and First Developments 1889-1935*, Rome: Missionari d'Africa, 1989 [re-edited by Kachere, 2006].
Vezeau, R., *The Church in Malawi: The History of Bembeke Parish*, Dedza: Private, 1982.
Wallis, J.P.R. (ed), *The Matabele Mission of John and Emily Moffat*, 1945.
Walters, W., *Life and Labours of Robert Moffat*, London: Walter Scott, 1882.
Wendland, Ernst R., *Buku Loyera – An Introduction to the New Chichewa Bible Translation*, Blantyre, Claim/ Kachere, 1998.
Wendland, Ernst, H., *A History of the Christian Church in Central Africa: The Lutheran Church of Central Africa 1953-1978*, Wisconsin: Mequon, 1980.
White, L., *Magomero: Portrait of an African Village*, Cambridge University Press., 1987.
Wills, A.J., *An Introduction to the History of Central Africa*, London: Oxford U.P., 1964.
Wilson, G. Herbert, *The History of the Universities' Mission to Central Africa*, Westminster: Central Afrtica House, 1936.
Zoobgo, C.J.M., *The Wesleyan Methodist Missions in Zimbabwe 1891-1945*, Harare: University of Zimbabwe, 1991.

Index

A

Abarohi movement, 147; 228
Abbasid dynasty, 26
Abdallah Marshambo, 39
Abeokuta, 77
abun of Ethiopia, 41; 42; 45; 46; 47; 48
Accrediting Council for Theological Education (A.C.T.E.A.), 183
Adeyemo, Tokunboh, 160
Adoptianists, 46
Adowa, battle of, 50
Aedesius, 40
Africa Evangelical Church of Malawi, 204
Africa Inland Church, 139; 172
Africa Inland Mission (A.I.M.), 82; 100; 101; 106; 138; 140; 168; 171; 172; 182; 251
Africa, James Mullan, 227
African Baptist Assembly, 204
African Greek Orthodox Church, 145
African Independent Churches Association (A.I.C.A.), 184
African Instituted Churches (A.I.C.), 140; 145; 148; 152; 153; 157; 162; 184; 228; 229; 230; 231; 246
African Lakes Company (Mandala), 192
African Methodist Episcopal Church (A.M.E.C.), 143; 215
African Methodist Independent Church, 216
African National Congress (A.N.C.), 156; 224
African Synod 1994, 130; 131
African Theology, 158; 162
African Traditional Religion (A.T.R.), 24; 28; 29; 56; 133; 145; 160; 161; 177; 178; 179; 180; 231; 241; 248; 250
Africanisation, 78; 79; 80; 152; 195; 207; 208
Afrikaander Volk, 87
Afrikaner, 97
Agaja, 31
Agape, 232
Agbebi, Mojola (David Brown Vincent), 144
aggiornamento, 130
Aggrey, J.E.K., 137; 144
Ahmad al-Mansur, 27
Ahmed, Imam, 44; 45
Ahmed, Muhammad, 50
AIDS, 180; 244; 245
Akan, 31; 52; 54; 158
Akinsowon (Christiana Abiodun Emmanuel, 147
Akinyele, Isaac, 147
Aladura movement, 140; 145; 147; 153; 228
Albert of Belgium, 81; 147
Alexandria, 19; 25; 38; 40; 41; 42; 45; 46; 47; 48; 50
Alfonso I (Mvemba Nzinga) of Congo, 55; 141
All Africa Conference of Churches (A.A.C.C.), 182
All for Jesus, 232
Almohad Empire, 27
Almoravid Empire, 27
Alvarez, Francisco (Portuguese diplomat), 45; 60
Alwa, 37
amaNazaretha Church, 148; 226
Amayi a Chifundo, 210
Amayi a Chigwirizano, 198
Amayi a Dorika, 210
Amayi a Mvano, 210
Amayi a Tereza, 210
Amayi a Umodzi, 210
Amde-Zion of Ethiopia, 43
American Board for Foreign Missions, 77
American Board of Commissioners for Foreign Missions, 99; 126
American Council of Churches, 181
Amharic language, 47; 48; 50
Amin, Idi, 151; 156
Andel, Van, 66
Andersson, Ida, 228
Angola, 33; 54; 55; 57; 61; 63; 82; 83; 84; 85; 107; 113; 114; 115; 116; 128; 129; 155; 164; 165
anti-clericalism, 98
Antiochene School, 19
Anzanea, 32
Aoko, Gaudencio, 151
apartheid, 87; 156; 159; 160; 234
Apostolic Faith Mission, 206; 226; 228
Aquinas, Thomas, 27; 176
Arckel, Johan van, 66
Arnot, F.S., 84; 90
Ashanti people, 31; 111; 134
Ashmun, Jehudi, 80

Assemblies of God, 85; 119; 207; 210; 226; 227; 229
Association of Evangelical Churches of West Africa, 183
Association of Evangelicals of Africa (A.E.A.), 160; 183
Athanasius, 19; 40
Auckland (New Zealand), 202
Augustine, 20
Augustinian order, 60
authoritarianism, 142; 200
Axum, 38; 40; 41; 42; 43
Ayyubid dynasty, 25; 39
Azusa Street (start of Pentecostalism), 225; 226; 228

B

Babalola, Joseph, 141; 147; 227
Bachmann, Traugott, 101
Badagry, 77
Baeta, Christian, 123; 162
Bagamoyo, 101; 128
Bagster, W.W., 84
Baily, A.W., 84
Balano, Alfonso de, 53
Balokole (East Africa Revival), 149; 150; 151; 153; 228
balubaala cult, 101; 102
Banana, Canaan, 222; 224
Banda, Hastings Kamuzu, 207; 212; 218
Banda, John Afwenge, 212
Bandawe, 192; 194; 196
Baptist Convention, 85; 204; 209; 235
Baptist Foreign Mission Society (B.F.M.S.), 126
Baptist Missionary Society (B.M.S.), 74; 77; 81; 82; 83; 126; 164; 202
Baqt, Treaty of, 37; 38
Barrett, David, 11; 108; 143; 162
Barro, 56
Barron, Edward, 81
Basel Evangelical Missionary Society, 77; 80; 123; 138
Batavian Republic, 68; 88
Bauern Mission, 51; 91; 127
Baviaan Kloof (Genadendal), 67
Bayudaya, 153
Bediako, Kwame, 11; 160; 162; 249
Beijing (1995), 243; 246
Belgian (Belgium), 117; 118; 119; 120; 129; 130; 135; 138; 147; 228
Bemba people, 33; 212; 214; 216; 217

Benin (Dahomey), 31; 53; 54; 55; 122; 227
Bennett, Dennis J., 230
Berber, 27
Berlin Conference (1884/ 1885), 83; 105; 107; 108; 110; 117; 120; 121; 123; 127; 134
Berlin Mission, 91; 101; 221
Bessieux, Jean, 81
Bet Abba Libanos, 43
Bethel Mission, 101; 124
Betsileo people, 102
Bevan, Thomas, 103
Beyers Naudé C.F., 156
Bhengu, Nicolas, 227
Biko, Steven Bantu, 159
Bingham, Roland V., 172; 174
Bismarck, Joseph, 195
Bismarck, Otto von, 122; 195
Black Theology movement, 142; 159
Blantyre Christian Centre, 232
Blantyre Mission, 188; 194; 195; 197; 202; 205
Blyden, Edward Wilmot, 79; 80; 144
Board of Commissioners for Foreign Mission, 81; 84
Boers, 64; 65; 66; 71; 87; 88; 90; 91; 92; 93; 96; 99; 108; 110
Boesak, Allan, 156; 159
Bokwito, Tom, 191; 194
Bonnke, Rheinhard, 231
Bonny, 77
Booth, Joseph, 136; 144; 169; 201; 202; 203; 204; 218
Boru Meda, Council of, 49
Bourget, Pierre, 200
Bradford Apostolic Church, 227
Braide, Garrick Sokari Daketima, 79; 146
Branch, Mable, 203
Bremen Mission, 80; 123
Brethren (Plymouth Brethren.), 67; 84; 89; 90; 95; 164; 165; 166; 167; 168; 174; 207; 214; 215
British/ Britain, 35; 48; 49; 65; 68; 69; 70
Brown, 19; 76; 144
Bucer, Martin, 180
Buchler, Johannes, 227
Buganda (in Uganda), 32; 101; 112
Buku Lopatulika (Holy Book), 198
Burkina Faso, 122; 160; 227
Burundi, 32; 120; 123; 124; 125; 227
Buthelezi, 159
Butscher, 76
Buys people, 220

270

C

Calabar, 77; 79; 146
Calvary Family Church, 232
Calvin, John, 180; 255
Cameroon, 80; 81; 113; 122; 125; 138
Candace, 36; 143
Cape General Mission (C.G.M.), 93
Cape Maclear, 191; 192; 194; 197
Cape of Good Hope, 53; 57; 70
Cape Town, 35; 63; 70; 90; 188; 191; 203
Cape Verde, 53; 115
Capitein, Jacobus Eliza, 61; 62
Capuchin order, 48; 54; 55; 56; 63; 81; 83; 128
Cardobo, Antonio, 199
Cardoso, Fr., 55
Carey, Lott, 80
Carey, William, 72; 126; 164; 181
Carmelites order, 103
Carr, Burgess, 182; 183
Cerullo, Morris, 231
Chad, 121; 122; 172; 174
Chagga people, 33; 101
Chakachadza, Mark, 203
Chalcedon, Council of, 37
Charismatic Movement, 149; 152; 184; 210; 215; 225; 228; 229; 230; 231; 232; 233; 238
Charismatic Renewal Ministries (C.R.M.), 233
Chaza (Mai Chaza), 151
Cherubim and Seraphim, 147
Chewa people, 33; 178; 189; 198; 200; 212; 235; 240; 241; 251
Chichewa, 94; 130; 143; 196; 198; 216; 217; 240; 250
Chigwirizano, 210
Chilangizo, 198
Childs, Gladwyn M., 83
Chilema, 209
Chilembwe, John, 136; 144; 166; 195; 202; 203; 204; 205; 207; 266
Chiluba, Frederick, 156
Chimurenga, 221; 224
China Inland Mission (C.I.M.), 165; 167; 168; 202
Chinguwo, Robert, 206; 228
Chinunu, Charles, 193
Chisumphi Cult, 240
Chitsulo, Cornelio, 208
Chitumbuka, 216
Chiwere (Ngoni Chief), 197
Chiwona, James, 208

Chiyanjano cha Azimayi, 210
Chrischona Lutherans, 49
Christ Apostolic Church (C.A.C.), 147; 227
Christaller, 80
Christian and Missionary Alliance (C.M.A.), 171
Christian Catholic Apostolic Church in Zion, 190; 226; 227
Christian Council of Malawi, 206
Christian Hospitals Association of Malawi (C.H.A.M.), 209
Christian Mission in Many Lands (Brethren), 84; 165
Christian Reformed Mission, 127
Christian Students' Society of South Africa, 93
Christian Union (C.U.), 230
Christiansborg, 62
Christoph da Gama, 45
Chuma/ Juma (Livingstone's servant), 190
Church Missionary Society (C.M.S.), 47; 48; 74; 76; 77; 78; 79; 80; 99; 100; 102; 124; 126; 135; 138; 141; 144; 149; 150; 182
Church of Central Africa Presbyterian (C.C.A.P.), 87; 164; 188; 196; 198; 205; 206; 208; 209; 210; 215; 216; 218; 223; 224; 235
Church of Christ in the Congo, 120
Church of God in Christ, 227
Church of God Mission International, 230
Church of Scotland, 87; 90; 92; 100; 123; 138; 191; 194; 198; 212; 215; 216
Church of the Twelve Apostles, 146
Church, Joe, 149
Churches of Christ, 151; 165; 203; 210
Clapham Sect, 71; 73; 76
Classical Missions, 74; 127; 140; 164; 167; 168; 169; 171; 189; 201; 202
Coillard, François and Christine, 90; 213; 221
Colenso, John William, 90; 91
Colonialism, 71; 85; 106; 108; 110; 119; 121; 126; 131; 132; 133; 134; 135; 136; 137; 142; 144; 151; 158; 221; 243; 244
Comber, Thomas, 82
Concordats, 114
Congo, 33; 53; 54; 55; 56; 61; 62; 63; 81; 82; 84; 107; 117; 118; 119; 120; 121; 122; 128; 129; 135; 138; 141; 147; 158; 164; 165; 171; 172; 228; 229; 230
Congo Free State, 71; 110; 117; 118; 119; 120; 129; 134; 135
Congregation of the Holy Ghost (Holy Ghost Fathers), 127
Congregational Theology, 160

Congress of Vienna, 88
Conrad, Joseph, 118
Consolata Fathers, 100
Constantinople, 25
continuity, 14; 158; 231; 253; 254; 255
Continuum, 254
Coptic Church, 19; 25
Council of Chalcedon, 19
Counter Reformation, 45; 129
Covenant (of Grace), 43; 87; 161; 256
Cox, Raymond G., 206
Cranmer, Thomas, 180
Creoles, 77
Crowther, Samuel Ajayi, 77; 78; 79
Crummel, Alexander, 80
Crusades, 21; 39
Cuguano, Ottobah, 73; 141
Curch Missionary Society (C.M.S.), 101
Currie, W.T., 83
Cyprian, 20

D

Dahomey (Benin), 31; 121; 122; 123; 227
Daneel, J.W., 220
Daneel, M.L., 148; 162
Danquah, Joseph B., 158
Darfur, 38
Daughters of the Blessed Virgin Mary, 211
Davies, 76
Debre Libanos monastery, 43
Debres Damo monastery, 41
Derr, Paul, 229
Dias, Diego, 102
Diaz, Bartholomew, 53; 57
Dictionary of African Christian Biography (D.A.C.B.), 15
Difaqane (Scattering), 65
Dingane of the Zulu, 34; 65; 87
Direct Rule, 131
discontinuity, 161; 253; 254
Doe, S.K., 155; 234
Domingo, Charles, 136; 202; 203; 207
Dominican order, 59; 219; 222; 251
Donatist upheavals, 21
Dondi, 83
Dongola, 36; 37; 38; 39
Donna Beatrice (Kempa Vita), 56; 230
Dowie, J.A., 148; 226
Doyle, Arthur Conan, 119
Dutch, 16; 35; 54; 55; 57; 61; 62; 63; 64; 66; 67; 68; 69; 70; 71; 86; 87; 88; 91; 92; 93;
94; 95; 97; 99; 108; 111; 127; 196; 197; 198; 200; 212; 214; 216; 220; 221; 223; 255
Dutch Reformed Church Mission, 66; 196; 197; 198; 205; 212; 223; 251; 253
Dutch West Indies Company, 61; 63
Dwane, James M., 143

E

East Africa Revival, 139; 149
East London Training Institute, 166; 169
echege of Ethiopia, 46; 48
ecumenical movement, 161; 181; 182
ecumenicity, 14
Ecumenism, 157; 180
Edinburgh Missionary Society (E.M.S.), 126
Edwards, Jonathan, 71; 164
Egypt, 19; 20; 21; 22; 23; 24; 25; 26; 28; 37; 38; 39; 41; 50; 107; 109; 112; 141; 143; 171; 184; 228
Ekwendeni, 193
Ekwikwi (Chief), 84
Ella-Amida of Axum, 40
Elmina, Fort, 54; 61; 62
Elmslie, Walter, 193; 197
Elton, Pa. G., 230
Emancipation, 35; 237; 239
Embangweni, 193
Emperor Haile Selassie I (Ras Tafari Makonnen), 50; 51
Enlightenment, 59; 71; 74; 131; 237; 238; 246
Equatorial Africa, 121; 122; 128
Equiano, Olaudah, 73
Era of the Princes, 47; 48
Erhardt, J., 99
Espirito Santo, Luis do, 219
Estifanites order, 44
Ethiopia, 21; 22; 26; 32; 36; 38; 40; 41; 42; 43; 44; 45; 47; 48; 49; 50; 51; 58; 60; 108; 110; 112; 141; 143; 157; 171; 174
Ethiopian Evangelical Church Mekane Yesus, 51
Ethiopianism, 12; 50; 80; 136; 142; 143; 144; 145; 151; 213
Eva (Krotoa), 66
Evangelical Alliance, 181
Evangelical Awakening/ Revivals, 72; 141; 180
Evangelical Brethren Church, 207
Evangelical Church of Malawi (Nyasa Industrial Mission), 202
Evangelical Lutheran Church in Southern Africa, 91

Evangelical Theology, 14; 159; 160; 161
Ewostatewos order, 44; 46
exorcism, 251
Ezana of Ethiopia, 40

F

Faith and Order Movement, 181
Faith Missions(Post Classical Missions), 74; 82; 99; 100; 117; 127; 164; 165; 166; 168; 169; 171; 172; 174; 201; 202; 203; 225; 235; 243
Faith of God, 232
Falashas, 48; 143
False Island (Kwaaihoek), 57
Fambidzano, 148
Fante, 52; 61; 62; 111
Faras, 36; 37; 38
Farrow, Lucy, 225
Fashoda incident, 109
Fasilidas of Ethiopia, 45; 46
Fatimids,, 25
Faulding, Jennie (Taylor), 167
Faulkner, Swam, 84
female circumcision, 245
Feminist theology, 159
Fernando Po, 81
fetishism, 55; 56
Filpos, echege, 46; 47
Finish Missionary Society, 124
First World War, 101; 109; 112; 123; 124; 125; 136; 137; 138; 204; 209
Fisher, Walter, 215
Flad, Martin, 47; 48
Flames of Victory, 232
Fort Dauphin, 103
Fort Hare University, 90
Fort Jesus, 58; 60
Fort Nassau, 61
Fourah Bay College, 76; 77; 79
Foursquare Gospel Church, 227
France (French), 66; 88; 105; 106; 107; 109; 118; 120; 121; 122; 123; 128; 139
Francis of Assisi, 22
Franciscan order, 22; 53; 128
Fraser, Donald, 93; 94; 193
Free Church of Scotland, 87; 90; 92; 126
Free Presbyterian Church, 210
Freeman, Thomas Birch, 77; 81
Freetown, 76; 77; 111; 144
FRELIMO, 115
French (France), 47; 48; 68; 69; 70; 81; 83; 88; 103; 105; 106; 108; 109; 110; 112; 118; 120; 121; 122; 123; 125; 127; 128; 129; 131; 139; 146; 158; 200
French East Indies Company, 103
French Revolution, 239
Frere, Henry Bartle, 99
Freretown, 99
Frumentius, 40
Funji people, 39

G

Gabon, 80; 81; 121; 122; 128
Galawdewos of Ethiopia, 45
Galla people, 47; 48
Gama, 232
Gambia, 29; 69; 113; 128
Garanganze Mission, 84
Garcia II of Congo, 63
Garcia III of Congo, 62
Garcia V of Congo, 81
Gare Maskal, 42
Gatu, John, 139; 183
Gaulle, de, 138
Ge'ez language, 40; 41; 48
Genadendal (Baviaan kloof), 67; 68
George, David, 27; 39; 67; 68; 71; 76; 166; 167; 191; 202; 235
Georgios II of Nubia, 38
Gereformeerde Kerk (G.K.) - Dopper Church, 87
German (Germany), 47; 67; 80; 81; 91; 101; 109; 110; 112; 122; 123; 124; 136; 138; 222
Ghana (Gold Coast), 27; 30; 31; 54; 61; 80; 81; 111; 112; 134; 138; 139; 141; 144; 151; 158; 160; 174
Ghana kingdom, 27
Glad Tidings, 232
Glasgow Missionary Society (G.M.S.), 90; 126
Gnosticism, 237; 238
Gobat, Samuel, 47; 49
Gold Coast (Ghana), 54; 61; 69; 70; 80; 111; 112; 123; 124; 125; 139; 144; 146; 182
Gomani (Ngoni Chief), 200
Gomer, Joseph and Mary, 80
Gomez, Diogo, 54
Gonakumoto, Justin, 210
Gondar, 45; 46
Gordon, Charles, 109
Govan, William, 90
Graft, William de, 81
Gray, Robert, 56; 63; 90; 91; 97; 203
Great Awakening, 71; 87; 164; 165; 166

273

Great Trek, 71; 87
Great Zimbabwe Ruins, 34; 222
Greek culture, 11; 19; 32; 36; 120; 145; 147; 169; 181; 237; 238; 240; 249
Grenfell, George, 82
Grubb, George, 94
Guinea Bissau, 115
Guinea Coast, 53
Guinness, Fanny, 82; 117; 127; 166; 169; 171
Guinness, Grattan, 166; 169
Gule Wamkulu, 201; 250; 251
Gutmann, Bruno, 101
Guyard, 200

H

Hagin, Kenneth, 231
Haile Selassie I (Ras Tafari Makonnen), 50
Hamasen Highlands, 50
Hannington, James, 102
Harare, 188; 206; 221; 223; 224; 251
Harare Synod of the C.C.A.P., 206; 223; 224
Harris, William Wadé, 122; 141; 145; 146; 230
Hausa, 28; 31; 77; 78; 155
Hawkins, William, 69
Hayford, J.E. Casely, 144
healing, 43; 56; 146; 147; 148; 151; 152; 214; 226; 228; 246; 250; 251
Heart of Africa Mission, 82
Henderson, Henry, 83; 194; 235
Henrique, Prince of Congo, 55
Henry Henderson Institute, 195
Henry of Portugal (Infante Dom Henrique, Prince Henry the Navigator), 52
Herero people, 64; 124; 125
Hetherwick, Alexander, 195; 196; 198
Heyling, Peter, 48
Historiography, 11
Hofmeyer, F., 99
Hofmeyr, L., 198
Hofmeyr, Stephanus, 220; 222
Holiness Movement, 95; 166; 169; 171; 193
Holiness Revival, 165; 166
Holy Ghost Fathers (Congregation of the Holy Ghost), 56; 79; 81; 83; 100; 101; 122; 123; 127; 128; 138
Hour of Freedom ministry, 230
Hova people, 102
Howells, Rees, 227
Huguenot Protestants, 66
Huntington, Selina, Countess of, 181
Hurlbert, C.E., 82; 172

Hutu people, 227

I

Ibibio people, 228
Idahosa, Benson, 230
Idowu, E.B., 161
Idris Alooma, 31
Ifriqiya, 26
Igbo people, 78; 138; 145; 146; 155; 248
Imasogie, 160
Indirect Rule, 131
Industrial Revolution, 237
International Council of Christian Churches, 181; 183
International Missionary Council, 181; 214
Islam, 21; 22; 24; 25; 26; 27; 28; 29; 31; 32; 35; 37; 39; 41; 44; 45; 47; 52; 80; 101; 131; 134; 155; 156; 157; 174; 180; 183; 208; 241; 248; 253; 254
Istanbul, 25
Ivory Coast, 121; 122; 141; 146; 230

J

Jacobis, Justin de, 48; 49
Jamaa Movement, 228
Jehovah Witnesses, 202; 209
Jesuits, 45; 48; 54; 55; 56; 57; 58; 60; 81; 98; 102; 118; 127; 213; 219; 222
Johannesburg, 223; 227; 230
Johanssen, Ernst, 101
Johera movement, 151
Johnson, James ('Holy Johnson'), 79; 136; 144; 190
Johnson, Mary, 228
Johnson, William Percival, 190
Jones, David, 103
Jones, William, 100
Jonsson, Anton, 50
Julius II, Pope, 53
Justo Mwale Theological College, 216; 217

K

kabaka, 32
Kachebere, 201
Kagame, A., 158
Kairos Document, 156; 159; 234
Kalambule, Lyton, 229
Kalden, Petrus, 66
Kaleb of Ethiopia, 41

Kalilombe, Patrick, 208
Kalonga Masula, 34
Kambalazaza, Mark, 232
Kamundi, 240
Kamwana, Elliot Kenan, 202; 203; 207; 218
Kanem-Borno, 31
Kaparidze, Mutapa Emperor, 58
Kapeni (Chief in Blantyre area), 194
Karanga language, 222
Kasavubu, Joseph, 120
Katchire, 232
Kato, Byang, 14; 160; 161; 183
Kaunda, David, 212
Kaunda, Kenneth, 151; 156; 212; 214; 215; 217
Kazembe dynasty, 33
Kebra Nagast text, 41
Kelly, John, 81
Kemp, Johannes Theodorus van der, 89; 95; 96; 97; 126
Kenya, 32; 48; 50; 76; 88; 90; 99; 100; 110; 111; 112; 113; 124; 127; 128; 138; 139; 145; 149; 150; 151; 161; 172; 182; 183; 196; 225; 227; 228
Keswick Convention, 93; 94; 95; 149; 193
Khambuli, George, 230
Kharijite, 26
Khoikhoi people (Hottentots), 34; 64; 66; 67; 68; 89; 96; 97
Khondowe, 194
Kibongi movement, 228
Kigozi, Blasio, 149
Kikuyu people, 33; 111; 138; 251
Kilham, Hannah, 76
Kilimanjaro, 99; 101
Kilwa, 32; 34; 57
Kimbangu, Simon, 120; 147; 148; 153; 228; 230
Kimbanguists, 120; 147; 184
Kimpa Vita (Donna Beatrice), 56; 141; 230
King's African Rifles, 109
Kitchener, Horatio, 109
Kitombo, battle of, 63
Klerk, Willem de, 156
Knight-Bruce, George, 222
Knothe, A., 221
Koelle, S.W., 77
Koi, David, 100
Kololo people, 213
Koyi, Isaac William Ntusane, 191; 193
Krapf, Johann Ludwig, 47; 48; 49; 99
Krio language, 76
Krotoa (Eva), 66
kuchotsa fumbi, 240

Kufa, John Gray, 195
Kuhnel, 67
Kuijper, 87
Kumalowho, Izak, 222
Kumm, Karl, 174
Kumm-Guinness, Lucy, 174
Kuruman, 89; 220
Kush, 36; 143

L

laager – mentality, 87
Lake Malawi, 33; 90; 191; 199; 200
Lakwena (or: Lekwana), Alice, 156
Lalibela of Ethiopia, 42; 43
Lambarene, 81
Lamu, 32; 57; 60
Lancaster House Agreement, 224
Lany, Emma de, 205
Lausanne Conference (1974), 161
Lavigerie, Charles Martial Allemand, 101; 128; 135; 199
Laws, Robert, 90; 191; 192; 193; 194; 196; 198
Lazarists order, 103; 128
League of Nations, 125
Lebna Dengel of Ethiopia, 45
Legio Maria, 211
Legion of Mary, 201
Legkangane, 227
Leipzig Mission, 101; 124
Lena (Moravian convert), 67; 141
Lenshina, Alice, 151; 217; 218
Lenten Pastoral Letter (1992), 208
Leopold II of Belgium, 107; 117; 118; 119; 129
Lettow-Vorbeck, von, 124
Lewanika of the Lozi, 213
Liberal theology, 157; 161; 162
liberalism, 87; 114; 150; 152; 162; 177; 181; 183; 239
Liberation Theology, 159; 162
Liberia, 80; 108; 144; 146; 155; 174; 182; 230; 233
Libermann, François, 79; 81; 128
Lier, Ritzema van, 67
Lijadu, E.M., 144
Likoma Island, 190; 227
Lion, Edward, 226
Litiya (Prince of the Lozi), 213
Living Waters Church, 210
Livingstone Inland Mission (L.I.M.), 82; 171

Livingstone, David, 57; 73; 74; 82; 84; 89; 90; 100; 117; 127; 166; 171; 188; 189; 190; 191; 194; 196; 220
Livingstonia Mission (Free Church of Scotland), 136; 137; 188; 190; 191; 194; 197; 205; 212; 215
Lobengula of the Ndebele, 135; 220; 221
Lolo, Dede Ekeke, 145
Lomwe people, 200
London Missionary Society (L.M.S.), 74; 77; 87; 89; 90; 95; 103; 105; 124; 126; 135; 188; 189; 213; 214
Louis XIV of France, 66
Louw, Andrew, 222
Louw-Malan, Cinie, 222
Lovedale College, 90; 100; 143; 144; 191; 192; 196; 203
Lozi people, 213
Lumpa Church, 151; 217; 218
Lunda people, 33; 215
Lusitanianism, 113; 129
Luther, Martin, 93; 180
Lutheran Church of Central Africa (L.C.C.A.), 206; 207; 210
Lutheran World Federation (L.W.F.), 181
Luwum, Janani, 151; 156

M

Maarsveld, 67
Macdonald, Duff, 195
Macedo, Henry de, 199
Machona Churches, 206
Mackay, Alexander, 102
Mackenzie, Charles Frederick, 100; 189; 190
macrocosmos, 250; 253
Madagascar (Malagasy), 64; 102; 103; 104; 105; 106; 120; 121; 122; 128; 171
Madima, Johannes, 221
MAF., 183
Maffuta, 56; 229
Maghrib, 26
Mahon, Edgar, 227
Makewana, 240
Makololo people, 89; 135; 188; 192
Makuria, 36; 37
Malagasy (Madagascar), 97; 102; 103; 106
Malawi, 11; 15; 23; 28; 33; 65; 87; 88; 90; 92; 100; 109; 110; 113; 124; 126; 127; 128; 130; 134; 135; 136; 137; 143; 144; 160; 166; 169; 178; 179; 180; 188; 189; 190; 191; 192; 193; 194; 195; 196; 197; 198; 199; 200; 201; 202; 203; 204; 205; 206; 207; 208; 209; 210; 211; 212; 214; 215; 216; 217; 218; 219; 222; 223; 224; 225; 226; 228; 229; 232; 233; 234; 235; 240; 250; 253; 264
Malawi Congress Party, 209
Mali, 30; 54; 122
Mali Empire, 30
Malikebu, Daniel, 166; 205
Malindi, 32; 57
Malinke people, 30
Mamluk, 25
Mandala (African Lakes Company), 192
Mandela, Nelson, 156
Mandovi, Joseph, 223
Mankadan, Sybrand, 66
Mansfield, Lord, 73
Manuh, Takyiwaa, 243
Maples, Charles, 190
Maples, Chauncy, 190
Maranke, Yohane, 227
Maravi, 33
Mariannhil, 91
Mario Legio of Africa, 145
Mariology, 56
Marists, 201
Maroons, 76
Martin V, Pope, 52
Maskal Kebra, 42
Masoha, Jozua, 222
Masowe, Yohane, 227
Massaja, G., 48; 49
Matecheta, Harry, 195
Matipwiri (Chief in Mangochi area), 199
Matoga, 232
Mattita, Walter, 142
Mau Mau movement, 139; 151
Mauritania, 20; 27; 52; 121; 122
Mauritius, 104; 122
Mbanza Congo, 55
Mbele (Ma Mbele), 151
Mbelwa (Ngoni Chief), 192; 193
Mbewe, 232
Mbila, Yohana, 138
Mbiti, John S., 158; 161
Mbona Cult, 23; 178; 219; 220; 240; 250
Meerhof, Pieter van, 66
Melbourne, 202
Mendez, Alfonso, 45
Menelik I, 41; 42; 43
Menelik II of Ethiopia, 50
Menghistu Haile Mariam, 51; 157
Mennonites, 119; 140
Merina people, 102; 103
Merkurios of Nubia, 38

276

Mesihafe Qedir book, 45
Mfecane (Crushing), 65
Mgala, 232
microcosmos, 250; 253
Middle Ages, 21; 23; 41; 238
Milingo, Emmanuel, 214; 215
Mill Hill Fathers, 100; 130
Miller, Clyde, 225
Miller, Samuel T., 84
Mindolo Ecumenical Institute, 214
Missionary Movement, 72; 74; 76; 140; 141; 142; 149; 152; 153; 164; 248; 249
Mliwa, Shadrack, 138
Mobutu, 147; 155
mobutuism, 155
Modernism, 162; 177; 182; 232; 252
Moffat, Robert, 89; 220
Mohammed bin Abdulla, 109
Moir, John and Alfred, 192
Mokamba, 213
Mokoele, Lukas, 222
Mokone, Mangena M., 143
Mombasa, 32; 48; 57; 60; 99; 111; 138; 172
Monjeza, Joshua, 207
Monophysitism, 19; 37; 41; 46; 47; 49
Monrovia, 80
Montanism, 229
Montfort Fathers/ Missionaries, 199; 200
Moravian Mission, 62; 67; 68; 89; 95; 101; 124; 141; 164
Morel, Edmund Dene, 118
Morgenster, 222
Morocco, 20; 26; 27; 108; 121; 122
Morudu, Jeremia and Petrus, 222
Mott, John, 94
Mozambique, 32; 34; 53; 57; 58; 64; 65; 88; 98; 99; 107; 113; 115; 116; 127; 129; 155; 199; 200; 209; 216
Mpingo wa Aroni, 250; 251
Mpingo wa Azimayi, 210
MPLA, 115
Mponda (Chief in Mangochi area), 191; 199; 200
Mtekateka, Josiah, 209
Mtuwa, Harry Apika, 195
Mua, 200
Mueller, Richard, 206
Muftaa, Dallington, 101
Mugabe, Robert, 224
Mugambi, Jesse, 162
Mulago, 158
Muocha, Leonard, 205
Murphy, J.B., 117
Murray Theological College, 223

Murray, Andrew, 84; 88; 91; 92; 94
Murray, Andrew Charles, 88; 92; 196
Murray, Annie, 94
Murray, Charles, 92
Murray, William Hoppe, 197; 198
Musa, 30
Museveni, Yoweri, 156
Mushindo, Paul, 217
Muslim, 25
Mutapa Empire, 34
Mutendi, Samuel, 227
Mutesa I, kabaka of Buganda, 101; 112
Muzorewa, Abel, 222; 224
Mvemba Nzinga (Alfonso I) of Congo, 55
Mvera, 197; 198; 205; 223
Mwalo, Yeremiya, 223
Mwanawasa, 157
Mwanga, Kabaka of Buganda, 102; 112
Mwari Cult, 23; 219; 251
Mwase, Edward, 210
Mwene Mutapa, 34; 58; 59; 219; 222
Mwinyi Mkuu, 32
Mzilikazi of the Ndebele, 65; 220
Mzimba, Pambani J., 144

N

Nagenda, William, 149; 150
Namalambe, Albert, 192; 197
Namibia, 34; 65; 88; 123; 124; 125
Napoleon, 88
Navigator, Prince Henry the (Infante Dom Henrique), 52
Ndebele people, 65; 135; 220; 221; 224
Ndovi, Stanley, 210; 232
Necessitades, Francisco, 57
Nederduitsch Gereformeerde Kerk (N.G.K.), 87
Nederduitsch Hervormde Kerk (N.H.K.), 87
négritude movement, 139
Netherlands, The, 16; 61; 67; 68; 70; 87; 88; 95; 126; 130; 210
Network for African Congregational Theology (NetAct), 184
Neukirchener Mission, 100
Ngola, 33; 57
Ngombe, Nguana, 213
Ngoni people, 65; 192; 193; 194; 197; 200; 206; 212
Ngunana, Shadreck, 191; 192
Nguni, 34; 64; 65
Ngunza (=Prophetic) Movement, 228
Nicolas V, Pope, 52

Niger mission, 78
Nigeria, 14; 73; 77; 79; 88; 111; 112; 125; 127; 128; 134; 136; 141; 144; 146; 147; 155; 158; 160; 161; 171; 174; 182; 227; 228
Nine Saints, 40
Njobvuyalema (Ngoni Chief), 200
Nkhoma Synod (C.C.A.P.), 87; 90; 183; 188; 196; 208; 210; 223; 235
Nkomo, Joshua, 222; 224
Nkrumah, Kwame, 139
Nku (Ma Nku), 151; 230
Nkunika, Elliot, 229
Nobatia, 36; 38
Nomiya Luo Mission, 145
Noo, Ishmael, 151
Norwegian Missionary Society, 91
Nsibambi, Simeoni, 149
Ntintili, Mapas, 191
Ntsikana, 97; 145
Nubia, 21
Nubian Christianity, 25; 28; 36; 37; 38; 39; 40; 141
Nyang'ori Mission, 225
Nyasa Industrial Mission (Evangelical Church of Malawi), 202; 205; 225
Nyasaland Christian Council, 206
Nyau Societies, 177; 201; 250; 251
Nyerere, Julius, 157
Nyimbo za Mulungu, 143; 206
Nylander, 77
Nzambi, Mama, 56

O

Obote, Milton, 156
Odubanjo, David, 147
Ojukwu, 155
Olowala, 160
Onitsha, 78
Oppong, Sampson, 141
Orange Free State Synod (of the D.R.C.), 212
Organisation of African Unity (O.A.U.), 154
Orimolade, Moses Tunolase, 147
Oromo people, 32; 44; 46; 47; 48; 49; 50; 51
Orthodoxism, 71
Oschoffa, Samuel Bilewu, 147
Osei Tutu, 31
Ositelu, Josiah, 147
Ottoman Turks, 25
Otumikira mwa Chikondi, 210
Overney, 66
Overtoun Institution, 194; 202; 212; 218
Oviedo, de, 45

P

p'Bitek, Okot, 159; 249
padroado, 52; 59
Paez, Pedro, 45
Paget, Edward, 222
Palmer, Phoebe, 166
Paris Mission Society, 81; 90; 105; 123; 127; 138; 213; 214; 221
Pax Britannica, 134
Pentecostal Holiness Church, 227
Pentecostal Movement, 147; 148; 152; 206; 207; 209; 210; 225; 226; 227; 228; 229; 231; 232; 233; 234; 246
Perfect, George, 227
Perrot, 200
Peters, Thomas, 76
Phelps-Stokes Commission, 137
Philadelphia Missionary Council, 172
Philafrican Mission, 85
Philip, John, 89
Phillips, John George, 190; 206; 227
Phiri, Hannock, 206
Phiri, Jim, 228
Phiri, Moses, 206; 210
Phiri, Wyson Chitsulo, 210
Pinto, Serpa, 199
Pirquet, Charles du, 83
Plessis, David du, 226
polygamy, 244
Pombal, 56
Portuguese/ Portugal, 22; 26; 27; 31; 32; 34; 45; 52; 53; 54; 55; 56; 57; 58; 59; 60; 61; 63; 64; 66; 69; 71; 82; 83; 84; 85; 98; 102; 107; 108; 111; 113; 114; 115; 129; 130; 131; 135; 136; 155; 199; 219
Positivism, 237; 238
Post Modern theology, 163
Post-Classical Missions (Faith Missions), 127; 171; 201
Post-Modernism, 177
Prasse, 76
Presbyterian Church in Kenya, 183
Presbyterian Church in Zambia, 216
Presbyterian Church of Malawi (P.C.M.), 233
Presbyterian theology, 160
Prester John, 22; 58
Pretorius, J.L., 197
Prezeau, Prezeau, 200
Principe Islands, 54
Prophet-Healing Churches, 142; 145
Prophetic Movement, 165; 166
Protten, Jacob, 62

Providence Industrial Mission, 136; 204; 205
Providence Industrial Mission (P.I.M.), 166; 203; 204; 205; 206; 210

Q

Qallabat, battle of, 50
Qua Iboe Mission, 228
Quaicoo (Quaque), Philip, 69; 70
Quakers, 76
Quinn, Edel, 201

R

Radama I of Madagascar, 103
Radama II of Madagascar, 105
Rafaravary, Mary, 104
Ragot, Miriam, 151
Ramushu, David M., 220
Ranavalona I of Madagascar, 103; 105
Ranavalona II of Madagascar, 105
Ranavalona III of Madagascar, 105
Rasalana, Rafavavy, 104
Rasolerina of Madagascar, 105
Raymond Lull, 22
Rebmann, J., 99
Reformation (of the 16th Century), 12; 22; 45; 61; 71; 129; 140; 153; 160; 164; 225; 229; 237; 238
Reformed Church in Zambia, 217
Reformed Church of East Africa, 183
Reformed Church of Zimbabwe, 223
Reformed Congregations Mission, 127
Reformed Ecumenical Synod, 182; 183
Reformed Mission League, 16; 127; 160
Reformed Presbyterian Church of Malawi, 210
Reformed Theology, 62; 157; 159; 160
Reformed/ Evangelical theology, 162
RENAMO, 115
Restorationist Revival, 165
Rhema Bible Church, 230
Rhenish Missionary Society, 124; 127
Rhodes, Cecil John, 110; 135; 212; 221; 222
Rhodesian Front, 224
Riebeeck, Jan van, 64; 66
Roberts, Oral, 231
Rogers, Cyrill, 203
Roman Catholic missions, 114; 121; 127; 199; 200; 201
Roman Catholic theology, 48; 157; 162
Roman Empire, 11
Romanticism, 238

Roosevelt, Theodore, 118
Roux, P.L. le, 148; 226
Rowland, J.F., 227
Rufinus, 37; 40
Rwanda, 32; 120; 123; 124; 125; 149; 150; 158

S

S.I.M. = Sudan Interior Mission, 51
Sabiti, Erica, 151
Saker, Alfred, 81; 123
Saladin, 25
Salvation Army, 172; 227
Sambani, Sam, 191
San (Bushmen), 34; 64; 96
Sanders, W.H., 84
Sanneh, Lamin, 162; 248
São Salvador, 55; 56
Sao Tomé, 53; 54; 57; 115
Savimbi, Jonas, 115
Sawyer, John S., 19; 21; 158
Scheut, Society of, 117; 128
Schmidt, George, 67; 68
Schweitzer, Albert, 81
Schwellnus, 221
Schwinn, 67
Scott, David Clement, 195
Scott, Peter Cameron, 100; 171
Scramble (The Scramble for Africa), 107; 108; 120; 122; 127
Scripture Union (S.U.), 152; 230; 232
Sechele of the Bakuena, 89
Second Coming of Christ, 72; 136; 146; 165
Second Vatican Council, 130; 158; 162; 181; 184
Second World War, 109; 112; 119; 150; 174; 179; 182; 239; 248
Secularism, 131
Selama, abun, 40; 47; 48; 49
Senegal, 30; 31; 80; 81; 121; 122; 128
Senghor, Léopold Sédar, 139
separatism, 142; 152
Seventh Day Adventists, 85; 119; 138; 203; 205; 206; 215
Seventh Day Baptist Church, 203
Shaka (Chaka) of the Zulu, 34; 65; 87
Sharp, Granville, 73; 76
Shaw, William, 90
Sheba, Queen of, 42; 43; 143
Shekanda, 39
Shembe, Isahah, 226
Shembe, Isaiah, 148; 230

Shembe, Johannes Galilee, 148; 153
Shembe, Londa, 148
Shimbra-Kure, battle of, 44
Shirer, W.L., 227
Shoa (in Ethiopia), 43; 99
Shona people, 34; 59; 148; 221; 224; 227; 251
Shonga people, 223
Sierra Leone, 70; 73; 75; 76; 77; 79; 80; 110; 112; 128; 141; 144; 171; 227
Silveira, Gonzalo da, 58; 219
Simond, Pierre, 66
Simpson, A.B., 167; 171; 172
Sisters of our Lady of Africa, 211
Sithole, Ndabaningi, 222
Siwale, Noah, 229
Siwi (priest), 213
slave trade, 31; 44; 57; 60; 70; 71; 72; 73; 75; 76; 89; 97; 98; 100; 108; 110; 111
slavery, 28; 35; 54; 55; 61; 63; 71; 72; 73; 74; 87; 103; 117; 133; 135; 141; 143; 195
Slessor, Mary M., 79
Small Christian Communities (S.C.C.), 184
Smith, Ian, 89; 158; 224
Smyth, Joseph, 81
Soba., 36
Society for the Propagation of the Gospel (S.P.G.), 69
Sofala, 32; 57; 58
Somalia, 109; 155; 174
Songhay country, 27; 30
Soninke kingdom, 27; 30
Sonni Ali, 30
Sontonga, Mankayi Enoch, 143
Sost Ledat, 46
Sotho people, 34; 65; 91; 213; 221
South Africa General Mission (S.A.G.M.), 85; 93; 203; 205; 214
South African Missionary Society, 67
Soviet Union, 114; 115
Soyo Congo, 55; 56; 62; 63
Spiritans (Holy Ghost Fathers), 127
St. Michael's and All Angels, 196
Stanley, Henry Morton, 73; 74; 90; 101; 118
Stellenbosch, 66
Stellenbosch University, 87; 91; 184; 188; 196
Stephanos Foundation, 210
Stern, H.A., 47; 48
Stewart, James (of Lovedale), 90; 100; 191; 196
Stober, M.Z., 84
Stoffels, 97
Stuart, C.E., 150; 189
Studd, C.T., 82
Student Christian Movement (S.C.M.), 230

Students Volunteer Movement (S.V.M.), 93
Students' Christian Organisation of Malawi (S.C.O.M.), 152; 232
Subordinatianism, 46
Sudan, 27; 28; 29; 30; 31; 36; 39; 40; 43; 44; 47; 51; 109; 112; 121; 122; 128; 139; 149; 150; 155; 164; 172; 174; 204
Sudan Interior Mission (S.I.M.), 51; 172; 174; 204
Sudan United Mission (S.U.M.), 174
Sufi orders, 39
Sukuma people, 228
Sulayman, 30
Sundiata, 30
Sunnite, 26
Supreme Being (in A.T.R.), 24; 178; 249; 250; 253; 254
Susenyos of Ethiopia, 45
Sutherland, William, 193
Suze/ Susi (Livingstone's servant), 190
Svane, Frederik Pederson, 62
Swahili Arabs, 28
Swahili, culture, 28; 32; 34; 53; 57; 99
Swedish Church Mission, 91
Syncretism, 14; 41; 55; 56; 161; 177; 178; 179

T

Tafari Makonnen, Ras (Haile Seleassie I), 50
Tanzania (Tanganyika), 32; 33; 65; 100; 101; 110; 112; 113; 123; 124; 125; 128; 139; 149; 150; 157; 172; 206; 227; 229; 251; 252
Taylor, James Hudson, 166
Taylor, Maria, 167
Taylor, William, 83; 85
Tear Fund, 183
Tekle Haymanot, 43; 46
Tembo, Ephraim, 210
Tembo, Mawelera, 193
Tempel, Placide, 139; 158
Tennent, Gilbert, John and William, 71
Tertullian, 20; 104; 229
Tewodros of Ethiopia, 47; 48; 49
Thembu National Church., 143
Theodora, Byzantine Empress, 37
Theologies of Reconstruction, 162
Theologies of the A.I.C.'s, 162
Thole, Peter, 193
Thomist philosophy, 176
Thompson, Thomas, 69
Tiénou, Tite, 160
Tile, Nehemiah, 143

Timbuktu, 30
Tippet, Barbara, 232
Todd, Garfield, 224
Togo, 122; 123; 125; 138
Tolbert, 155
Tomani, 197
Tonga people, 192; 193; 194; 212; 223
Tordesillas, Treaty of, 53
Tozer, William, 100; 190
Traditional Religions, 22
Translation Theologies, 162
Triangular Trade:, 70
Trotha, Adrian Dietrich Lothar von, 124
Tshatshu, Jan, 97
Tshibangu, 158
Tswana, 34; 64; 65; 89
Tubman, 155
Tucker Theological College, 150
Tunisia, 20; 121; 122
Ture, 30
Turner, Harold, 162
Turner, Henry M., 143; 225
Tutu, Desmond, 156; 159
Twain, Mark, 119

U

Ubangi-Shari, 121; 122
Uganda, 32; 99; 100; 101; 102; 111; 112; 113; 119; 134; 135; 139; 141; 145; 149; 150; 151; 153; 156; 168; 172
Ugandan Martyrs, 102
Ukpabio, Esien, 79
Umanyano, 210
Unctionists, 46; 48
UNESCO, 36
Union of South Africa, 88; 110; 125; 138
Unionite view, 42; 46; 48; 49
UNITA, 115
United Church of Zambia, 214; 215; 216
United East Indies Company, 64; 70
Uniting Presbyterian Church in South Africa, 216
Universities' Mission in Central Africa (U.M.C.A.), 100; 101; 126; 189; 205; 206

V

Vanneste, Alfred, 158
Varley, Henry, 94
Vasco da Gama, 45; 53; 57
Venda people, 223
Venn, Henry, 78; 133; 136; 144

Vermeulen, Dick, 210
Verstraelen, 11
Villa-Vicencio, Charles, 162
Vincent, David Brown (Mojola Agbebi), 144
Vineyard, 232
Virginia Theological Seminary, 204
Vlok, Theunis C. Botha, 92; 197; 223
Volta, 121; 122

W

Walton, Spencer, 93
Warren, 76
Washington, Booker T., 93; 119
Waterboer, 97
Wauchope, Isaac, 191
Wesley, John, 71; 109; 164; 206
Wesleyan Methodists' Mission, 77
Westminster Abbey, 191
White Fathers, 101; 102; 127; 128; 129; 135; 199; 200; 214
Whitefield, George, 71
Wilberforce, William, 73
Wilkinson, Moses, 76
Williams, Daniel P., 227
Williams, William J., 227
Winnen, Antoine, 200
Wishard, Luther, 93
witchcraft, 24; 56; 145; 147; 149; 179; 217; 241; 250; 256
Word of Life Evangelical Church, 51
Work and Life Movement, 181
World Evangelical Fellowship, 181
World Alliance of Reformed Churches (W.A.R.C.), 181
World Bank, 180
World Christian Fundamentals Association, 181
World Council of Churches (W.C.C.), 114; 148; 159; 181; 182; 184; 214
World Mission Conference (Edinburgh 1910), 93
World Relief, 183
World Vision, 183
Wylant, Willem, 66

X

Xhosa people, 34; 64; 65; 89; 96

Y

Yao people, 34; 100; 138; 195; 204
Yaqob, abun, 43
Yekunno-Amlak of Ethiopia, 43
Yohannes IV of Ethiopia, 49
Yonamu, 223
Yoruba, 31; 77; 78; 79; 144; 155
Young, E.D., 191; 233
Yusuf bin Hasan, 60

Z

Za-Dingil of Ethiopia, 45
Zagwe kings of Ethiopia, 42; 43
Zaire (Congo), 80; 81; 120; 155; 213
Zalimba, 232
Zambezi, 34; 53; 58; 59; 65; 98; 189; 205; 223; 225
Zambezi Evangelical Church (Z.E.C.), 202; 225
Zambezi Industrial Mission (Z.I.M.), 202; 205; 223
Zambia, 33; 65; 90; 110; 113; 151; 156; 161; 165; 190; 193; 206; 209; 210; 212; 213; 214; 215; 216; 217; 218; 221; 224
Zanji, 32
Zanzibar, 32; 48; 57; 60; 74; 99; 100; 101; 105; 111; 112; 123; 157; 190
Zar'a-Ya'qob of Ethiopia, 44; 45
Zenj (Zanj) Empire, 32; 111
Zimbabwe, 23; 28; 34; 58; 59; 88; 90; 110; 113; 148; 151; 206; 209; 210; 216; 217; 219; 220; 221; 222; 223; 224; 227; 251
Zimmerman, 80
Zinzendorf, Count von, 67; 181
Zionism, 140; 145; 147; 206; 225; 226; 228
Zomba, 11; 12; 16; 19; 21; 66; 68; 89; 94; 136; 178; 179; 190; 195; 196; 201; 203; 204; 206; 209; 210; 211; 216; 224; 228; 235; 236; 250
Zomba Theological College, 11; 16; 68; 178; 209; 216
Zulu, 34
Zulu people, 65; 87; 88; 90; 91
Zwangendaba of the Ngoni, 65
Zwingli, Ulrich, 180

Kachere Series
P.O. Box 1037, Zomba, Malawi
email: kachere@globemw.net
web: www.sdnp.org.mw/Kachereseries

This book is part of the **Kachere Series**, the publications arm of the **Department of Theology and Religious Studies of the University of Malawi**. A range of books on religion, culture and society in or regarding Malawi is published under the categories: Kachere Books, Kachere Monographs, Kachere Texts, Kachere Studies, Kachere Theses, and Mvunguti Books.

James N. Amanze, *African Traditional Religion: The Case of the Bimbi Cult*
D. Bone (ed.), *Malawi's Muslims: A Historical Perspective*
Joseph Booth, *Africa for the Africans* (ed. Laura Perry)
J.W.M. van Breugel, *Chewa Traditional Religion*
Beryl Brough, *Saint Johnson of Lake Malawi*
J.C. Chakanza (ed.), *Collection of Pastoral Letters*
J.C. Chakanza, *Wisdom of the People*
J.C. Chakanza, *Voices of Preachers in Protest*
J.C. Chakanza, *Islam Week in Malawi*
J.C. Chakanza and Kenneth R. Ross, *Religion in Malawi: An Annotated Bibliography*
Felix Chingota, *The Use of the Concept of Fear in the Book of Deuteronomy*
Masauko Chipembere, Robert Rotberg (eds), *Hero of the Nation*
Henry Church, *Theological Education that Makes a Difference: Church Growth in the Free Methodist Church in Malawi and Zimbabwe*
Rijk van Dijk, Ria Reis, Marja Spierenburg (eds), *The Political Aspects of Healing in Southern Africa*
Harry England, *A Democracy of Chameleons*
Klaus Fiedler, *Christianity and African Culture: German Protestant Missionaries in Tanzania*
Klaus Fiedler, Paul Gundani, Hilary Mijoga (eds), *Theology Cooked in an African Pan*
Klaus Fiedler, *Joseph Booth in Melbourne*
Peter G. Forster, *T. Cullen Young: Missionary and Anthropologist*
Richard Gordon, *Transforming Psalms*
Clara Henderson, *Rolling Away the Stone: The Africanisation of Christian Music by Presbyterian Mvano Women in Southern Malawi*
David Hulme and Marshal Murphree (eds), *African Wildlife & Livelihood: The Promise and Performance of Community Conservation*
Patrick A. Kalilombe, *Doing Theology at Grassroots: Theological Essays from Malawi*
Janet Kholowa and Klaus Fiedler, *In the Beginning God Created them Equal*
Janet Y Kholowa ndi Klaus Fiedler, *Mtumwi Paulo ndi Udindo wa Amayi Mumpingo*
Janet Y Kholowa ndi Klaus Fiedler, *Pachiyambi Anawalenga Chimodzimodzi*
Harry Langworthy, *'Africa for the African' – The Life of Joseph Booth*
Ian and Jane Linden, *Catholics, Peasants and Chewa Resistance* (reprint)
Patrick Makondesa, *Moyo ndi Utumiki wa Mbusa ndi Mai Muocha wa Providence Industrial Mission*
John McCracken, *Politics and Christianity in Malawi 1975-1940: The Impact of the Livingstonia Mission on the Northern Province*
Hilary Mijoga, *The Pauline Notion of Deeds of the Law*
Owen Kandawire, *Chiswakhata Kandawire of Livingstonia*
Fulata Moyo and Martin Ott, *Christianity and the Environment*
David Mphande, *Nthanthi za Chitonga za Kusambizgiya ndi Kutauliya*
Stephen Kauta Msiska, *Golden Buttons: Christianity and Traditional Religion among the Tumbuka*
Augustinus Musopole, *Being Human in Africa*

Yesaya Zerenji Mwase, *Essential and Paramount Reasons for Working Independently*
Silas S. Ncozana, *The Spirit Dimensions in African Christianity : A Pastoral Study Among the Tumbuka People of Northern Malawi*
Silas S. Ncozana, *Sangaya : A Leader in the Synod of Blantyre*
Silas S. Ncozana, *Sangaya : Mtsogoleri wa Sinodi ya Blantyre : Mpingo wa CCAP*
M.S. Nzunda, Kenneth R. Ross (eds), *Church, Law and Political Transition in Malawi*
Patrick O'Malley, *Living Dangerously: A Memoir of Political Change in Malawi*
Peggy Owen (ed.), *When Maize and Tobacco are not Enough: A Church Study of Malawi's Agro-Economy*
Martin Ott, Kings M. Phiri, Nandini Patel (eds), *Malawi's Second Democratic Elections: Process, Problems and Prospects*
Martin Ott, *Theology in Images*
Martin Pauw, *From Mission to Church: The History of Nkhoma Synod of the C.C.A.P. 1889-1968*
Isabel Apawo Phiri, *Women, Presbyterianism, and Patriarchy*
Kings M. Phiri, Kenneth R. Ross (eds), *Democratization in Malawi: A Stocktaking*
Hubert Reijnaerts, Ann Nielsen, Matthew Schoffeleers, *Montfortians in Malawi: Their Spiritual and Pastoral Approach*
Edwin D. Roels and others, *Mayankho Odalirika – Answers to Live By* (ed. Steven Paas)
Andrew C. Ross, *Blantyre Mission and the Making of Modern Malawi*
Kenneth R. Ross, *Church, University and Theological Education in Malawi*
Kenneth R. Ross, *Gospel Ferment in Malawi: Theological Essays*
Kenneth R. Ross (ed.), *Christianity in Malawi: A Source Book*
Kenneth R. Ross (ed.), *Faith at the Frontiers of Knowledge*
Kenneth R. Ross (ed.), *God, People and Power in Malawi: Democratization in Theological Perspective*
Kenneth R. Ross, *Here Comes Your King: Christ, Church and Nation in Malawi*
Matthew J. Schoffeleers, *Guardians of the Land*
Matthew J. Schoffeleers, *In Search of Truth and Justice*
Matthew Schoffeleers, *Religion and the Dramatisation of Life: Spiritual Beliefs and Rituals in Southern and Central Malawi*
George Shepperson, Thomas Price, *Independent African: John Chilembwe and the Nyasaland Rising*
Boston Soko, with Gerhard Kubik, *Nchimi Chikanga: The Battle Against Witchcraft in Malawi*
Boston Soko, *Chikanga: A Traditional Healer*
T.Jack Thompson, *Touching the Heart: Xhosa Missionaries to Malawi*
Zacharias Ursinus and Caspar Olevianus, *Katekisma wa Heidelberg – Heidelberg Catechism* (ed. Steven Paas)
Ernst R. Wendland, *Bukhu Loyera: An Introduction to the New Chichewa Translation*
Ernst R. Wendland, *Preaching that Grabs the Heart: A Rhetorical-Stylistic Study of the Chichewa Revival Sermons of Shadrack Wame*

Kachere Series Editors: J.C. Chakanza, F.L. Chingota, Klaus Fiedler, P.A. Kalilombe, S. Mahomed, Fulata Moyo, Martin Ott; For Mvunguti Books also: Saidi Chiphangwi, Joel Manda, Silas Nyirenda

www.ingramcontent.com/pod-product-compliance
Lightning Source LLC
Chambersburg PA
CBHW031547300426
44111CB00006BA/202